Paymaster John Harley wrote his memoirs in the mid to late 1830s, some fifteen years after he had left the army under questionable circumstances. He apparently published this memoir privately in two volumes in 1838 a few years before his death – quite possibly as he had not found a mainstream publisher because of its potentially libellous content – and only four hundred copies were apparently printed.

John Harley had a varied and interesting military career, serving in the Tarbert Fencibles, the 54th Foot in Egypt, and then the 47th Foot with Wellington in Spain and Southern France. He also served during the Miguelite War of 1823 and is a rare witness to this little-known conflict. However, the greatest joy of these pages is to be found in the various scurrilous incidents mentioned in these memoirs, which have all been found to be fully established in fact. Duels, bigamy, abductions, women tricked into marriage, sinking boats, cowardice, larceny, murder, corruption, human tragedy, bankruptcy, forgery, suicides, privateers, debtors prison, card sharks, highwaymen, prisoners of war, and Garryowen Boys, indeed the whole gambit. It truly exposes the seedy underside of the Georgian age both within the army and in civilian life too.

John Harley's memoirs are a total joy and a real eye-opener on many levels – once you have read them, you will never look at Wellington's army in the same light ever again.

John Harley was born in Cork, Ireland on 18 November 1769 and lived with his mother for most of his youth in the area of Kilkenny. At the age of fourteen he was put to work at a merchant house in the city but soon chose to pursue a military career with the Tarbert Fencibles. He later served with the 54th Foot in Egypt and the 47th Foot in the Peninsular War. He went on half-pay in 1814 and later joined the British volunteers who went out in 1821-23 to serve in the Miguelite Wars under Sir Robert Wilson. He resigned his commission for a commuted allowance on 20 January 1832 and then lived in Bristol and Liverpool until his death around 1843.

Gareth Glover is a fifty-seven year old former Royal Naval officer who has studied the Napoleonic wars for the last forty years. He has become renowned as the foremost expert on memoirs of participants in the Napoleonic Wars, editing over sixty of them to date. Gareth lives with his wife Mary in Cardiff and has two grown up children.

The Veteran or 40 Years' Service in the British Army

The Scurrilous Recollections of Paymaster John Harley 47th Foot – 1798-1838

John Harley, with New Introduction, Notes, and Commentary by Gareth Glover

Helion & Company Limited

Helion & Company Limited
26 Willow Road
Solihull
West Midlands
B91 1UE
England
Tel. 0121 705 3393
Fax 0121 711 4075
Email: info@helion.co.uk
Website: www.helion.co.uk
Twitter: @helionbooks
Visit our blog at http://blog.helion.co.uk/

Published by Helion & Company 2018
Designed and typeset by Mach 3 Solutions Ltd (www.mach3solutions.co.uk)
Cover designed by Paul Hewitt, Battlefield Design (www.battlefield-design.co.uk)
Printed by Lightning Source Limited, Milton Keynes, Buckinghamshire

ISBN 978-1-912390-25-0

British Library Cataloguing-in-Publication Data.

A catalogue record for this book is available from the British Library.

Contents

List of Illustrations

List of Maps

New Introduction

By Gareth Glover

I am constantly searching for rare or unpublished memoirs of soldiers who served during the Napoleonic Wars to bring to a modern audience and this is one that I have recently re-discovered. Paymaster John Harley wrote his memoirs in the late 1830s, some fifteen years after he had left the Army under somewhat questionable circumstances – we will come back to this issue later. He apparently published this memoir privately in two volumes in 1838 a few years before his death – quite possibly because Harley had not found a mainstream publisher because of its potentially libellous content – and only four hundred copies were apparently ever printed.[1] For this reason alone, it would be rare, but searches of worldwide bibliographies reveal no known copies anywhere, apart from the one copy that I have discovered in the British Library, making it very rare indeed. I am very glad to be able to rescue it from such obscurity.

John Harley was, according to his own account, born in Cork, Ireland on 18 November 1769 but his father then died within a few weeks of his birth, and he therefore lived with his mother for most of his youth in the area of Kilkenny. At the age of fourteen he was put to work at a merchant house in Cork but he never really settled in this role and when offered the opportunity of obtaining a lieutenancy in the military if he could procure fifteen volunteers, he jumped at the chance. He achieved this, just, and was duly appointed as a lieutenant in the Irish Tarbert Fencibles on its formation in 1798.[2] Fencible regiments were raised at time of threat of invasion, to bolster the defences, freeing up regular, better trained troops for other operations. They had first been raised in 1759, and had then been raised again during the War of American Independence and now during the Irish Rebellion of 1798 when there was the very real threat of a French invasion. The

1 Published as *The Veteran or Forty Years in British service: Comprising adventures in Egypt, Spain, Portugal, Belgium, Holland and Prussia by Captain John Harley, late Paymaster of the Forty-Seventh Regiment* in 1838.

2 Because of the name Tarbert, many mistakenly believe that the regiment hailed from Tarbert in Scotland, but it was raised at Tarbert House in Ireland.

fencibles were viewed as militia, but officered by regulars, hence the value put on his new appointment by Harley.

The Tarbert Fencibles soon sailed from Ireland, staying at a number of garrisons in South Wales, Gloucester, Poole and then Southampton, having experienced a number of adventures along the way. At this period, Harley gained a commission as Quartermaster of the 54th (West Norfolk) Regiment of Foot on 12 June 1800 and joined his new regiment at Winchester. Soon after, they were ordered to proceed abroad and within a year Harley found himself trudging through the hot sands of Egypt in the campaign of Sir Ralph Abercromby to oust Napoleon's French army from North Africa. Following the campaign, they formed part of the garrison of Gibraltar and were there during the infamous mutiny against the governor the Duke of Kent. Soon after, the signing of the Peace of Amiens brought the war between Britain and France to a temporary end and in the government's clamour to reduce the size of the armed forces John Harley was placed on Half Pay on 24 June 1802.

Harley soon found a new position however, becoming Quartermaster to the 60th (Royal American) Foot on 12 February 1803, but it seems that this appointment had hardly been announced when he exchanged again to become Quartermaster of the 27th (Inniskilling) Foot on 2 April and then exchanged again as Quartermaster in the 1st Battalion of the 47th Foot on 2 June 1803. It is therefore very unlikely that he ever physically joined either the 60th or the 27th.

The 47th (Lancashire) Regiment of Foot had recently returned from a ten-year stint garrisoning the islands of New Providence and the Bahamas. A second battalion was now raised as well in 1803. The two battalions of the regiment remained together at Colchester when Harley joined them and they continued to move together to garrison Woodbridge and then Liverpool, before they embarked for Dublin in January 1804, the 1st Battalion then marching to Kilkenny and the 2nd Battalion to Clonmel. On 11 July 1805 John Harley gained the position of Paymaster to the 2nd Battalion and moved with it around Ireland for the next three years, staying for short periods at Cork, Cahir, Belfast, Enniskillen and finally Omagh in March 1807. The 1st Battalion sailed from Cork in May 1806 for the East Indies, but was diverted at the Cape of Good Hope to participate in the attack on Montevideo in 1807, but after this disaster, they did continue on to India, where they served for the next twenty-one years.

John Harley's battalion proceeded to Preston in May 1807 and to Chelmsford in the autumn, where they remained until 1809 when they were finally ordered for foreign service. They sailed for Gibraltar in October 1809 and were then transferred to Cadiz, which was under siege, and they also became involved in the defence of Tarifa in 1811. The following year the siege of Cadiz ended; the battalion marched to Seville and then joined in the difficult retreat to Portugal at the end of the 1812 campaign. The following year the battalion was at the Battle of Vitoria, where Harley received the awful news of the death of his son, who was serving in the same regiment as a lieutenant; he then took part in the siege of San Sebastian.

In 1814 the battalion was engaged in the crossing of the Bidassoa, the battles of the Nivelle and the Nive and finally involved in the sortie from Bayonne, when the war ended. The 2nd Battalion of the 47th Foot was not involved in the war in America or at Waterloo and was disbanded at Liverpool on 24 October 1814 and those effective men and officers were sent to India to join the 1st Battalion there.

John Harley went on half pay in 1814 and he continued on half pay until he resigned his commission for a commuted allowance on 20 January 1832. He then lived in Liverpool until his death around 1843 (there is a death recorded at Liverpool that year but there are not enough details to prove it is our man). John Harley had by his own statement married and had children, but all searches have proven fruitless in finding records of any wedding or births.

Memoirs of soldiers serving in the 47th (Lancashire) Regiment of Foot are very rare, despite their extended period serving in the Peninsula, only one other having surfaced to date and that also published by the current editor in 2012.[3] This alone would make John Harley's memoirs important, but they are also essential reading for anyone wishing to gain a real insight into life in the British Army in the Napoleonic Wars – for they are like no other.

As a Paymaster, Harley was rarely in the fighting, but he was certainly close to the action at times and also saw much of the terrible aftermath. However, some of the greatest and most entertaining memoirs have already come from non-combatants, including the bawdy tales of Commissary August Schaumann, Surgeon Henry's trifles, and the stories of Commissary John Daniel, Surgeon Charles Boutflower, Paymaster John Dayes, Robert Cooke of the Pay Corps and the Reverend George Stonestreet. It is a simple truth that if you want to know what it was really like serving in the British army for the ninety-nine percent of the time when there was no fighting, read the memoirs of such men, who had opportunity to enjoy the best of times, partook in many of the greatest adventures and thankfully had the spare time to record them for posterity. I have no doubt that the memoirs of John Harley will join these hallowed ranks once they are republished and gain a wider audience.

John Harley was a rumour monger. He loved scandal and enjoyed recounting it at great length, whilst his own life was hardly run of the mill itself. Although he did not write his memoirs until the 1830s, Harley remembered a great deal: names, personalities, incidents and tragedies, and although his memory might occasionally forget the correct ranks or some of the finer details, every one of the major incidents he records is to be found in the records.

This memoir has however been a real challenge, almost certainly the hardest I have ever had to deal with as an editor. This is because, when published, as often done in Victorian books, many names are obscured with only the first letter shown

3 *Seven Years on the Peninsula. The Memoirs of Private Adam Reed, 47th (Lancashire) Foot 1806-17.* (Godmanchester: Ken Trotman; 2012).

to avoid both embarrassment to the living and also probably to avoid serious libel action. This however, makes it very difficult to be certain with identifications when working back and it requires a great deal of checking and re-checking to be certain. I am very pleased that in the end, well over 97 per cent of these individuals have now been identified with high levels of certainty and in these situations I have completed the full name in the text indicating by [-] the letters I have re-inserted. However, a very few have proven particularly stubborn or impossible to identify with any certainty at all, often where unfortunately Harley does not give enough information to be exact. The other issue is that he sometimes rambles off with a good story and breaks his sequential narrative, this also makes it difficult sometimes to identify when an incident happened. I have therefore when necessary added the odd short passage – set in italics to differentiate it from the original text – to help the reader keep to the path when necessary.

As with any such material, there does need to be some note of caution used. In some of these cases John Harley was involved personally and he clearly had a vested interest in portraying events in a light favourable to himself. In these, and only these few, cases, he may well be guilty of distorting the truth and hiding his shadier side. This is particularly true of an incident that occurred in 1814 toward the end of the war.

Paymasters handled a great deal of public money, but they also had plenty of opportunities to act as unofficial loan agents – indeed they were sometimes not far off loan-sharks. They were often the only source of ready cash for officers in the regiments, when on foreign duty far from home and these loans were often left outstanding for many years, indeed decades in some cases with usurious levels of interest incurred. I have recently been able to view the records of another Paymaster, William Deane of the 18th Hussars, which show that twenty and thirty years after he made loans to officers, some still remained unpaid. Paymasters were officer's best friends when they needed funds, but their worst enemy much of the rest of the time and that must be borne in mind regarding the complicated case I will try to untangle. It does however include claims of false accounting, dodgy dealing and bankruptcies.

But the greatest joy of these pages are the various scurrilous incidents mentioned in these memoirs, which have all been found to be fully established in fact. Duels, bigamy, abductions, women tricked into marriage, sinking boats, cowardice, larceny, murder, corruption, human tragedy, bankruptcy, forgery, suicides, privateers, debtors prison, card sharks, highwaymen, prisoners of war and Garryowen Boys, indeed the whole gambit. It truly exposes the seedy underside of Georgian life both within the army and in civilian life too.

John Harley's memoirs are a total joy and a real eye-opener on many levels – once you have read them, you will never look at Wellington's army in the same light ever again.

Acknowledgements

I must initially thank the staff at the British Library for providing a copy of this material for me to work on and Andrew Bamford, Commissioning Editor at Helion & Company, who saw the potential in this book when many others did not. A project of such complexity cannot be tackled alone with any hope of achieving any significant success. In reality it can only be achieved with a huge amount of help from a great number of people, each utilising their expertise to unravel the various strands. I have however, one person to thank more than anyone else for single-handedly helping me identify many persons in Harley's memoir. Ron McGuigan has generously given a great deal of his time to suggest numerous avenues to investigate and possible answers and has been a fantastic sounding board to numerous off the wall suggestions from me in my desperate attempt to identify people and events. I can say with great confidence that Ron and I have turned over every stone to attempt to fill in these blanks and know that we have gone as far as possible, but that does not mean that someone somewhere does not know better than I, and I will happily receive any corrections with real appreciation. Any errors in this work are however of course mine alone. Many others who frequent the Napoleon Series Website have helped me with their expertise on specific questions and I thank them all for their generous help. This more than any other has been a real team effort.

I must as always, also thank my wife Mary for her unceasing and unquestioning support, without which I could not have achieved what I have.

Gareth Glover
Cardiff

1

Early Life

From the earliest period of my recollection, the army was the profession I wished to follow, and I always looked forward with the pleasing hope of being, one day or other, enrolled amongst those who were then fighting the battles of our country. I was a child of fortune. At the age of six weeks, I was, by the sudden death of my father,[1] left, together with an only sister, to the care of a mother, who, with unremitting solicitude, strictly fulfilled all the duties of a kind and affectionate parent. If she had a fault it was a weakness too common with parents – but almost excusable in her case – over-indulgence. Being her only son, and probably on that account her favourite child, I was frequently gratified in many wishes, incompatible with my true interest and welfare; so that, in after-life, I have often had occasion to regret her partiality for me, as it left me too much my own master.

I need scarcely say that by the death of my father, who was at the time but thirty-three years of age, we sustained a severe – an irreparable loss. He was what the world terms an independent man, and very much inclined to speculation. Some time previously to his death, foreseeing that in all probability, and at no very distant period, a bridge would be built across the River Lee for the purpose of uniting the north suburbs of Cork with the city, he purchased a property (upon which he afterwards resided, and where I was born, on the 18th of November 1769) from a highly respectable Quaker family of the name of Alby,[2] whose present representatives are the wealthy family of the Manders, now resident in Dublin.[3]

As my father was a Roman Catholic, and the penal laws were at this time in force, and in many cases strictly carried into execution, my father was advised to have the title-deeds, &c. prepared and drawn up in the name of his trust-worthy friend John L[ane], Esq, a Protestant gentleman of the highest respectability,

1 This would appear to be a William Harley who died in Cork in 1769.

2 The earlier Quaker House of Cork stood on the same site of the present temple building built in 1833 on Grattan Street, which is now a medical dispensary.

3 The Manders family had risen in wealth through manufacturing (bakeries) in Dublin. Richard Manders was Mayor of Dublin 1801-2.

Map 1 A map of Ireland c.1800. (Authors collection)

which was accordingly done.[4] During Mr L[ane]'s life, he regularly and punctually paid my mother the profits arising from this trust property; but, after some time, dying suddenly intestate, his widow, who had a family by a former marriage of the name of R[oberts], possessed herself not only of his property effects, but also of our property which her husband held in trust. Thus, my mother and her children were suddenly bereft of their means of subsistence, with the exception of a small annuity allowed her by her uncles, the late John and Michael Heffernan, Esquires, of the county of Limerick, who were men of considerable fortune.[5] The property we were thus deprived of is at present in the hands of the Messrs. W[estropp],[6] of Cork, they having obtained possession of it by a marriage with a grand-daughter of John L[ane]'s, widow. I have been advised, by very competent authority, to take legal proceedings for the recovery of this land; in consequence of which I am determined, should I survive any time, to appeal to the *present* laws of my country for redress for myself and my children.[7]

My mother being unable from want of means to bring me up to a learned profession, as had been intended by my father, placed me in a mercantile house in Limerick, at the age of fourteen years, where I continued during the remainder of my boyhood, occasionally spending my time very pleasantly between my mother's and my uncle's at Liskennett, in the county of Limerick.

It is impossible for me to call to recollection the many curious scenes I witnessed, and the extraordinary occurrences that took place at this period in the neighbourhood in which I lived. Some of them, however, are still fresh in my memory, and may not be unworthy of being related, as they exhibit traits of the Irish character half a century back, when jokes were practised with greater freedom, and laws violated with more impunity, than at present.

The priest of our parish (Ballingarry),[8] the Reverend Gilbert James O'Grady,[9] who was a relation of my aunt's, and constantly at her house, and also related to the late Chief Baron of Ireland,[10] was a most excellent and worthy character, highly respected and esteemed by people of all ranks and persuasions. Having been summoned to Dublin, where the parliament was then sitting, as a witness

4 The only John L at Cork was the Barrister at Law John Lane of Mary Street, Cork.

5 They lived at Liskennett in Limerick.

6 There were two barristers with a surname starting with a W, (John White and Michael Westropp) but the number of dashes indicates a long name, hence I believe he refers to Michael Westropp of South Parade. The Westropps were linked with the Roberts family for a number of generations.

7 In the 1820's most of the restrictions on Catholics owning property et cetera were relaxed, culminating in the Roman Catholic Relief Act of 1829, which finally gave landowning Catholics the vote, although the value of land required to qualify to vote was increased significantly for all.

8 In Kilmallock, County Limerick.

9 He died in 1829.

10 The Chief Baron of the Irish Exchequer, was a senior judge of the Court of Exchequer (Ireland), one of the Four Courts at Dublin. The position lapsed in 1916. Barry Yelverton (later Viscount Avonmore) was Chief Baron from 1783-1805.

on a contested election, and having a great aversion to stop at inns or hotels, he expressed his anxiety to one or two of his young country friends who travelled with him, never having been in the metropolis himself, to get into some snug, quiet lodging, where he might be free from interruption or noise. The young wags, who knew Dublin well, immediately volunteered to procure one for him, and on their arrival placed him in that highly fashionable and select lodging-house, kept by Mrs B[rowne],[11] in Trinity Street, a house well known and much frequented in those days. The poor priest was greatly pleased with the attention paid him by the lady of the house and her inmates, and, being fatigued by his long journey, he retired to rest at an early hour, highly gratified with the selection his friends had made and the reception he had met with.

On the following morning, having risen at an early hour, as was his usual custom, he stood at the street door in his slippers to breathe the pure fresh air, and sharpen his appetite for his morning's repast. He had not been many minutes in this situation, when some of his acquaintances from the county Limerick happened to pass, whom he saluted in the most friendly manner, utterly unconscious of the injury his moral character momentarily sustained in their eyes, and of the unpleasant reflections his being seen on such familiar terms in such a house, naturally gave rise to.

Several persons had already passed him, contented with barely returning his salute with apparent respect, when one gentleman, more thoughtful than the rest, and very probably placing a greater degree of reliance on the virtue and innocence of his worthy pastor, at once addressed him, and asked him, with seeming unconcern, how he happened to lodge in that house, and how long he had been an inmate of it. 'It was,' said the poor old man, 'at the recommendation of one or two young friends, who travelled with me yesterday, that I came here. I have been in it of course but one night, but I can truly say that kinder or more polite attention I have never received from any family, than I last night experienced from the lady of the house and her charming and interesting daughters.' 'Good Heavens!' exclaimed the gentleman, 'do you know, Father O'Grady, where you are? can you be aware that you are in a house universally noted for its infamy? Quit it instantly, sir, or your character is lost for ever.' He then explained to him the nature of Mrs B[rowne]'s establishment, and very kindly offered to conduct him to more reputable lodgings. It is almost unnecessary for me to add, that he immediately left the house, and was so exceedingly indignant at the treatment he had received, that the authors of this ill-timed trick were obliged to keep out of his way for several months afterwards.

The village of Ballingarry, in the county of Limerick, where the above-named worthy old priest resided, was, and I believe is, still remarkable for the periodical

11 It has proven very difficult to be absolutely certain, but later directories do show a property owned in Trinity Street by a Mrs Browne.

struggles that usually took place between rival factions at the different fairs held in and about the neighbourhood. It was always a maxim with the country people, *no fight, no fair*; that is, a fair could not be good unless it ended in a battle; and, accordingly, there were in general more people assembled for that purpose, than for the disposal of cattle or the vending of goods.

On one of the evenings of those fairs, Dr Mollowney, who was the village doctor, and a most singular character – no man a better judge of a glass of good whiskey nor a pinch of real Lundyfoot,[12] although he was considered by all who knew him as a skilful practitioner, so that no other medical man was employed in that neighbourhood – was called upon to attend a man, whom I recollect very well, named Darby Shehan, who had just got a desperate beating in the fair, and was then speechless. The doctor, on seeing him, looked grave, gave his head a professional shake, and immediately bled his patient copiously; and, on taking leave, told the woman of the house to keep the blood until he should call again on the next day. When he arrived on the following morning, he was informed that poor Darby was dead – 'and as brave a fellow,' said the woman, 'as ever handled a cudgel at fair, or patroon.'

'Very well,' said the doctor, 'I thought so; but show me the blood I gave into your charge yesterday.' It was instantly exhibited, and appeared to be in a very bad state. The doctor, as soon as he had examined it, and given a nod or two, indicative of his skill and wisdom, exclaimed with unaffected seriousness – 'Well! well! Dead or alive, Darby, poor fellow, you are the better for that being taken from you; and I am sure you are easy, now'.

At the following assizes of Limerick, some of the party who had been opposed to Darby in the fight, were put on their trial for murder. The doctor was of course subpoenaed as a principal witness, to prove the cause of his death. He, however, refused to answer a single question until he received a fee, and, addressing the judge, he told him, that he had come that morning from Ballingarry, in compliance with his lordship's subpoena, but that he could not give evidence unless his fee was forthcoming. The judge, smiling, told him he thought he was perfectly right, and ordered two guineas to be given to him. The celebrated John Philpot Curran, who was counsel for the prosecution, examined him.[13] After the doctor had accurately described the injuries the man had sustained, the apparent cause of his death, and the state of his blood on the next day, Mr Curran, with his usual powerful wit, said – 'Then, doctor, as the taking of the blood from him was so beneficial to him, dead or alive, what did you next do for him?' 'Oh! Nothing, Mr Curran, at all at all,' replied Mollowney; 'sure, Darby was then out of my sphere'.

12 A variety of snuff.

13 John Philpott Curran (1750-1817) was an Irish orator, politician, lawyer and judge who defended many of the famous treason cases around 1800 and later became Master of the Rolls in Ireland.

The judge, the late Baron Yelverton,[14] was almost convulsed with laughter, and enquired with a half malicious smile, if Mr Curran had any other questions to put to the witness. 'No, not one, my lord,' replied the witty barrister, 'the doctor has given a final answer.'

It was, as I stated before, a general remark with the country people, that there could be no good in the fair – or rather, to express what I suppose to be their meaning, no fun, unless it concluded with a fight. Accordingly, whenever it occurred, as it sometimes did, that the hostile parties did not soon become into collision, or that the evening advanced without a fair opportunity of entering into their favourite diversion, one of the peasantry would take off his great coat, trail it along the ground, however inclement the season might be, and, dragging it after him through the fair, utter shouts of defiance against any person who dare to lay a foot or a finger upon it. If any person, either by accident or design, happened to touch or step upon any part of the coat, it was enough, the owner turned on him, and, whether he was foe or friend, as was sometimes the case, instantly knocked him down. In a moment, the row was general, one or two hundred able bodied fellows on a side, knocking each other's brains out with every kind of weapon, for, in a protracted contest, legs of tables, tent-poles, and even shafts of cars,[15] would inevitably be put into requisition. And all this bloodshed more for amusement than through bad feeling, or for the honour of some townland or barony. In vain would country gentlemen or magistrates interfere, or even the landlords of the parties themselves: there was but *one person* who could exercise influence over them – the parish priest; and I have often seen that good-natured man, Father O'Grady, at those fairs, rushing into the midst of the most desperate fights, taking their shillelaghs from them, and striking right and left (for there could be no time for reasoning), disperse them in a few minutes to their respective homes. And it is remarkable what a peculiar sense of honour those combatants had, however severe the injuries they sustained on such occasions, they never, except in case of foul and wilful murder, instituted a prosecution against any of the parties engaged in the row. On the contrary; it was their custom, on their return home, to place their cudgels of oak or blackthorn in their chimneys for safe keeping, and that they might be well seasoned against the next fair-day, when they expected to retrieve their lost honours, or to reap fresh laurels.

Although it may seem almost incredible, the country was perfectly quiet in those days; no Whitefeet,[16] no nocturnal outrages or visitations, no plundering of

14 The Chief Baron; see Note 9, above.

15 The word cars, derived from carriages, is not a modern word.

16 The Whiteboy groups began to rise as early as 1750 and stood up against the 'Agrarian Revolution' which threatened the livelihoods of so many peasant farmers. One such group raised in Leinster in the 1820's was called the Whitefeet. They carried out night raids to destroy newly raised fencing, destroying farm machinery and occasionally driving out those who stood up against them, particularly local priests.

arms, no religious animosity, no sectarian feeling, none of those numerous evils which afflict my unhappy country at the present day.

There was another celebrated place in my immediate neighbourhood, the inhabitants of which even exceeded those of Ballingarry in their fighting propensities, inasmuch as scarcely a day passed that they had not a rencontre of one description or another, either with the authorities or with strangers, but very seldom amongst themselves. I mean the far-famed Garryowen, a district in the south suburbs of the city of Limerick, inhabited by a fearless race of men, who spend most of their time in drinking and fighting.[17] I remember, when a lad, that they were held in such dread by the inhabitants of Limerick, that it was considered a most serious thing to give the slightest offence to one of them. If they happened to receive any insult or the least annoyance from those who lived without their district, pots, pans, and kettles beat to arms; their forces were instantly collected, marched into the city, the streets of which would be immediately cleared of magistrates, constables, and inhabitants; they would then, after holding possession for a short time, return in triumph to their stronghold, quite satisfied with the bloodless capture of the city, and the awe they had inspired.

Should a prisoner from the country be conducted to the gaol of Limerick through their district, they would stop the escort and inquire his crime; if it were only a riot, an assault, or debt, they would instantly set the man at liberty, for resistance was out of the question; any attempt to oppose them would only prove useless, and might possibly lead to fatal consequences.

In 1792, when the Irish militia force was organised, the city of Limerick regiment was quickly filled up and completed, almost exclusively by the Garryowen boys, six-hundred of them having immediately enrolled themselves in the corps; and they were considered the smartest, best disciplined, and also the most wicked regiment in Ireland. They had been but a short time embodied, when they were led against the French, who had landed at Killala.[18] They fought the battle of Collooney under their brave Colonel Vereker, now Lord Gort,[19] conducting themselves with

17 'The Garryowen Boys' were infamous for their lawless behaviour including drunken rampages through the area, but rather surprisingly they consisted mostly of the bored sons of well-to-do merchants. They are immortalised in the well-known song *Garryowen in Glory*, which names Johnny Connell (whose father owned two breweries) and Harry O'Brien (whose family were horse traders).

18 The French force under General Humbert landed in nearby Kilcummin Harbour and seized the village of Killala on 22 August 1798. The same village was to see the final battle of the 1798 expedition when a combined force of some 1,000 Frenchmen and 4,000 United Irishmen were defeated by a British force some 1,200 strong on 23 September 1798.

19 Colonel Charles Vereker, 2nd Viscount Gort, was colonel of the Limerick City Militia which distinguished itself in this action. Vereker was heavily outnumbered and was eventually forced to retreat in good order but without his cannon and losing about one hundred prisoners. However, the stiff resistance his militia made impressed the French general and convinced General Humbert that this was merely an advance party of a larger force and thus he failed to make an attempt on Sligo. Humbert paid due

Contemporary print of Limerick Castle. (Author's collection)

testimony to Vereker whom he described as the only British officer he had encountered in Ireland who was capable of commanding a hundred men.

The Gallant Limerick Militia; Or, Garryown Heroes. From *Lord Howe's Victory Over the French,* published in Limerick in 1800 by W. Goggin.

You stout Irish heroes that ne'er was dismayed,
Or of any enemy was never yet afraid ;
Attend to my story, while shall unfold,
Our intrepid Limerick boys who are stout hearts of gold.
The fifth of Sept. the year eighty-nine,
The Rebels and French both together did join,
Naer the town of Sligo, our force to subdue
While balls they in showers were pouring like rain,
We stood them like Trojans and never did flinch,
Tho' they were ten to one boys we ne'er gave an inch.
But being outnumbered were forced to retreat.
We still fought like lions, ne'er feared a defeat.
We are the boys that did clearly make known,
That we were loyal heroes of bold Garryown.
And ravage our country and make us to rue.

Brave Colonel Vereker, appriz'd their scheme,
Went with his Limerick heroes those gallants of fame,
Who was always courageous and still did make known
That they would shew them play as from sweet Garryowen,
Our foes at Coloony assembled they were,

all the coolness, steadiness, and bravery of an old regiment of the line.[20] Their conduct on this occasion obtained even the admiration of their enemies; for the French commander, General Humbert,[21] is said to have remarked, on his arrival at the Castle of Dublin, that General Vereker, as he called him, and his regiment of Garryowen boys, were the best soldiers in Ireland.

The Garryowen boys, when at home, had always a chief commander who resided in their district, and to whose orders they, in general, paid implicit obedience. In my early days about fifty years ago, I remember perfectly well their leader or chief, Johnny Connell: he was the son of a very worthy and respectable man, a brewer, who lived in the district. Johnny had some deputies or inferior officers under him, particularly a man named Jemmy O'Brien, with whom he was on habits of intimacy. Old Mr Connell made every effort in his power to reclaim his wild and thoughtless son; and, after trying many expedients, but in vain, he contrived to send him, much against his will, to some friend in Cork, with the expectation that, by separating him from his associates for some time, and introducing him into another society, a reformation might be possibly brought about in his character and conduct. Shortly after young Connell's departure, his quondam friend, Harry O'Brien, was taken up, committed to prison, and brought to trial at the ensuing assizes, in the City Court House of Limerick, for some misdemeanour.

As soon as the indictment had been read against him, and just at the moment that the clerk of the crown, Mr E. Parker,[22] had called upon him to plead, he prevailed upon one of his fellow prisoners to stoop down, stood upon his back, and, with one active spring, jumped out of the dock clear over the iron spikes and the soldier's bayonets, alighting amongst the crowd in the body of the court house, and finally escaping, to the astonishment of the judge, jury, and all who witnessed the transaction.[23]

And to salute them we straight did repair
We gave to them a breakfast, and speedily make known,
We were the rare heroes of sweet Garryown.
We fought them two hours, and our pass did maintain,
Vereker our brave Colonel may God him preserve,
Who made it his study his men to reserve
To face those proud Frenchmen and rebels also,
We shew'd Limerick heroes could give 'em a blow.
And now to conclude boys we'll forever sing,
A health to brace Vereker and great George our King,
Likewise our gallant Limerick boys that did make known,
They were all gallant heroes from sweet Garryown.

20 The Battle of Collooney (also known as Carricknagat) occurred on 5 September 1798, it was a defeat for the local British forces.

21 *Général de Brigade* Jean Joseph Amable Humbert (1767-1823).

22 Mr Edward Parker of Thomas Street, Limerick.

23 This escape of Harry O'Brien was a famous incident.

Johnny Connell, after having remained in Cork for some years, returned home quite reformed, to the great joy and satisfaction of his poor father, who, soon dying, left him the property and brewery at Garryowen.[24] Johnny very prudently married, and, devoting himself entirely to business, became, in a short time, a most useful and respectable member of society, accumulating a very considerable fortune by honourable industry. And, although any further intimacy with his old friends, the Garryowen boys, could not of course be permitted, he did not neglect administering to their necessities, and relieving their wants, whenever proper objects of charity were presented to his notice.

When I was last in Limerick, about five years since,[25] I spent a very pleasant day with him, and was surprised to find that, though then nearly eighty years of age, all his faculties were in full vigour, and he had a perfect recollection of every incident that occurred in his early days. After dinner, he related many anecdotes to me, one or two of which may not be uninteresting to my readers.

A man who lived in the neighbourhood of Limerick, and had been once in possession of a comfortable farm, called upon Mr Connell, a few days previously to my seeing him. He told him that he came to apply for a small debt, that was now so long due to him that he almost feared it might have escaped Mr Connell's memory, and that he would not think of making the demand were he not driven to it by absolute necessity. 'My claim, sir', said he, 'is for fifteen guineas, which you and your boys forced from me for drink, on a Saturday night, on Ball's bridge, in the city of Limerick.[26] Had it been treble the amount, I should not have thought anything about it then, nor would I on any account have made a complaint to your father, but now, as I am in reduced circumstances, it, or any part of it, would be the greatest object to me.' Mr Connell instantly recollected the circumstance, though after the lapse of many years, and ordered his cashier to pay the farmer the sum of thirty guineas, double the amount of his claim, which the poor man received with tears of gratitude.

Another circumstance, which he mentioned as having only occurred the week before, exhibits, in a striking light, the ingenuity of the lower classes of the Irish. Another person made a claim upon Mr Connell, to which he objected, being conscious that he did not owe the man a farthing. The fellow, however, continued calling every morning at the counting-house, still demanding his money. There is a high tree in front of the brewery, upon which, on one of those occasions when the man was urging his claim, a crow had perched. The bird during the argument, took wing; when Mr Connell immediately said, between jest and earnest, 'look, my good fellow, at that bird flying away; now, until you bring me back the crow, I will never pay you your unjust demand; so, spare yourself the trouble of coming

24 He owned Connell & Fitzgerald Brewery at Greenhill, Limerick.

25 That is to say, in 1833.

26 Ball's or Baal's Bridge in Limerick connected the areas of English Town and Irish Town.

A contemporary print of Baal's Bridge, Limerick by William Bartlett. (Author's collection)

to me again.' The man went off grumbling, and Mr Connell saw no more of him for the space of three weeks, when he returned one morning, and, running into the office, a crow being then perched upon the same tree, hastily exclaimed, 'Now Mr Connell, I have brought you back the crow, after travelling round the world in pursuit of the black devil, and therefore I expect your Honour will give me three weeks wages, as well as my claim on you, for, sure enough, I have earned it well'. Mr Connell could not avoid laughing heartily at the fellow's artful contrivance to obtain the money; and, though he was unwilling to submit to his imposition, he could not help rewarding his ingenuity by giving him a pound before he dismissed him – the rogue still continuing to tell Mr Connell that it was himself had the trouble, day and night, watching that crow, until he coaxed him back to the tree; as he knew he would not get his money unless that identical same bird was brought back to his Honour.

Nothing was more common in the south of Ireland in those days, particularly in the counties of Cork, Waterford, Limerick, and Clare, than abduction. Wherever a snug farmer had a daughter with a prospect of a reasonable portion,[27] she might be certain of being carried off some night by force and married, against her consent, to a man with whom, very probably, she had no previous acquaintance. And yet,

27 Dowry.

notwithstanding in many instances, not only the parties themselves, but their families, soon became reconciled, and lived together in mutual harmony and peace. When any idle young fellow in the country took a fancy to a girl that was likely to have a fortune, and whose consent he thought he could not obtain, he assembled his friends and companions, and easily prevailed upon them to assist him in carrying her off by force; and, if the unfortunate girl had no particular admirer, it was not unusual for those fellows to play cards for her, and he that won was sure of the hearty co-operation of his lawless companions in obtaining the prize for him, for which they had unsuccessfully contended.

When it was determined to carry off a girl, the party came by night, well mounted and armed, to the house in which the young woman resided. If the door were not immediately opened for them, they entered forcibly, seized on the fair one, took her up in their arms, and placed her on the horse behind her intended husband, who was generally mounted on a swift charger, and had a pillion or kind of saddle provided for the accommodation of his bride. The whole party would then gallop off at full speed to the mountains, or to some remote and intricate part of the country, where, by threats or persuasions, they would prevail upon the girl to marry the young fellow, having always a man at hand, called Father 'Tack'em' or 'Couple-beggar', to perform the usual ceremony.

In some cases, the family and friends of the young women would pursue the party and succeed in recovering her before the marriage ceremony had taken place; but, in general, the robbers contrived to evade the hottest pursuit, and to get clear off with their booty.

This lawless custom was beginning to prevail considerably amongst the higher classes, until, at length, in consequence of a Mr Massy carrying off a Miss Ingoldsby, a rich heiress,[28] an act was past [sic], called the Ingoldsby Act, making it felony for any person to take away a female by force. I remember well the first unfortunate man who suffered under this act. He was a Mr Sullivan,[29] a man of some respectability; he had carried off a Miss O'Malley, who was, however, recovered by her friends, after having been detained by him for two days. Having been prosecuted by her friends, he was tried and convicted at the ensuing assizes. I was present upon the occasion, and recollect that the judge, previously to passing sentence, addressed Miss O'Malley, and calling her attention to the prisoner, who was a very fine young man, urged her, in the most persuasive manner, to spare his life, by consenting to marry him. She was determined, she said, to let the law take its course, and, accordingly, sentence was passed, and the unfortunate young man executed on the following week. Thousands of the country people attended, under the impression that she would yet relent and save him at the gallows; and deep and dreadful were the execrations that were poured upon her head when they

28 In 1785 Hugh Fitzjohn Massy was married to Frances Ingoldsby.
29 Either Mr James or Jeremiah Sullivan of No. 19 Clare Street.

saw Sullivan suffer death – since one word from her was sufficient to have saved him. Another occurrence of a similar nature took place when I was at school in Limerick, which, however, did not terminate so fatally as that which I have just related. A widow Villiers, a lady who had nearly approached the meridian of life, and whose sole attraction was the possession of £20,000, was attending divine service, on a Sunday, in the month of June, at a church called Killmurry, between Limerick and Castleconnel,[30] when she was forcibly taken out of the church by a natural son of one of the Massey family, and carried off by him and his party to the Galtee mountains, which divide the counties of Cork and Limerick, a wild and lawless place, and the frequent scene of many similar and desperate exploits.[31] The alarm soon reached Limerick, and the 47th Regiment, then in garrison (a regiment in which I afterwards served for many years), were suddenly called out of the cathedral, in the middle of divine worship, and despatched in pursuit of the fugitives, accompanied by the City of Limerick Volunteer Cavalry, under the command of Colonel Pery, the present Earl of Limerick,[32] and father-in-law to the Right Honourable Thomas Spring Rice, Chancellor of the Exchequer.[33] After a close and diligent search of three days, the lady was discovered in a cabin on the side of the mountains, but unfortunately the culprit escaped, and was never taken afterwards. Mrs Villiers, who was very religious, died lately, leaving her immense fortune to build alms-houses for distressed respectable females in Limerick, and for other charitable purposes equally laudable.[34]

Another case of abduction occurred about the same period in the County Waterford, when two young men, brothers, lost their lives, having been betrayed by the basest treachery. A young lad of rather respectable connexions, assisted by his brother and some friends, carried off a young girl into some distant part of the country, where he had her concealed for more than two months before her family discovered the place of her retreat. Upon learning it, the mother of the girl wrote to the young man, saying, that she forgave the act he had committed, that she would willingly receive him into her house as her son-in-law, if he would restore her daughter to her, and consent to marry her. The young fellow, who was really fond of the girl, and had treated her while she was in his power, with every respect and kindness, was overjoyed at the proposal, and most gladly embracing the offer, arrived, in a day or two, at his intended mother's-in-law's house, accompanied by his brother and the young woman.

They were all, on the night of their arrival, partaking of an excellent supper that had been prepared for the occasion, and they were just about making arrangements

30 Castleconnel lies 3 miles north east of Limerick.

31 The Galty Mountains or Galtees lie in Munster.

32 Edmund Henry Pery, 1st Earl of Limerick, (1758-1844) was styled Lord Glentworth from 1794-1800.

33 Thomas Spring Rice, 1st Baron Monteagle of Brandon, was Chancellor of the Exchequer from 1835-9.

34 Mrs Hannah Villiers, left her money for charitable purposes, her trustees establishing a school and maintaining alms houses she had established during her lifetime.

for the marriage of the parties on the following day, when the house was suddenly surrounded by a party of dragoons, sent out by the Mayor of Waterford, the women of the house having given private information to the mayor of the intended visit. The young men, in despair, defended themselves gallantly, and were only captured after a most desperate resistance, during which one of them was very severely wounded. They were prosecuted at the following assizes by the treacherous woman and her ungrateful daughter, and both convicted and sentenced to be hanged. One of them, however, died of his wounds a day before that appointed for his execution; and the other underwent the extreme penalty of the law with becoming fortitude and submission, while the wretched authors of his premature death very narrowly escaped falling a prey to the irritated feelings of the indignant populace.

During my apprenticeship in Limerick, I naturally spent many days with another uncle of mine, a merchant in that city. Mr Terence McMahon, who had considerable dealings with many gentlemen in his own and the surrounding counties.[35] Among the rest, there was a Mr D[enny] of Tralee, in the county Kerry, uncle to the present Sir [Edward Denny][36], who, in the course of business, became indebted to my uncle in the sum of £1,000, a single shilling of which he found it impossible to obtain in liquidation of the debt.

Mr D[enny] had a landed property of some value, but it was under settlement, and he was what I believe the law terms tenant for life; that is, that after his death the property was not liable to his debts, but descended, free of all encumbrances, to his heir. In addition to what Mr D[enny] owed my uncle, he was otherwise deeply involved and had, therefore, frequent applications made to him for money. Annoyed a good deal by the repeated claims upon his empty purse, he very ingeniously contrived a stratagem which would at once release him from his debts, and rid him of his importunate creditors. He feigned illness – took to his bed – had it reported through the country, particularly in Tralee and Limerick, where his principal creditors resided, that he was so dangerously ill it was impossible he could recover – and then to all appearance died – taking his departure, not into the next world, but into a neighbouring kingdom. A funeral procession, supposed to be his, moved, in solemn array, from his house to the churchyard, attended by some sham, and some real mourners, for he was generally esteemed; while his inflicted widow, in well-feigned grief, put on her dark weeds, and the whole family appeared in the deepest mourning.

Some years after this occurrence, my uncle went to France to purchase wines, when, what must have been his astonishment at meeting in Bordeaux, his old

35 Mr Terence McMahon, of Mungret Street, was a flour and meal dealer.

36 The Denny family owned most of Tralee. Sir Edward Denny, 4th Bart of Tralee Castle had inherited the title in 1831, on the death of his father, also Edward, who had inherited from his elder brother Barry in 1794. His father had five younger brothers and any of these could have been the uncle referred to – Henry, Arthur, Maynard, Thomas or William Denny.

friend and debtor Mr D[enny], in good health and spirits, living there comfortably with a part of his family! This stratagem was so ingeniously designed, and so well carried on, that none ever suspected the trick that had been practised upon them; and it is probable they never would have heard of it until he had really died, if my uncle, by mere chance, had not thus met the old gentleman.[37]

There then resided close to the town the celebrated M[orgell], an attorney, who is well remembered by the people of the neighbourhood.[38] I knew his father, who had been a farmer, at Dromcoler. This artful attorney contrived to set all the families in the county by the ears, and, as attorneys were not then so numerous as at present, he was employed on all occasions. M[orgell] soon drove his coach and four, and was one of the first men in the county, from the extent of his landed property. But there never was a man who obtained a fortune so rapidly, and fell so suddenly.

He had two sons and one daughter; what became of his sons I know not, nor have I ever taken the trouble to inquire. His daughter, a fine girl, was much admired for her personal beauty, as well as for her manners and amiable disposition.[39] Her father, naturally anxious to get her well married, encouraged the addresses of Sir [Barry Denny], a man of large fortune. They were married a few days previously to a contested election in the county Kerry. Sir [Barry Denny] being one of the candidates, M[orgell] strained every nerve to assist him in the election, and by his so doing involved himself to the extent of twenty or thirty thousand pounds. As disputes frequently arise between the contending parties on these occasions, particularly in Ireland, so it unfortunately occurred in this case; and Sir [Barry Denny] was shot dead by his opponent,[40] and, being tenant for life, his estates devolved to the present Sir [Edward Denny].

The effect that this shock had upon M[orgell] was overwhelming. He was then at his town house, in Dublin, and, well knowing he was now defeated in all his plans by the death of Sir [Barry Denny], his property having gone out of his family, and that the heavy expenses he had been at to get him returned member for the county, were utterly ruinous to him, he resolved to settle all his affairs at once, and deliberately went down to the Pigeon House, near Dublin, filled his pockets with large stones, walked into the water, and was soon drowned. He was observed by many who could not for a moment suppose such was his intention. His body was soon taken up and brought on a car to the Police Office, in Exchange Street. I remember

37 I have been unable to establish that any of the Denny brothers named above faked their death and lived in Bordeaux.

38 Mr Crosbie Morgell of Mount Morgell, MP for Tralee.

39 Anne Morgell his daughter.

40 Sir Barry Denny (the sitting member) was shot in a duel with Mr John Gustavus Crosbie, in an argument over the election of the second MP for Kerry in 1795. They met at Oakpark when Crosbie, who apparently had never fired a pistol before, fired first, shooting Denny in the head and killing him instantly. Crosbie won the election, but died within the year by a fall from his horse at night. The local populace was not slow to blame the ghost of Sir Barry Denny for 'spooking' the horse.

at the time being in Dame Street, in conversation with the old Lord Muskerry, who well knew M[orgell], in consequence of the loss of property he had sustained by him.[41] The car passed with the body on it, covered by a blanket, except the legs, which were completely exposed, with the shoes and breeches. M[orgell]'s legs were most remarkable, being bowed, with large lumps on the shin bones. When Lord Muskerry, who had reason to know them, exclaimed to me aloud, 'By God! Harley, dead or alive, wherever they have come from, there go M[orgell]'s legs,' pointing to the car as it passed. In a few hours after this, his having drowned himself was spread over Dublin.[42]

The situation of Lady [Denny], his daughter, was deplorable, she not having any settlement, in consequence of the estates being entailed. She was a fine young woman, and shortly afterwards repaired with her mother to Dublin, where she remained until she married the late General Sir J[ohn] F[loyd], a gentleman of considerable fortune, which he had acquired in the East Indies.[43] She retained some of the cleverness of her father, for, before she married Sir J[ohn] F[loyd], she made him settle a jointure on herself, and a handsome allowance on her mother. Sir J[ohn] F[loyd] had a daughter by a former marriage, a very lovely and amiable person.

When living with my mother in Newcastle, in the county Limerick, being then not more, I should suppose, than ten years of age, I recollect J[ohn] F[itzgerald], a barrister, coming to dine at my uncle's, Michael Heffernan, Esq, of Liskennet, and also at the Reverend Mr Lock's, the protestant clergyman. This celebrated man, whose features I still bring to memory, was of a sallow complexion, nearly copper colour, with piercing black eyes, slender in person, and a little above the middle size. He wore a close scratch wig. His family's rise was uncommon. They were indebted for it to the cleverness, or rather cunning, of his grandmother, Norah Quain, or, in English, Honour Quinn. This woman's abilities in bargain-making were astonishing: she sold milk in Limerick, and constantly rode in with it, in two churns slung on each side of her horse, from Ballysheda, where she lived. By degrees, she accumulated money, and was enabled to take some land. Among the number of her transactions (all of which were very shrewd) there was one in

41 William Power Trench Lord Muskerry was head of the McCarthy dynasty which could trace its lineage back to the Kings of Desmond. He became the 1st Earl of Clancarty in 1803.

42 The *Anthologia Hibernica* for 1795, records that on 10 November, Crosbie Morgell was discovered drowned near the first wharf at the South Wall, his pockets laden with stones.

43 Sir John William Floyd had joined the Army in 1760 and had risen steadily to become lieutenant colonel of the 23rd Light Dragoons serving in India. In the Third Mysore War (1790-2) he led all the cavalry forces against Tipu Sultan. He was promoted to major general in 1794 and became colonel of the 23rd Light Dragoons in in 1800, when he returned to Ireland. He became a lieutenant general in 1801 and transferred to the colonelcy of the 8th Light Dragoons in 1804. He became a full general in 1812 and was made a baronet in 1816. He was the Governor of Gravesend and Tilbury from 1812 until 1818 when he died.

particular that, at this time, was the topic of conversation in that country. She made a purchase of two hundred ewe sheep, and the bargain she made with the farmer was, to send home a male with every five sheep. Her terms were agreed to: the farmer supposing that she was an oddity, as she wished him to send home one of his men, or herdsmen, with five sheep at a time. I must explain to my readers that this clever woman made her agreement in Irish; the word *farr* signifies *husband*, and she artfully made it appear, that by her bargain she was entitled to a male sheep or ram for every five she bought, thus making an increase of forty in the number. An action was brought against him by Norah Quain, and it was decided in her favour, from the manner in which she worded her contract. Numerous are the acts of this description, handed down to this day in Limerick, of Norah Quain.

2

The Tarbert Fencibles

As it had been, from my very boyhood, the highest object of my ambition to join the army, I soon got tired of commercial pursuits, and a favourable opportunity in a short time presenting itself to me, I applied to Colonel Sir Edward Leslie (who had just obtained letters of service to raise a regiment) for a commission,[1] which he very kindly granted, with a promise of giving me a lieutenancy, provided I could raise or recruit fifteen men.[2]

It was now, indeed, that my troubles commenced. None but those who have raised men in this way, can have the least idea of the fatigue and anxiety attendant upon it, and the disagreeable situation in which one will sometimes be necessarily placed. When I had received from my colonel the beating orders and necessary instructions, I proceeded, accompanied by a sergeant, drummer, and fifer, to the different markets and fairs in the neighbourhood, and, after enduring indescribable annoyance for some time, being frequently obliged to associate with persons of the lowest description, and as often returning home minus several guineas in consequence of desertions, I at length, with the greatest difficulty, procured thirteen men, nearly all clean well-looking young fellows. But what was to be done? I was still two men deficient of the complement. The day of inspection was near at hand, and, unless I furnished my full quota, I could not expect my lieutenancy.

As I was returning one day through the celebrated village of Cahir-Conlish, after an unsuccessful tour through the country, greatly depressed in spirits in consequence of the very unfavourable aspect of my affairs, I was accosted by a tall thin, meagre-looking man, an exact counterpart of the ghost-like apothecary in Romeo and Juliet, who declared his inclination to enlist under my banners, and his readiness to fight against the enemies of his country. Really shocked at his

1 Colonel Sir Edward Leslie, 1st and only Baronet (1746-1818), established the Tarbert Cavalry and the Tarbert Infantry Fencibles. The 'Loyal Tarbert Regiment' were raised on 27 July 1798, his ancestral home being Tarbert House, near Tarbert in County Kerry. The regiment was disbanded at Plymouth on 19 June 1802.

2 Recruiting to gain a commission was a recognised method of raising regiments quickly.

appearance, and apprehensive that he could not possibly survive to reach headquarters, for he seemed as one who had just risen from the dead to pay a short visit to his former abode, I was declining his services in the best manner I could, when my sergeant, who was an old soldier, and what was in those days termed a crimp,[3] came up to me, and, as in most cases I acted under his counsel, persuaded me to receive Timothy O'Halloran, Knight of the Thimble,[4] into his Majesty's service, to whom I accordingly gave a guinea in the King's name, ordering him at the same time a good meal of bread and meat, with an allowance of beer, in the vain hope of improving his condition against the day of inspection.[5]

As I was still in want of one man to complete my number, and the inspection was to take place on the following day, I was almost about to give up the enterprise, when I accidentally met with a stout, well-made little man, named Jemmy O'Brien, but who was unfortunately two inches under size.[6] Circumstanced as I was there was no time for consideration, I therefore, with the advice of my prime minister the sergeant, received him into our ranks, and thus in one manner or another completed my number, although with a conviction that my last two recruits would be certainly rejected by the inspecting officer, General Morrison, who was remarkable for strictness and severity.[7]

On my arrival at headquarters with my quota, I was invited to spend the day at Sir Edward Leslie's. During the evening, his amiable and kind-hearted daughter, observing my low spirits, and fearing that I might have been unwell, inquired the cause. Charmed by the solicitude that she so kindly yet delicately evinced for one whom she supposed to be ill, I candidly told her that as one of my recruits, a tailor, was so pale, thin, and miserable looking, and another so considerably under size, I was almost certain of their being rejected, and had, consequently, but faint hopes of being able to procure my commission. Miss Leslie entreated me not to feel any uneasiness on that account, and, with an arch smile, desired me to have the tailor brought to the butler's room before twelve o'clock next morning, the hour appointed for the inspection, and that she would engage to pass him; but that she would leave it to the ingenuity of myself and the sergeant to raise Jemmy O'Brien's height to the necessary standard. Next morning, in compliance with Miss Leslie's instructions, I waited upon her, attended by O'Halloran. On seeing him, she desired me to conduct him into the butler's room, and having sent for her paint-box, she and her servant Molly laid on very gently such a proportion of

3 A man employed to 'find and persuade' recruits.

4 A tailor, as taken from *The 1811 Dictionary of the Vulgar Tongue*, by Francis Grose.

5 All recruits were required to be passed by the colonel's inspection before they joined the regiment.

6 At this time, the official minimum height for the army was 5 foot 7 inches (1.7 metres), although many were allowed in who were under this height. As the war went on, the height limit reduced down to 5 foot 4 inches (1.63 metres), as it became more difficult to recruit enough men.

7 Major General Edward Morrison, colonel of the 4th Battalion of the 60th Foot, was on the staff in Ireland and commanded the Limerick District in 1798.

colour on his cheeks, as made so great an alteration in him for the better, that his wife on his return to the lawn exclaimed, 'Och! Tim, honey, is that yourself that's in it? By the powers of delph, you look so well that the devil a one of the neighbours would know you, my jewel.'

We were now to *make up* Jemmy for inspection. Here I must remark, that the system of recruiting then was very different from what it is at present. In measuring recruits formerly, particularly in time of war, there was not that strictness that is observed now, nor were the men ever required to strip.

My trust-worthy crimp sergeant, who really felt interested for me, was sincerely rejoiced to see such an evident improvement in O'Halloran, who looked the very picture of rude health, and, having congratulated me on his appearance, he hurried off with little O'Brien to the colonel's stable, where, assisted by O'Brien's wife, which was rather singular, as in general the women could not bear the idea of their husband's enlisting, he stuffed his shoes with hay, until he had raised him to the regulated height. The hour of inspection having arrived, the general made his appearance, accompanied by his aid-de-camp Captain Brand, now Colonel Brand of the Guards,[8] on the lawn in front of Tarbert House, where, with mingled feelings of hope and despair, I had drawn up my little party to the best advantage, placing Tim the tailor, as he was the tallest of my men, on the right, who looked as well in his slop red coat (which, by-the-bye, we took care to stuff) as we could possibly wish. The general, attracted by his appearance, regarded him for a moment through his glass, and remarked aloud, 'What a fine looking fellow;' and then having viewed the remainder of the party, pronounced without hesitation the happy sentence – 'A fine set of recruits Lieutenant Harley has got – note him down, Brand, for his commission.' The words had scarcely passed the general's lips when I flew to my amiable young friend, to whom I communicated my good fortune, returning her thanks, as being the sole cause of my success. She was delighted that the stratagem succeeded so well, and with unaffected joy called out to Lady Leslie, who happened to be in an adjoining room, and told her that Lieutenant Harley's painted tailor had passed the inspecting officer.

Thus, with the assistance, I should rather say by the contrivance of a young and delicate female, I obtained my commission, but not without cheating our good and gracious sovereign, the beloved and regretted George the Third, of one soldier, by substituting the person of Mr Timothy O'Halloran, of Cahir-Conlish, tailor, a man whose services for his king and country were of such little value, that as soon as I saw myself gazetted in Gloucester, I applied to General Whitelocke,[9] who then finally inspected us, to have him discharged as a useless soldier; one, in fact, totally unable to perform his duty. I certainly cheated his Majesty in the manner

8 Lieutenant and Captain the Honourable Henry Otway Brand, Coldstream Guards, who later became a general and was made Lord Dacre just before he died in 1853.

9 Lieutenant General John Whitelocke commanded the South West District from 1799-1806.

I have related, but such things then were of frequent occurrence, and not regarded as criminal. I am now of a different opinion and only trust that my error in this case has been fully compensated by my subsequent services and privations in different parts of the world.

Portrait of Lieutenant General John Whitelocke by Hopwood. (Public Domain)

In fact, the cause of our second inspection in England arose from the frauds that were then practised in raising regiments in Ireland. It is a well-known fact, that about this period there were one thousand men produced at the inspection of a new regiment in the County Clare by a colonel of that county, whom the inspecting general declared to be as fine a body of men as he had ever seen, and for whom the colonel drew from government sixteen guineas a man; but, as soon as the inspection was over, every weekly return from the colonel to the War-Office reported from ten to twenty and even twenty-five desertions, until the regiment was reduced to a mere skeleton. This can easily be accounted for. The colonel persuaded his own tenants and the neighbouring farmers, by whom he was much beloved, and who being in general very wealthy, had not the least idea of entering into the King's service, to put on the uniform for the day of inspection only, that he might become entitled to the bounty, with the understanding that they might be at liberty to return to their farms after the inspection, which they accordingly did, although, to avoid suspicion, the returns made it appear that the decrease was gradual. And, however incredible it may seem, it is nevertheless true, that several tall masculine looking women were dressed in the regimental clothing, and passed muster on the day of inspection. Indeed, so great was the popularity of the colonel, that his tenantry and friends would have done anything for him he required, to enable him to complete the number he had engaged for, and for which he was to be so handsomely paid.

The occurrences which took place in those times were truly laughable, and one cannot but feel astonishment that they were, even then, allowed to pass without any notice being taken of them. I will here relate a circumstance that came within my knowledge. A regiment was raised in the County of Limerick by Sir Vere Hunt, Bart.[10] Nearly all the officers who joined him in the undertaking, many

10 Sir Vere Hunt, 1st Baronet, (also known as Aubrey de Vere Hunt), an Irish politician and landowner, founded the village of New Birmingham in County Tipperary. He was a heavy gambler and spendthrift, once purchasing the Island of Lundy, which he soon regretted. He raised the 135th (Limerick) Regiment of Foot in 1796 but it was disbanded in the same year and the recruits were passed into other regiments.

of whom I knew very well, were, although men of high respectability, much reduced in circumstances, and labouring under pecuniary embarrassments. The sentries, therefore, at the barrack-gate had strict orders not to admit any person in coloured clothes,[11] lest they should be visited by a limb of the law. And, when the recruits once entered, they were never allowed to go out until they were sent on foreign service. An old acquaintance of mine, Morgan O'Dwyer,[12] a captain in the regiment, and as good a fellow as ever lived, being considerably in debt in Limerick, kept close quarters within the barrack-gates at the Curragh,[13] where the regiment then lay. One of those ingenious fellows called a sheriff's bailiff, of the name of Hartigan, from Limerick, devised a curious stratagem. Having procured a soldier's old coat, he obtained admission, and immediately arrested poor O'Dwyer. Although completely taken by surprise, O'Dwyer did not lose his self-possession, but observed to the bailiff that he was not at all displeased with him for doing his duty, 'and as a proof of it,' said he, 'here is a shilling, get whiskey at the canteen, and I will accompany you wherever you wish.' When Harrigan had sufficiently refreshed himself, he returned for the captain, in order to escort him to prison, when, to his astonishment, he was handed over by O'Dwyer to the sergeant-major, as having been enlisted by the shilling he had given him. Nor had O'Dwyer any other alternative, as he would have been ultimately ruined had he gone to prison.

Hartigan was immediately conducted to the orderly-room, where he was measured, and his name entered upon the muster-roll and regimental books; and, when he exclaimed that he did not want to be a soldier, and on his knees entreated to be let out again, he was frightened into silence by being told, that if he continued to annoy them, he would be put into the black hole and severely punished for mutiny. He was then fitted by the master tailor with regimentals, and had a stiff leather stock clasped about his neck; and was finally handed over to the strict, old drill-sergeant, to be instructed in the manual and platoon exercises. I dined at the mess on the day this singular scene occurred, and saw the unfortunate bailiff led in with the other recruits to be shown to the colonel; and was, I must confess, very much amused with his stiff appearance, with the broad leather stock and the rueful expression of his countenance. He made one or two efforts to complain, but was instantly stopped by the drill sergeant with the usual threat of the black hole and mutiny.

From that day to the day of his embarkation, he was regularly drilled and exercised from six o'clock in the morning until nine, then from ten till two, when the

It seems unlikely that Sir Vere received his money for raising the regiment. He spent most of 1803 in Fleet Prison claiming that the British government owed him a great deal of money.

11 Civilian clothing.

12 Little is known about Morgan O'Dwyer, beyond the fact that he had previously served in the local yeomanry and had married a Miss C. Keating in 1798.

13 The Curragh is a large flat open plain of common land of some 5,000 square acres in County Kildare, between Newbridge and Kildare. A training camp was set up here for the training of militia units.

recruits dined, and again from three until eight o'clock at night. He embarked with his regiment for the West Indies, but, fortunately for him, the transport he was in, encountered a storm, was blown into the Bristol Channel, and, in consequence of the injury the vessel received, the detachment was obliged to land. On his arrival at Bristol, he made application to the mayor to be released, stating his situation and the manner of his detention. The mayor was not a little surprised, and very probably amused, at the recital of his adventure, but thought it prudent to take no further notice of it than ordering his immediate discharge, which was instantly complied with. When he obtained his liberty, he lost not a moment in bidding adieu for ever to a military life, and, crossing over to Waterford, he walked from thence to Limerick in his red coat, relating to his friends his campaign, and declaring his determination never to enter a barrack again to arrest an officer.

The final inspection of our regiment was ordered to take place in the city of Gloucester, for which destination the 1st division marched from Tarbert on the 1st of February 1798,[14] being the year of the Irish rebellion, to embark at Waterford, and proceed by way of Milford [Haven], in Wales. On our arrival at Clonmel (Sir Charles Asgill commanded there),[15] and in the absence of Captain Taylor, who was quarter-master, I was appointed to act for him.[16] As the rebels were then supposed to be organising on the Kilkenny side of the River Suir, the general advised me to send the women and baggage by water to Carrick-on-Suir,[17] to prevent their falling into the hands of the insurgents. I, accordingly, hired three lighters, or large flat boats, in which I embarked women, children, baggage, and escort. I was detained, very fortunately for me as the sequel proved, from accompanying them myself, in consequence of an attempt at gross imposition on the part of the carmen who had conveyed our baggage from the last stage. Happening on my return to the inn to inquire whether it was possible to procure a conveyance from Clonmel to Carrick, a respectable gentleman, Wm. Smyth, Esq who resided in the latter town, feeling for me as I was a stranger, addressed me at once, and informed me that there would be no public coach on that road until the next day, proposing that if I were anxious to proceed and had no objection to company, we should post it together.[18]

We had scarcely reached within two or three miles of the town, when Mr Smyth, who was a magistrate, universally known and greatly beloved by the country people, was informed by some who were returning from the market, that a large boat had been lost coming from Clonmel, conveying baggage belonging to the army, and that all on board perished. Scarcely believing the report to be true, I

14 He states 1798, but means 1799 as can be seen by the following incidents.

15 Brigadier General Sir Charles Asgill, 2nd Bart. commanded the Eastern district of Ireland.

16 Captain-Lieutenant and Quartermaster William Taylor. Captain-lieutenant was the rank of the senior lieutenant in a regiment.

17 In Waterford.

18 Mr William Smyth resided on Main Street in Carrick Mor according to the 1799 Census, he was a merchant and unmarried. He appears to have had two married brothers Lawrence and Francis.

hurried on; what were my feelings on entering the market-place to find the bodies of all my people lying stretched on the ground, colourless and lifeless! It was really agonizing to witness the scene, for some of the women had their lifeless children firmly clasped in their arms. We lost on this unfortunate occasion thirty women and forty children, besides the escort, consisting of a sergeant and twelve men.[19] Our poor sergeant I understood lost his life in endeavouring to save the boat from striking against the bridge. The current was so rapid that it carried the boat against the pier of the centre arch, by which it was dashed to pieces. The sergeant, poor young fellow, could readily have saved himself by jumping out before the boat and pier came in contact, and swimming to shore. He would not, however, desert his charge, but remained to afford every assistance, and was endeavouring to save the wretched women and children by putting his hands against the pier to lessen the shock, which he saw was inevitable, when he was overwhelmed in the general destruction. He was the son of a reduced gentleman of the county Limerick, of the name of Lacy or De Lacy, and was a near relative of the Generals De Lacy in the Austrian and Spanish service.[20] In consequence of my acting both as adjutant and quarter-master, I had the heart-rending duty to perform of having their bodies removed for interment, a work in which I am bound in honour to acknowledge I was most materially assisted by the inhabitants of Carrick-on-Suir of every class, who evinced the deepest sympathy on this melancholy occasion. Nor must I forget the Protestant and Roman Catholic clergymen, who co-operated in the good of charity, without any reference to the religious persuasion of the wretched victims.

On the following morning, we learned with surprise, that two female infants had floated on the water lower down than the bridge, were thrown by the current on an island, and picked up by some boatmen, who had been in search of plunder of the wrecked baggage. As soon as this circumstance as made known to some ladies of fortune in the neighbourhood they sent for the orphan children, for whom they handsomely provided, nor was it ever known to which of the poor soldiers those children belonged. After visiting my brother officers, Captain Hewson,[21] Macnamara,[22] and Sands,[23] who had reached Carrick before me, and who deeply felt for the severe loss our regiment had sustained, I accompanied Mr Smyth

19 The three boats made their way from Clonmel to Carrick on Suir on 8 February 1799, but the river being swollen from thawing snow, one of the boats carrying 111 men, women & children smashed against the bridge and broke apart. It is usually stated that only four men and six women survived, but Harley records that two young girls also survived.

20 The De Lacy family of Ballingarry, Limerick was the family source of a Spanish branch which included General Patrick de Lacy, the hero of the Siege of Oran in 1832, and General Luis Roberto de Lacy who fought during the Peninsular War; the Austrian branch included the Austrian Field Marshal Franz Moritz Graf von Lacy, whose father had been the Russian Field Marshal Count Peter von Lacy.

21 Captain John Hewson.

22 Volunteer John Macnamara was appointed to the 49th Foot as an Ensign in 1799.

23 Lieutenant John Sands appears to have left the regiment in 1800.

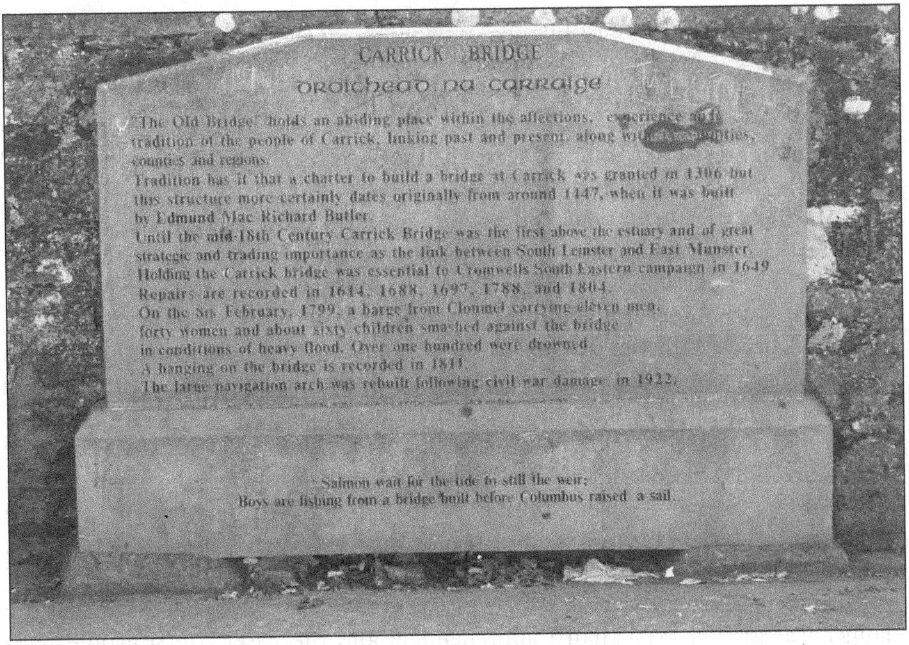

Memorial to those who lost their lives near Carrick Bridge in 1797, amongst others. (Author's collection)

home, where he introduced me to his wife, son, and daughter, by whom I was most hospitably entertained. The next morning at an early hour, a person called to inform Mr Smyth that a large quantity of the baggage which was thrown by the stream on a place about four miles down the river, had been taken possession of by the country people and carried off. Upon hearing this, Mr Smyth decided that he and I, accompanied by his clerk, should proceed at once, and without any guard, to endeavour to recover the property, as the state of the country was such, that it would not be prudent to take less than a whole regiment, and even with that force our efforts might be unavailing, so that it was thought better to depend upon advice and remonstrance, and Mr Smyth's influence with the people.

When we reached the village, we found all the people, men and women, at home, it being Sunday, and a finer race of peasantry I have never met with. Mr Smyth having desired me privately, as we were entering the village, not to open my lips upon any account, took very kindly the whole trouble upon himself, and, addressing the people in the most feeling manner, on the melancholy loss of so many lives, he implored them to give up all the baggage they had got, telling them that the property lost belonged to the officers and their families, who were not willing to injure them, and to the friends of the poor creatures who had been drowned; and at the same time warning them, that if they did not take his advice, and resign quietly the property in their possession, the garrisons of Clonmel and

Carrick-on-Suir were determined to come down on the following day with artillery to level their houses and burn the village.

While Mr Smyth was thus admonishing the people, and endeavouring, at one time by coaxing, and at another time by threats, to persuade them to restore the baggage, I observed a woman address the men in Irish, saying, '*Cur a pickie un*,' in English, 'put the pike into him.' As I understood the Irish language tolerably well, of which, of course, she could not be aware, I could not be deceived as to the import of the expression; and guessing, too, from the dark looks of the people, that something unpleasant was about to occur, I immediately apprised Mr Smyth of the woman's observation, and the fears that I could not but entertain for our personal safety. With the utmost composure, although he was certainly placed in a very hazardous situation, he desired me to mount my horse instantly, and retire to his house, leaving him and his clerk to manage matters: 'for,' said he, 'the people of this country will not, I think, injure either of us – their hostility seems directed towards you and your profession – it would be fool-hardy for you to remain, as they may, in the present excited state of the country, be easily led by any evil-minded person to commit some outrage.' Feeling the justness of this remark, I mounted, and retraced my steps at a rapid pace; nor did I consider myself safe, until I had reached the precincts of Carrick. It afterwards appeared that the danger was greater even than I apprehended, and the wiser course would have been to have remained; for some of the men seeing me ride off so suddenly, and naturally supposing that I was gone to bring out the army against them, thought to have intercepted me; and, had they succeeded, they would, in all probability, have murdered me.

Mr Smyth, some time after I left him, more, indeed, by reasoning than by using threats or intimidation, at length prevailed upon them to give up all the property they had concealed. And, such was the influence that this amiable man had in that country, that they sent in, on their own cars, in the course of the evening, whatever they had belonging to us, without so much as a single box or trunk having been opened by them.

We proceeded to Waterford the following day, where we met the venerable General Johnson,[24] who afforded us every assistance in his power in enabling us to embark, without delay, for Milford [Haven], South Wales. In fact, our men were deserting so fast, that it was an object of the highest importance to us not to lose a moment in embarking, as every officer was interested in bringing over his full complement of men for the final inspection at head-quarters, in Gloucester.

After a delightful passage of a few hours, we landed at Milford, and proceeded the same day four miles farther, to Haverfordwest, where we waited for a route from the war office, and a remittance from our agent, the late Colonel Brown, of

24 Major General Henry Johnson was colonel of the 81st Foot when he defended successfully New Ross in 1798. The following year he became a lieutenant general and governor of Ross Castle in 1801.

Contemporary print of the Monnow Bridge at Monmouth; Harley would have crossed this. (Public Domain)

King Street, St James's, London. A few weeks having elapsed, we were in readiness to proceed, when we were prevented by a robbery at a watchmaker's shop, which was instantly laid to the charge of our men. The mayor of the town sent his deputy to request politely, that the commanding officer would permit the men's knapsacks to be searched by the constable; a request with which, although so degrading to the pride of a soldier, we immediately complied. The search was made, but none of the stolen articles were discovered; and we left the town much annoyed at the unjust suspicion, but highly pleased with the result; and, in a few days after, we had further gratification, while we were at Monmouth, of receiving a polite letter from the mayor of Haverfordwest, apologising to our commanding officer for having caused the soldiers to be searched, and informing us that the robbers were now found to be two of the inhabitants of the town, who had planned and effected the robbery while we lay in it, in order that the suspicion might fall on our men, to whom, being wild, and undisciplined Irishmen, every improper act that occurred would be attributed.

While we remained for a day or two at Monmouth, we had a strong suspicion that one of our men, named Frewin, had an intention of deserting on the first favourable opportunity; and, as the sequel proved, we were not wrong in our conjectures. The plan by which he endeavoured to effect his object was singular. At the public house where he was quartered, a party of soldiers belonging to a regiment stationed in Jersey, were billeted for the night, being on their route to Ireland, Frewin becoming acquainted with some of the party, proposed to the corporal to take him up as a deserter from his regiment, with a promise of a reward of five shillings when he should by that means obtain his liberty. The corporal, without hesitation, consented; but the arrangement between the parties being overheard by my servant, he immediately came to the inn, and informed me of it. It was evening when the corporal led his pretended prisoner to the inn where all our officers messed, and where Colonel Elford of the South Devon Militia was then dining with us.[25] The two worthy confederates having been ushered into our presence, the corporal made his charge, stating that he felt it his duty to take up the prisoner, whom, having met accidentally, he at once recognised as a deserter from the regiment in which he had the honour to serve. Frewin being called on to answer the charge, with seeming sorrow, acknowledged his guilt, and entreated our interference to procure a mitigation of punishment when he should join his old regiment; but, to the utter confusion of both parties, I introduced my servant, who so clearly detailed the whole plot, that the corporal confessed the truth, and earnestly entreated for pardon. As it subsequently appeared that Frewin, by false representation, had worked on the credulity and good nature of the corporal, we dismissed the latter with a severe reproof, but kept the former in close custody during the remainder of our route to Gloucester.

Leaving Monmouth, we marched at our leisure through beautiful principality, South Wales, halting at Carmarthen and Ross, and other romantic places.[26] Amongst my recruits was the son of a Dr B[rody], a physician of respectability in Limerick.[27] This young man, who was at the time twenty-five years of age, had received a very liberal education, and had been only a few months called to the bar when, in consequence of his drunkenness and profligacy, he was obliged to enlist as a common soldier. This unfortunate fellow often occasioned me more trouble on our march than all the rest of my party. He has frequently laid himself down on the road and refused to march, unless I gave him liquor or the money to purchase it withal, well knowing that the absence of even one man at head-quarters would be a most serious loss to me, and might deprive me of my commission, as we were not yet gazetted; and, unfortunately, I had no remedy but to bear all patiently, having no power to try the recruits by court martial.

I shall never forget a scene that occurred in Brecon, in which our young counsellor was a principal actor, although I must acknowledge a passive one. When we arrived in the town, B[rody] was missing, and also a Sergeant Colloppy.[28] When I

25 Lieutenant Colonel Sir William Elford, banker and politician, commanded the South Devon Militia during the Irish Rebellion.

26 Carmarthen being in West Wales, they had passed through there many days before their arrival at Monmouth.

27 Mr Michael Brody of Cecil Street.

28 Sergeant James Colloppy.

had procured billets for my men and sent them to their respective quarters, I went to dine with some gentlemen at the inn, though I could not avoid feeling somewhat uneasy at the absence of two of my party.

The cloth had not been removed when, to my agreeable surprise, the sergeant staggered into the dining room with B[rody] on his shoulders, exclaiming, 'Here, lieutenant, I have brought you the counsellor, and, bad scran to him, I'm after carrying him four miles upon my back (Colloppy was a large powerful man), for he sat down on the road and swore he wouldn't budge an inch unless he got whiskey, and I had none to give him, so I whipped him up on my back like a sack, and here he is for your Honour.' 'Oh! His *Honour*,' roared out B[rody], who was quite drunk, 'I beg his *Honour's* pardon,' This curious exhibition caused much laughter and merriment, not only amongst the company at dinner, but also the inhabitants of the town, who followed the sergeant in crowds to the inn door, to witness the novel scene.

Having at length arrived, in May 1799, at head-quarters, in Gloucester, I found myself greatly relieved when I had given up my men, who were, fortunately for me, highly approved of.

A few days after, happening to meet B[rody] in the street, at an early hour in the morning, quite drunk, and talking familiarly to a gentleman named Windle, I remonstrated with him in the mildest manner, on the great impropriety of his conduct in exhibiting himself to the public I such a shameful state of inebriation. At the time, he made no reply, and I desired him to return to his quarters; however, in a few hours after, I received a letter from him, of which the following is a copy.

> To Mr John Harley,
> *Now* Lieutenant, Gloucester.
>
> Gloucester, 6th May, 1799
>
> Sir,
> On going to market this morning, accompanied by my friend Dr Windle, your *Honour* was pleased to address me in language very strange to me. But I have seen yourself, even your *own Honour,* to use a new-coined expression, as simply grogafied as myself; but, as your *Honour's* situation veils many indiscretions, and least any casualty may occur, I beg you will order your purse-bearer, alias Fitzgerald, your Pay-Sergeant, to pay me off my arrears of pay, marching money, billet money, beer money, fuel money. &c. &c.
>
> I have the honour to remain,
> Sir, with profound respect,
> Your *Honour's* most obedient servant,
> John Stephen Brody,
> Private Soldier,

As the above letter was written in a moment of great excitement, I took no notice of it. It appeared that the unfortunate fellow's feelings were deeply wounded by my remonstrance before a respectable stranger, as he imagined, and that, from my acquaintance with his connexions, I should not only have treated him with indulgence, but overlooked all his faults.

He remained with us for some time, but at length we were obliged to have him discharged, to his great annoyance and disappointment, as he became every day more troublesome and useless. When sober, his demeanour was that of a perfect gentleman, and his manners were refined and polished; but when drunk, he was a complete nuisance to everyone who had anything to do with him. While we were quartered in Gloucester, the assizes commenced, and as by the laws of England the military are prohibited remaining in the town while the judges are sitting, we were ordered out into cantonments in the neighbouring country – some companies to Tewksbury, some to Cheltenham, and the third division to Painswick.[29] There was no captain with this division, and as I was the oldest lieutenant, the command of it devolved on me, a circumstance that placed me in an awkward, and, at the same time, ludicrous situation.

At this period, a spirit of raising volunteer corps existed in England to a great extent, each town vying with the neighbouring towns in furnishing fine, well-looking men, the greatest anxiety being evinced that they should be properly disciplined. We were at the head inn of the village,[30] when the waiter announced to me that Captain Loveday, commander of the Painswick Volunteers, wished to have an interview with me.[31] He was of course ushered in, when, to my astonishment and confusion, he said that he called with a request that I would be good enough to review his corps (supposing me to be an experienced officer), which should be ready for my inspection at any time I wished. When I was about to reply and confess my inexperience in such matters, my brother officer, Lieutenant Sands, a pleasant waggish fellow, quickly answered for me, by saying that I should feel great pleasure in reviewing them, but would leave the hour to himself. Captain Loveday, quite rejoiced at his success, named six o'clock in the evening for the review, and, thanking me for my ready compliance with his request, took leave of us.

He had scarcely gone when Sands, who was an old officer, gravely assured me, that were I to decline reviewing the volunteers, I should run the risk of losing my commission, if his Majesty heard of it, as it was only a part of my duty. Deceived, therefore, by his arguments, put forth too with such confidence, and urged in the strongest language, I consented, though not without reluctance, to become inspecting field officer, as I was fully sensible of my unfitness for the task thus imposed on me. I had

29 A small village three miles north of Stroud.

30 He does not mean that it was called *The Head*, but that it was the chief inn. This was the 'Falcon Inn' which still exists today.

31 Captain Charles Loveday.

a drummer attached to my division, named Larry O'Hare, an honest, faithful creature, though, by-the-bye, he had deserted from different regiments of the line before he joined us. Upon hearing of the circumstance, and knowing how inadequate I was for such a performance, he watched my leaving the inn, and begged of me to have nothing to do with the inspection, as I had been such a short time in the army, and was of course unacquainted with the duties of a field officer.

By this time, the Painswick Volunteers, consisting chiefly of the manufacturers and clothiers of the village, were drawn up in line, on the bowling green, at the rear of the inn, in their best uniforms, and really making a very handsome appearance, while their families, and the ladies of the neighbourhood, were also in attendance to witness this grand review. I must confess, that when I saw the corps thus drawn up under arms, 100 strong, and commanded by a captain and two lieutenants, that my heart failed me, and I felt at a loss to know what to do – with Sands on the one side urging me on, and the drummer on the other side keeping me back, until I at length found myself in the middle of the green, and exactly opposite to the formidable array, where the rogue Sands then left me, that he might the better enjoy my confusion. Confused, indeed, I was, nor do I at this moment know how I could have been extricated from the difficulty in which I foolishly allowed myself to be placed, had it not been for the poor drummer, who, finding that I could not now retreat, gave me a few hasty instructions, at the same time endeavouring to inspire me with confidence. 'Never mind, lieutenant, honey,' said he, 'it will be all over in five minutes. Just go and stand in the centre in front of the line for a couple of seconds, then take off your hat, hold it for a moment over your head, but not very high, and put it on again; then go to the right of the line and walk down (looking very close at them) to the left, and turning to the commanding officer, tell him, that in the course of your service (then about a month) you never saw a finer or better disciplined body of men'. Sands being all this time opposite to me enjoying his joke, I strictly followed the instructions of my friend Larry, going through the several manoeuvres he had suggested. As soon as I had finished the inspection, with mock gravity, Captain Loveday gave the word to order arms and stand at ease, and then addressing the corps, said, 'Gentlemen volunteers, the commanding officer of his Majesty's troops desires me to express to you his high satisfaction with your state of discipline, and his admiration of your fine appearance, and to say that in the course of his military experience he has never inspected a finer body of men. In conclusion, I must thank you for the attention to your duties, which has obtained for you so distinguished a mark of approbation, and most sincerely congratulate on the pleasing result of this day's review.'

At the conclusion of this speech, the volunteers and their friends moved off the ground quite delighted with the evening's proceedings, and the review being now over, the captain and his two lieutenants came forward, and, having thanked me for the honour I had conferred upon their corps, requested that my brother officers and myself would give them the pleasure of our company to supper that night at the Falcon Inn. I was about to accept the invitation, when Sands again interfered, being apprehensive that I might decline the treat, and, popping his head over my shoulder, briefly replied that we should *all* do ourselves the honour of waiting on them. We accordingly met them at supper, and really spent an exceedingly pleasant evening. Thus terminated a review, probably remembered by many of those who were present on that day, and which gave as much satisfaction and pleasure to the Volunteers of Painswick, and probably answered as well as if Lord Wellington himself had inspected them.

This ridiculous review brings to my recollection a similar occurrence at Limerick, when I was quite a youngster. I remember witnessing the following scene, which appeared to cause much mirth to the bye-standers.

A regiment was at that period embodied called the Munster Provincials, or Fencibles,[32] and, on a company of this regiment coming to relieve the main guard, commanded by a Captain F[itzgerald], who knew little or nothing of military tactics (as commissions in this corps were given to private gentlemen), when he had to give the word of command to his guard, he forgot what it was.[33] After a delay of some minutes, he turned foolishly round, and, assuming a look of great military importance, said, 'Do as you used to do, boys.' The soldiers, laughing at this new style of command, shouldered arms, faced to the right and marched away, with their experienced captain at their head, who made short work of guard mounting, to the evident amusement of the spectators, amongst whom were several half-pay officers.

I shall never forget two of the recruits we had then; one, a country schoolmaster and poet, the other a strolling player, dubbing himself comedian. Each was vying with the other in praising his favourite officer; for the comedian was Captain Tooker's recruit,[34] while the schoolmaster was mine. During our march on our return from Painswick to Gloucester, the comedian amused his comrades with extempore verses in praise of Tooker, occasionally interlarding[35] them with the most ridiculous quotations from dramatic authors; while my poet, who, through sheer envy, pretended to look down upon his rival, committed the effusions of his prolific brain to paper, and handed it to me on my arrival at Gloucester. I remember a few words of this ludicrous composition.

'To Painswick brave Harley led the way,
His great commands the troops did obey;
From him till death they ne'er will stray
Sing, Garryowen, and clear the way,'

32 There were six Provincial Regiments raised in Ireland in 1782/1783. Two were raised in Munster, one being the 1st Munster Provincial Regiment, commanded by Colonel Arthur Blennerhassett. They ranked as Fencibles although not referred to as such. They appear to have been disbanded in late 1783.

33 This would appear to be Captain John Fraunces Fitzgerald the son of Colonel John Bateman Fitzgerald, 23rd Knight of Glin, colonel of the Glin cavalry regiment and artillery company raised in 1777.

34 Captain Richard Tooker.

35 Interspersing.

And oh! Such troops as I had on the march to and from Painswick; they consisted of a set of ragged recruits, among whom a counsellor, an actor, a poet, sweeps, tinkers, and tailors. So motley a crew had not I am convinced been collected since the days of the renowned Sir John Falstaff.

In June, we proceeded from Gloucester to Poole in Dorset-shire, and, as the weather was unusually hot, we deemed it most prudent to march by night, and rest by day. On passing over Salisbury Plain, where we made a halt for some minutes, I was surprised to observe the men regaling themselves with gin, being aware that they had no means to purchase it: the mystery, however, was solved on our reaching Poole, for we were quickly followed by an old woman from Salisbury Plain, from whom the men had obtained the liquor. She first applied to a magistrate, Mr Jeffreys,[36] producing a number of bad sixpences, which she alleged she had received from the soldiers who had just marched into town. The magistrate promptly communicated her complaint to us, and an inquiry being immediately set on foot, it was discovered that one of our recruits, named Totty O'Neill, a tinker by trade, had furnished himself and his comrades with the means of purchasing gin in the following very ingenious manner. Happening to call at the old woman's house for a drink of water during our halt on the plain, he spied a new tin lantern hanging up behind the door, which she had only purchased that morning in Salisbury market. Finding that she sold gin, and having no money to purchase some, he slipped out the lantern without her perceiving it, and with his tinker's shears, cut it quickly up into small pieces, shaped like sixpences, and then bending them to make them resemble as much as possible the coin then passing, he generously distributed them amongst his comrades, who soon became good customers to the old lady, purchasing in a few minutes her entire stock of gin. Totty having been examined, for we guessed that it was the work of some clever tinker, he readily confessed what he had done, and humorously said, 'Faith, gentlemen, I could not be in distress for a drop for myself and my comrades, but as the new coin I gave her don't please her, why sure there is £3*l*10*s* of my bounty yet in hand, in the name of St Patrick pay the old damsel out of that money, though she gave us such horrid confounded bad stuff.' In addition to the sum which poor Totty was obliged to allow her out of his bounty, we made up a subscription for her, as she had travelled sixty miles after us; so that she returned home with three times the amount of the price of her keg of gin. The magistrate, on learning the trick, laughed heartily, and was so pleased with Totty O'Neill's ingenuity, that he interceded for him with the commanding officer, who consented to pardon him in consequence of his interference.

During our stay at Poole, which was but short, we were very near getting into a serious scrape, that was likely to end in a general riot. Captain Rose,[37] of our regi-

36 Mr John Jeffreys, who also became an MP.

37 Hickman Rose was certainly a lieutenant at this time.

ment, who was remarkably fond of good ale, and had in vain tried to procure it in different parts of the town, at length learned that there was some of a superior description to be had in a house, called the King and Queen,[38] situated in a remote part of the town, near the quay, and frequented by fishermen and sailors (Poole at that time carrying on a considerable trade with Newfoundland). He and I, therefore, accompanied by Captain Taylor, repaired to the house in question about nine o'clock at night, with the intention of ordering some of the best ale to our quarters. Immediately on our entering the house, Rose, who had a very great impediment in his speech, addressing the landlady said, in the best manner he could. 'My goo-goo-good woman, I want some of your mi-mi-mild ale.' When the landlady, whom, to our utter astonishment, we found to be similarly afflicted, replied in evident anger, 'You va-va-va-vagabonds, you only come here to mo-mo-mo-mock me.' The more, poor Rose endeavoured to explain his object in coming there, the worse he made it, as his impediment increased with his confusion, and she only became more enraged, concluding from our manner that we came for the mere purpose of turning her into ridicule. At this moment, two of our young officers, Macnamara and Raymond entered,[39] and could not refrain from laughing when they witnessed the altercation. This confirmed her in her opinion. Explanations were offered by all of us, but in vain, and she burst out into complete violence.

Some sailors, fishermen, and porters, who had been drinking in the tap-room, rushed out on hearing the noise, and espoused the lady's cause, as was natural. Rose still stammered and stuttered away, but to no purpose, as the fellows made a most desperate attack on us, compelling us, after an unavailing resistance, to run for our lives; and pursuing us as far as the market-place, where, very fortunately, some of our soldiers happened to be at the moment, by whom we were protected from a good drubbing, occasioned merely by Captain Rose and the landlady of a tavern being unhappily subject to the same affliction. It was a long time before Rose could be perfectly reconciled to us, particularly the young officers, as he attributed the disaster to our laughing. Laugh, indeed, we did, and that heartily, at the commencement of the scene, and until matters assumed a more serious aspect, and, had the weeping philosopher himself been present, he could not have refrained from at least smiling on the occasion.

38 The 'King and Queen' Inn, East quay, Poole, no longer exists.
39 Captain James Raymond left the regiment in 1800.

3

A Murder and Transfer to the 54th Foot

We left Poole in September for Botley,[1] where we were reviewed by General Whitelocke on our arrival. The general, seeing the great number of women that accompanied the regiment, for we had as almost as many women as men, which was then generally the case with Irish regiments, immediately reported the circumstances to government, and in consequence an order came down in a few days from the commander-in-chief, directing all the women, with the exception of six for each company, to be instantly transmitted to Ireland, their native country. It was likewise ordered that they should be sent to Bristol, under charge of an officer, who was to see them embark for Ireland from that port. This unpleasant duty devolved upon me, but I had no way of avoiding it, and I undertook the charge, (with great reluctance I must allow,) of nearly four hundred women. The allowance from government was very liberal. I was instructed to pay each woman one shilling per day, and each child sixpence, and, on their embarking, a guinea was to be given to each woman, and half-a-guinea to each child. It was really distressing to behold the misery of these poor creatures on being thus separated from their husbands. The greater number of them had been married but a short time, and many of them having displeased their friends by marrying soldiers had not a home to return to. We of course did everything in our power to alleviate their distress, and to reconcile them to their situation. Previously to my setting out, it was requisite to have a route signed by the general of the district, to entitle them to billets, and I was therefore obliged to go over to Winchester to General St John for that purpose.[2] When the route was ready to be filled, a difficulty arose as to what term should be used, as we could not call them a regiment, detachment, or party. The general suggested that they should be styled 'the useless baggage', but Mrs St John, who was present, objected to the use of either of the words, so that finally it was determined to denominate them a detachment.

1 Botley is a small village three miles east of Southampton.

2 Major General the Honourable Frederick St John, who had served in Ireland during the 1798 Rebellion and was soon to sail for India in 1800 where he served at the Battle of Delhi in 1803.

Every necessary arrangement having been made, I proceeded, in full regimentals, with my battalion of women, accompanied by a sergeant, who was to assist me in procuring billets for them on the march. The first day we reached Romsey, where the constable, on seeing my detachment, refused to give any billets, alleging that it was a fraudulent route, women not being entitled to billets. I should have been placed in an awkward situation by this fellow's overstrained adherence to the letter of the law, although very probably, like the Pharisees, he cared very little for the spirit of it; but the innkeeper's wife fortunately took compassion on them, and lodged them comfortably in her outhouses until the following morning. We continued our march from Romsey, travelling through Hampshire and Wiltshire, not a little annoyed by the ribald jests and impertinent remarks of every low fellow, upon my regiment of *she soldiers*, as they called them, until we at length approached the city of Bath. Here I must confess my fortitude entirely forsook me; and, as I had many friends and acquaintances in Bath, it being then the height of the season, whose jokes on my marching into the city at the head or tail of a regiment of women, I could not bear the idea of, I left them within about a mile of the city, in charge of the sergeant, giving him the day's pay to distribute amongst them. I had just sat down to dinner at the ordinary in the White Hart, about five o'clock, when one of the waiters running in, called out aloud to me, with a sneer upon his countenance – 'Colonel, some of your women are below in the hall, and want to speak to you.' I was greatly confused, there being at the time between twenty and thirty gentlemen at the table, but seemed to take no notice of what the waiter had said. In a few seconds, before I could compose myself sufficiently to determine how I should act, the door was opened, and forty or fifty of my followers rushed into the room, headed by the wife of one of our black drummers, demanding payment of their day's allowance, and threatening, that if I did not give it to them, they would that moment set out on their return to their husbands. Confused and terrified, I started from the table, ran out of the room pursued by the mutinous party, and fortunately made good my retreat to the York House.[3] Having given strict orders to the waiters not to acknowledge to any person that I was in the house, I sent for the sergeant, and desired him to inform the women, that if they followed me again in that disorderly manner, I would leave them at once, and not render them any further assistance. This determined message had the desired effect, and they conducted themselves with tolerable propriety during the remainder of the journey.

On my arrival with my *corps des femmes* at Bristol, I hired a vessel to convey them to Cork, assisted by a gentleman of the city, Mr Savery, a banker, who also gave me cash for my bills without charging discount, and instructed me how to proceed in

3 The York House Hotel, in George Street, Bath, later the Royal York House Hotel which still exists as a Grade II Listed Building.

obtaining three day's provisions for the women and children.[4] Indeed, I shall ever hold his kindness, on that trying occasion, in grateful remembrance. Not anticipating any further delay or obstruction, I put them on board on Saturday evening, and engaged a boat to convey me down the river to Lamplighter's Hall,[5] where I slept that night, for the purpose of seeing the vessel set sail the next morning. But a disappointment awaited me. In the morning, the captain called to inform me that his ship had been seized, and detained by the Custom House officers, in consequence of his not having a permit from the collector of the port.

This intelligence was a great mortification to me, after all the trouble I had taken, in making, as I thought, every necessary arrangement. However, something was required to be done immediately. I therefore went to Bristol, and, although it was Sunday, made application to Mr Collins, the collector,[6] for the requisite certificate. He told me that he could do nothing for me, unless I would promise to dine with him; but, on my saying that I should feel pleasure in doing so, he instantly granted the permit, with which, after dinner, I returned to the vessel, and had the gratification of seeing the poor women and children sail the same evening, with a fair breeze for old Ireland.

As soon as I had thus got rid of a charge, which had occasioned me more trouble and uneasiness than any circumstance either before or since, I returned to Bath without any farther delay, and took my seat in the Southampton coach, to join my regiment, then stationed at Botley. My fellow passengers were two fine boys, who had each a card fastened to the cape of his coat, with a direction on it – 'To be left at Mr [Nowe]'s school, near Warminster, in Wiltshire.'[7] This novel mode of sending children to school surprised me not a little, particularly when an old maiden aunt, who had escorted them to the office, requested that I would be good enough to have them dropped according to the direction; a request, with which I, of course, complied.

As the night was unusually cold, I wrapped myself closely in my cloak, and, being overcome by the fatigue, both of body and mind, that I had suffered during the last few days, I quickly fell into a sound sleep, out of which I was, however, disturbed in a short time, by the entrance of a respectable looking elderly gentleman, who, the moment he had taken his seat, commenced making common-place observations, to which, as I was annoyed by his unseasonable interruption of my slumbers, I paid

4 Mr John Savery of the firm of Savery, Towgood, Yerbury, and Towgood, Wine Street, Bristol, was the banker who worked with John Rennie in 1799 trying to fund the Southampton and Salisbury Canal. His sixth son Henry Savery was tried in 1824 for forgery and was transported to Tasmania, where he became a celebrated novelist.

5 The 'Lamplighter's Hall' was a public house at Shirehampton from around 1760 where the Pill ferry went from and it became a favourite resort for pleasure parties. It still exists as Lamplighters.

6 The collector of custom dues.

7 This almost certainly refers to a school run by Mr John Nowes, who set up a school at Fisherton Anger in 1721 for forty boys under 13 years. It is now Fisherton Anger Church of England Junior & Infants School.

no attention. At length, he asked me from whence I came. I answered, sullenly, from Bristol. He then inquired if I had heard any recent news from Ireland, and on my replying in the negative – 'Do you think,' said he, 'that the Union' – the question being at that time pending – 'will pass the Irish Parliament? If I were to have the management,' he continued, without waiting for my opinion, 'I would cram it down the throats of the Irish scoundrels with English bayonets; for they are guilty of every crime that can disgrace human nature. Have you heard, sir,' said he, with all the seriousness imaginable, 'that the rascally Papists have roasted Protestant children on spits, and actually eaten them? I assure you, sir, I am credibly informed that such is the fact; and I am, therefore, of opinion, that that country can never enjoy peace, nor the rising generation be tamed, or brought to any state of civilisation, until all the old Papists are driven out it, and colonies of English settlers placed in their stead.'

At this part of his observations, and while I was conjecturing who my fellow traveller might be, not doubting but that he had lost the use of his reason, the coach stopped to change horses. On hearing me call for a glass of Wiltshire ale, which is considered the best in England, he requested me not to drink such poisonous, pernicious stuff. 'You shall sup with me to-night,' said he, 'and I will give you some home brewed ale, far superior to any of the kind you can obtain here, the making of which is always superintended by my wife or my daughters.' This kind invitation, soothing my irritation a good deal, and removing much of that repulsive feeling with which I had been previously disposed to receive his observations, I became more familiar with him, and now and then offered an opinion, neither coinciding, nor yet directly at variance, with his. As we proceeded to Romsey, he resumed the conversation on Irish topics; and, after a slight discussion, in which, as I did not wish to offend the old gentleman, I merely ventured to doubt that the Irish were really so bad as they were generally represented, he exclaimed, little knowing that he was speaking to an Irishman, 'Oh! You have no conception, my dear sir, of their villainy; they are capable of crimes of the blackest dye; as a proof of it, I only need assure you, that there is an Irish regiment stationed in my neighbourhood, who have stolen nearly all my fowls, so that I have been scarcely left a single hen, goose, turkey, or duck.' I told him that if he made the circumstances known to the commanding officer of the regiment, he would obtain immediate redress. 'No, no,' said he, 'redress is unfortunately out of the question; for, though the soldiers steal my fowls, it is the officers who eat them.'

When the coach stopped at Romsey, this worthy, but mistaken and credulous old man, did not forget to renew his invitation, which, however, I was reluctantly obliged to decline. While he was taking leaving of me with a hearty squeeze of the hand, the hostess of the White Horse Inn,[8] the same that had been so kind to the women on our route to Bristol, came forward to the coach-door, and addressing

8 The White Horse Inn, in Market Place, Romsey, a 600 year old coaching inn which still exists today.

me by name, said, 'Welcome back, Lieutenant Harley,' and my cloak opening at the same time, he saw my uniform, and inquired where my regiment lay, and how far I had to go. I replied, 'to Southampton.' 'Do you go no further?' said he. And, on my answering to Botley Barracks, and telling him that I had the honour to belong to the Irish regiment, the men and officers of which stole and eat his fowls, the old gentleman decamped as speedily as possible, and without bidding me a final adieu.

I subsequently learned that he was the rector of Romsey, and as worthy a man as ever lived; beloved by all his parishioners, and held in general esteem by all who had the pleasure of his acquaintance.[9] His accusation against our regiment, and his confusion, when he learned that I was one of the officers, caused many a hearty laugh at our mess-table; and, for some time after, we were frequently in the habit of inquiring of our cook, if he had any of the doctor's fowls for our dinner. I have often regretted since, that I did not call and pay my respects to him, before I left the neighbourhood. As he was so misinformed on Irish affairs, and so foolishly prejudiced against the Irish people, I ought, in justice to my countrymen, to have disabused the mind of this worthy, well-disposed man of those unjust prejudices and mistaken notions under which he appeared to labour.

A circumstance occurred at Botley, about this period, which annoyed the regiment very much, and very probably strengthened the opinion the worthy rector of Romsey entertained of the Irish character. An account reached our barracks about nine o'clock one evening, that an old man, upwards of seventy years of age, had been murdered on the Common by two soldiers. An investigation immediately took place, but we found all our men in barracks. Two of them, however, Pendergrass and Deigan, being out constantly together, at late hours, our suspicions fell on them, and they were accordingly put in close confinement. As it appeared subsequently, that the poor man was killed with a bayonet, part of which remaining in his neck, was extracted and brought to the barracks, a closer inquiry was instituted, and it was discovered that our shoemaker's bayonet was missing; and, although it was well ascertained that he had not left his room the entire day, he was confined on suspicion, as was also Sergeant Colloppy, a pay sergeant, from having a few drops of blood upon his shoulder-belt for which he could not account.

Next morning, a public investigation was held at the Head Inn, in the presence of several magistrates; and, after the several witnesses had been strictly examined, the prisoners were remanded until the following day, and ordered to be confined separately. In the interim, my washer-woman communicated to me, privately, that she had just seen Pendergrass, who had sent a message by her to Deigan, desiring him to keep all he knew secret and there was no danger. I lost not a moment in taking her before the magistrates, who were still sitting in consultation, before whom she made the same declaration. Deigan was again brought before the magistrates, and made a voluntary confession of the murder, and explained all the

9 John Woodburn was the Rector of Romsey from 1780 to 1807.

circumstances attending it, acknowledging, also, that he had been concerned in many highway robberies.

He stated, that he and Pendergrass were in the habit of committing petty robberies on the roads, and that, at the last fair of Romsey, they had robbed a farmer of £2/13s. – that, on the night of the murder, it was their intention to stop and rob me, on my return home from a friend's house to my quarters, and, in the event of their not meeting with me, to lie in wait for Sergeant Colloppy, who, they were aware, had charge of the company's pay; but, being disappointed in their intended attack upon us, and seeing an old man decently clad, making some purchases in a shop in the village, whom they supposed to be a wealthy farmer, they followed him until he had reached the Common, where they attacked him, and took from him six eggs (which they carried home unbroken) and seven pence in change. The poor man, instead of being a rich farmer, was supported by the parish; Pendergrass stabbed him in the neck with the bayonet, which broke on his attempting to pull it out, and, hearing a carriage driving up, they threw him into a ditch among some briers, and returned to their quarters. As he also confessed that it was with the shoemaker's bayonet (which they had obtained without his knowledge) that the inhuman murder was committed, the man was released from custody, and the handle of his bayonet was found the next morning under the bridge, where they had thrown it in their retreat. But poor Colloppy, who was no way concerned in the transaction, was, in consequence of his not being able to account for the spots of blood, committed to Winchester gaol with Pendergrass and Deigan, to stand his trial at the following assizes. The unfortunate Deigan expressed great contrition for his crimes, and acknowledged that he deserved to suffer; but that he had one consolation – that he did not give the fatal blow; nor ever had an intention of committing murder. He appeared to think, that it was by the special intervention of Providence, he was brought to justice; for their poor victim, desperately as he was wounded, contrived to crawl along more than a mile upon his hands and knees, until he reached his house, when he threw himself on the floor, and had just life and strength enough to declare that he had been murdered by two soldiers, when he expired. While our poor sergeant was in Winchester gaol, awaiting his trial for the awful charge of murder, a circumstance came to his recollection, which immediately obtained his release. On the day of the murder, he had called on me, at Mrs Tinny's house, for the company's pay. She detained him to dinner, and while he was picking a bone, with his knife in his hand, he gave his ear a slight cut, which caused it to bleed. As soon as this circumstance was made known to the magistrates, and confirmed by Mrs Tinny's testimony, Colloppy was discharged out of custody, and returned to his regiment, with unsullied reputation.

When Deigan's trial came on, he pleaded guilty, and was sentenced to be hanged and gibbeted on the Common where the murder was committed – a sentence which was fully carried into execution; but Pendergrass, pleading his own cause, was, strange to say, acquitted for want of evidence. He then returned to his regiment, with all the confidence of innocence, notwithstanding the confession of his less guilty accomplice, and refused to do any further duty, unless he got the arrears of pay that had accrued while he was in confinement, which was incompatible with the regulations of the army. He was, therefore, tried by a regimental court martial for disobedience of orders, and sentenced to receive three hundred lashes, and to be drummed out of the regiment, both of which were carried into execution. And here I cannot but remark the glaring inconsistency of the inhabitants of Winchester. They first accused the officers of our regiment of being too lenient and partial to the men, particularly to this fellow; and took every opportunity of insulting us in the streets; but, when they saw him punished, and turned out of the town, they followed him, brought him back, and made a handsome subscription for him. Thus, the principal in the murder escaped for the present – I say for the present – for justice, either from Heaven or earth, must at length overtake him; while the unfortunate man whom he had seduced into the commission of crime, and led in to the paths of guilt, forfeited his life to the laws of the country.[10]

I shall never forget my first visit to London. It took place while our regiment lay in Botley. Colonel Anstey,[11] son of the celebrated Doctor Anstey, who wrote the Bath Guide,[12] being kind enough to feel a partiality for me, gave me a seat in his curricle; and we stopped together at Hatchet's Hotel, Piccadilly, in those days, a house remarkable for its moderate charges; beds being only one shilling per night, and dinners, very excellent ones, but one shilling and sixpence.[13] These prices, however, reasonable as they were, did not satisfy me. I was at that time an economist, not a political, but a domestic one; and, as I deemed even those charges to

10 According to *Bell's Weekly Messenger* this murder occurred on 2 March 1800. Three soldiers of the Tarbert Fencibles reportedly came across a travelling man named Thomas Webb from Swanmore, whom they robbed of a few shillings after which they stabbed him numerous times, then threw him into a ditch and stamped on him. Despite his terrible wounds, Webb found the strength to crawl to the cottage of a Daniel Barfoot, nearly a mile away, where a surgeon was sent for, who removed a part of a bayonet in his body, six and a half inches in length.

According to the *Evening Mail* all three accused appeared before the Lent Assizes at Winchester that lasted from eleven in the morning until midnight. Pendergrass and Colloppy were released for lack of evidence, but Deigan (often spelt Diggins in the newspaper reports) was found guilty of murder and sentenced to execution on 17 March 1800. Pendergrass was later given 600 of a 1,000 lash sentence by a court martial for disobedience of orders. He received the remaining 400 later and was then drummed out of the regiment.

Deigan is recorded as having shown remorse and begged Webb's wife's forgiveness. He was hung at the gibbet on Curdridge Common, the body was then taken back to the place where the murder occurred and his body hung there in chains. He was only 22 years of age when he died. There is a memorial stone to Thomas Webb at the side of a drinking fountain in Botley which had been erected by 1801.

11 Lieutenant Colonel Robert Anstey of the Tarbert Fencibles.

12 Christopher Anstey (1724-1805) actually gained an MA at Cambridge but was not awarded a doctorate, having written an article which offended the university authorities. He lived the last thirty-five years of his life at Bath and wrote the celebrated *The New Bath Guide – or Memoirs of the B_n_r_d Family in a series of Poetical Epistles.*

13 Hatchett's Hotel and Coffee House in Piccadilly was renowned.

Photograph of the memorial to Thomas Webb. (Author's collection)

be too high, I resolved to find out some other house more suited for a subaltern's pocket. I therefore, sallied forth, on the second or third morning, at an early hour, on my tour of discovery; and meeting in Covent Garden with an Irish basket-woman, I requested she would be good enough to direct me to a cheap house to dine at; and show me where the playhouse was, being resolved to see one play at least, before I left London. My countrywoman, expressing her willingness to serve me in any way, shewed me the door of Covent Garden Theatre, and, pointing out the Bedford, which she said was a mighty decent place to dine at, asked me for some silver for all her trouble, 'and,' said she, 'to drink the health of Ould Ireland, your Honour, and St Patrick.'

On my entering the dining room of the Bedford, I was surrounded by several well-powdered waiters, who soon *smoking* me,[14] from my broad Irish accent, and knowing me to be a fresh arrival, unacquainted with the ways of the town, were determined to have a bit of fun with me. Three of them came up to me together; one asking what I would like for dinner; another producing a long bill of fare, nearly as long as a bill of costs; and the third, waiting to know at what table his *Honour* would wish to dine; each of them with a broad grin upon his countenance, such as those with which Liston has frequently amused the play-going folk of London;[15] or, as my readers may have seen happily delineated, on the cover and frontispiece of 'Hood's Comic Annual.'[16]

Not knowing well how to make a selection from such a variety of good things, I told the waiters I would leave it to themselves, to provide a good dinner for three; and, as near the hour of five as possible as I and my two friends purposed going to the play. 'You shall have a good dinner, sir,' said one of the fellows; 'but as to the play, your Honour need not be in a hurry on that account, as we will make it wait for your Honour, until any hour you wish.' On saying which, they bowed themselves away, turning me into ridicule all the time – though I was too stupid to perceive it – and I departed with the prospect of enjoying a cheap and good dinner, and of seeing the play.

Meeting in the course of the day, with my two colonels, Sir Edward Leslie and Colonel Anstey, I communicated to them my good fortune, in having discovered an excellent and cheap house, called the Bedford, quite contiguous to the theatre; and asked them if they would join me at dinner, and accompany me to the play. They, smiling at each other, assented; and, as it was then after four o'clock, and we were in a distant part of the city, we proceeded, after a short delay, to Covent Garden, and arrived at the Bedford exactly at the hour appointed.

14 An archaic word for making fun of somebody.

15 The comic actor John Liston (1776-1846). He made his first appearance at Covent Garden in 1805 and continued playing there regularly for the next twenty-five years.

16 The *Comic Annual* was published each Christmas by Thomas Hood from 1830 with a mixture of comic poetry, prose and illustrations; it went on for sixty years.

In a few minutes, dinner was served up, consisting of a little soup meagre, four marrow bones, three herrings, and a small joint of roast mutton; and they placed wine on the table, although it was not ordered. During dinner, Sir Edward [Leslie] and Colonel Anstey were rather silent; and, as I observed them now and then smiling at each other, and a significant nod or wink occasionally passing between them, I felt extremely mortified, supposing them to be annoyed with me, for not having providing a more substantial dinner.

The matter was, however, soon cleared up; for on the bill being called for, after dinner, I found a separate charge made for everything, even the wax-lights, fire, &c.; and that instead of my having used economy, my proportion of the bill amounted to seventeen shillings. Provoked beyond measure at my own foolishness, and the ridiculous figure I must have cut, I vowed I would leave London the next day, and declined going to the theatre. The colonels laughed heartily at my plan of saving, in leaving a cheap and comfortable house for one of the most fashionable and expensive in London; and only prevailed upon me, after much persuasion, to accompany them to the play, where I had the pleasure of witnessing Miss Melon's first appearance, now Duchess of St Albans.[17] On our return home from the theatre that night, the expensive dinner was so annoying to me, that I never ceased cursing English extortion; telling Sir Edward, that if I were in Limerick, I could get the herrings and marrow bones for five-pence, and the mutton equally cheap. To this, his only reply was, 'Don't annoy yourself, my dear Harley, about such trifles, but be more knowing in the future.' Determined on returning at once to my regiment, I called in the morning for my bill, when I was informed that Sir Edward Leslie had discharged it the previous night, on his return from the play; an act of friendship I feel proud in acknowledging, for a better-hearted or a more generous man than Sir Edward never lived.

Some days after my return from London, I went over to Winchester, accompanied by Captain Hefferman,[18] to receive a large sum of money. We returned across the common about ten o'clock, on a fine moonlight night, and were engaged in an interesting conversation, when the postilion suddenly stopped. On our looking out to ascertain the cause, we perceived a well-dressed, gentlemanly-looking man, mounted on a very fine horse, speaking to the postilion, and, after a moment's delay, galloping off in the direction from whence we had come. At the next stage, where we obtained fresh horses, the postilion informed us that he had been stopped by a highwayman, who, presenting a pistol at him, demanded who was in

17 Harley's memory is slightly out here. The actress Harriett Melon had already acted for some time and her debut at Drury Lane had occurred in 1795. Whilst on tour in Cheltenham in 1810, she met Mr Coutts, who pursued her amorously until his wife died in 1815, when he immediately offered to marry her. They did marry and she left the stage immediately, they appear to have been happy together until his death in 1822. In 1825, she was introduced to the much younger (by 20 years) Duke of St Albans at Sir Walter Scott's Abbotsford and they soon married. She was at the coronation of William IV and died in 1837.

18 Captain John Hefferman of the Tarbert Fencibles.

the carriage; that, on his replying there were two officers, he said, 'curse them, they are not worth the trouble of stopping,' and immediately rode off. He represented the man, as we judged ourselves, from the view we had of him, to be of a very respectable appearance, and his horse to be worth not less than £100.

John Harley transferred to the 54th (West Norfolk) Regiment of Foot as Quartermaster on 12 June 1800 when a second battalion had begun forming at Winchester on 16 May. Both battalions of the regiment then sailed in August, arriving at Gibraltar by the end of the month and went on to Minorca in the November, before sailing for Egypt in the December. The regiment landed at Aboukir Bay in March 1801 and was involved in the Battle of Alexandria and remained in Egypt until late that year when they sailed to Minorca. They sailed from Minorca in February 1802 and then proceeded to Gibraltar where the second battalion was disbanded in the May; at this time Harley went on half pay and returned to Britain. The first battalion remained on the Rock until 1805.

During this short visit to Winchester, I was solicited, by the late General Darby, then colonel in command of the 54th, to join that regiment, which was stationed at that time in Winchester.[19] The request having been made in terms so flattering, and the exchange from a fencible into a regular regiment holding out, under such circumstances, a prospect of considerable advantage, I parted from my old comrades with great regret, and, joining the 54th in Winchester, passed the spring very pleasantly in that town.[20]

A few days after I had joined the 54th Regiment at Winchester, the recruiting sergeant brought me in two recruits; and, as I was always zealous to obtain men for my regiment, he brought them first to me. I gave them some money on account of their bounty: and from their youth and appearance I was completely satisfied as to their fitness for the service. On Colonel Darby seeing them, he said to me, 'Harley, why should we encourage such young men to enlist? I never wish to have gentlemen's sons in that capacity, for they presume too much on their former rank in life, and are seldom good soldiers.' They turned out very different from what I supposed them to have been; they were both lieutenants of the line, who had been lately dismissed for improper conduct. The unfortunate Mac[ombe], the best behaved of the two, was cashiered for his propensity to indulge in liquor. He had been in the 52nd regiment, and was the nephew of a general of the same name.[21]

19 Lieutenant Colonel Christopher Darby was in command of the 1st Battalion.

20 John Harley transferred into the 2nd Battalion 54th (West Norfolk) Regiment of Foot on 12 June 1800, to be their quartermaster.

21 Lieutenant John Macombe, or M'Combe, of the 52nd Foot had transferred to the 48th Foot but was cashiered on 22 December 1801. His relation General Alexander Macomb (1782-1841) became the general commanding the United States Army in 1828.

Nothing else was attributable to him but his unfortunate propensity for drinking. D[ixo]n had been a lieutenant of the 89th regiment, and was cashiered and struck out of the army list, without a court martial, for a most atrocious crime. He was on duty in the neighbourhood of Buttevant, in the county Cork, in Ireland, during the disturbed state of the country, in 1798; a farmer's daughter was left under his protection by the magistrate and her friends, in the guard-house; D[ixo]n was the officer on duty; but instead of protecting her, as a man of honour would have done, he acted towards her as a villain. The circumstances becoming known, he was dismissed by the King, without court martial.[22] The colonel was perfectly right in his remark to me, for D[ixo]n deserted, and behaved like a scoundrel. The unfortunate Mac[ombe] died on our passage to Egypt.

About this period, Edmond O'Brien B[utler], a relation of my wife's, joined our regiment as a volunteer from the Tipperary Militia.[23] Previously to his leaving Ireland, he called at Cashel to take leave of his maternal uncle, the late Lord D[unboyne], Roman Catholic Archbishop of Cashel;[24] and, as soon as he had received his benediction, he informed his mother that he intended walking, his means being limited, from Cashel to Cork, a distance of sixty miles. The good woman, feeling for her promising son, ordered her old coachman, Mick Flanagan, though not, indeed, without some hesitation, to saddle one of her favourite carriage horses for Master Mun and to ride the other himself, and accompany him to Cork, where he was to embark for England; 'but above all things, Mick,' said the old lady, 'take good care of my poor horses, that we have had now more than fifteen years in the family.'

They accordingly set out together, and reached Cork in due time; but, on their arrival there, Master Mun on one pretence or another, detained poor Mick from day to day, until one evening missing his master, and proceeding to the livery stables to inquire after him, found to his great surprise, that Master Mun had sold the old carriage horses that morning; and set sail for Portsmouth, leaving him only the two saddles and a bridle to carry home to his mistress. As Mick was something of a stoic, he bore the loss with great fortitude, and disposing of one of the saddles to obtain the means of subsistence on the road, and putting the other with the bridle on his back, he pursued his wearisome journey home, where he arrived on the following evening. No pen can describe the appearance of poor Mick; trudging up the lawn in front of the house with his heavy load, which he had thus carried sixty Irish miles; nor could any but the pencil of Hogarth, give a faithful and true picture of Mrs B[utler]'s countenance, when informed by Mick – the saddle still on

22 This must be Robert Dixon who had been an ensign in the 89th but transferred into the 83rd as a lieutenant but simply disappears from the Army List in late 1798. There was also an Ensign John Dixon in the 89th, who never rose to the rank of lieutenant and who resigned on 15 December 1798. I discount the latter as he never became a lieutenant and was allowed to resign, thus would get his commission money back.

23 Lieutenant Edmond O'Brien Butler.

24 Archbishop James Butler, Roman Catholic Archbishop of Cashel 1774-1791.

his back – of the loss of her favourites, and the disgraceful conduct of her hopeless son. After the first paroxysms of rage had subsided, anger gave way to revenge, and she felt herself somewhat satisfied by making a solemn declaration that she would never forgive him! While the old servant, who thought that his mistress might be satisfied when she did not lose himself, endeavoured to console her, by showing the hazard he ran in being carried off to the wars by the soldiers, and by declaring his willingness to serve her to the end of the world, whether she had carriage horses or not.

Lieutenant Edmond O'Brien B[utler] reached Portsmouth in the *Dictator* man-of-war,[25] with the last division of his regiment. The night before they disembarked, having made too free with some grog, in company with one of the ship's officers, he overslept himself, so that on going on shore in the morning, at rather a late hour, he found that the division had already marched, but to what place, or for what destination, he could not tell, having forgotten the name of the town, and being as ignorant of geography as a native of Owhyhee.[26]

As he could just recollect that the first syllable was Win, one of those loiterers about the inn doors, to whom Master Mun had made known his embarrassment, told him it must be Windsor; for which place he immediately took a seat by the first coach.

As they were entering Windsor, one of his fellow-passengers, to whom he happened to mention that he was going to join his regiment, the 54th, then quartered in Windsor, remarked, 'there must be some mistake, sir, as there never is any regiment stationed here, except the Guards; but if I recollect well, I saw your regiment, the 54th, marching this very morning into Winchester.' '*By de dod!* You are right, sir,' exclaimed B[utler], 'and how far is that from us?' 'About ninety miles,' said his companion. 'Oh then, *by de dod*, sir, I can never get there, as I have no money,' said B[utler], letting his voice fall to the lachrymose key, as he spoke of the needful. The gentleman, having some of the milk of human kindness, took pity on our young soldier, and invited him to his house that night, where he entertained him most hospitably; and, lending him five pounds in the morning, enabled him to join his regiment, after a further delay of two days, occasioned by the mistake he had made.

He proceeded with us to Egypt, and, after the conclusion of the campaign in that country, returned to England, and going up to London, took his abode in Hatchett's Hotel, Piccadilly. Never having been in London before, he was at a loss to find his way through the streets; he therefore hired, as he thought very wisely, the son of the boots of the hotel, a boy about twelve years of age, at 5*s*. per day, who was to show him London, point out the streets and buildings, and accompany him everywhere he wished through the metropolis. As the Haymarket Theatre, the favourite resort of his late Majesty, George the Third, was then open,

25 HMS *Dictator* was a 64-gun warship.
26 Old English name for Hawaii.

he determined upon going to the play, and accordingly proceeded thither with his guide, to whom, previously to entering the house, he gave a pound note, as he supposed to pay for himself only. He had not been very long in the theatre, where he had taken a front seat in the centre box, when, turning to his guide, who was stationed behind him, he demanded his change, and when the boy, who had paid for himself as well as his master, handed him six shillings, he exclaimed, '*Oh dod!* Here are only six thirteens, where are the rest?' The lad then told him that he paid fourteen shillings for their two tickets – seven shillings each. Upon hearing this, he made a great noise, abusing the boy, so as to attract the attention of his Majesty, who, seeing him in such a rage, and observing his Egyptian medal, sent one of the Lords in waiting to him, to inquire who he was. 'Tell him,' said B[utler], 'by *de dod,* (a favourite expression of his) that I am O'Brien B[utler], of de 54th regiment, just home from Egypt, and on my way to sweet Tipperary.' The good-natured monarch was highly amused at the incident, for he was also made acquainted with the cause of his anger, and laughed heartily at B[utler]'s eccentric reply.

As in a few days his cash began to run rather short, he was anxious to get home while he still had the means; and, upon consulting his guide, it was determined that he should go to the Royal Exchange to look out for some ship that was homeward bound. He accordingly went there, and, after reading several advertisements for shipping to almost every port in the world, without meeting with the one he wanted, he asked different persons whom he met, if there was any ship bound for the town of Tipperary. Being very naturally turned into ridicule, and sent about, for their amusement, from one person to another, he was almost out of patience, when a gentleman, feeling pity for him, told him not to take notice of anything that had been said to him, but to take his seat in the morning, for Bristol, in one of the coaches, from whence he could proceed to Waterford in the packet, and then on to Clonmel and Tipperary.

When he had paid his bill at the hotel, he found that he had but £10 remaining; he, therefore, set his wits at work to know what he could take home to his mother as a present, that would please her, and still leave enough to bear his expenses on the road. As the old lady was very religious, he fixed upon making her a present of prayer books, thinking that such a peace-offering would induce her to forgive him for having sold her favourite horses. He, therefore, went to a bookseller's, and ordered three pound's worth of the best gilt prayer books, which were that evening packed and sent to him.

As I happened to be at his mother's when he arrived, I was present at the meeting. As soon as the usual congratulations had taken place, the family flocked round him, each expecting a present from some foreign country, and supposing that he had brought home wonderful curiosities. When his trunk was opened, all it contained was an old regimental coat, a pair of Maltese trousers,[27] and the

27 Loose nankeen trousers.

parcel of prayer books, which he opened, and presented to his mother, with filial reverence, observing, that he should have felt shame if he had forgotten her, and trusted that the present he now offered, would meet with her approbation. The poor woman, delighted at seeing the prayer books, exclaimed, with rapture, 'Oh, Mun! my child, although you were always a wild boy, I never gave up the hope of seeing you, one day or other, become a religious character, and profit by the instruction you received in your youth'. 'This present,' said she, 'amply repays me for all the trouble you have ever occasioned me; and I am sure when I give one of these good books to Mick Flanagan, he will join with me in forgiving you for having sold our poor carriage horses.' She then anxiously opened the prayer books, which, to her horror and consternation, she found to be rituals of the protestant church. Nothing could equal her rage, for she was a violent bigot. His brother and I did everything in our power to appease her, but in vain; she would not listen to anything we could in his favour; nor would she believe it to have been a mistake of the bookseller's, as we told her. 'I forgave him,' said she, 'all his bad acts, even his selling my horses, but his purchasing heretic prayer books for me, and then presenting them to me, is an insult to my religion that I never can forgive.' She was as good as her word; and this poor fellow, whose good nature could not be exceeded, and whose eccentric character, and manner of speaking, caused much innocent mirth amongst his brother officers, died, in a short time after, of drinking, at Mallow, in the county Cork; about the same period, indeed, that his uncle, the Roman Catholic Archbishop of Cashel, caused so much noise in the world by his conversion to the Protestant religion.

This old gentleman was seventy years of age when he took it into his head to abjure the errors of Popery and take a wife, a Miss B[utler], an ugly old maid, about forty-five years of age, and by becoming Protestant, he obtained the title and estates of Dunboyne. The honey-moon, however, was scarcely over, when the old man began to repent of the foolish step he had taken; and, again recanting, returned to the bosom of the mother church, but not to his former see, from which he was for ever excluded. By the advice of his confessor, and in order to make atonement for the heinous crime he had committed, he separated from his disconsolate bride, and went into retirement for the short time he survived, attended only by his chaplain.[28]

During his last illness, he made a will, conveying over all his estates and property to Government, for the benefit of the Roman Catholic college of Maynooth;

28 James Butler the Catholic Archbishop, had inherited the Barony of Dunboyne from his nephew, but he was aware that the family line would end there unless he had a son. As a Catholic cleric, he could of course not marry, so he resigned his position as bishop and appealed to the Pope for special dispensation to marry. Even though this was refused, he married Maria Butler and he took the Protestant faith. The couple had a daughter, who unfortunately soon died and his house was attacked in the 1798 Rebellion. In 1800, he wrote a letter of repentance to the Pope and made a confession to a Catholic priest, before he died in Dublin.

thereby excluding his nephew, Peirce O'Brien B[utler], of Blancha, from all he had possessed. His family, however, being, of course, dissatisfied with such an arrangement, contested the bequest, and commenced a suit to recover the estate in the right line, during which his confessor was imprisoned twelve months in Newgate, Dublin, to force him to divulge a trust reposed in him; and, after a protracted and expensive litigation, carried on by the nephew, a compromise was at length effected, by which he obtained the Dunboyne estates, leaving the College of Maynooth in possession of the remainder of the property; but as for the title, he would not accept of it, preferring to remain a plain but respectable country gentleman.

To return to my regiment. About the latter end of May, 1800, we left Winchester for Netley Common, near Southampton, where we encamped; and where an army consisting of nearly 30,000 men were then assembled for foreign service, under the command of Sir James Pulteney.[29] Better or braver troops could not be seen, being composed of the flower of the Irish militia regiments, that had then, for the first time, got permission to volunteer, as the old regiments of the line were perfect skeletons, and men were not to be had in the usual way by recruiting. We lay encamped in this delightful situation for a month, within view of the Isle of Wight, and close to the beautiful town of Southampton, the New Forest, and the celebrated Netley Abbey;[30] and, on the 1st of July, we suddenly embarked and proceeded to Portsmouth. The day before we were to set sail, Mr F[irmin], the well-known military tailor of London, unexpectedly made his appearance among us, to the great annoyance of many of our young subs, who were more or less in Mr F[irmin]'s debt. Upon holding a council of war, to consider how the enemy could be defeated, for they shrewdly suspected that the tailor had been making arrangements with two gentlemen, called John Doe and Richard Roe[31], it was thought advisable to prepare a masked battery[32], and send him a friendly invitation to dinner: a compliment by which he felt highly honoured.

From the moment dinner was placed on the table, Mr F[irmin] was scarcely allowed time to eat a morsel, each of his young friends pledging him in bumpers of madeira, port, and sherry, of which he purposely obliged to drink alternately. By the time the cloth was removed, the poor tailor was, in the language of the fancy, *done up*, being quite unable to move. While in this state, one of the wags searched his pockets, and actually discovered writs marked against every one of those who were in his books, which, no doubt, he intended to put into execution on the following

29 Lieutenant General Sir James Murray Pulteney (1755-1811) commanded the Ferrol expedition in August 1800.

30 A ruined Cistercian Monastery founded in 1239.

31 John Doe and Richard Roe were often used to disguise a person's real name, but in this case it is just possible that Harley is referring to Lieutenant John Aldgeo, who joined the 54th from the 4th Foot 3 July 1800, and Ensign Robert Rowe.

32 Preparing a trick or a surprise for him.

morning. There was but one course for the lads to pursue, now that the enemy was in their power. His weapons of offence were destroyed, the writs were burned, and the poor tailor himself, quite stupid, given in charge of the guard of a coach starting for London, with whom they arranged that he should be delivered according to a direction on a card which was pinned on the cape of his coat, and addressed 'To Mrs F[irmin], Bedford Street, Covent Garden,' where he arrived next morning at six o'clock, to the astonishment of all his family, as well as to his own surprise, and not yet quite recovered from the effects of the previous evening's carouse. In the meantime, before he could take any further steps, the regiment embarked, and many of our subs saved their commissions by this *ruse de guerre*, as in all probability they would have lost them, had they been detained by the sheriff's officer. Nor was Mr F[irmin] any loser by this innocent trick, as the first money our officers received, was remitted to him in payment of their respective debts.

In Portsmouth, we were joined by a Captain Standish,[33] whose promotion from the 27th into the 54th was rather singular. There was an encampment on Swinley Common, near Windsor, in 1800. As the 27th Regiment, among others, was passing in review before his Majesty George the Third, he took particular notice of one officer of that corps, and immediately inquired his name. Upon being informed by Colonel, now General Graham,[34] that it was Standish – 'Standish! Standish!' he repeated; and then turning to the Duke of York, said, 'Frederick,[35] give him a company – give him a company.' In vain, did his Royal Highness remonstrate with him, telling his Majesty that Standish was only a very young lieutenant. The King was peremptory, and Standish was appointed to a company in the 54th. He did not, however, remain with us any time, but effected an exchange into some other regiment, in consequence of the harsh treatment he received from some of our old lieutenants, who felt annoyed at his being put over their heads.

This anecdote brings to my recollection having once met that worthy old King, while marching with a party of recruits, in company with another officer, from Weymouth to Winchester. We had made a halt, and our men, who had received large sums of bounty-money the day before, and who had got intoxicated, were lying on the ground, when his Majesty happened to pass on horseback. On seeing the men, he stopped suddenly, and asked 'What regiment?' 'The 54th, please your Majesty,' we replied. 'The 54th – 54th – all drunk – all drunk – poor fellows – poor fellows – put them to bed – put them to bed. Good morning, gentlemen,' said the King, and then rode off. I need not say that this kind address of his gracious Majesty completely dispelled the fears we entertained of being censured for suffering our

33 Lieutenant Henry Standish was in the 27th Foot and is recorded as transferring to the 54th Foot in the London Gazette dated 27 July 1800 as a captain. He was then gazetted back to the 27th from the 54th Foot on 19 August 1800. However, he is also gazetted as having been removed to the 27th Foot on 15 November 1800 which would agree more with Harley's story.

34 General Thomas Graham, 1st Baron Lynedoch.

35 Frederick, Duke of York, the second son of King George III, was Commander in Chief of the Army.

men to be inebriated on the march; for, had we met with a strict general officer, we should, no doubt, have been severely reprimanded.

We were also joined at Portsmouth by a Captain Taylor, who volunteered from the Flintshire militia, and was appointed paymaster of our second battalion.[36] This gentleman, having, unfortunately for himself, fallen desperately in love with a lady in the Isle of Wight, when we had proceeded to sea, remained almost constantly on the deck, casting longing looks behind him, as the Isle of Wight disappeared from his view. As we had formed an intimacy, he soon confided in me, and told me of his unalterable attachment, and the anguish he felt on being separated from the object of his affections,

> 'Dragging at each remove a lengthened chain.'[37]

It was in vain I attempted to reason him into sense; the strength and ardour of his attachment had so completely mastered him, that his despondency and low spirits were observed by everyone on board our ship, the *Ariadne*,[38] and became in a short time the subject of general conversation and enquiry. Many a night we spent hours on deck conversing on the never-ending subject, and he only became more inconsolable as the distance lengthened between him and his lady-love, while every other person on board enjoyed with delight our sail up the Mediterranean under easy way, particularly at night, the time poor Taylor felt most, when the moon shone with great splendour.

Even after we landed in Egypt, his state of mind remained the same, if it did not really become worse. Oft-times we walked arm in arm through the lines at midnight, when all was silent as the grave, looking at the stars that rose or set in the direction of the Isle of Wight; and, although I generally accompanied him in these nocturnal excursions, fearing something fatal might occur from the disordered state of his mind, we often walked for hours together without exchanging more than two or three words; and he would sometimes become so wrapped up in gloomy contemplation, that the occasional cry of the sentinels would make him start as if he had been suddenly awakened from a dream.

Whenever I visited his tent, I invariably found him busily traversing the maps, and calculating the number of miles between Alexandria and the Isle of Wight, often repeating to himself the immense distance of 3,200 miles,[39] and then sinking into a fit of despair. Sometimes, indeed, when the signal was made that letters had arrived in the bay from England, his cheeks would be flushed with a momentary

36 Paymaster John Taylor. Paymasters ranked as the most junior captain in a regiment.

37 A slightly altered quote from Oliver Goldsmith's *The Traveller*, which should read 'And drags at each remove a lengthening chain'.

38 The transport *Ariadne*.

39 This would be the distance by sea; the distance 'as the crow flies' would be about 2,100 miles.

joy. And, mounting his horse, he would gallop off to the beach at the utmost speed, but usually returned again, whether he received letters or not, with slow and solemn steps, as if he was accompanying a funeral. As it was evident that he was sinking a prey to this fatal attachment, I endeavoured to persuade him to retire from the army, and return home. At first, he was unwilling to do so, fearing that it might be imputed to cowardice, as he was then opposed to the enemy; but, after some time, feeling that his happiness, nay, his life depended on it, he resigned his commission, returned to England, and married the lady who had unwillingly been the cause of such sufferings.

I accompanied him to the sea-shore on his leaving Egypt, and parted from him with deep regret; for I lost in him a faithful, true, and grateful friend. It may be well imagined that, from the distracted state of poor Taylor's mind, his paymaster's accounts must have been badly kept. The sequel proved it. On my arrival in London, after I had returned from Egypt, I was waited on by Taylor, who stated that government made a demand against him on their settlement of £800, and that immediate steps were to be taken against his securities, Samuel Taylor, Esq of Holywell, Flintshire, and another gentleman, for the recovery of that sum, or the amount of the security.

As I knew well that Taylor was not by any means extravagant, but, on the contrary, observed the most temperate habits, never exceeding his pay, I felt convinced that he could not have spent the money, and that the present demand must have originated in some mistake, on either side.

Before my arrival, he had employed clerks to look over the accounts, but as no error could be discovered on the part of government, the crown solicitor received instructions to proceed against his securities, and all further investigation into the accounts was dropped by Taylor and his friends. It occurred to me, on being consulted about it, that the issue of batt and forage money amounted to about the sum of £800, and which, as it was received from the Quarter-Master-General's department, had no right to be inserted or taken notice of in the regimental pay-list.[40] I therefore called upon Taylor, and made him accompany me to the Army Pay-Office, and looked over the lists of May 1801, when, to our great gratification, we discovered that my surmise was correct, as he had credited that sum erroneously. This fortunate discovery exonerating him and his securities, we procured a certificate from the Pay-Office to that effect; and thus this mistake, which occurred from the distracted state of his mind, at being separated so far from the idol of his affections, and which threatened to involve himself and his family in considerable difficulty, was at length, through my interference, fortunately rectified. I must say, his friends were most grateful to me for the happy discovery I made, and sent me repeated invitations to spend some time with them. Batt and forage are extra

40 Batt and forage money was an allowance made to officers to cover the costs of feeding their animals, both riding horses and pack animals.

allowances to the army, and should never be entered in the regimental accounts, which are intended solely for the pay; being, in fact, a gift from the government to the officers.

The night before our departure from Spithead, in the midst of the confusion of embarking, we were joined by an old gentleman, in the uniform of the West Middlesex militia. Of course, no notice was taken of him then, and we sailed next morning. When we got half way down Channel, our colonel asked him what was his object, and where was he going; upon which he then, and not till then, produced a letter of introduction, recommending the bearer as a volunteer to accompany the expedition.[41]

At this moment I think (though now so many years have passed by) I see the colonel stare at the old volunteer, who was then at least fifty years of age, and turning round to me, exclaimed, 'Good Heavens, Harley, what a strange fellow my friend must be, to send this man, unfit for anything!' The colonel would have sent him back if in his power, but that was impossible, and he could not bear to see him. But the mystery was soon solved respecting W[eatley]'s coming to us.[42] He had a handsome wife, and he was provided for on foreign service by a certain gallant officer, whilst she remained at home as his housekeeper. W[eatley] was not calculated for an officer on active service, from his bulky appearance and age, as well as from his vulgar habits. Fortunately for him, the Quarter-Master B[ody] was left behind sick at Minorca,[43] and W[eatley] was appointed to do duty with the regiment in his absence. This man was a native of Ireland, and not having received any education, the young officers found an everlasting fund of amusement in hearing his odd expressions in conversation, always applying the wrong word to the meaning; for instance, at one time he had occasion to make some excuse for himself, and in endeavouring to explain he was an injured man, and offering to take his oath to the fact, he called aloud, 'I will swear, colonel, I am a perjured man,' not knowing the difference in the meaning of the words. They were constantly playing tricks on him, whenever they had a leisure hour in the camp; in fact, he was a never-ending source of amusement to the young wags. All this he endured with great patience and good humour; I can well bring to memory a scene in particular, as he lay in his tent one morning west of Alexandria. I had a very large and ferocious buffalo, that I had purchased the day before; it was blindfolded, in order that no injury should be done by him, nor make his escape. Some of the young officers, without my knowledge, cut the rope by which he was

41 The volunteer system allowed a gentleman who was unable to afford to purchase a commission or without friends to gain him one for free, to accompany a regiment abroad in the hope of being granted a commission by the colonel if there was a death in the regiment. The volunteer would mess with the junior officers, but would be expected to fall in with the ranks and fight as a private soldier with a musket.

42 Volunteer William Weatley became an Ensign in the regiment on 5 April 1801.

43 Quartermaster Samuel Body who had joined the regiment on 5 October 1799. Port Mahon on Minorca was then in British hands, but was returned to Spain at the Peace of Amiens in 1802.

fastened to a stake, and let the animal loose, to steer his course to W[eatley]'s tent, which was not far distant, in order to have a laugh at his expense, well knowing he had a female companion with him inside. The buffalo, on getting entangled among the ropes of the tent, became enraged, and rearing on its hind legs, with all the weight of its ponderous carcase came down on W[eatley]'s tent, levelling it to the ground, with hideous roars. My readers may well suppose the astonishment of W[eatley] and his companion, and the continued fits of laughter of the lads outside. W[eatley]'s head at last appeared, thrust out under the canvas, with a red night cap on, calling loudly for assistance, and the Arab female endeavouring to make her escape on the other side. This scene was droll beyond description, and all who witnessed it, officers and soldiers, were convulsed with laughter. I thought it time to have him released from his perilous situation, and hastened down to his assistance, and, with three or four pioneers, soon extricated him and secured the animal, W[eatley] declaring there was a conspiracy against his life.

4

Egypt 1801

But to return once more to the regiment. After a short delay in Portsmouth, we proceeded to Spithead, where we were joined by more troops, and from which we finally set sail on Sunday morning. It is totally impossible for me to give a just description of the beauty of the scene as we went down Channel, and I shall not therefore attempt it. The weather was remarkably fine, and our men were in the highest spirits; our fleet, which consisted of 300 sail of transports, had on board 30,000 of the flower of the British army – artillery, cavalry, and infantry.

Off Ushant, we fell in with the grand fleet of England, then blockading the French off Brest, and commanded by Lord Howe.[1] As we approached them, they opened in two lines, through which we passed in full sail, the sailors, dressed in their blue jackets and white trousers, it being Sunday, manning the yards and cheering us as we sailed by, and the different bands of the men-of-war playing the national air of 'God save the King' while our men, to return the compliment, crowded the decks, gave cheer for cheer, and our regimental bands struck up the inspiring air of 'Rule Britannia.'

Having touched at Houat and Belleisle,[2] where we met with some little delay, we proceeded across the Bay of Biscay, and arriving near Ferrol, disembarked there. Unfortunately, the attack on this place was so badly managed, that after having been two days before it, and losing some men, we were compelled to embark again, without having effected any advantage, although the town and arsenal would certainly have been taken, had sufficient promptness and decision been shewn on the occasion.[3]

1 He is in error as Richard Lord Howe, Admiral of the Fleet had died in 1799. Earl St Vincent then commanded the Channel Fleet.

2 Both islands off the southern coast of Brittany.

3 The naval force had cannonaded the coastal batteries whilst a force of 8,000 men landed to attack the port from the landward side. After a brief conflict, the British captured the hills overlooking the defences of the town. It was only then that they realised that the defences were too strong and the decision was made to re-embark.

From Ferrol we proceeded to Vigo Bay, where we encountered a severe storm, in which we lost the *Stag* frigate.[4] The captain, greatly to his credit, succeeded in saving all the crew, and then, to prevent the ship falling into the hands of the Spaniards, he set fire to her, on leaving her. It was really an awful sight, and as grand as could be witnessed, the night being extremely dark, and, of course, the volumes of flame appearing much plainer. The *Stag* mounted 28 guns, which were all shotted, and, as the devouring element reached each gun, it exploded, rendering our situation very perilous, as every shot passed quite close to us, until, at length, the fire reaching the magazine, the wreck blew up with a terrific explosion, and the scattered fragments fell in showers around us. It is somewhat singular, that on visiting Vigo, many years afterwards, in 1823, I saw part of the mainmast of that fine frigate, of the loss of which I had been a spectator, at the house of Mr Menendez, the British consul.

This was the place that gave rise to that well-known bubble called the Vigo Bay Company, by which hundreds of credulous speculators, throughout England, were unfortunately duped. As many of my readers may not be aware of the origin of this company, I will briefly explain it.

In the reign of Queen Anne, and when we were at war with Spain, a rich fleet of Spanish galleons – large vessels employed in bringing home treasure to old Spain, from Lima and Mexico – were chased into Vigo Bay by the British admiral, when many of them were destroyed and sunk. In the rage which existed, some few years since, for speculation companies, certain gentlemen proposed to form one to raise sunken ships, and to recover the lost treasure. Shares were accordingly issued, for which, in a few days, the demand became so great, that they rose from £10, the original price, as high as £150; and, indeed, so very feasible was the scheme made to appear, that it was considered by far the best speculation in the market.

As soon as every preparation had been made, divers and engineers were sent out, with various implements, to raise the supposed treasure; and general expectation was at its utmost height, when it was fully ascertained, by documents and records in the custom house of Vigo, that all the specie, and everything of value on board the galleons, had been landed, and forwarded to Madrid, before they were attacked by the British admiral, so that nothing was now to be found but the rotten hulls of the vessels. Thus ended the Vigo Bay Company, by which numbers were beggared, and a few knowing ones enriched.[5] I had almost forgotten to state, that we lost another vessel in the storm we encountered in Vigo Bay – a Guernsey-man, that followed our fleet as a tender, and supplied us with different necessary articles.

4 HMS *Stag* of 32 guns, Captain Robert Winthrop, was wrecked in Vigo Bay on 6 September 1800; happily the crew was saved.

5 The Battle of Vigo Bay occurred on 23 October 1702, between an Anglo/Dutch squadron and the Spanish treasure fleet supported by a French squadron. The entire Franco/Spanish squadron was either captured or burnt/sunk, however almost all of the treasure had already been landed before the battle, so the scheme to recoup the lost treasure was a scam.

This vessel having been driven ashore in the gale, was immediately plundered by the country people, who were also disposed to treat the crew with severity. They were, however, rescued by the governor of Vigo, whose generous conduct on the occasion reflects the highest credit on him. Instead of making the master and crew prisoners, he treated them with the greatest attention and humanity – had, by his exertions, the greater part of the money and property of which they had plundered, returned to them again, and finally sent them and their property on board our admiral, in a vessel of his own.

From Vigo, we proceeded to Cadiz. On our anchoring before that city, the governor sent out a flag of truce, apprising the admiral that the plague raged violently in the city, and that he was sure the English were too generous a nation to add the horrors of war to that scourge of Divine Providence; we therefore sailed, on the next day, for Gibraltar, when we were joined by the ever-to-be-lamented Sir Ralph Abercromby, who succeeded Sir James Pulteney in command.[6]

As soon as the army had been newly brigaded, and some regiments that were for limited service, sent home to England, Sir Ralph, in an order of the day, strongly recommended the ladies to return home, as they were liable to so many inconveniences and hardships in foreign countries, assuring them that every accommodation and facility should be afforded for that purpose, an offer, of which all the ladies, except two, gladly availed themselves; but neither persuasions nor entreaty could induce these two to forgo the resolution of accompanying the army.

From Gibraltar, we proceeded to Tetuan Bay, on the coast of Barbary,[7] where we were in the act of taking in a supply of fresh water, when a storm drove us out of the bay, and continued to harass us afterwards, until we reached Malta. At this island, we remained for a fortnight, refreshing ourselves, and getting our vessels cleaned – a duty which was inspected by the commander-in-chief in person, who was always most anxious for the comfort of his officers and men. From Malta we sailed for Marmorice [Bay], in Turkey, and, after a rough and tedious passage, anchored in Marmorice Bay. The entrance into this beautiful bay is exceedingly narrow, but finely wooded, from the water's edge to the tops of the lofty mountains which line it on both sides; so much so, indeed, that we could, without the slightest difficulty, throw a biscuit from the decks of our ships, as we sailed through, to the shore on either side. What, then, must have been our astonishment and admiration, after passing through such a narrow channel, that appeared but as the mouth of a mountain stream, to find ourselves, in a short time, in a most splendid and extensive harbour, at least twenty miles in circumference, having the appearance of a grand amphitheatre, being surrounded with lofty hills, which rose one above the other, and covered with the most verdant foliage!

6 Lieutenant General Sir Ralph Abercromby (1734-1801) commanded the troops during the invasion of Egypt.

7 Tetouan in Morocco.

The scene we witnessed seemed rather the work of enchantment than of nature; and, as the whole expanse of the water was as smooth as a pond, the contrast between it and the rough billows we had been traversing for some days before, was so great, that we felt the change delightful. Having landed our sick under the charge of some medical officers, we remained at anchor in this romantic harbour until sometime after Christmas, spending the interval pleasantly enough, in paying and receiving visits from our friends, on board the different ships in the fleet. The delay here was unfortunate. We were ordered to wait for a reinforcement of the Turkish army, who were unaccountably tedious in their movements, and for a supply of horses for our cavalry, who had left their own in England, and thus, two or three months were lost, during which the French had full time to make preparations to receive us; whereas, had we proceeded direct from Malta to our destination, our conquest of Egypt would have been much easier, and attended with less bloodshed on our side, for, as it will afterwards appear, our Turkish auxiliaries were of little or no service to us. Although it might be supposed, as this bay was surrounded on all sides by the loftiest hills, with the exception of its narrow entrance, there could be scarcely a possibility of a breath of wind gaining access sufficient to disturb the tranquillity of its waters, yet we experienced, on the 8th of February, a tremendous storm, the awful grandeur of which we could not avoid admiring, notwithstanding the danger that threatened us. The darkness, the loud and repeated claps of thunder, the vivid flashes of lighting, and the howling of the wolves and jackals, which the storm had driven from the tops of the mountains, reminded many of us strongly of the battle-smoke, the deep roar of the cannon, the blaze of artillery, and the thrilling groans and cries of the wounded and the dying, and seemed, indeed, a grand rehearsal of that fatal tragedy in which we were soon to be engaged as actors.

Being, at length, upon the 23rd of the same month, joined by the Turkish army, we sailed for the coast of Egypt, with a favourable breeze. The day was remarkably fine, and the weather moderate; and, as each vessel of our fleet, which appeared to cover the sea, endeavoured to out-sail the other, the brave men on board partook of the emulative spirit of the seamen, encouraging each other with cheers, as ship passed ship, and one sentiment of ardour and patriotism pervaded the whole British army. It was altogether a scene peculiarly calculated to overcome all reflections upon the awful destiny that awaited so many of us, who were doomed never to see country, home, or friends, again.

We arrived, in high spirits, after a short and agreeable passage, in Aboukir Bay, on the 6th of March,[8] but without the Turkish flotilla, which took very good care to remain aloof, and allow us to proceed alone, and effect a landing without their assistance. On our anchoring in the bay, we perceived a small vessel making for the

8 The fleet actually arrived in Aboukir Bay on 2 March, but heavy seas and high winds delayed any attempt at a landing until 7 March.

harbour of Alexandria, which, after a short chase, we captured. As we expected, from the efforts it made to escape, that it contained despatches, or something of importance, for the French army, we considered the capture of the greatest consequence, until, to our disappointment, we learned that it only contained a party of comedians, actors and actresses, who were on their way from France, for the amusement of the French army. On this circumstance being made known to the commander-in-chief, he ordered the vessel with her precious cargo to be liberated, and sent into Alexandria, the governor of which very humorously sent them back to us next day, saying, that we were very welcome to their services, as he would not deprive his soldiers of the provisions they would consume, and that he had provided further amusement for us; but our admiral returned them again, with a similar message in reply, and we heard no more of them.

Every arrangement having been made for our landing, by that gallant officer Sir Sydney Smith,[9] and all things being in readiness, on the night of the 7th of March, we received orders to prepare to disembark on the following morning (Sunday) at day-break. The orders had been scarcely issued, when they were, with a single exception, obeyed with an alacrity that showed the eagerness of officers and men to engage in the approaching deadly contest. There was, unfortunately, an instance of cowardice, and that too attended by breach of discipline, which, it must be acknowledged, even by our enemies, is of very rare occurrence in the British service. There was one of our officers, who had volunteered from the City of Dublin militia, and who, from the time he joined the 54th, was remarkable for his temperate habits and great dislike to spirituous liquors, being very seldom persuaded to exceed two glasses of wine at our mess-table, upon whom the dread of meeting the foe in mortal combat had such an effect, that to drown fear and all sense of danger, he drank so plentifully of ardent spirits before he left the ship, that on his landing he staggered about on the beach, and was scarcely able to stand. Unfortunately for him, the boat in which he came ashore happened to be between the commander-in-chief's boat and that of our colonel, and as the crews of these three boats landed at the same moment, his situation was immediately observed by Sir Ralph Abercromby, who exclaimed in a reproachful tone, 'Colonel Darby, look at that officer of the 54th.' Upon which, the colonel struck him with the flat of his sword, and ordered him to return on board the transport, and await further orders. And, in a few days afterwards, on a message being conveyed to him by the adjutant, to know whether he would stand a court martial, or resign, he very prudently chose the latter alternative, and retired from the army.[10]

Notwithstanding the disadvantageous circumstances under which we laboured, the men not being able to load until they had formed on the beach, sustaining a heavy fire from the batteries on the hills, as well as from the castle of Aboukir,

9 Captain – later Vice Admiral – Sir William Sidney Smith (1764-1840).

10 This must be Lieutenant James George Thornton, who resigned from the army on 26 May 1801.

Contemporary print showing British troops landing at Aboukir in 1801. (Author's collection)

which was on our right, and charged by the cavalry, who rode up to their saddle-girths in the water, cutting at our men as they hastened out of their boats, our brave fellows effected their landing in gallant style, and drove the enemy before them, taking in their way the guns which had played upon them from the heights.

On landing, I beheld a most distressing scene; two young officers of the Guards – one of them stretched on the sands, dead; his brother officer, a fine looking youth, apparently about fifteen or sixteen years of age, lamenting over his friend in the most agonizing manner. The deceased was a son of Admiral Sir John Borlase Warren, whose division of the fleet was only at that moment come into the bay;[11] and the young officer who so bitterly deplored the loss of his friend and companion, was Lord Delvin, the present Marquess of Westmeath.[12]

We lay for that night on those sand-hills where the enemy had formed their batteries; and, on the following morning, the 9th of March, advanced about four miles, without anything material occurring, except an occasional skirmish of the outposts of the hostile armies. We had a man pardoned this day, who attempted

11 Lieutenant George John Borlase Warren, Coldstream Guards, was killed at Aboukir Bay.

12 Ensign George Lord Delvin, Coldstream Guards, later became the Marquis of Westmeath.

The Landing of British Troops at Aboukir 8 March 1801 by Philip de Loutherbourg. (Public Domain)

to desert while we lay in Marmorice. He had conceived the absurd idea of being able to make his way back to London; but, being taken in the mountains, and brought back to us by the Turks, he was tried by a court martial, on board our ship, the *Ariadne* transport, and sentenced to be shot. As he had, by the advice of Sir John Moore, who was president on his trial, thrown himself upon the mercy of the court, he was, in consequence of Sir John's interference and humane recommendation, reprieved, and now finally pardoned, and permitted to return to his duty. Sir John Moore had a very high opinion of the Irish regiments. 'Are you not an Irishman?' said he to me, as I was giving testimony on this man's trial, having been appealed to by him for a character; 'your countrymen, Lieutenant Harley, are excellent soldiers – I know them well. An English soldier requires to be well fed, a Scotch soldier to be well paid, but the Irishman a cold potato and a little whiskey, but not too much, and he will fight for you while he has life.'

We remained stationary for three or four days, in order to have our artillery and cavalry landed, together with the necessary stores and provisions, until the morning of the 13th, when our army moved forward in line, extending from Lake Mareotis,[13] to the Bay of Alexandria, the enemy occupying a very strong position

13 Lake Mareotis was a huge inland lake which restricted the land connection between Aboukir and Alexandria to a thin strip little more than a mile wide.

on the hills between us and the city of Alexandria. On the approach of our line, they boldly advanced to meet us; but were, after a well-contested battle, forced to abandon the heights and retire.[14] We then took up their position, in front of Alexandria, which city we now for the first time saw, and where we remained until the memorable battle of the 21st of March.

During the battle of the 13th, I perceived the paymaster of the Royals stationed behind a large date tree, and anxiously looking out for the wounded officers belonging to his regiment, as they were carried to the rear, and then as anxiously inspecting each side of a small card which he held in his hand.[15] As I could not divine what his motive could be for this extraordinary conduct, I had curiosity enough to ask him, when he at once told me, that, on one side of the card he had the names of the officers who were in credit, and on the reverse those, principally subs, who were on the wrong side of his books. When an officer was borne to the rear, with a leg or an arm off, or likely to be amputated or otherwise badly wounded, he would, on ascertaining his name, pronounce his satisfaction that he was in credit, or deplore that he was in his debt, as the case might be. Such mercenary and unfeeling conduct really astonished me, particularly under such awful circumstances, nor do I believe there was another officer engaged in that action, on either side, who would have acted in a similar manner.

I was encamped, for a day or two after the battle, near one of the sand-hills, attended by one of our pioneers, named Bryan O'Toole, one of my old men from the county Limerick. I had some chocolate in an old tin pot, but having no other vessel of any description, I intended, as soon as the pot had cooled (for we had made a fire under it that soon warmed it), to make it answer the double purpose of pot and cup. My careful man, however, not wishing that his master should have his breakfast in such an uncomfortable way, said that he would engage to procure me both a cup and saucer, comforts to which I had been for some days unaccustomed, and which, situated as we were, I could not expect. He accordingly left me on his search, and to my surprise, returned in a few minutes with a china cup and saucer, and a silver spoon, crested. Having asked him how he obtained such articles, he replied without hesitation, that he had borrowed them from our friend Sir Sydney, meaning Sir Sydney Smith, whose tent was but a few yards distant from mine, and who was such a favourite with the army, that they often trespassed in this manner on his good nature. I was a good deal annoyed at O'Toole's presumption in daring to make such a request of Sir Sydney, and sent him back immediately with the articles, apologising at the same time for O'Toole's conduct. I would have as soon sent

14 A French force of five thousand men under *Général de Division* Lanusse, defended a ridge which crossed the isthmus at Mandora. Despite a strong defence, Abercromby's force forced the French to retire on Alexandria on 13 August 1801.

15 Paymaster Charles Gordon of the 2nd Battalion 1st Foot (Royals).

to the grand seignior himself to ask such an accommodation, for I had too high a respect for Sir Sydney Smith to take such a liberty with him.

On the 17th, as I had charge of the provisions of our regiment, about halfway from the landing place to the lines, I was met by a foreign officer in a very exhausted state, who addressing me in broken English, informed me that he was a captain in the *Chasseurs Britanniques,* a foreign corps in our service, that he landed that morning at an early hour from a transport, and had been ever since travelling about in quest of rations, having been refused by the commissariat depot to which he had applied, as he had no return nor document to show them.

Knowing that his regiment was in front of the lines, and that he was unable from fatigue and want of refreshment to reach them, I willingly produced my store, and we sat down together to partake of it. When he had eaten a hearty meal of cold pork and biscuit, and taken a glass or two of rum and water, of which I usually contrived to have a tolerable supply, he turned to me with joy beaming on his countenance, and said, 'I have dined at the table of princes, but may truly say, I never enjoyed a dinner before; and I only wish, my dear sir, that I may, one day or other, have it in my power to show my gratitude.' He then told me that he was the Baron Capolle, and that before the French revolution he was a colonel in the old Swiss Guards in Paris, and had fought in the defence of the unfortunate Louis the Sixteenth.[16] The Baron was a man of his word, for having been, in a short time afterwards, appointed commandant of Alexandria, he did not fail to find me out, and entertain me repeatedly in the most handsome and hospitable manner.

On the morning of the 20th, I was rambling along the banks of the canal, accompanied by my friend Dr O'Dwyer,[17] when we fortunately met with an Arab, who sold us a sheep for a trifle, which being small and rather lean, we easily managed to carry home between us to the camp. As we had not tasted a morsel of fresh meat for many months, we congratulated each other on our good fortune, and had it immediately killed, and one half of it made into broth, which we thought delicious. As the other half of the sheep belonged to O'Dwyer, it was laid aside until he could conveniently send for it, and I prudently reserved a camp-kettle full of the broth for my own use on the following day. The attack of the enemy, however, commencing before day-break the next morning, a six-pound cannon-shot entered my tent, struck the ground near me, and dashed the sand into my face, as I lay on a mat upon the ground in my clothes, having taken off nothing but my boots, which now, for the first time since our landing, I had stripped off, as my feet had become much swollen and very painful.

16 Harley's memory has let him down slightly here. This is most certainly Captain Philip Baron de Capol who was actually in de Roll's Regiment rather than the Chasseurs Britanniques. He became Town Major at Alexandria rather than Governor.

17 Surgeon James O'Dwyer.

Starting up in the dark, I laid hold of one of my boots, which with some difficulty I drew on, but, while groping in search of the other, I popped my leg into the pot or kettle of broth, so that when I found the boot, in a minute or two afterwards, I in vain attempted to pull it on. While in this dilemma, the firing increasing every moment and approaching nearer and nearer, Dr O'Dwyer appeared at the tent door, calling to me for his side of the mutton, and telling me if I had anything else, to take with me, as 'God only knows,' said he, 'where we will be this night.' Obeying the doctor's injunctions, I hastened out with a bag of dollars on my shoulder, and the boot under my arm; and, being joined by O'Dwyer with his side of mutton on the saddle, proceeded to the rear, the subject of mirth with all who met us, and of general merriment amongst our officers when the battle was over.

It was, as I before remarked, on the morning of the 21st of March, about an hour before day-light, that the enemy commenced their attack on our outlying picquets on our left, which they drove in with a smart fire. It was soon manifest that this was a feint to draw our attention from the main point of attack, which was our right, and against which quarter they sent large columns, intending to turn our right, and force us into the lake. They were bravely resisted in this manoeuvre by Sir John Moore and the reserve, and finally repulsed with considerable loss by the gallant 42nd and the other corps which formed our right wing. Finding themselves defeated in this attempt, they directed a most furious attack on our centre, where the 54th were stationed, who gave them an equally warm reception, obliging them once more to retire from the contest They, however, effected their retreat in good order, as we had not sufficient cavalry to harass them, until they secured themselves under the guns of Alexandria.

As we were but 25,000 strong, and the enemy at least 40,000, under the command of General Menou, we considered it a complete defeat of the French, though they reckoned it but as a drawn battle.[18] The victory, for such it really was, cost us very dear, and among many valuable officers, we lost our esteemed commander-in-chief, General Sir Ralph Abercromby; a man universally beloved by both officers and men, and whose death was as generally deplored. The fatal wound he received in his groin, from a pistol shot which caused almost immediate death.[19] Such was the esteem and veneration in which he was held, that the fatal occurrence was kept a secret from the army for some time, under an apprehension that it

18 Harley overstates the size of the forces involved in the Battle of Alexandria. A French force of just under 10,000 men commanded by *Général de Division* Jacques-Francois Menou made a pre-dawn attack on the British encampment. The brunt of the attack fell on Moore's troops, particularly the 28th Foot, and the fighting rapidly became confused amidst the half-light of dawn. The British forces involved actually outnumbered the French at around 14,000. The French lost some 1,200 killed and 3,000 wounded whereas the British only lost about 1,500 killed and wounded.

19 Sir Ralph Abercromby (1734-1801) was wounded at the Battle of Alexandria and he was taken on board HMS *Foudroyant* for treatment. Unfortunately, he died of his wounds seven days later, not quite as rapidly as Harley suggests.

The Battle of Alexandria 21 March 1801 by Philip de Loutherbourg. (Public Domain)

would cast a damp and gloom upon the spirits of the men. I once had an opportunity of conversing with Sir Ralph, and of experiencing his kindness. While we lay in Marmorice Bay, I was sent on board the *Foudroyant*, commanded by Lord Keith,[20] to apply to the commander-in-chief for an authority to obtain a supply of flannel shirts, which had been sent out by the Ladies of England.[21] The general was walking on the quarter-deck when I boarded the ship, and perceiving me, immediately called me to him, and, in the most-friendly way, asked me, 'had I any commands for him'. On my telling him the nature of my business, he was kind enough to say that the order should be made out instantly, and that, in the meantime, I should take some refreshment. I may truly say, the reception I met with was most courteous; nor have I ever known a man of his rank more free from pride and ostentation.

20 Admiral George Keith Elphinstone, 1st Viscount Keith, commanded the naval forces in the Mediterranean. HMS *Foudroyant*, an 80-gun two-decker, was his flagship during the Egyptian Expedition.

21 The Ladies of England were a patriotic group, set up to support the troops abroad, just as was done in the First World War. They also paid for the statue of Achilles in Hyde Park, the first public nude statue in London, which commemorated the Duke of Wellington.

When Sir Ralph Abercromby was commander-in-chief of Ireland, he visited Kilkenny, and stopped a few days there. In early life, Sir Ralph had been quartered there, then a subaltern officer. He was in the habit of going down the river to fish: there was a young man and his wife, of the name of Dunfy, who invariably invited him into their cabin, near the river, and was so partial to him, they gave him, on many occasions, the best fare they had, such as potatoes, eggs, and milk, which he, with pleasure, partook of with them. His regiment left Kilkenny, and he never had an opportunity of visiting it after, until this period. The day after Sir Ralph arrived, he walked down, unaccompanied by any one, to his old haunt, and, stopping at the door of his once kind friend, Dunfy, found him and his wife living, then an old couple, with a family grown up. Sir Ralph asked them if their names were Dunfy, they replied in the affirmative; he then said, 'Do you recollect an officer of the name of Abercromby, that frequently visited your cottage when fishing in the river, some years ago?' 'Recollect!' said the old man, 'we do, indeed, sir, and often inquired for him; at last, we heard he was dead, and heartily sorry for him we were, for he was a good creature, and had no pride in him: he used to sit down with us in our poor cabin, and sometimes taste our humble fare.' 'In troth' said the old woman, 'we would share with him now, was he alive' – at the same time giving an expressive look at her husband, as if in sorrow for him. To the generous and kind heart of Sir Ralph Abercromby it gave sincere pleasure to find, in the breasts of these humble people, such kindly feeling. To their great surprise and joy, he told them that he was the same Abercromby that they had known. He then put a one hundred pound into the old man's hand, and wishing him, his wife, and family, all happiness, expressed his grateful sense of their former kindness to him. Judge their surprise, on going into the town of Kilkenny, to hear that their kind benefactor was then commander-in-chief of Ireland. The daughter of Dunfy served my family with milk, in Kilkenny, in the year 1804.

Immediately after the action, we missed one of our grenadiers, who was neither among the dead nor wounded; and, as it was impossible for him to have been taken prisoner, as the enemy made such a precipitate, though regular retreat, we naturally concluded that he must have deserted; but, after some time, we perceived an odd shot to be fired, now and then, from a hollow ground near the enemy, which seemed to cause a picquet of theirs to move; and, while we were busy in conjectures about it, we saw the missing man emerged from the hollow, and hasten to join us. As soon as Paddy O'Carroll, which was his name, and who was a volunteer from the Tipperary militia, was asked to account for his absence, he replied, with an air of triumph, that he had been down firing at the French picquet. 'I have popped sixty rounds at them,' said he, 'and all did not go for nothing. Make haste, and give me a fresh supply, for I am determined to send them fellows away out of that, in a hurry.' I need not say that Paddy was not indulged in his request, but immediately ordered to join his company, and not to quit his ranks again in any future battle, under pain of punishment.

During the action, and while, to an observer, the issue was yet doubtful, we perceived a large body of Arab cavalry stationed at a considerable distance, and, to all appearance, waiting to see which side victory would turn; and no sooner were the French on the retreat, and victory declared on our side, than they instantly galloped down to us, crying out, 'Tibe John' – meaning good Englishman; John, being a general name for the English, with the Arabs, and, brandishing their swords, congratulating us, and offering to join us against the enemy, whom, however, they did not care to pursue.

The day after the battle, a very fine dog was observed lying down on a particular spot, from which some of our men had endeavoured to bring him, by coaxing and by threats, but all in vain. The poor animal remained there all night, scraping away the sand, and disturbing us by his piteous howls. On enquiring, the following morning, a French prisoner told us that he belonged to one of their captains; and we learned from one of our pioneers, that the body of a French officer had been buried there after the action; so, no doubt remained, but that it was the body of his master which this faithful creature had been vigilantly guarding for two days and two nights. Our sergeant-major had him forced away, after a good deal of trouble, and, taking proper care of him, brought him safely to England.

We now moved to the west of Alexandria, and encamped near Pompey's pillar,[22] where I was but a short time, when I was sent on duty on board the admiral's ship. Being unable, when I landed, on my return, to reach the east side of Pompey's pillar, the enemy being between me and the main body of our army, I took up my quarters, for that night, in a swamp that the retiring waters of the Nile had made.

At daylight, I was awoke by a brisk fire of musquetry, and, on leaping up, was informed by my sergeant, that the 30th Regiment were attacking the green hills. In a few minutes, I saw that brave corps ascend the hill with fixed bayonets, charge the enemy, and, after a desperate struggle, ultimately succeed in gaining the heights. Their work, however, was not yet half done; and the regiment, which was not above 200 strong, had to shelter themselves against the shells and grape shot, which were poured on them from the other batteries on the hills; and to prepare to receive a body of 500 picked men, whom the enemy detached against them, together with two pieces of ordnance, for the purpose of retaking the hill. The gallant 30th, however, would not flinch, but, collecting in a small but firm band, and animated and led on by Colonel Lockhart and Captain Grey,[23] they rushed on the enemy with fixed bayonets, without firing a shot, or waiting for their near approach, and putting them to immediate rout, drove them back in confusion, taking ten prisoners on the spot, for they were not at liberty to pursue them.

22 This large Roman triumphal column which stands 27 metres high, was misidentified as being of the time of Emperor Pompey (106-48 BC) but was actually built in AD 297 for Emperor Diocletian.

23 Brevet Lieutenant Colonel William Lockhart, who commanded the 30th (Cambridgeshire) Foot in Egypt, and Captain George Grey also of the 30th.

Had the regiment been in the least confusion, or once commenced firing, they would have been inevitably lost; nor could the regiments in the rear, the 50th and 92nd, who were hastening to their assistance, come up in time to save them; and thus, not only would the 30th have been annihilated, but the hill must have been retaken. The cool, steady, and intrepid conduct of the small corps, was witnessed and admired by General Hutchinson and the whole army.[24]

The distinguished manner in which Captain, afterwards Lieutenant-Colonel Grey, of the 30th, acted upon that day, is so well known, having been highly eulogised by Sir Robert Wilson and others, who have written histories of the campaign in Egypt,[25] that it is almost unnecessary for me to add a single word, although I might probably be excused for doing so, having since had the honour of being allied to his family, by a marriage with one of my sisters, in 1829.

It is painful to me to state, that this brave officer, who had been in thirty-two general engagements, without having received the slightest wound, was, subsequently, killed at the storming of Badajoz, in the act of entering the breach, at the head of his regiment, being the lieutenant-colonel commanding the 30th.

> London Gazette Extraordinary,
> Friday, 24 April, 1812.
>
> The following is an extract from a dispatch from the Earl of Wellington.
>
> Camp before Badajoz,
> 17 April, 1812
>
> It was impossible for any men to behave better, than those in the Fifth Division. I must mention Lieutenant-Colonel Brooke, 4th Regiment,[26] the Honourable Colonel Carlton, 44th Regiment,[27] and Lieutenant-Colonel Grey, of the 30th Regiment, who was unfortunately killed.

The following inscription is on a plain marble tablet, erected to his memory by his then widow, (now Lady Godfrey Thomas),[28] in the church of Newtown Fartullagh,

24 Major General John Hely-Hutchinson, later 2nd Earl of Donoughmore, took command of the army on the death of Abercromby.

25 Sir Robert Thomas Wilson served with the army in Egypt and Spain and was then sent as an observer with the Russian army in 1812. He published his own history of this campaign in 1803.

26 Lieutenant Colonel Francis Brooke was not wounded at Badajoz and survived until 1826.

27 Lieutenant Colonel the Honourable George Carleton 44th Foot was wounded at Badajoz, but recovered and was killed at Bergen op Zoom in 1814.

28 Elizabeth Anne Vignoles had married George Grey in 1808 and then re-married the Reverend Sir John Godfrey Thomas, 6th Baronet, on 10 March 1817.

diocese of Meath, the rector of which place is the Reverend Charles Vignolles, senior chaplain to the Marquis of Wellesley, and brother to Lady Thomas.

Sacred to the Memory of
Lieutenant Colonel George Gray,
Of the 30th Foot,
Who fell at the Storming of Badajoz,
On the night of the 6th of April, 1812,
In the 33rd year of his age,
This Memorial of
The esteem, affection, and sorrow of his afflicted Widow,
(Who unceasingly laments him,)
Is the humble record of those virtues by which, though dead, he yet liveth. Though absent, he is yet present in the remembrance of all who valued him as a Christian, a Husband, and a Friend.

It had been always his most anxious wish, that in case he met with his death in the field of battle, it should be from a similar wound as that which occasioned the death of the brave and much lamented Sir John Moore, between whom and Colonel Grey an intimate friendship had subsisted for some years; and, singular to relate, it was precisely such a wound he received. He expired in nine hours, from loss of blood, having lain nearly all that time amongst the dead and wounded. He was, at length, however, discovered, in a dying state, by Surgeon Frazer, a relation of his;[29] but, at that period, all human skill was vain; and, requesting to be affectionately remembered to his beloved wife, Eliza, who was his sole earthly consideration in his last moments. He, in a short time after, breathed his last, perfectly resigned to that fate which cut short his career of glory.

Mrs Grey's maiden name was Vignoles. She was the daughter of a clergyman in Portarlington, and was equally lovely in form and amiable in disposition. Her husband was extremely attached to her; and such was her affection for him, that neither toil nor privations, much less the entreaty of friends, could dissuade her, from accompanying her husband in all his campaigns, and almost sharing with him the dangers of the field, as she was seldom more than two or three miles distant from the scene of action.

Her anxiety for his safety was so great, that she always prevailed upon him, when going into a general engagement, or on an expedition likely to be attended with danger, to take a tourniquet with him, to be applied in case of haemorrhage. And it is remarkable, that the occasion on which he neglected to take it with him, was the only time he ever had any use for it; but he unfortunately forgot it on the

29 The only surgeons named Fraser or Frazer in the Peninsula in early 1812 were both in the Royal Artillery, so this must refer to either Assistant Surgeon John D. Frazer or John W. Frazer.

last fatal day, although Mrs Grey, with her usual carefulness, had not failed to remind him of it.

His melancholy death was, of course, a severe shock to her, and is supposed to have hastened the birth of a son, whom she named George, after his father, and who is now a subaltern in the 83rd Regiment, and bears a strong resemblance to Colonel Grey.[30] Although her regret for his loss was deep and sincere, she has since married Sir Godfrey Thomas, an English baronet and clergyman, who had made proposals of marriage previously to her union. With George Grey, to whom she gave a decided preference, although Sir Godfrey's pretentions were favoured by her family: Grey had no friend to speak for him, but love itself.

We suffered extremely from want of water in Egypt, and were obliged to send Arabs for it, five or six leagues in our rear, who conveyed it to us in large skins, on the backs of camels and dromedaries. They generally arrived in the evening, the water having been exposed, during the day, to a hot burning sun; and, although it was such as any European would turn from in disgust in his own country, I can well recollect it was considered by us a most delicious draught, and esteemed such a treasure, that it was portioned out with the most economy.

Our usual plan was to send to the men on the advance posts and outlying picquets, their proportions, after which, the guards and different regiments were supplied, and then, if any were left, it was distributed amongst the women, who were generally very importunate, and would sometimes, on its arrival, endeavour to force it from the Arabs. On one of these occasions, I was under the necessity of having them kept off with bayonets, until the men had obtained their supply. 'Oh, sir,' cried one of those poor wretches, with despair pictured on her countenance, 'If I was at home with your Honour, near Limerick, you would not refuse me a drink out of the Shannon!' – an exclamation that, bringing with it a sudden recollection of home and friends, procured for her half of my own share.

Indeed, the scarcity of water was such, that I was induced to defraud Colonel Sir E. Paget of a camel load of it.[31] The Arab driver came, by mistake, to the 54th, instead of the 28th Regiment, for whose use it was intended. I took advantage of the mistake, and divided it amongst our own men, but with the intention of repaying them at a future period, when they might have more pressing occasion for it; but this occurred the following day, when they sent to us for the loan of a camel load of water, being in great need of it. I, of course, gave it to them, and it was regarded as a particular favour, though, if they had known the truth, it was but what was justly due to them.

It was during the time we were encamped on the west side of Alexandria, that I first met Sir Robert Wilson, who commanded a corps of dromedaries, which

30 George was born at Lisbon on 14 April 1812, only eight days after his father was killed. He was gazetted to the 83rd Foot in 1830 and rose to become Governor General of New Zealand.

31 Lieutenant Colonel the Honourable Edward Paget commanded the 28th Foot in Egypt.

he had organized with infinite trouble. He was then a very young man, but was, nevertheless, in high esteem for his military talents; nor could our whole army boast of a finer or more martial-looking officer. And, about the same period, I first saw Sir John Milley Doyle, then a mere boy, and an ensign in the 92nd regiment, with whom I was fortunate enough to form an intimate friendship, which, I feel pleasure in saying, exists to this day.[32] He was generous and open-hearted to a fault, and, young as he was then, his kind disposition and prepossessing manners, gained him many friends, who have not since ceased to regard him with affection.

The Ancient Irish arrived about this period, but all the fighting was then over.[33] There is a singular circumstance connected with the history of this regiment, that I cannot forbear relating.

When we arrived in Malta, on our way to Egypt, the commander-in-chief ordered all the women who had accompanied the army to return, except such as were absolutely necessary to supply the hospitals with nurses; and, accordingly, two large transports were fitted up, in which above 300 women were embarked for England; but having sailed without convoy, they were taken by the French, and carried into Marseilles. They were then sent, in a cartel, to Minorca, at that time garrisoned by British troops, and amongst the rest, the Ancient Irish. Reports having reached them, while there, that the plague had swept away most of our army, and that the few whom it spared had been killed, such of the women as believed, or wished to believe them, got married to men in the garrison; and it so happened, that most of the wives of the men of our regiment, were married to men of that noted one, called the Ancient Irish, commanded by Sir Judkin Fitzgerald.[34]

It was truly laughable to witness the meeting of the women with their former husbands, when this corps landed in Egypt; there were a thousand expostulations and recriminations on both sides, loud and angry, but the matter was finally settled by all the former husbands, save one, refusing to take back their wives; and that one belonged to our regiment, and ever afterwards lived a miserable life, from the manner in which his comrades treated him.

The Ancient Irish were really an extraordinary regiment. It was chiefly composed of Irish rebels, and was raised under peculiar circumstances.

32 John Milley Doyle originally joined the 107th Regiment but exchanged to the 92nd Foot by 1801 as a lieutenant. He was aide de camp to his uncle Major General John Doyle during the Egyptian campaign. He later commanded Portuguese brigades in the Peninsular War.

33 The Ancient Irish Fencible Regiment was raised in 1799 and like all fencible regiments, they were raised for 'Home service' only. However, the Ancient Irish did proceed abroad, travelling to Egypt via Minorca where they stopped to be trained and armed, but missed any fighting there, although one man was killed. They then returned to Britain via Malta in 1802.

34 Sir Judkin Fitzgerald, a magistrate from County Tipperary, was colonel of the regiment. He was later made Baron of Lisheen.

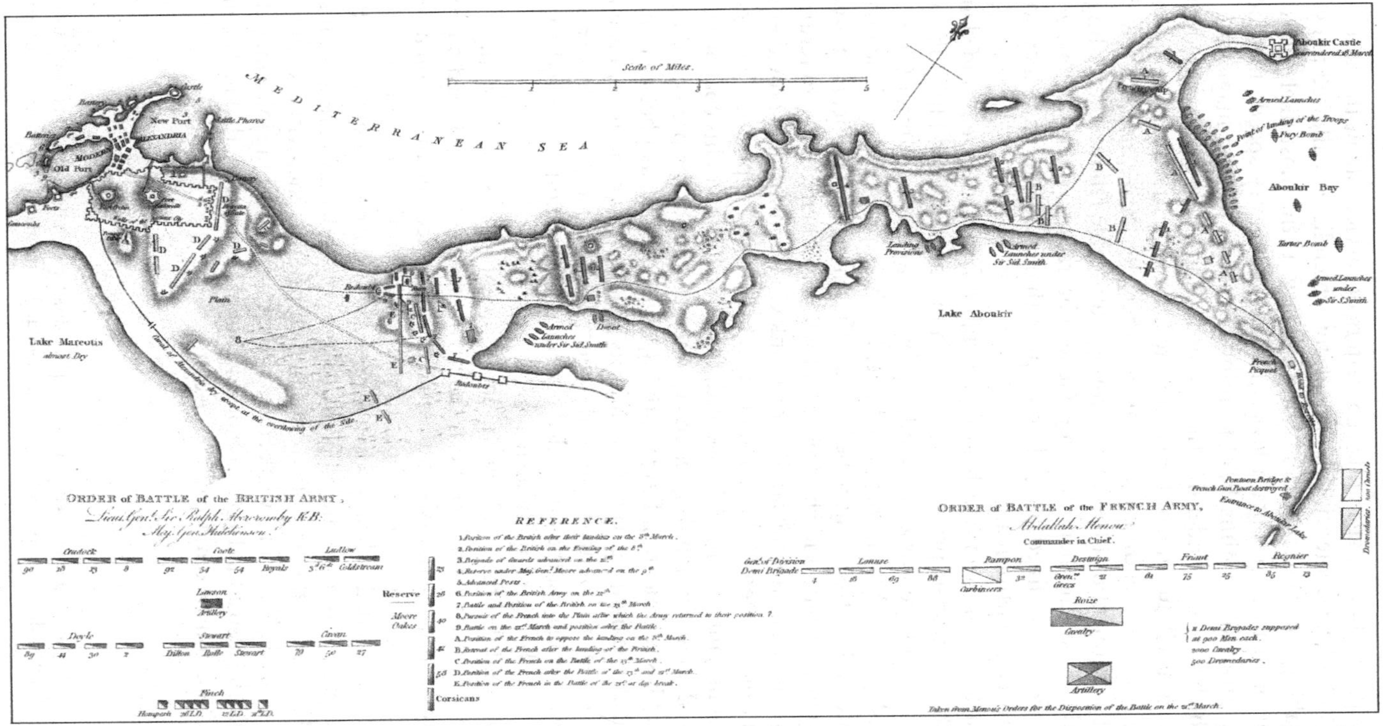

Map 2 'A plan of the Operations of the British Forces in Egypt from the landing in Aboukir Bay on the 8th of March to the Battle of Alexandria March 21st inclusive.' Map by William Fadden. (Public Domain)

The late [Sir Judkin Fitzgerald],[35] got letters of service, about the latter end of the year 1798, to raise a fencible regiment, for which he was allowed ten guineas a man. Making choice of the county of Tipperary, as the most likely place, from his connexion with it, to obtain levies, he adopted a very speedy method, and not a little profitable to himself, of forming his corps. Being a magistrate of the county, which was then under martial law, he took up every man accused, or even suspected, of rebellion; and, by threatening to hang the unfortunate people, if they refused to enlist, pretending there was no other alternative, he, in a few weeks, completed a regiment of 1,000 men – young, stout, able fellows. According as he obtained them, he sent them into New Geneva barracks, Waterford,[36] where they were kept closely confined, more like culprits than soldiers, until they were all ready to proceed to Minorca.

Many of the men, who had held comfortable farms, were entrapped in this manner. To my great surprise, I met one man in Egypt, named Philip Fitzgerald, whom I knew to have possessed landed property to the amount of £300 a year; upon my asking him how he happened to enlist, he explained the whole matter to me, and said, 'It is better for us to be here, sir, than hanged at home. I left my lands and cattle with my wife and children, and I will have them if I live to return; but, if I never see home again, my family are, thank God, comfortably provided for.'

The first time I visited Tipperary after my return from Egypt, I saw [Fitzgerald]'s carriage coming into town, and observed, that, in addition to his coat of arms, he had assumed some foreign devices in commemoration of his pretended exploits and those of his regiment, in Egypt, although they did not, as I before remarked, arrive until all the fighting was over; and this gallant officer had never been there, nor, I believe, seen a shot fired against the enemies of his country, unless, indeed, it might have been against the misguided peasantry of the south of Ireland, to whom it would be hardly fair to apply such a term.

About the middle of April, I left the encampment for a few days, being sent on duty on board the *Ariadne* transport, then lying in the bay. I selected one of our men, Paddy Carrol, as a trusty, confidential person to accompany me on my expedition, and was provided with a boat to take us down the lake into the bay. We had scarcely proceeded half way when we were hailed from the shore by a British officer, who placed some wounded French prisoners under my care, with instructions to take them to the first of our hospital ships that I met with. As they were very badly wounded, and in a weak state, I gave them some lime juice mixed with water; to which I also added a portion of rum out of my canteen, that had been well replenished previously to my leaving the camp.

35 He died in 1810.

36 Geneva Barracks was originally a settlement (set up for disaffected inhabitants of Geneva) which had soon been abandoned. It was converted into a barracks and particularly used to hold rebel prisoners in 1798.

As it was now late, and we found that we could not reach the *Ariadne*, or any of the hospital vessels, until after nightfall, which was just approaching, we thought it prudent to wait the return of day before we proceeded further, lest we might be run down by some vessel in the bay; and, accordingly, came to anchor, for the night, in three or four fathom water.

My man, Paddy Carrol, placing himself in the stern of the boat, and fixing his knapsack between his knees, so that when I lay down, my head might rest upon it, pressed me to take a sleep after the fatigues of the day; promising, at the same time, to keep a good look out during the night, to take care of the prisoners, and prevent the occurrence of any unpleasant accident. Relying on Paddy's professions, and obeying the dictates of nature, I soon fell sound asleep, which I enjoyed, undisturbed, until morning; but on my awaking then, what was my surprise to find my confidential soldier, who had made such promises, and upon whom, in some measure, our safety during the night depended, lying quite intoxicated, behind me, after having finished the contents of my canteen while I had slept. When I spoke to him about his conduct, with the most unblushing effrontery he told me, that knowing my feelings for the poor wounded prisoners, he had now and then given a drop out of the canteen, to keep the life in them; 'because,' said he, 'I knew that if your Honour's self was awake, you would refresh the poor perishing creatures; and as I did not wish to disturb you out of your fine sleep, I thought it best to help them myself.' As the fellow was guilty of falsehood, not having given the unfortunate Frenchmen one drop, as well as of drunkenness and neglect of duty, I took good care to punish him in a way the most likely, above all others, to be felt by him – stopping his allowance of grog until we returned to the regiment, and then, for some days after, only giving him half the quantity allowed to the other men.

While we lay encamped outside the walls of Alexandria, Captain Frederick, of our regiment, and late lieutenant-colonel of the 55th Regiment,[37] joined with me in inviting a master of a transport, who had been extremely civil to us during our passage to Egypt, to dine with us in the camp. Frederick having, some time before, obtained a large centipede, put it in a bottle half filled with rum, for the purpose of preserving it; and as it had been incautiously left among the empty bottles in his tent, it was, with others, filled up for dinner, out of a small barrel of wine that we had procured. After we had drank two or three bottles, this was produced, and our guest took a bumper of it; but as he remarked that it differed very much from the wine we had been drinking, it was ordered off the table, and other bottles introduced. In the meantime, the Maltese boy who attended us, gave the rejected bottle to a sergeant outside the tent, who did not take it from his mouth until he had drained it to the bottom – so delicious did he esteem it – but when he saw the reptile it contained, he flew into a violent passion, and exclaiming, 'I am poisoned! – you Maltese rascal, you put these vipers in the bottle on purpose to kill me, and

37 Captain Robert Frederick became a major in the 55th Foot in 1808 and a lieutenant colonel in 1814.

I will have my revenge' – drew his sword, and ran after the boy into our tent, with the bottle in one hand and the naked weapon in the other. When the cause of the disturbance was made known to us, the master of the transport turned pale; and crying out, 'I am a lost man,' started up, ran off like a madman to his boat, and rowed, with all possible expedition, to his ship, in order to procure medicine to counteract the poison. The sergeant also, became very alarmed, and, as well as one or two others who had merely tasted it before it was given to him, expected immediate death. Our regimental doctor, O'Dwyer, was quickly in attendance, and prescribing his usual medicine, and never-failing remedy, a couple of glasses of good grog, speedily effected a cure – there being nothing but fright in question, as the liquor itself was perfectly innocuous.

About the same period, a circumstance occurred, which, at another time, might have been attended with serious, if not fatal consequences, to the parties concerned. I was acquainted with a Turk of respectability, in Alexandria, at whose house, however, I had never been; but passing it one night, accompanied by Captain Featherstone,[38] after we had enjoyed our wine rather too freely, and perceiving a light in it, I entered the courtyard, and prevailed on Featherstone to come with me into the house, telling him, and almost persuading myself, that I was sure of a hearty welcome from my friend the Turk; whereas, we were about to commit an act of most daring presumption, particularly being Christians, and what, in our sober hours, we could not dream of attempting. The slave, at the entrance of the door which led to the stairs, was well armed; but knowing me to be personally acquainted with his master, and supposing that we came by invitation, he allowed us to pass without interruption, many guests being expected, as this was the wedding day of the Turk's *sixth living wife*, all inhabiting the same house. On entering the room, we found him and his friends seated, cross-legged, on a sumptuous carpet, smoking their long pipes, and occasionally singing in turn – but there were no females to be seen.

My reception, at least, was gratifying. When the Turk saw us enter, he gave instructions to one of his attendants to place me near him, keeping poor Featherstone, in consequence of his coat and epaulette not being as new and as brilliant as mine, at the lower end of the room, just inside the door, and not suffering him to approach nearer – a distinction that annoyed him very much. After some time, the host made me sit down close to him, and, taking his pipe out of his mouth, thrust it into mine, as a particular mark of friendship – one, indeed, I did not covet, but to which I was nevertheless, by etiquette and politeness, obliged to submit.

Having ordered supper, a slave entered with two silver basons, one containing lumps of soft bread, and the other filled with some sweet stuff resembling treacle, but of a more greasy nature. As the Turks never use anything at their meals but their fingers, their manner of eating is not the most cleanly, at least, it does not

38 Actually he was then Lieutenant Francis Featherstone.

appear so to one accustomed to European habits, and I must confess it almost disgusted me. He first dipped a lump of soft bread in to the liquid stuff, and then, putting it to his mouth, bit off such part as retained a portion of the liquid, continuing afterwards to dip the bread, and bite off part in turn until he had finished the piece.

He then pointed to me to follow his example, and, as I did not immediately do so, he, in order to instruct me how to eat, supposing that the delay arose from ignorance, rather than reluctance, took a large lump in his fingers, and dipping it into the other bason, first took a bite out of it himself, to show me the way, leaving on it, at the same time, the impression of his teeth; and then dipping into the sweet stuff again, tried to cram it into my mouth with great kindness, but I involuntarily closed my teeth against its admission, and the clammy stuff, with which the bread was besmeared, fell on the lace and facings of my new regimental coat, and completely destroyed it.

As I thus had cause to dread a repetition of such specimens of Turkish civility, I shortly afterwards withdrew, not a little annoyed at the loss of my coat, which I had only worn once or twice before. Featherstone enjoyed my misfortune above all things; and the vexation, which I could but ill conceal; seemed to make ample amends to him, for having been placed at the lower end of the room, amongst the inferior classes of guests, while I was ranked even above the highest – a distinction he unjustly attributed to my interference; but which was, in fact, entirely owing to the worn-out state of his regimentals, and the spruce appearance of mine. Few of our brother officers would believe us, when we told them of our adventure, on the following morning, as admission into such a place, and at such a time, particularly for Christians, they considered utterly impossible.

5

Mutiny, Ireland Again, and Joining the 47th

Peace was at length declared in 1802, and I embarked at Alexandria, in the *Lord Hood* transport, with about seven other officers, belonging to different regiments.[1] The weather was remarkably fine, and we had a favourable breeze for the first few days; but, on the fifth or sixth day, the wind chopped round, and blew a gale right against us, which increased every hour, until it became a perfect hurricane, which continued without any intermission for six or seven days, during which period we suffered much both in mind and body; for, as we had sprung a leak, and there were not less than seven feet of water in the hold, we were every moment in expectation of the vessel's going down; and, in consequence of the violence of the storm, we were unable to cook any provisions. The poor soldiers and their wives were in a state that cannot be described; the men working the pumps day and night, to keep the ship above water, and the women obliged to shift for ourselves, under such awful circumstances. One of the pumps became choked at last, and then we gave up all hope of being saved, as one pump could not possibly keep her clear. Such of us as had been at all seriously inclined, now devoted themselves earnestly in preparing for that death we all thought unavoidable. Even the captain, who was a religious man, retired to his cabin, resigned to his fate, saying, all was now over with us, and entreating us to think no more of this world; but make our peace with God.

One of our officers, who had a passion for obtaining curiosities, had, with much labour and perseverance, made his way into the mummy pits while we were in Egypt, and procured a child in a perfect state of preservation, which he was now taking home with him, with the intention of presenting it to his Alma Mater, Trinity College, Dublin, where he had been educated. When the storm was raging with its utmost violence, one of our servants informed the sailors that it was on board; they, with their usual superstition, attributed the violence of the storm to the circumstance of the dead body being on board; and, coming to the cabin-door, required, in terms that admitted of no resistance, that it should be given up to

1 Britain agreed to remove all troops from Alexandria as part of the Peace of Amiens.

them. Their demand was of course immediately complied with, and the mummy was quickly consigned to the waves.

Still we were no better off; and, whatever faith the sailors might have in the destruction of the mummy, they, too, soon gave up all hope, when they found the storm continuing; and, notwithstanding the precautions taken by the captain and by us; they gained access to the spirit stores, and became, in a short time, in a dreadful state of intoxication.

As there was no effort now made to keep the ship afloat, the leak gained on us considerably, and the vessel was every moment sinking deeper and deeper, when it pleased providence to direct the gale to abate by degrees, until the wind soon died away nearly altogether. Pouring our grateful thanks for the prospect we now had of being snatched from the jaws of death, we set to work at the pumps again with renewed vigour; and at length succeeded, after length succeeded, after much labour, in keeping the leak under, until, with the greatest exertions, we were enabled to reach Malta in safety, where we had been scarcely changed into another transport, when the *Lord Hood* sunk in the harbour.

Remaining a few days at Malta, to recover the fatigue we had undergone in the late storm, we again set sail in our new transport, on our passage to Gibraltar; but, as we sailed down the beautiful coast of Sicily, another gale set in from the westward, which drove us back, so that we were obliged to take shelter in Syracuse harbour. It was night when we came to anchor, and, as it was extremely dark, and Mount Etna was then pouring out volumes of burning lava, we had a favourable opportunity of witnessing one of the most magnificent spectacles that could possibly be imagined. On the following day, we landed and visited the town; and an American frigate coming into the harbour, the officers entertained us handsomely, inviting also many of the principal inhabitants, who in turn gave a grand masquerade, it being then the carnival, in which the Sicilians, particularly the ladies, performed their different parts, and sustained their characters in a superior manner. The scene was altogether so gay and enchanting, that our party could scarcely credit that we were the same individuals who had been, but a fortnight before, in such imminent danger in the *Lord Hood* transport.

We paid a visit to the principal nobleman in the town, the Baron de Bosco, who received us with politeness, and directed his servants to conduct us to the apartments of the Baroness, who, according to the custom of the country, saw us in her bed room, where she ordered up refreshments of every description, of which we partook, remaining of course a considerable time, during which the Baron never made his appearance.

We visited many places of note during our stay here. The cathedral,[2] part of the wall of which forms a portion of the Temple of Diana;[3] also the Ear of Dionysius,

2 The Romanesque Cathedral of Syracuse.
3 The Temple of Diana in Cefalu in Sicily.

where the tyrant used to confine his victims;[4] and our guide, who appeared extremely intelligent, and very well versed in the ancient history of the country, pointed out to us the spot where he lay, that he might have the gratifications of hearing the groans and the clanking of the chains of the unfortunate wretches whom he had confined.

We then proceeded to view the most extraordinary place we had yet seen in the island, a convent built partly underground, where we were received with great politeness, and even marked attention by the monks, who seemed to vie with each other in their endeavours to gratify our curiosity, showing us the splendid gardens, and all the other parts of the monastery, that might be thought worthy the notice of a stranger. One part was arranged as a sepulchre for the brotherhood, nor were the remains of any others admitted, with the exception of the first class of grandees, and those only with special leave.

The bodies, being preserved by some process known only to the monks, had the appearance of life. Every feature was perfect, and I might almost say the very expression of the countenance was unaltered. They were placed in an upright position, in niches in the walls; the hand of each extended, to which a small piece of paper was attached, containing the name of the deceased, his age, birth, and date of his death, in legible characters; and, however it was contrived, though this place was considerably underground, there was sufficient daylight to trace the letters distinctly.

The monks also showed us the body of a young nobleman, about nineteen years old, which was then lying on a table in the middle of a room, undergoing the usual process, which they informed us was very expensive and tedious; occupying at least three months before the body could be said to be sufficiently preserved from decomposition.

Parting from these benevolent and seemingly happy men, we returned to Syracuse, highly pleased with our day's excursion; and, on the following morning, a few of us, who had more courage than the rest, travelled to the foot of Mount Etna, with the intention of proceeding up the mountain, and viewing the crater of this remarkable volcano; but in consequence of the thickness of the atmosphere, occasioned by the clouds of ashes it vomited forth, we were obliged reluctantly to relinquish the further prosecution of our journey, which might probably have been attended with fatal results; as the burning lava was pouring down the sides of the mountain in torrents, and large cinders and half-burnt stones fell in showers around its mouth.

As the wines of this island are very fine, and of various kinds, I was anxious to procure some of the best, and prevailed on Colonel Ramsey, of the 2nd or Queen's Regiment,[5] who was one of our passengers, to join with me in the purchase of

4 A huge limestone cave formed from an ancient limestone quarry at Syracuse.
5 Brevet Lieutenant Colonel the Honourable James Ramsay, 2nd Foot.

a thirty-gallon cask of the first quality, being a rich, sweet wine, resembling the finest Constantia.[6] Having procured it, we had it carefully put on board, and placed for safety in the steward's cabin; and then, as the weather had become sufficiently moderate, we proceeded to Gibraltar, our destination. After having spent a fortnight so pleasantly at Syracuse, that notwithstanding our anxiety to join our respective regiments, we all left it with regret.

One morning, during our passage, I found two of our soldiers and one of the seamen near the cook-house in a state of intoxication; but the latter was besides deadly sick, and exclaimed in my hearing, and yet I little suspected what had occurred; 'Damn my eyes, if I will ever recover after that cursed sweet stuff. I should never have taken the trouble of boring that there barrel; but I was told it was rum.' In the course of a day or two we arrived at Gibraltar; and, as Colonel Ramsay and I were most anxious to get the wine on shore to divide it, each of us naming the lady in England to whom we intended to present it, we had the barrel immediately hauled up; but, to our consternation and astonishment, it was quite empty. The conversation I had overheard at the cook-house instantly recurred to my memory. The captain ordered an investigation, and, on the sailor being examined, he candidly declared the truth; that the soldiers, the very men we had employed to stow it away, had informed him where the barrel was, and that it contained rum – that they had got at it by raising the boards of the steward's cabin – that they did not drink much of it, as it was so sweet; but as it sickened them, they took no trouble in stopping the hole they had made, and he supposed that all the rest had leaked out. Thus, we foolishly lost our valuable wine, and our friends their presents.

At Gibraltar, the lightning is awfully destructive at times. I remember a circumstance that occurred there. A sergeant and guard, who were stationed on the top of the rock, in the morning on the new guard going up to relieve them, were found dead, having been killed during the night by the lightning, and on the table in the guardroom was found the guard report, which the poor sergeant had written, of course intending to hand it to his successor when relieved. The report was as follows – 'Nothing extraordinary since guard mounting.' Little did the poor fellow then suppose that it was the last report he would ever make for himself or his companions.

About two months before our arrival at Gibraltar, the Governor-general died, a most eccentric individual, yet possessed of various amiable qualities.[7] I had the honour of being personally known to him, and, when we landed at Gibraltar,

6 A sweet desert wine grown in South Africa. It was exported to Europe in great quantities in the 17th and 18th Century.

7 General Charles O'Hara died on 25 February 1802 from complications in his old wounds. The low morale on the Rock in 1798 led to a plot to hand over the defences to the Spanish, O'Hara discovered it and had up to a thousand civilians exiled from Gibraltar.

The Defences of Gibraltar seen from the Spanish Lines, by Henry Aston Barker, dated 1804. (Aberdeen University)

his death had been so recent that his oddities were still the subject of general conversation. He was a strict disciplinarian; yet, strange to say, he delighted in seeing the garrison drunk, provided the guards and men on duty were sober. But the reason was evident; as governor, he derived a duty of ten dollars on each pipe of wine consumed in the garrison; therefore, drunkenness was a source of considerable profit to him; and I have often seen him, when in Gibraltar on a former occasion, take no notice of men who actually lay down in the streets from the effects of wine.

He was very rough in his demeanour towards the officers, and would not hesitate sometimes to abuse them in no measured language; yet still his heart was kind, and there was no man more capable of a generous act. The following noble trait is strikingly characteristic of his disposition and manner. There was a captain in the garrison who had his wife and family with him, and who, in addition to his company, had an excellent staff employment. His sister also resided with him, a young and amiable creature; but as she was dependent on them for support, he and his wife treated her with shameful neglect, did not allow her to go into company nor mix in their society, but kept her as a mere children's maid.

This young lady, being very handsome and interesting, won the affections of a young ensign of the garrison, who saw her occasionally, as she accompanied her unfeeling brother's children in their daily walks. After some time, the attachment became mutual, and the young lovers had frequent interviews; explanations followed of course, and the matter ended with a resolution to be married as speedily as possible.

The practice in Gibraltar is, or at least was, for the individuals to apply to the governor for licence. As soon as Mr R[aleigh], the secretary,[8] had informed the general of the names of the parties, who in this instance applied for licence, he desired them to be ushered into his presence. The trembling pair had barely crossed the threshold of the door when the governor began in his usual *polite* tone. 'Why, you beggarly pair of wretches, what do you mean? you will be both starving before long, and the devil mend you, you pair of brats – why should such as you think of marrying? A fine thing, indeed, Mr Ensign, with your 4*s*. 8*d*. a day, to think of supporting a wife, and to-morrow or next day half a dozen squallers. Get you gone, both of you, out of this – I will give you no licence.'

The young lady, with her handkerchief to her eyes, and the intended Benedict, hanging down his head, moved slowly towards the door in utter despair. They had even reached the hall-door, and were about to proceed into the street, when the general cried out, 'R[aleigh], call them back, I want to speak to them again.' On their reappearance, he hastily exclaimed, 'So, you will be married – I suppose you must, I know all the bad treatment you have received, young lady; you cannot fall into much worse hands than those you wish to escape from; and, while I am over him, this young chap shall not treat you badly: R[aleigh], make out a licence at once – give her 1,000 dollars (£250 British) – let them have a small house on the hill – tell the barrack-master to furnish it comfortably – and put this boy on duty on the works, at five shillings a day. And now, young couple, you may go to the devil, and take care of yourselves. But don't attempt to go near your sister-in-law, that treated you so ill, nor her rascally husband'. This was precisely the general's manner; and this is but one of many similar generous acts.

As soon as the general's death became known in England, His Royal Highness the Duke of Kent was sent out as Governor;[9] and immediately on his arrival, in May 1802, he set about reforming the garrison, which he found, from the cause before assigned, in a state of complete insubordination; and, although such reform would occasion a great loss to himself, in a pecuniary point of view, as the revenue derived from the wine was immense, he was so determined, however, on putting a stop to inebriety, that he issued an order prohibiting soldiers from drinking in wine-houses or public-houses; directing that each man should be supplied with a pint of good wholesome wine at his dinner in the barracks, which wine was to be furnished by the mess or canteen man within the gate.

As this arrangement completely spoiled the trade of the public-houses in the town, the owners of them gave plenty of wine to the soldiers for nothing, and encouraged, by every effort in their power, that spirit of mutiny they saw arising, and of which they themselves had been very probably the origin.

8 Mr John Raleigh, Secretary to the Governor.

9 General Prince Edward, the Duke of Kent and Strathearn, was renowned as a very strict disciplinarian.

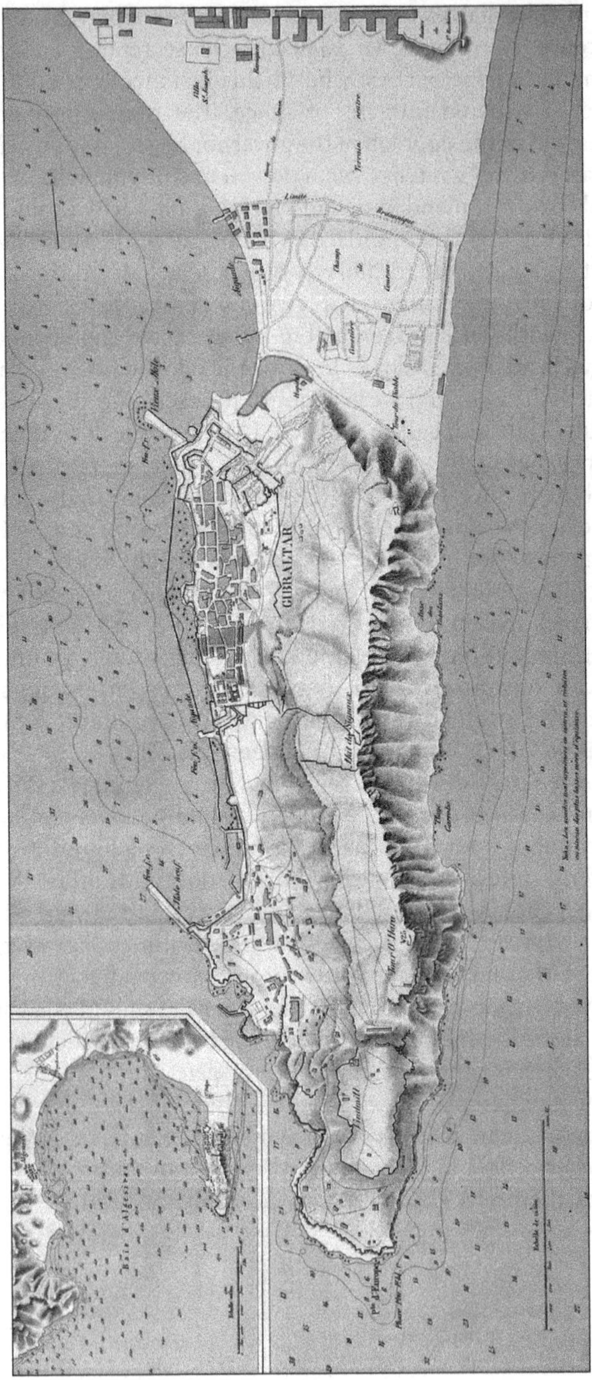

Map 3 A French map of Gibraltar circa 1800. (Author's collection)

There were eight regiments in the garrison at the time. The mutiny had been going on privately for a few days, the conspirators endeavouring to extend it to each regiment; but, from what cause I cannot say, ours (54th) was not consulted by them, nor were our men at all aware of it until it actually broke out. It has often occurred to me since, that as we were an Irish regiment, and, of course, wild and fond of drink, they considered it needless to consult our men till matters were fully ripe for a revolt; thinking the Irish would be ready to join them at all times, in anything of such a nature; but, if this was their expectation, they were woefully mistaken.

We lay in the south barracks, outside the town. About six o'clock in the evening, as the officers were proceeding to the mess room, Colonel Ross, who then commanded our regiment,[10] arrived in haste from the town, and, collecting the officers around him – dinner being at the time on the table – he said, 'Gentlemen, we must not sit down to dinner, there is a mutiny in the garrison. We have not a moment to lose in putting it down, if possible. I trust, our men are not concerned in it – let us have them all on parade.' We were thunderstruck: the drum beat to arms, and, in a few minutes, the whole regiment was drawn up – not one man was missing. The Colonel then addressed them – told them of the enormity of the crime of which the mutineers had been guilty, and, in a few words, entreated them to stand by their officers, who would not desert them. He had scarcely finished his address when a shouting was heard, as if from a large body, and the mutineers appeared in a few seconds, approaching our barracks from the town, and calling on the brave 54th to join them. Lieutenant Conran, the late General Conran, who commanded the grenadiers,[11] instantly faced his company about, without giving his men time for reflection, and poured a volley on them, which killed and wounded several, and dispersed the rest.[12]

At this time, the Duke and his staff were in the government house, which, considering the excited state of the garrison, it would have been the extreme of folly to leave. Colonel Ross lost no time in marching the entire regiment down to the town, and surrounding the governor's house. The mutiny was at once quelled by these decisive steps, and some of the ring-leaders were taken up and executed on the following morning. Various opinions have been afloat, and many different causes assigned for this mutiny; but such is, in a few words, its entire history.

10 Lieutenant Colonel Andrew Ross, 54th Foot, played a significant role in stopping the mutiny at Gibraltar.

11 Lieutenant William Conran 54th Foot. I believe that Harley may have confused two officers named Conran, as the 'late' General Conran would be Henry Conran, originally of the 52nd Foot, who died in 1829.

12 One man was killed on this occasion when the mutiny collapsed on Christmas Eve 1802. A second attempt on Boxing Day was foiled by the artillery turning the guns on the walls to fire on the mutineers which killed another two. The twelve ringleaders were tried and condemned to death, whilst two others were sentenced to receive 1,000 lashes. The Duke of Kent transmuted all but three of the death sentences to transportation for life to Australia. The three executed by firing squad were named Pastoret, Teighman and Reilly. The first two were Dutchmen whilst the third was Irish.

Gibraltar from Spanish lines by Henry Aston Barker. (Author's collection)

Notwithstanding the false colouring of prejudiced persons, and the stigma attempted, by those who know not his worth, to be attached to his character, I can assure my readers there never was a better hearted man than his late Royal Highness.

His anxiety for the discipline of the army did not prevent his wishes and exertions for the happiness and comfort of his soldiers, for whose welfare he had more consideration than his own emoluments.

When I had been about three months in Gibraltar, I was taken very ill of a nervous fever; and, as my recovery was tedious, my physicians recommended my trying my native air; I, therefore, applied to the Duke of Kent for leave, and he not only ordered me a passage immediately, but told me, in the kindest manner, not to delay an hour, as he could perceive that I was in a bad state of health. I accordingly embarked in the first vessel for England, a transport attached to the Ordnance, and bound from Minorca to Woolwich, having on board six passengers; a lady, four officers, and myself.

As the weather was fine and the wind favourable, we calculated on a quick passage, and only laid in what we deemed a reasonable supply of provisions for a fortnight's voyage; but we had not reached St Vincent, on our way home, when we encountered a violent storm, which drove us nearly to the Western Islands; and, as the wind continued blowing very fresh from the point, for several days, we made but little or no head against it; particularly as our vessel was heavily laden with shots and shells. On a sudden, the weather changed and became squally, being sometimes a dead calm, and the next half hour a heavy gale, until at length we were finally becalmed in the Bay of Biscay for several days. As it was now six weeks since we left Gibraltar, our sea stock was completely run out, and we were anxiously looking out for a ship, in the hope of obtaining relief, when, to our great joy, we at length fell in with one, a large outward-bound Indiaman. We sent a boat on board, with a request for a few provisions, as we were now in a state of actual starvation, having had nothing to eat for nearly two days, and on very short allowance for three or four weeks. To our utter dismay, the boat returned empty, with an answer, that they were going a long voyage, and could not spare any – telling us, at the same time, by way of consolation I suppose, that we were near home.

This cruel, unfeeling conduct of our countryman roused our indignation so much, that, for a moment, we forgot our own misery in our execration of the individual; but the demands of nature became at last so insupportable, that the master of the transport advised us to remain in bed as much as we could, as he had not a morsel to give us; and he knew that exposure to the fresh, keen air, created and irritated the appetite. Next day, however, we fortunately observed another sail, at some distance, to which we instantly sent a boat, with an officer and money, to purchase any species of food that could be procured. She turned out to be a Frenchman, from Bordeaux, bound to the West Indies. On our officer boarding her, and stating our melancholy situation, the captain ordered his steward to put into our boat at least two hundred weight of very fine new bread, two large hams, some vegetables, two gallons of brandy, a small barrel of about twenty gallons of excellent Bordeaux wine, and another barrel of water; he also ordered refreshments for the officer and crew, who, poor fellows, stood in much need of them. And, on being asked what was to be paid, the noble French captain answered, 'Nothing. I am happy to have it in my power to oblige the English. I was once a prisoner of war in England, and then received kindness from your people which I shall ever remember with gratitude; and, besides, I am quite sure, that if our situations were changed, you would be equally ready to assist me.'

We were thus rescued from a dreadful death by the noble benevolence of a stranger; nay, one whom we might almost call the natural enemy of our country, while we were inhumanly left to starve by the captain of a British East Indiaman.

In the course of another week, we arrived in the Channel, and, on passing the Isle of Wight hailed a pilot boat, the master of which agreed to take our passengers to Portsmouth for ten guineas, as the transport could not enter the harbour, being bound for Woolwich, with ordnance stores. We accordingly got into the boat, taking all our luggage with us, but, on approaching the point at Portsmouth,[13] and almost in the act of setting our feet on shore, we were hailed by the custom house officers, who demanded where we came from; and, on one of our party unfortunately replying, the Mediterranean, we were instantly ordered off to the Mother Bank, to perform quarantine, and had volleys of abuse poured on us for attempting to land.[14]

This was a dreadful disappointment to us, for we had been, but a few minutes before, congratulating each other on the narrow escape we had from death, and the happy prospect of soon meeting our dearest friends; but now, as the pilot was

13 Portsmouth Point or 'Spice Island' was the area just north of King Edward's Tower. It was originally outside the fortress walls but in the 18th Century, the area was built on, with numerous bars and brothels opening up, hence the name Spice Island. The area is now part of Historic Portsmouth.

14 The Mother Bank is a shallow water anchorage north east of the Isle of Wight between Cowes and Ryde. It was used as an anchorage for merchant ships for centuries.

obliged to hoist the yellow flag,[15] no boat dare approach us with provisions, and we had none with us in the boat, with the exception of half a dozen biscuits.

At the very moment, however, that we were ordered away from the point at Portsmouth, Captain Campbell hastily wrote, on his card, in pencil, 'The 54th Regiment in distress, and hungry,' and directing it to Miss Palmer, of the George Inn, Portsmouth, threw to a boy, with an entreaty that he would immediately take it to her.[16] This passed unnoticed by any of us, nor did he apprise us of what he had done, lest some disappointment might occur, and then we should only feel the more. Our evening was spent in misery. I had, very fortunately, a tent or marquee, in which I had lived during the campaign in Egypt, and which, thrown across the boom, served to protect us from the heavy dew of the night. We all lay down under it, resigned to our miserable fate, yet longing for the return of day; while the poor pilot and his son were almost frightened to death, lest they might take some plague or contagious infection from us, and dreading the forfeiture of their boat for such a breach of the quarantine laws; as there was an order against their taking passengers out of any vessel from the Mediterranean. About midnight, as we lay awake, ruminating on our unhappy fate, a small boat came alongside us, with a noiseless motion of the oars, as if there was danger in their being heard, and, in a minute, three hampers were handed into our boat, with Miss Palmer's compliments, containing every necessary article we could require; she even sent us the latest newspapers, army lists, &c., and desired her messenger to inform us, that if we wanted anything more, it should be sent to us on the following night.

At the end of four days, we were released by an order in council, and, on arriving on shore, the first person we met was General Whitelocke, then governor of Portsmouth, afterwards tried for his conduct at Buenos Ayres, who humanely told us that we ought to be shot for breaking through the quarantine laws. Without paying much attention to the general's unfeeling observation, we repaired to Miss Palmer's hotel, where we remained some days, as a recompense – a trifling one indeed – for her attention to our wants when in distress, and then proceeded to our respective destinations.

I should have mentioned before, that being at a great loss, previously to my leaving the transport, to know how I could land some valuable things I had purchased abroad for my family, and elude the lynx-eyed vigilance of the custom house officers, an old sergeant, who learned the cause of my uneasiness, offered to manage the matter for me. 'Leave them to me, sir,' said he, as I was stepping out of the ship into the pilot boat, 'and I will insure their safe delivery in Limerick.' As there was not a moment to be lost in deciding, I at once consented. He immediately called down the drummer of a recruiting party, then on route to

15 The quarantine flag was plain yellow, it later became chequered yellow and black.

16 Captain John Campbell, 54th Foot. The George Inn, built in 1780, still exists today just outside the historic dockyard.

the south of Ireland, into the cabin, and having taken off the drum head, filled it with the different contraband articles I had, and placing it again on the lad's back, cautioned him to be careful of the contents until he reached Limerick, when he was to deliver them according to a direction given to him, reminding him that he had no occasion to beat his drum until he arrived at his destination. The drummer strictly adhered to the sergeant's injunctions, and, passing through the custom house of Portsmouth and Dublin without detection, delivered them to my family, in Limerick, perfectly safe and uninjured.

We had a subaltern officer in the 54th Regiment who caused much amusement, Lieutenant John G[alpine]. We often made him describe how he came into the army. He commenced by telling us, 'that his mother was a farmer-ess, in Surrey, not many miles from London; his father had been dead some years, and his mother having sent him frequently into London to sell hay at the Haymarket, he had seen the soldiers mounting guard at St James's, and took a great fancy to the army as a *trade*, and, as Johnny said, 'no longer wear the smock frock, flourish the long whip, and drive his waggon to the Haymarket, but change it for a red coat and sword, and go to the wars.' He returned to his mother one day, after selling his hay, full of this idea, and proposed to her to become 'a soldier officer, or gentleman soldier; for be so as how, mother, this band of music is so fine, that, *dang* it, I will have no other *trade*.' His mother, wishing to get rid of him, (having large funds of his in her hands, left him by his father, which she was not inclined to account for) quickly purchased for him an ensigncy, and by his getting into the army, she concluded she had done with him for ever. Shortly after he joined the 54th Regiment, he embarked in that unfortunate fleet of Admiral Christian's, which, it must be remembered, met with such disasters in the Channel.[17] The transport that Johnny G[alpine] went in, among many others, was wrecked on the coast, near Plymouth; he got on shore with nothing on him but his trousers, an old red jacket, without lace or epaulet, and a foraging cap belonging to one of the soldiers. He was met on the road by the constables, who instantly took him up as a deserter; and in vain did Johnny remonstrate with them, and tell them, in his Surrey dialect, 'that be so as how he was no *disarter*, but a soldier officer of the 54th Regiment.' But they not believing it, from his appearance and conversation, put him into the Bridewell,[18]

17 Rear-Admiral Sir Hugh Cloberry Christian (1747-1798). In 1796 he was given command of the Leeward Islands and was ordered to sail with a squadron and a fleet of merchant ships, numbering over 200 ships in total, carrying 16,000 troops. The fleet sailed from Spithead on 16 November 1796, but soon struck terrible weather, with a number of merchant ships foundering with a large loss of life. A second attempt was made on 9 December with the fleet being scattered, some reaching their destination, a number being lost and a large number being forced to turn back again. These storms were then often referred to as 'Christian's gales'. Christian successfully reached the islands on the third attempt and participated in the successful capture of St Lucia, St Vincent and Grenada with General Abercromby.

18 Bridewell Prison in London had been established in 1553 in a former royal palace, the term subsequently being applied to a prison or lock-up.

where he remained two or three days, and, of course, faring on the prison allowance. Captain Neynoe, then of the 34th Regiment, and latterly Lieutenant-Colonel of the 27th,[19] fortunately for Johnny G[alpine] was passing by the prison; G[alpine] perceiving him, called to him through the bars, 'Captain Neynoe, be so as how I am here, and they will not be for letting me go.' Captain Neynoe instantly went to the prison door, but at the moment did not recognise him, from his beard being so much grown, and the ludicrous figure he presented altogether. The poor fellow was released from prison, and he joined his regiment. He afterwards purchased a lieutenancy; and a short time after, a company being for sale, as he well knew there were sufficient funds in his mother's lands, of his own, he instantly gave in his name for purchase, which was forwarded to the agents. His mother accordingly called at their office, where she was well known to be a woman of property, and promised to pay the purchase-money. He was gazetted, the notification came out to the regiment, and we were embarked for Egypt. We all congratulated Johnny on his promotion: he gave us a pleasant entertainment on the occasion, and commenced doing duty as a captain, and continued to do so until we arrived in Malta, where, to our great surprise, an order was received from the War Office, that Lieutenant G[alpine]'s, promotion had not taken place in consequence of the low cunning of his mother, who, upon hearing he was gazetted, supposed she need not pay the purchase money, and that he could not be deprived of his captainship, as she called it, exulting in having taken in the agents; but, of course, the commander-in-chief cancelled the commission, and Johnny found himself once more an humble lieutenant. The disappointment naturally fretted and annoyed the poor fellow, and we all felt for him. He vowed vengeance against his mother, who had married his father's steward, and robbed him, and sent him from being a captain, back to the ranks; as he used to say a lieutenancy was nothing better. He cried like a child; but nothing could improve this simple fellow, for he still retained his honest country manners and ideas. He honourably served the campaign, returned to Gibraltar, and died of the plague, greatly regretted by his brother officers.[20]

I now went on half pay, at my own request, as my constitution was a good deal shaken by the fatigue I had undergone for more than two years; and I was anxious to obtain some civil employment, that might, in addition to my half pay, enabled me to retire, with comfort, into the bosom of my family, until I had recruited my health.[21]

I had not been many days in London when I saw, in one of the morning papers, an advertisement offering appointments under government, from £100 to £1,500

19 Captain William Brydges Neynoe, 34th Foot, later became a lieutenant colonel in the 27th Foot.

20 John Galpine was appointed captain by purchase on 9 August 1800, but this appointment was annulled in the gazette of 28 October of that year, presumably for the reasons stated by Harley. He was appointed captain by purchase again on 26 March 1803.

21 Harley went on half pay on 24 June 1802.

per annum; application to be made at No.-, Northumberland Street, Strand. As this appeared a fit opportunity to carry my intentions into execution, I determined on laying out a few hundred pounds I had then saved, in procuring an adequate appointment, and accordingly repaired to the above-mentioned address. Here I was ushered, by a clerk, into a waiting room, in which I found two or three respectable-looking gentlemen, very probably on the same business as myself.

After having been detained in the anti-room more than an hour, before I could procure an audience with the principal – a thing done, no doubt, with an idea of impressing my mind with a deep sense of the respectability of the establishment, and of attaching importance to its proceedings – I was at length introduced into a room occupied by an elderly, respectable-looking man, wearing glasses, whose name I understood to be D. His table was covered with letters, documents, and cards of various descriptions, which he seemed to be very busily perusing when I entered the room. On seeing me, he asked me, with an assumed air of consequence, the object of my visit. I told him, that having read his advertisement in the papers, I had now called with the intention of purchasing an appointment. 'To what amount?' said he. I replied that my finances would permit my purchasing one of £200 a-year. He then deliberately turned over the pages of a large book, and after appearing to examine it closely, expressed his regret that he had none then vacant under £400 a-year. 'I have a capital appointment to that amount, now vacant,' said he, with the most serious countenance, 'it is of the utmost importance at Court, and must be filled up within a week. I advise you, sir, to think of it; it is deserving of your notice; such an appointment is not to be had every day. You will be constantly about the King's person, have your children provided for, if you have any, and brought up and educated in the palace of St James's; and there can be little doubt but that you will be knighted before long, as his Majesty cannot but be highly pleased with a gentleman of your manner and appearance.'

Thanking Mr D for the flattering opinion he was good enough to entertain of me, I stated, in reply, that I had no wish whatever for a title – that I was not at all ambitious – my only object was to get an appointment, for which I was willing to give the full value, to the amount of 100. At length, after much manoeuvring on his part, during which I urged him to come to a decision one way or the other, he told me, to my astonishment, that if I gave him £10, he would inform me of the vacancy in question, which he had no doubt I had sufficient interest to obtain. I looked at the man with amazement, asking him, in an angry tone, whether his informing me of the death of the Lord Chancellor, or of the Archbishop of Canterbury, could procure either of the appointments for me? I took up my hat and left the office, with my money safe in my pocket. Mr D accompanied me, very politely, to the door, saying, he should be glad to be honoured with my commands at any time, and reminding me that his office was open every day, from ten o'clock in the morning until four in the afternoon. Some days after this occurrence, this same Mr D was brought before the police magistrate, at Bow Street, charged with obtaining money from several individuals, under pretence of procuring them situations in Somerset

House, and was, I believe, committed to prison, to stand his trial at the following quarter sessions.[22]

Such were, and are, at this moment, some of the many tricks practised in London, by designing men, on the credulous or unwary. I know not how it happened, or whether anything occurred to excite my suspicion, but I was particularly cautious and observant in my interview with Mr D; and it would have been a fortunate circumstance for myself and my family, if I had been as guarded in other transactions in after life.

During this visit to London, I met my cousin, Captain McMahon, who had been aid-de-camp to Sir Thomas Trigge, in the West Indies, and was since colonel of the 53rd Regiment.[23] McMahon entered the army in the French service, although he preferred the British; but, at the time he joined, no Roman Catholic officers were admitted into the British army, and he was of that religious persuasion. While serving in France, he married a French lady, a countess in her own right, who was highly connected, and by whom he had one child. The regiment to which McMahon was attached, was the Irish Brigade, then in the service of France, and commanded by Count Walsh.[24] In the revolution, which took place at the conclusion of the seventeenth century [sic], nearly all the officers of the Irish Brigade emigrated, not wishing to join the republic, and among them McMahon, leaving the countess and his child at their chateau, near Paris.

He was, at the time I met him, preparing to return to France and join his wife, after an absence of eight years. I accompanied him to Long Acre, where he purchased a splendid carriage for the countess, and to Rundle and Bridges, where he bought plate and jewellery to the amount of £1,000.[25] I saw the poor fellow leave London for Dover, with a light heart, at the happy prospect of so soon embracing his dear wife and child.

On his arrival at the chateau, he was kindly received by Madame, who declared herself highly pleased with the presents he had brought her, which she put up very carefully, and informed him, after dinner, that she would be always happy to see him whenever he visited France, but that, situated as she was then, he could not remain, even that night, as she had been married during his absence, under the laws of Robespierre. McMahon's feelings and astonishment cannot be expressed.

22 Diligent searches of the archives of the newspapers of 1802-4 have failed to identify either an advertisement or a court case regarding this scam and therefore Mr D has unfortunately not been identified to date.

23 Captain Terence McMahon, later lieutenant colonel of the 53rd Foot; the officer whose aide he served as was General Thomas Trigge (1742-1814).

24 Walsh's Regiment was one of three regiments in the French Irish Brigade serving in the American War of Independence.

25 Long Acre in London runs from St Martin's Lane to Drury Lane and was famous for its carriage builders; Rundell and Bridge silver manufacturers were based at 32 Ludgate Hill and by 1803 had become suppliers to the King and the Prince of Wales.

He returned home in disgust with the whole sex; and having taken some legal advice how to proceed against her for the restitution of conjugal rights, he was on his way to Paris, when he was made a prisoner of war, at Calais, and sent on, with other English subjects to Verdun.[26]

It happened to have been McMahon's good fortune, some time before, while stationed in St Lucia, to meet Madame Le Clerc, the widow of General Le Clerc, and sister of Bonaparte, who was then first Consul.[27] She had put into that island from distress of weather, where she was detained some days, during which period McMahon paid her every mark of attention, and procured her a passage home. His conduct was not unrequited; for, on his writing to her from Verdun, she not only obtained his parole and liberty to reside at Toulouse, in the south of France, but also had his daughter restored to him. He continued at Toulouse till 1814, when the Duke of Wellington took that city, and released him.

I now left London for Ireland; and, as the intercourse between the two countries was not so frequent as it is now, I posted it with a friend through Chester, which was then the usual route, and, stopping a couple of days at Parkgate,[28] sailed for Dublin, and arrived at the Pigeon House a night or two after.[29] My fellow passengers were, a Captain McCullagh of the navy,[30] another gentleman, and a Miss Henry.

McCullagh and I, being strangers in Dublin, we were easily persuaded to get into a boat, and go up to the city by water, on reaching which our boatman directed us to, what he called, a good inn or hotel, on the quay, where we took up our quarters for the night. We were busily employed after supper in opening our parcels, and arranging the articles in our trunks, when the servant maid, on seeing them, exclaimed in an alarmed manner, 'Oh dear! gentlemen, you do not know where you are. My master is a custom-house officer, and if he knows what you have, he will seize all; therefore, for God's sake, pack them up again, and go to your beds, for you ought to be tired.'

We took the poor girl's advice; called for our bill, and discharged it; and leaving the house at an early hour in the morning, removed to an hotel in Dawson Street, kept by a person named Falkener;[31] but not without proving to the servant girl how grateful we felt to her for her good-natured hint.

26 When war was resumed Napoleon ordered the arrest of any British males of an age to be able to serve in the British forces, then in France or French occupied countries, to be detained indefinitely. Many were civilians on the Grand Tour but were kept at inland fortresses such as Verdun for many years, many not being released until the end of the war in 1814.

27 Pauline Bonaparte had married General Charles Victoire Emmanuel but he died at Saint Domingue of Yellow fever in 1802.

28 Parkgate on the River Dee.

29 Pigeon House is an area of Dublin at Clontarf.

30 This must be Lieutenant Thomas McCulloch RN.

31 Mr Francis Falkner owned an Irish Whiskey shop at No. 36 Dawson Street in Dublin. Presumably he also owned a hotel in the street.

Leaving Dublin, after a stay of a few days, I proceeded to Limerick, where my family resided, and was immediately visited by a number of friends, who thought I had returned home as rich as a nabob (it having been reported that I possessed £20,000 in specie), and who favoured me with several applications for loans and accommodations, which I politely declined. One gentleman, however, whom I had known many years, Mr Thomas Wilkinson, sheriff of the city, having persuaded me to attend a sale of a place called Castle Park, belonging to Major Ormsby,[32] I became, by his advice, the purchaser, and placed a steward in it, who attended more to his own interest than to mine; he and his family robbing me every night, and then coming the following day to report such and such a robbery on the lands, houses, or gardens. I became so disgusted, that I relinquished the property altogether, and, bidding adieu to farming, at the loss of my purchase money, I returned once more to London, and commenced a negotiation with the late Sir Thomas Roberts, Bart., of Cork, banker,[33] for the purchase of some land in the county of Limerick, that had been ninety years in my wife's family. Concluding that I had fully completed the agreement, I gave directions to my bankers, Messrs. Whitehead and Howard, to sell out £1,600 for me of my 3 per cent consols, in order to pay Sir Thomas for the intended purchase.

At this period, the negotiations for the peace of Amiens were going forward, and, on the day my stock was sold out, there was a hoax imposed on the Lord Mayor of London, by a counterfeit letter, purporting to come from ostensible authority, that the terms of the peace had been concluded by Lord Whitworth,[34] in consequence of which the consols rose up to 72; but the fraud having been discovered in the course of the evening, they fell again to 63. On my going to my bankers, I found that my consols had sold at 72; and, as after some consideration I declined the purchase of the land, I directed my money to be again vested in the funds, and gained, by this trick which had been played on the Lord Mayor, £144. Whoever invented this hoax, it served me materially.

John Harley soon found a new position, becoming Quartermaster to the 60th Foot on 12 February 1803, but it seems that this had hardly happened when he exchanged again to become Quartermaster of the 27th Foot on 2 April and then exchanged into the 1st Battalion 47th (Lancashire) Regiment on 2 June 1803 as Quartermaster. The battalion moved to Colchester in the

32 When the Ormsby family bought the property in 1789 they renamed the house Blackland Castle. The house was unfortunately gutted in a fire in 2001 and remains derelict today.

33 Sir Thomas Howland Roberts, Bart. of Brightfieldstown. He ran the private bank of Roberts & Co.

34 Harley's memory again fails him slightly. Charles Whitworth, 1st Earl Whitworth, was a senior diplomat. He was sent as Ambassador to Paris in 1802 after the Peace Treaty with France had been signed at Amiens on 27 March. He arrived in Paris in December and was the recipient of some serious tirades by Napoleon before he returned home and war was resumed on 18 May 1803.

September where a second battalion was formed. The two battalions then moved together via Woodbridge and Liverpool to arrive in Dublin at the end of the year. They moved on from Dublin in February 1804, the first battalion to Kilkenny and the second to Clonmel.

Finding a difficulty in procuring a situation suited to my wishes, I regretted leaving the 54th, and, after a short time, effected an exchange into the 47th, then stationed at Battle in Sussex.[35] In September 1803, we left Battle for Colchester, where we quartered for some time, and were joined by the present Lieutenant-General Sir Edward Blakeney, who was then promoted to a majority in our regiment; he only continued with us until we arrived in Clonmel, in Ireland, the following summer, when he obtained further promotion into the 7th Foot. We regretted him very much, for his kind disposition and gentlemanly demeanour, caused him to be beloved by both officers and men. He subsequently distinguished himself highly in the Peninsular war, and now commands in Dublin, where he is esteemed by all classes, civil as well as military.[36]

In October 1803, we were also joined at Colchester by Captain Farmer, the oldest captain in rank, and yet the youngest in years – being only seventeen – in the British army; having obtained his commission while he was actually in his cradle;[37] previously, of course, to the regulation introduced by his Royal Highness, the late deeply lamented Duke of York; the soldier's father and friend.[38]

As Farmer had never joined any corps before, he knew nothing of the regulations observed in the army; but considered that, from his seniority, he had first choice of quarters in any garrison; and, although really a good-natured and well-disposed young man, he was so elated with the idea of being the oldest captain, that he was, for the first few days after he joined us, regarded with some degree of jealousy by the veteran captains and lieutenants who had served many years in foreign countries, and had seen severe service. It was his duty to wait on the colonel as soon as he arrived, yet he never made his appearance to any of us until dinner, when, entering the mess room, he announced himself to Colonel King as Captain Farmer, the oldest captain in the army, who had come to join his

35 Harley skips over a few personal events, as it is clear that his return to the army was not quite as simple as he describes here.

36 Major Edward Blakeney returned from half pay on 11 July 1803; He exchanged into the 7th Foot on 7 April 1804, but remained a major. In his later career Blakeney became Commander in Chief, Ireland in 1836 and later became a Field Marshal in 1862.

37 Captain Maurice Farmer had seniority as a captain as of 8 February 1795, in the 107th Foot. If he was 17 in 1803, he was 9 when given his captaincy. Farmer was second senior captain in the battalion when he joined the 47th.

38 The Duke of York did impose some restrictions on officer promotions to stop the worst abuses in 1809, but he did not impose a minimum age. He did however make the rule that an officer had to serve three years as a subaltern before they could become a captain.

regiment.[39] Colonel King very good-humouredly said, 'You are welcome, Captain Farmer, to the 47th; sit down and eat your dinner.'

This was a remarkable day with us. The officers of the 18th Dragoons dined with us, and as Betty Landy, our mess-woman, left us that morning, on her return to Bermuda, her native country, with a large fortune she had acquired in our regiment, we were obliged, in such an awkward predicament, to accept the services of one of our sergeants, who was so ignorant of cookery and of furnishing a dinner, that he placed on the table three large pieces of roast beef, and had everything else in admirable confusion. We were, therefore, in rather an ill humour, particularly as we had so many guests, who had a few days before entertained us in the handsomest style, and we were, consequently, but little disposed to yield to the pretensions of our young captain.

He had not been long at dinner, when, addressing me, he asked where he was to sleep, reminding me that he was a captain of 1790.[40] I bluntly referred him to the quarter-master; but some of the old officers, who wished for a little fun to make up for their bad dinner, joined him in urging his claim, and telling him that he was right, and that he should not allow himself to be imposed upon. One of them, more waggish than the others, told him there were no quarters within the barracks fit for him, but that at the entrance into the town, there was a large house where two sentinels were placed, which contained apartments for officers of his standing in the army.

Poor Farmer sallied out, accordingly, at half past eleven o'clock, in quest of the house to which he had been directed, accompanied by a couple of men with his luggage. On entering the hall, his luggage was laid down, and he was shown into the parlour by the housekeeper. As he was preparing to take his boots off, at the same time making inquiries about his bed, respecting which he seemed to be very particular, telling the woman of his rank, and his being the oldest captain of the army, she, supposing him to be the aide-de-camp who had preceded the general, asked him what day he expected Sir James Craig down from London.[41] As he appeared to know nothing about him, but still continued to urge his claim and rank, the housekeeper saw there was some mistake, and exclaimed, 'Bless my soul, sir, do you know where you are? You must have made a mistake. This is the house of Sir James Craig, the general commanding the district; you cannot stop here, sir, without his orders; and I beg that you will leave the house.' Upon which, poor Farmer was ushered into the street.

39 Lieutenant Colonel Fielder King exchanged into the 47th from the Cape Regiment on 9 July 1803 but exchanged out again to the 7th Foot on 21 January 1804.

40 He was a captain of 1795 according to the Army List; he sold his commission in April 1805.

41 Lieutenant General Sir James Henry Craig (1748-1812) commanded the Eastern District until he went out to the Mediterranean in 1805.

It unfortunately happened that it was both assizes and race week at Colchester, and all the inns were crowded, and it was too late in the night to procure private lodgings, so that Farmer had to walk about the town during the entire night. About seven o'clock in the morning, as I walked into the town, it being my usual custom to rise early, I met the unfortunate fellow in a deplorable condition, wet to his skin, as it had rained the greater part of the night; he was in a very exhausted state, from fatigue, and want of sleep. I immediately took him to my quarters, and furnished him with a dry change, and, as soon as we had breakfasted, sent for the quartermaster, and had suitable apartments prepared for him. Whatever were his faults, ingratitude was not one; we were ever afterwards intimate friends, and he constantly avowed the obligations he was under to me for having, as he said, preserved his life.

This young man was, unfortunately, too susceptible of female charms, being always in love with some beauty or another. His first adventure, in this way, was falling in love with the daughter of a Mr Bantry, of Colchester, whom he accidently saw at a window, and for whom he proposed, immediately, without having had any previous acquaintance with her, or one of her family, referring her father to me, as to the amount of his property. When Mr Bantry, a highly respectable gentleman, applied to me on the subject, I candidly told him that I knew nothing of Captain Farmer's fortune, or family; that he had been but a short time in our regiment; and, at the same time, remarked, that, though I considered him a well-disposed young man, his daughter might, in my opinion, make a more eligible match, as he was too young to have yet acquired sufficient steadiness for the marriage state. Mr Bantry expressed his acknowledgements to me, for my candour, and said, he perfectly agreed with the observations I had made, and would beg to decline the honour Captain Farmer wished to confer upon his family.

Shortly after this occurrence, we were *en route* for Ireland, where he fell in love with every pretty face he saw in any town or village through which we passed, and, had he sufficient time, would, no doubt, have proposed for them in turn, until he had been accepted by some one of them. At length, the regiment was ordered to take up its quarters in Clonmel and Cahir.

When we had completed our men at Colchester, out of the army of reserve, we proceeded to Ireland;[42] and, on arriving in Dublin, received orders to march to Kilkenny. In the meantime, while the regiment pursued this route, I obtained leave of absence, before I left England, to go to London for a few days, to see some friends, whom I had not met for a considerable length of time. One of them was the late O'B[rien].[43] Being anxious to meet him, I hastened to the coffee-house which

42 To boost numbers, the Army of Reserve was announced in 1803 which was designed to raise 50,000 men for 'Home Service' only. The project only achieved the recruitment of 35,000 before it was abandoned.

43 I believe he refers to Mr Murrough O'Brien (1726-1810) who became 1st Marquess of Thomond; he was a renowned drinker and gambler. He died from a fall from his horse in Grosvenor Square in 1808.

he generally frequented; and, while waiting here, met the late George Hanger, since Lord Coleraine, whose humour created general amusement.[44]

O'B[rien] at length joined me, and asked me when I intended leaving town; and, on my telling him, the following morning, I could easily observe, that it was with great reluctance he invited me to dine with him that day, at six o'clock. I met at his house, at dinner, the celebrated W[orcester],[45] a Mr O[rchard],[46] and a young gentleman, whose name has escaped my memory, of about twenty-two years of age, a native of the West Indies, and then transacting business for his father, to a large amount. He resided at the Percy Coffee House, where, I suppose O'B[rien] first acquainted with him.[47] He was attended by a black servant. On this day, W[orcester], who was then resided in [Gloucester], called on him, and took him to O'B[rien]'s, in his splendid carriage, where every preparation had been made to receive him, in the style becoming a nobleman. The dinner was superb, the wines were of the best quality, and every delicacy of the season, in profusion.

We were not very long at our wine, when it was proposed that we should retire to the drawing-room, where we had tea and coffee; O'B[rien] presiding at one table, and I at the other; a celebrated lady, named M, who enjoyed an annuity of £1,200 a-year, and resided with O'B[rien], not making her appearance.[48] After some time, cards were introduced; piquet was the game fixed on; and, being a fifth person, I was only a looker on.

The play got very high: the stranger at first won, amusing his new acquaintances, at intervals, by the many strange adventures which he said had occurred to him. His manners and conversation were highly agreeable. He dwelt very much on his father's wealth; said, that several of his ships were in the docks, laden with coffee, sugar, and cotton, and that he was determined to make the old boy's money fly before he left London, adding, 'though it is a fixed maxim with me not to win or lose more than from £1,500 to £2,000 at a sitting.' This intelligence, of course, delighted his new friends, who, seeing a prospect of reaping a golden harvest, redoubled their attention to him, and treated him as a being of superior rank; while he, not to be outdone in civility, ordered his servant, who was in attendance on him, to go to his hotel, and bring him over a few jars of preserved ginger, which

44 George Hanger, 4th Baron Coleraine (1751-1824). Having risen to the rank of lieutenant colonel of the 82nd Foot, he sold his commission to become an ensign in 70th Foot because of financial problems (gambling?). He was imprisoned in King's Bench Prison, but getting out he began life as a coal merchant. In 1806, he was appointed captain-commissary of the Royal Artillery and retired on full pay in 1808.

45 Henry Charles Somerset was known as the Marquess of Worcester until he inherited the title of 6th Duke of Beaufort in 1803. He was well known in the gambling joints of London when he was not serving as an MP.

46 The only well-known gambler recorded in White's gambling book who was not gentry – hence simply Mr – was Mr Richard Orchard.

47 Percy Coffee House was situated in Percy Street, but no longer exists.

48 I have been unable to identify this lady.

he immediately, on the servant's return, presented to O'B[rien], telling him at the same time that he had some very fine pine-apple rum, and would make him a present of a puncheon of it, to divide among his friends in the room, adding, 'and you must not forget your military friend here (meaning me), although he has not joined in our amusement.'

On their commencing play, after supper, he inquired, with seeming nonchalance, how the play stood; and when informed that he had won £100, he requested to be paid that sum, as it was his usual habit, at play, at once to be paid, on losing or winning money to that amount. This he again repeated, in the most gentlemanly manner, and hoped his friends would not wish him to deviate from a rule that he universally observed, although he had often lost £2,000 in a night. In fact, he acted his part so well, and assumed such an appearance of simplicity and truth, that he completely threw the knowing ones off their guard.

O'B[rien], not having so much money about him, sent to Mrs M for it, who instantly enclosed him two £50 notes, which I saw him hand to the young West Indian, who carelessly rolled them up and put them in his pocket. They then commenced in earnest, and played until two o'clock, when he again inquired how the play stood, and was informed that he had lost £1,800. 'Never mind,' said he, 'the old fellow's sugars shall pay for this in the morning; the worse luck now, the better another time.' Then rising from the table, he said, he would play no more that night; and that if his friends would do him the honour of calling on him the next day at the Percy Coffee House, at one o'clock, he would give them a check on the old gentleman's banker for the amount; but hoped they would afford him an opportunity of winning it back. The sound of the check seemed delightful to the ears of the gamblers; and the party broke up in excellent humour with each other; W[orcester] ordering his carriage, and setting the young stranger down at his hotel. The party met the next day at Bedford Square. I was present; and, on deliberating as to the hour at which they should call on the West Indian, they agreed that it would not look well to be there to the minute; and, therefore, deferred their visit until an hour later, much against Mrs M's inclination; who, for the first time I had ever seen her, now made her appearance, and seemed very uneasy about her £50 notes, which she was to be repaid out of the £1,800 won from the stranger. When the hour arrived, they sallied forth to the Percy; and I, having some suspicion of the disappointment that awaited them, accompanied them through curiosity. The waiter, on being asked, was such a gentleman at home, referred us to the bar-maid, whose words, as well as the doleful countenances of the parties, I never can forget. 'You mean,' said she, 'the young West Indian gentleman, who stopped here for some days. Bless your heart, sir,' addressing herself, to O'B[rien], whose face began to assume an ashy, 'demanded his bill, changed a £50 note to pay it, treated us all well, and, having ordered a coach, took off all his luggage, and his servant; and has, before this, embarked for the West Indies.

To picture the gloom that overspread the countenances of the three sharpers, for such, in reality, they were, however high their rank, would be utterly impossible,

A contemporary print of gamblers. (Author's collection).

particularly that of O'B[rien], who was doomed to encounter the severe reproaches of his friend Mrs M, who did not seem to be a lady likely to bear such a loss, as £100, with good humour or indifference; and which, as I subsequently heard, poor O'B[rien] learned, to his cost.

Thus, were these three knowing ones outwitted by a young West Indian, a mere simpleton, compared to them; but who, nevertheless, contrived to enjoy a good dinner, and pocket £100. O'B[rien], never could bear to hear this circumstance mentioned afterwards; and, whenever I touched on the subject, as I sometimes did to annoy him, or alluded to the puncheon of pineapple rum, he became outrageous.

6

Ireland Again

As my leave of absence was on the point of expiring, I now prepared to leave London; but, previously to my doing so, I called on my friend Captain C[umming],[1] at the New Exchange Coffee House, in the Strand; a place which I had been in the habit of frequenting after my return from Egypt, and where I had always experienced the kindest attention, from both the landlord and landlady, whose singular history I am about to relate to my readers.[2] C[umming], who was a captain, on half-pay, of the British service, lodged several years ago in the Exchange Coffee House, which was then kept by an old couple, whose age prevented their attending properly to their business, obliging them to confide in the management of a bar-maid, upon whom they placed much dependence, and to whom they paid a liberal salary.

As C[umming]'s circumstances were not very affluent, as is generally the case with *half-pays*; and he was, besides, of an extravagant turn of mind. Necessity often compelled him to borrow money, at different times, from the bar-maid, who was a prudent woman, and had laid by the savings of a few years. He lived in the house for several months together; during which time he paid great attention to her, making love to her every opportunity, and always promising marriage, of which, by-the-bye, he had not the slightest notion.

As he was continually making one excuse, or another, for delaying the nuptials, and as he was now upwards of £200 in her debt, for cash lent to him. She determined on having either the man or the money; and, going into his room one morning, as he lay in bed, demanded that he should either pay her what she had lent him, or immediately fulfil his oft-repeated promise of marriage. C[umming], as usual, made some excuse; but it would not do, she was resolved, she said, to be no longer trifled with, as she had been, for months back, but to have justice immediately done. She then produced a marriage licence, which she had previously

1 From the records, this would appear to describe Lieutenant Francis Cumming (Harley calls almost everyone captain) who was half pay in the Irish Brigade from 1800. He exchanged into the 54th in August 1801, went back on half pay in 1802, and remained on half pay beyond 1805.

2 The New Exchange Coffee House stood on the present site of No. 69 The Strand.

procured, and informed C[umming], that the clergyman was then waiting at the church to marry them; and that, unless he complied, and honourably redeemed the pledges he had so often made, she would have him arrested and sent to prison, from which it was no easy matter to get out, by two bailiffs, whom she had on the stairs, outside the room, waiting to see if their services would be required. At this moment, C[umming] heard the men on the stairs cough; and knowing, from their being in the house, that her resolution was taken, he began to think seriously of his situation; and, after a few minute's consideration, reluctantly yielded to her demand, requesting, at the same time, that the ceremony might be deferred until evening. To this, however, she would not agree; nor would she quit the room, until accompanied by him. It was, certainly a curious scene to behold the captain, with the fair and fat bar-maid leaning upon his arm, marching down the Strand, at slow time, towards St Martin's Church, now and then casting a mournful look behind him, and as often encountering the keen and watchful glances of John Doe and Richard Roe,[3] who failed not to bring up the rear, and that too in close order. As soon as the ceremony had concluded, the same gentlemen, politely taking off their hats, made each of them a low bow, and wishing the newly married couple every happiness, immediately retired. C[umming] and his bride returned to the coffee-house, where they were received with great kindness, by the master and mistress, who, notwithstanding the short notice, had a comfortable wedding breakfast prepared for them.

They had a high esteem for Mrs C[umming], who had lived with them many years, and served them faithfully; and being an old couple, and having no family, they, after a little time, disposed of their house, furniture, stock on hand, &c, to Mrs C[umming], for a very trifling – a mere nominal consideration – and retired into the country, having acquired sufficient means to maintain them in comfort the rest of their days. Mrs C[umming] made a most excellent wife. I spent many evenings with them, when in London, on a former occasion, and I never met with a happier couple.

I now left London to join my regiment in Ireland, and on my arrival in Dublin had the honour of an invitation to dinner from Dr Fitzgerald, then Vice Provost of Trinity College.[4] At his table, I met the venerable Bishop of Elphin, also the present Bishop of Ferns, and Dr Browne, both of whom were fellows of the college; and, among some others, the late celebrated Dr Duigenan.[5] I happened to sit next to him at dinner, and, as he knew me to be an officer just arrived from England, and

3 This is a generic term and indicates here the two men sent to ensure the nuptials whose names Harley did not know.

4 It is likely that Harley is ahead of himself here, as the Reverend Gerald Fitzgerald (1740-1819) was not Vice Provost of Trinity College until 1806 to 1819.

5 John Law was the Bishop of Elfin from 1795 to 1810, when he died in office; the Bishop of Ferns at the time that Harley wrote his memoirs in 1838 was James Keatinge; Arthur Browne was Senior Fellow at Trinity College at Dublin from 1795 until his death in June 1805; Dr Patrick Duigenan (1735-1816) was MP for Armagh and Professor of Civil Law at Trinity College.

therefore supposed me to be a stranger to the country, he took infinite pains in describing to me the evils of Ireland, and the unfortunate state of the country; not at all aware that he was speaking to a person who was much better acquainted than he could possibly have been, having been reared amongst them, with the ideas and feelings of the people whom he abused. The doctor particularly exclaimed against the priest and papists, assuring me that they were the cause of all the poverty and troubles of the country – an observation which the Bishop of Elphin overhearing, he said in a good humoured way, 'do not believe all the doctor tells you, sir, as,' said his lordship, 'the priests are more to be pitied than blamed – having no fixed income, they are too much under the control of their flocks, and I only wish that their situations were more comfortable, and we should soon find them less to yield to the prejudices of the people.' The doctor, however, still maintained that the fault was theirs, and that the country was over-run by papists, in consequence of the priests marrying the peasantry too young, in order to get the marriage fees. Now, it is a well-known fact, that notwithstanding the doctor used this language, his wife was at the time, a Roman Catholic;[6] and he himself had protected, and for aught he knew, screened from justice, a Roman Catholic priest, who, being accused of rebellion, and other treasonable matters, took refuge in his house, in 1798. But the fact was, it was by violent harangues against the papists, that Dr Duigenan first brought himself into notice in the House of Commons and obtained the high situation of Vicar General of Ireland; and he had now policy enough, to carry on the farce which he had so successfully enacted.[7]

I met him at a subsequent period, in 1815, at the Duke of York's levee, at the Horse Guards, and on inquiring how matters went on in Ireland; his reply was, 'Indeed, my dear sir, the Irish are just going on in the same way these last five hundred years, they have never been without their white boys and right boys; nor will they ever be quiet until popery is finally extinguished – and I only wish that I might live to see that day.' On my asking, rather too inquisitively I confess, what business he could have at the Horse Guards, he informed me, that he had come to apply for a commission for a young friend of his in Ireland, and expressed a wish for the usual form, with which I furnished him; and was glad to hear that he succeeded. Although an agreeable companion in private society, in his public situation, his manners were so rude and unpleasant, that there was no man in England or Ireland more disliked or less regretted. The enlightened Protestants, knowing his hypocrisy, despised him; and the Roman Catholics, believing his apostasy, detested him.

From Dublin we proceeded to Kilkenny, Captain Polhill, an excellent good-natured fellow, obtaining leave to travel with me in my gig.[8] There was an impres-

6 He married a Miss Cusac, a Roman Catholic.

7 He became a member of the Irish Privy Council.

8 Captain Fraser Polhill, 47th Foot.

sion upon his mind, that the people of Ireland were particularly savage, and that all he met with were rebels, having read a prejudiced narrative of the insurrection in 1798. He was, consequently, in continued dread the whole journey; and our meeting but two or three people together, was quite sufficient to excite his alarm. We slept the first night at Naas. The next day, as we were about midway between Balitore and Carlow, we perceived a large crowd coming towards the road; returning, as it afterwards appeared across the fields, from some burial ground. On seeing them, Polhill became much alarmed, and asked me were they not rebels? I told him I believed they were, and that I observed there were female rebels amongst them. 'Oh! Heavens, Harley, let us turn back, we shall both be murdered,' cried Polhill, in evident agony of mind. 'No, said I, it is too late to retreat now, they could easily overtake us, by taking short cuts across the fields; you may see with what ease they are now leaping over the highest fence – resistance is also in vain, therefore, our only plan is to meet them peacefully, and make the best terms with them we can.'

The crowd, having by this time reached the road, divided, one part preceding us on the way to Carlow, the other, which was a larger body, moving to us in dense masses. As the road was very miry, rain having fallen in great abundance a day or two previously, I drove quietly through them; addressing several of the most respectable looking in the Irish language, which seemed to surprise them very much, and asking whom they had buried. Delighted at hearing me speak in their own language, they all stopped, and, crowding round me, informed me that it was a very respectable farmer, to whom the people had been greatly attached.

I told them, I regretted to hear that the minds of the people were yet unsettled; and exhorted them to be quiet, peaceable, and amenable to the laws, and the day would not be far distant, when their condition must be bettered, as I was sure the English Government were determined to do everything in their power to promote peace and prosperity amongst them; but they replied, they cared little for anything they had to complain of, but that abominable tax upon the industry of the poor, called tithes. After a few words more, in which perfect good humour prevailed, I wished them a good morning. And making way for us to pass through, the women curtsied, and the men exclaimed, flourishing their hats in the air, 'Long life to your honour, it's the likes of you the country wants---God send you safe to your journey's end!'

During the conversation, which was carried on in Irish, my fellow traveller sat back in the gig – a silent spectator, now and then casting suspicious glances around him, and not a little uneasy in his mind. When we had got on some distance from them, 'Oh! My dear friend,' said he, 'how shall I repay you for your interference, how can I be ever sufficiently grateful to you, for I certainly owe my life to you – what did the fellows say to you? How did they know you? Or how did you contrive to obtain such wonderful influence over them? For, before they recognized you, they were determined on having our lives.' All this he said in a breath – his agitation not having yet subsided. I told him that they all knew me well, that I had been a rebel general myself, and had commanded at Vinegar Hill, and that if he had not been under my protection, they would have taken him off to the mountains, where they generally kept their arms concealed, or perhaps have killed him on the spot with their *skeins* or long knives, which they usually carried about them; but, as I had been an old friend of theirs, they considered themselves bound to obey me as before, and that they had all now gone home at my request.

He was so much pleased at the escape he thought he had had from so formidable a body of rebels, that he said he considered himself safer travelling in my company alone, than if he were escorted by a regiment of soldiers, and would, if I permitted him, always accompany me in every march while he remained in the country, which should be as short a time as possible. When we arrived in Carlow, he told the colonel, now General Cumming,[9] that we had been surrounded by a large body of rebels in arms; but, owing to my influence over them, his life was preserved. He also mentioned the circumstance in a letter to his father, the following day, who then resided near Seven Oaks, in Kent, informing him of the escape he had had, and attributing it to my interference. And, if I mistake not, the affair in its serious light, was published in a Kentish paper, and from thence copied into many of the metropolitan and provincial newspapers.

We were now quartered in Kilkenny, and, as there was good society in the city and neighbourhood, we passed our time very pleasantly, having a constant round of invitations to every gentleman's house within ten miles of us. There were some of our lads, however, who, having little or nothing to do but to pay and return visits, felt their time hang heavy on their hands, and, by way of removing the *ennui* with which they were affected, amused themselves occasionally at the expense of their neighbours, regardless of the inconvenience or trouble they occasioned.

There were a lady and gentleman of high respectability in the vicinity, who were so unfortunate as never to have had a family, and were consequently, as is generally the case, very unhappy, though extremely attached to each other. As those lad's brains were fertile, and ever employed on ingenious contrivances, they procured on a dark winter's night, a man and horse with a pillion, which they sent to the principal female in the town, who attended ladies in their *accouchement*, with a note not to lose a moment in hastening to the house of Mr S[hea],[10] whose lady was in hourly expectation of presenting him with a son and heir. It was about twelve o'clock, of a dark winter' night, when Mrs Meehan was roused from her bed to obey this pressing call; and, as the messenger had received particular instructions to be urgent, the old lady muffled herself up, and, seating herself on the pillion behind the horseman, arrived about one o'clock at Mr S[hea]'s house, and calling up the family, who were all quietly at rest, not in expectation, of course, of such a visitor, was admitted, and ushered by the servant into the parlour, when

9 Lieutenant Colonel James Cumming, 47th Foot.

10 It is impossible to be certain of this unfortunate couple, played such a cruel trick, but by far the most likely was a member of the Shea family who was one of the greatest families of Kilkenny.

she requested to see Mr S[hea] without a moment's delay. The horseman, in the meantime, decamped as quickly as possible, having received directions from his employers, not to delay an instant when he had set down the old lady. When the old gentleman entered the parlour, he was naturally greatly surprised at meeting Mrs Meehan, with whose person and occupation he was well acquainted, and asked was she mad, or what on earth had brought her out to his house at such an hour of the night – Mrs Meehan all the time putting questions to him, asking, how long was his lady ill, how she felt herself now – was there an accoucheur in attendance?[11] He again, more surprised than before, demanded, in a peremptory tone, what had brought her to his house. And, on the poor woman producing the forged note, he was outrageous, abused her grossly, and all who were concerned in the trick; and it was only after much entreaty that he permitted the unfortunate dupe to sleep in his house that night. Mrs Meehan returned next day to Kilkenny, disappointed, and vowing vengeance on the authors of the hoax, if she could discover them.

I will give my readers another instance of the unceasing pranks of these wicked young fellows. A captain of the 17th Dragoons, while quartered in Kilkenny, got an order from the castle of Dublin to repair to the Curragh of Kildare, with his troop, in order to be inspected at a grand review that was to be held by the Lord Lieutenant in person. This order he communicated to some of those wags, who instantly laid a wager with him of a supper and wine, for a certain number, that the Lord Lieutenant would not review them: a wager which the captain took up without hesitation, as the orders from the castle were so distinct and peremptory. The young fellows, after holding a consultation on the subject, had an anonymous letter written to the Lord Lieutenant, stating, that if he came to the Curragh he would certainly be fired at by some of the soldiers, who were determined to shoot him if possible, and advising him not to venture his person on that day. A privy council was immediately held on the receipt of this letter, and it was determined, after they had in vain endeavoured to sift the matter, to send down Lord Cathcart to review the troops,[12] and not the Lord Lieutenant; the wags, consequently, won the supper, which the captain very cheerfully gave on his return to Kilkenny, being totally ignorant of the cheat that had been practised upon him. And, although Captain Featherstone[13] and I were of the party who partook of the supper, we were not informed of the stratagem that had been made use of, for several months after the circumstance occurred.

At this period, I had a servant living with me about twelve years old, an honest, faithful creature, the son of a poor widow in Kent, whom I had taken in my service as an act of charity – and never was a master blessed with a better servant. Young

11 Accoucheur: Midwife.

12 General William Schaw Cathcart, 1st Earl Cathcart (1755-1843), who was Commander in Chief in Ireland from 1803-5.

13 Then Lieutenant Francis Featherstone of the 47th Foot.

as he was, he was as careful of me as a parent or guardian, watching me closely, and following me whenever any of the officers called to ask me out, lest I might get tipsy, and some accident might occur. He has often borne, with unflinching steadiness and patience, volleys of abuse, and not unfrequently blows, from the officers, on such occasions, while endeavouring to prevail me to return home.

One evening, at Mr Laughlan's, the banker, where we were constantly in the habit of dining, my faithful boy came into the room when we were at supper, having heard that we were about to commence drinking freely, and said to me, in a whisper, 'Master, it is time for us to go home.' 'Be off, you young scoundrel!' cried Featherstone, who overheard him 'your master shall not go.' 'But I will not go, sir,' said the boy, determinedly, but respectfully, 'until master comes with me.' And then, turning to me, said, 'Come home, master, like a good gentleman, for you be making a damned fool of yourself when you be drunk.' The poor lad was forced out of the room, but could not be prevailed upon to leave the house without me; and no one wished to use violence towards him.

As he was so young, I began, after some time, to feel uneasy lest he might be corrupted in the regiment, and taught evil practices by the soldiers; I therefore judged it better, on the lad's own account, to send him back to his mother while his mind was still pure, and parted from him with little less regret than from a favourite child.

From Kilkenny, I went on a tour to receive volunteers from militia regiments, and amongst many other places, visited Wexford, Enniscorthy, Carlow, Limerick, but, unfortunately, with no success, in consequence of the act of parliament allowing militia-men to volunteer, and permitting colonels of militia to set aside half their men, and the volunteers for the time to be only taken out of the other half. Such a regulation had this affect, that the militia colonels kept the best of their men back, and only allowed the old and married men to volunteer; so that those who would come to us, we would not take.[14] Owing to this circumstance, I returned without a single man, which annoyed me very much, as Colonel Backhouse had purposely selected me for the duty,[15] thinking, that as I was an Irishman, I should be more successful than any of the English officers.

My disappointment in obtaining volunteers was very near bringing me into a serious scrape. As I was a good deal excited at the time, I wrote off, without considering for a moment, to no less a personage than the then prime minister – the ablest man that ever yet guided the reins of government, the Right Hon. W. Pitt,[16] stating to him the absurdity of the act allowing half the men to be retained

14 The militia, which was conscripted by ballot, was an ideal recruiting ground to obtain trained recruits for the Army and there were regular drives to persuade militia men to volunteer into the line and recieve the bounty.

15 Lieutenant Colonel Thomas Joseph Backhouse of the 47th Foot.

16 William Pitt, the younger, (1759-1806) had been Prime Minister 1783-1801 and was again from 1804-6.

by the colonels of militia, by which means no fit men could be procured for the line, and suggesting the propriety of immediately altering the act, and allowing young militia officers commissions in the line for bringing such a number of men with them.

I heard no more on the subject until Colonel Backhouse sent for me one morning, and said, with a smile, 'Why, Harley, you have been corresponding with the Premier; what could possess you to write to Mr Pitt?' handing me a correspondence containing my letter to Mr Pitt – his to the Duke of York – the Duke's to Lord Cathcart, and Lord Cathcart's to Colonel Backhouse. I was, I confess, surprised, and knew not what to say for a moment. The Duke, in his letter to Lord Cathcart, expressed his displeasure at the militia colonels taking advantage of an uncertain phrase in an act of parliament, and keeping back the best men, because they were entitled to retain half; a circumstance which it thus appeared I was the first to communicate. The Duke also wrote to me, saying he was pleased with my zeal for the service, and informing me he had referred the matter to Lord Cathcart, then Commander-in-Chief in Ireland, whose letter to Colonel Backhouse was most severe against me, stating that, however just my communisation might be, any remark I had to offer should have been addressed to him, through my commanding officer; and calling on Colonel Backhouse to demand an immediate explanation from me for such irregular conduct, and breach of military etiquette.

I had, therefore, to write an apology to Lord Cathcart, stating that the letter of which he complained had been written on the impulse of the moment, and not out of any disrespect to him. This was enclosed by Colonel Backhouse in a letter he himself wrote to Lord Cathcart, making further apology for me, and bearing testimony to my general good character as an officer.

For several months afterwards, this occurrence was a fund of amusement for the officers, who made it a practice to tease me with applications for introductions and letters of recommendation to my friend the Premier, with whom I was in the habit of corresponding. However, I bore all their quizzing very well, particularly as I had the gratification of seeing the act altered the following session of parliament, after which we obtained as many men as we could require.

A curious circumstance occurred during our stay at Kilkenny, which afforded considerable amusement amongst our men for a length of time. One evening, as I stood in the barrack-yard with Colonel Backhouse and Major Johnson,[17] a corporal and five men, who had just returned from Carlow, were followed into the yard by a countrywoman, who, the moment she saw us, exclaimed, 'My drake! my drake! Oh Colonel, honey, I have been robbed of my drake,' without knowing who the colonel was, or whether he was there or not. The poor woman, however, happened to address the colonel, who asked her who had robbed her. 'One of these men, your Honour,' said she, 'that came in now.' He immediately ordered them to halt, and

17 Major William Clarke Johnson 47th Foot.

asked again, 'Which of these men, my good woman, has robbed you; point out the man, and I engage to have him punished.'

As she could not tell the particular man who had stolen her drake, the soldiers only laughed at her; but, as the colonel saw that she still persisted in attributing the theft to some one of them, to satisfy her, he ordered the knapsacks of the privates to be searched, but neither drake nor duck was to be found. She then called out, 'If your honour, colonel, my jewel, would make that gentleman, the corporal, open his bag, maybe my poor bird might be found.' The colonel, rather angry at her importunity, desired her request to be complied with, and lo! When the first strap was unbuckled, the drake, in good health and spirits, thrust out his head and neck, to our great amusement. The poor woman was rejoiced at the sight of her bird, and, returning thanks to the colonel jewel, as she called him, for restoring her drake; and giving her half a crown for her trouble, she trotted off merrily, after her march of seven miles in pursuit of the soldiers. The corporal, it is almost needless to remark, was reduced to the ranks, and was, while he continued in the regiment, dubbed by his comrades the thief of the drake.

From Kilkenny, we were ordered to the Curragh of Kildare, where we were encamped for some time, and became acquainted with a country gentleman, [William] Delaney Esq [in fact Henry Flower – see footnote] who resided at Castle Durrow, in the Queen's County,[18] not very far from the Curragh, to whom our officers showed some little attention, having him to dine at the mess upon three or four occasions. On our regiment returning to Kilkenny from the camp, our route lay through the town in which Mr Delaney [Flower] resided, and of which he was chief magistrate. Hearing of our march, he met us within two or three miles of the town, and invited all the officers of the corps to dine with him – at least thirty in number. I mentioned to him that we were too numerous, and begged leave to apologise for some of us; but he said he would take no excuse, and that all should dine with him. On our arriving at Castle Durrow, the general gave orders that the brigade, consisting of the 28th and 47th Regiments of the line and a militia regiment, should immediately encamp in Lord Ashbrook's park,[19] which was enclosed by a high wall – that none of the men should be allowed to leave camp, nor go into the town, and that all the officers should remain with the men.

At this time, our friend Mr Delaney's [Flower's] dinner was nearly ready – several ladies invited – the tables laid out, &c., and I was sent from the camp to communicate the order we had received, and to thank Mr Delaney [Flower] for his hospitable intentions. He in vain made application to the brigade major for liberty

18 He has mixed two people up here. Castle Durrow (now a high class hotel) was owned by the Flower family and was then owned by Henry Jeffrey Flower, 4th Viscount Ashbrook, who had succeeded his brother in 1802. This is almost certainly who he meant, because the Delaneys owned the flour mill at Durrow, David William Delaney being the miller from 1798 to 1855.

19 This confirms that he means Henry Flower, Viscount Ashbrook.

for the officers to come to his house; the general's orders were positive, and the brigade major declined interfering, but in a polite manner. 'Then, by Jove,' said Mr Delaney [Flower], 'there can be no order against the officers' eating their dinner in the park.' He, accordingly, had all the requisites removed to the camp in a short time, accompanied by himself and family, and a large party of ladies, where he gave us a most sumptuous dinner, and with as much comfort as if we had partaken of it in his own house; such was the hospitality of an Irish country gentleman.

During the time we were encamped on the Curragh, my family resided in Dublin. I was very anxious to go and visit them, and, as no officer could obtain permission to leave the camp, I took leave myself, and going in my regimentals into the village of Kildare, to meet the coach, I stepped into the first that passed, which happened to be the Limerick day-coach. Meeting in it with a Mr Bourke, a respectable brewer of that town, whom I had known well for years, I conversed with him on different subjects, asking him, amongst other inquiries, could he inform me if any person lived at Castle Park, the farm which, I before mentioned, I had purchased near Limerick. Before Mr Bourke could make a reply, a lady who sat next to me, but who had hitherto lain back in the corner, turned about and said, 'I will inform you, sir, all about it. That place belonged to a Captain Harley, a small, but stout-built little man, whom I remember well, but I believe he is dead.' Mr Bourke said, 'I think not, and,' smiling at me, 'I have reason to know that I am correct.' 'Oh! He is indeed dead, sir,' said she; 'he died of the plague in Gibraltar, and the farm is let to Dr Larry, who will never pay the rent for it, for he makes it a point never to pay one shilling he owes.' She then told Mr Bourke that she knew Captain Harley better than most people, and could relate all and many things about the same little chap, and then commenced telling truths and untruths – what did, and what did not happen; in fact, she told me about half of my own story and much relative to disagreeable family matters. Mr Bourke, who sat opposite to me, being now and then obliged to indulge in a hearty fit of laughter, ostensibly at the good stories with which she thought she was amusing us; but in reality at the awkward situation in which she unconsciously placing herself.

The Lady, who was a Miss Franklin, a native of Limerick, and a facetious spinster of fifty-two,[20] engrossed all the conversation to herself, from the moment she began to speak of Captain Harley until we came in front of the camp on the Curragh, upon which the sun shone at the time in great splendour.[21] Upon perceiving it, she exclaimed, in such rapture as an old maid is capable of feeling upon such an occasion, 'Oh! What a beautiful sight a camp is, with the thousands of young and gay men who reside in it. I should like, above all things, to see it on my return from Dublin.' As this was too broad a hint to be passed over without rudeness, I offered to shew it to her. She asked to whom she was indebted for this kindness, that she

20 Very probably a relative of John Franklin, attorney, of No. 15 Grand Parade, Kilkenny.

21 A large camp was established at the Curragh in 1805.

might know for whom to inquire. I told her it was only necessary for her to ask to be shown to the Paymaster's marquee of the 47th to which any of the soldiers could direct her; that I was to be found there at any time, and would feel much pleasure in paying her all the attention in my power, and taking her through the lines. She thanked me repeatedly, and said she would gladly avail herself of my kind offer, and have the pleasure of visiting the encampment on her return from Dublin.

Thinking that the history she gave me of the little captain pleased me, and wishing to gratify me further, she again commenced it, and continued telling me the most absurd stories about myself, which had not even the shadow of truth, until we arrived at Rathcoole, when, while they were changing horses, I left the coach for a few minutes, Bourke having promised me that he would not undeceive her, but leave her to suppose that I was dead. During my absence, however, he informed her who I was; and, as she had not a word to say during the remainder of the journey, and there was a general restraint upon us, we were as stupid as owls. When we reached the coach-office in Dublin, she did not give me time to renew the invitation to the Curragh, but tripped off in a hurry. On our return from the Curragh to Kilkenny, part of our regiment, one of the [two] battalions, was ordered to Cahir, where a circumstance occurred that made us all very unhappy. Lieutenant Lennon and Lieutenant Wormall, two officers universally beloved in the regiment, had some dispute late in the evening at the mess table, during which the latter used some irritating expressions. A hostile message was the consequence, which was accepted, and the following morning at five o'clock, appointed for the meeting.[22]

Previously to the hour, poor Wormall, feeling that he had been the aggressor – for, though passionate, he had noble and generous principles – sent an apology by his second to Lennon; but the heartless scoundrel through whom it was sent, wishing for mischief, never delivered that apology which one of the parties cheerfully gave, and the other would as gladly have received. The meeting took place – Wormall was unfortunately wounded at the first discharge, and, having been conveyed to his barrack-room, was laid upon his bed, expressing the greatest anxiety to see Lennon. As soon as Lennon entered the room, he stretched out his hand to him, and said, 'Shake hands with me; I know I am a dying man; but from my heart I forgive you; but, oh! Lennon, why did you not accept my apology?' Lennon, on hearing this, became nearly distracted, declaring in the most solemn manner that it was the first intimation he had of it; and, indeed, so great was the shock such intelligence occasioned, that he never recovered his spirits afterwards.

Poor Wormall, who survived the fatal occurrence but one day, had been some time married to a titled lady in Devonshire, where she was residing at the time of

22 This refers to Lieutenant Alexander Wormald or Wormall who joined the regiment on 14 July 1804 as an ensign and became a lieutenant on 7 May 1805; and William Homman Lennon who joined the regiment as an Ensign on 26 January 1805 from being a Lieutenant in the North York Militia.

the duel.[23] The day after his interment, a letter arrived addressed to him, which the colonel thought proper to open in the presence of some of the officers, as is usual in such cases. It was from Wormall's wife, and expressed fears that he had got into some dispute or quarrel, as she had dreams to that effect for several nights, entreating of him, as she knew the warmth of his temper, not to hesitate in apologising, if in error, to whatever gentleman whom he might have a dispute, for if not, she dreaded the worst consequences.

The colonel answered her letter, and in the most delicate manner informed her that her apprehensions were justified, as her husband was no more; and at the same time declared how much the officers of the regiment sympathised with her in her affliction for the loss of one who was so generally beloved and esteemed by all who had the pleasure of his acquaintance; but more particularly by his brethren in arms. The parties were afterwards tried and acquitted, at Clonmel assizes; but they were not released from military arrest for twelve months after.[24]

John Harley does not mention it specifically, but he was appointed Paymaster of the 2nd Battalion on 11 July. At the end of 1805 this battalion proceeded to Cork and then to Cahir and Belfast, whilst the first battalion remained at Cork preparing to sail to the East Indies.

In 1805, our regiment left Kilkenny for Cork, about five o'clock in the morning of the 20th of October. As I had some business to transact, I was detained the greater part of the day, so that it was three o'clock in the afternoon before I was able to leave town. I had my own carriage, for which I hired post horses; but the innkeeper, a fellow named Magennis, imposing on me, gave me a pair of wretched hacks, that appeared as if they had just come off the road, although he assured me, and I was fool enough to believe him, that they had not been out of his stable for a week.

Having proceeded on our journey for some time, at a snail's pace, we arrived about nightfall at a lonely place at the foot of Kilcash Hill, in the county Tipperary, at that time a noted resort for robbers, when the horses became tired and were unable to proceed up the hill. In this predicament, I got out of the carriage, and handed my wife and her maid out also, for the purpose of lightening the draught and enabling the wretched hacks to surmount the hill, leaving them but little more than the empty carriage to drag after them.

23 Alexander Wormall is recorded in the London Gazette of 14 May 1805 simply as deceased. With respect to his wife, Harley has again mixed up two people. Wormall had married Harriet Anstruther Leslie at St Martin's in the Field on 13 September 1802. A Lady Harriett Leslie married William Courtenay, 10th Earl of Devon in 1804. This is not the same person.

24 There appears to be no evidence of a court martial, but Lieutenant William Homman Lennon died on or before 19 January 1809: did he die of guilt?

While we were in this disagreeable situation, an October night fast approaching, and no house at hand where we could find shelter, a stout-built man, rather under the middle size, and in the dress of a country schoolmaster, came down the road towards us in such manner as to excite my immediate apprehension, particularly as I wore my regimentals, which, in such times, and in such a place, would prove but a bad passport for me.

He passed pretty close to us on the right-hand side of the road, apparently viewing us all the time with a sharp penetrating eye; and then, turning back again on the left-hand side, he got before us, and, after a pause of a few minutes, returned again, and stood looking at the post-boy, quite a young lad, who was in vain endeavouring by whipping and scolding, and at another time by coaxing, to get the poor animals forward.

I confess I became very much alarmed now, as I had always heard that there were robbers on that road, and exclaimed in Irish, 'Us monia athru shin,' which in English means 'we are to be pitied.'[25] He looked at me with astonishment when he heard me speak in Irish, and immediately asked whence I came and where I was going; I told him from Kilkenny, and that I was on my way to Clonmel. He then inquired who the lady was, and on my replying that she was my wife, he expressed a wish to know her maiden name; I told him that she was one of the O'Brien's, of the county Limerick. 'A good name, sir,' said he, 'and one of the old families; I thought as much. But where did you hire these rascally horses, and from whom?' 'In Kilkenny,' said I, 'from a person named Magennis.' 'Oh! I know the fellow well,' said he, 'and he is a great scoundrel for treating you so badly, for those horses have been ploughing all the morning; – but stay – may be, if we put them on the good level road, they might contrive to creep to the next stage.' Then, placing one of his fingers in his mouth, he gave a loud whistle, which was promptly answered by some persons near us, and, in less than two minutes, seven or eight stout, well-looking fellows, bounded down the hill towards us, from some place where they had been lurking in the heath. These he ordered to remove the horses from the carriage, and pull it up the hill; at the same time, handing my wife and servant into it. With a ready obedience, they took the horses from the carriage, and giving them in charge to the post boy, proceeded up the hill with the vehicle, and apparently without being much distressed, the leader and I following them at our leisure. During the walk, he told me that my regiment had passed early in the morning, and asked why I should have remained so long after them. On my informing him that I had got permission to remain to transact some private business, and in consequence of my having a family, 'that was very fair,' he observed; 'but why did you ever join the army?' 'I did so,' said I, 'to gain a livelihood.' He then became very inquisitive, and asked me several questions about my family – some of whom, he said, he knew to belong

25 This is a mistranslation; the phrase given by Harley translates as 'let us go back there'. The Irish for 'we are to be pitied' would be 'ni mor duinn trua'.

to the good old stock of the country – and about my profession, wondering, and appearing much pleased that I had so well retained my native accent and language, after having been so long unaccustomed to speak it, or hear it spoken. He inquired particularly if I recollected a deserter's having been rescued from a party of our regiment while passing over the mountain, about a month before. And, on my replying in the affirmative, he informed me that he was the man who had rescued him; and that he never allowed a deserter to pass in custody, whom he could set at liberty. 'But I hope,' said he, 'that the corporal and the two soldiers with him, were not punished, as they could not avoid it.' On my informing him that they were not, although condemned, as my wife had obtained their pardon, he seemed greatly pleased, and said that he was glad it now lay in his power to serve her.

We now reached the top of the hill, and I offered the men some money for their trouble; but he would not permit them to take it; telling me, at the same time, who he was – and that his name was Brennan. 'And holloa, lad,' said he, addressing the post-boy, 'tell your rascally master my name, and assure him, that if he ever comes in my way, I will repay him for the manner in which he has treated this gentleman;' then, bidding us a safe journey, he and his men jumped over the ditch of the road, and disappeared. This Brennan was, at this time, the terror of the surrounding country, effecting many robberies with impunity. He was, at length, however, taken, about three months after my rencontre with him, and was executed in a short time afterwards. He was the most noted robber that had been in Ireland for some years; and I may, with truth, say, my escape from him is to be entirely attributed to my knowledge of my native language; though, in all probability, this would not have saved me, had he been aware that I had upwards of £2,000 of public money in my writing desk.[26]

26 Willie Brennan was the highwayman. There is a traditional song about him, called 'Brenan on the Moor':

'Tis of a brave young highwayman this story I will tell
His name was Willie Brennan and in Ireland he did dwell
It was on the Kilwood Mountain he commenced his wild career
And many a wealthy nobleman before him shook with fear

Chorus
It was Brennan on the moor, Brennan on the moor
Bold, brave and undaunted was young Brennan on the moor

One day upon the highway as young Willie he went down
He met the mayor of Cashiell a mile outside of town
The mayor he knew his features and he said, Young man, said he
Your name is Willie Brennan, you must come along with me

Now Brennan's wife had gone to town provisions for to buy
And when she saw her Willie she commenced to weep and cry
Said, Hand to me that tenpenny, as soon as Willie spoke
She handed him a blunderbuss from underneath her cloak

Now with this loaded blunderbuss – the truth I will unfold -
He made the mayor to tremble and he robbed him of his gold

In November 1805, the second battalion of our regiment, then stationed in Cahir, received orders to proceed to Belfast; but, previously to this, the gazette appeared, announcing a Mr William Ryan as ensign in the 47th. A day or two before our intended march, two gentlemen of that name arrived at our headquarters, each claiming the commission. One of them, a young man of extremely prepossessing manners and appearance, asserted that he must be the individual gazetted, as he had lately applied, and had been promised an appointment to the first vacant ensigncy. The other, who had come from Dublin, as positively contended that he must be the person, as he had strong claims on government, his brother, the late Captain Ryan, having been killed by Lord Edward Fitzgerald, in Thomas-street, in 1803,[27] on which account he had been promised a sinecure situation, which he was given to understand was the ensigncy in question. Under these circumstances, Colonel Skerrett found it necessary to write to the War Office to ascertain which gentleman had been appointed (the officers, in the meantime, paying them every attention, and entertaining them at the mess), and, in the course of a post or two, received a reply, stating that Mr Ryan, whose brother had been killed by Lord Edward, was the person appointed to the ensigncy in the 47th. The other gentleman, of course, left us immediately, to the regret of all our officers, who, short as the acquaintance with him was, felt more than an ordinary regard for him, which, too, was naturally increased by the disappointment he had met with.[28]

The following morning, we marched for Belfast, I have seldom witnessed such a day. The clouds, which appeared surcharged with rain, hail, and sleet, opened over us, and the watery element came pouring down upon us as if the flood-gates of heaven were unclosed. Ryan, who was at least thirty-five years of age, was, as

One hundred pounds was offered for his apprehension there
So he, with horse and saddle to the mountains did repair

Now Brennan being an outlaw upon the mountains high
With cavalry and infantry to take him they did try
He laughed at them with scorn until at last 'twas said
By a false-hearted woman he was cruelly betrayed

They hanged Brennan at the crossroads, in chains he hung and dried
But still they say that, in the night, some do see him ride
They see him with his blunderbuss, all in the midnight chill
Along, along the King's highway rides Willie Brennan still!

27 Lord Edward Fitzgerald, a son of the Duke of Leinster, had embraced revolutionary principles. The government discovering that Fitzgerald was one of the leaders of the United Irishmen, on 9 May 1798, a reward of £1,000 was put up for his arrest. On 18 May, five days before the planned uprising, his hiding place in Thomas Street, Dublin was betrayed. Captain William Bell and Captain Daniel Ryan entered his room to arrest him, but Fitzgerald stabbed both, Ryan fatally. He was then shot in the shoulder by Major Swan and captured. He was imprisoned at Newgate prison, where his wound became infected and he died on 4 June 1798, not 1803 as stated by Harley.

28 This incident must have happened earlier in the year than Harley remembers. Ensign Ryan appeared in the 47th in the February 1805 Army List, but by September 1805 it had been amended to William T.M. Ryan.

junior ensign, the officer appointed over the baggage guard, and had charge of nearly one hundred cars – so many being required to convey, in Ireland, as much baggage as could be conveniently placed on ten or twelve waggons in England.

Ryan was, upon this day, initiated into some of the inconveniences of his new profession, having to march a distance of twenty-one miles, from Cahir, in the County Tipperary, to Ballyspellan, or Johnstown, in the county Kilkenny, under unceasing torrents of rain.[29] About three hours after our arrival at the latter place, he joined us, with the baggage, dreadfully fatigued and wet, being scarcely able to stand, or sustain the weight of his wet and miry clothes. He came into the room at the inn where we had just breakfasted, and threw himself on a chair in a desponding state, opposite the table, which was covered with egg shells and empty cups, and broken pieces of bread; and, after looking round at the officers, who were regardless of him, running to and fro, each on his own business, he fixed his eyes on me as I was sitting by the fire, and seemed to say, 'have you no commiseration for me?' I therefore remarked to him, 'you have had a dreary, disagreeable march of it, Mr Ryan;' to which he replied, with a sigh, 'Oh! You may safely say that, sir.' And then, after a moment's pause, 'what may be the amount,' he inquired, 'of my day's pay' – as I was paymaster. On informing him that it was 4s. 8d. he looked astonished, stood up, walked about the room for a minute, and then threw himself on the sofa, exclaiming, 'I have been greatly deceived; let people say what they will, an ensigncy is no sinecure. I was always promised, and of course expected one, but this is an extraordinary way to be rewarded by the government for acknowledged services.' From that day Ryan, who was really a pleasant, good kind of fellow, went by the name of *sinecure* in the regiment.

The battalion started the year 1806 in Belfast and early in the year they moved to Enniskillen to recruit.

We arrived in Belfast in due time, but after a very fatiguing harassing march, and spent the winter there very pleasantly; nothing particular occurring worthy of notice during our stay; and, in the beginning of 1806, proceeded to Enniskillen, to endeavour to complete our regiment; to facilitate which government promised commissions to such gentlemen as could procure a certain number of recruits.

At this period, an elderly gentleman, the Reverend Mr Cochrane,[30] came to Enniskillen for the purpose of applying to the colonel for a commission for one of his sons, but having no introduction to him, he was at a loss how to act, when he accidentally met two of our officers in the street, Captain Featherstone and Captain

29 Johnstown is two miles from Urlingford, very near to Ballyspellan Spa.

30 The Reverend James Athol Cochrane, 6th son of the 8th Earl of Dundonald, vicar of the Parish of Belleek until 1805. He died in 1823.

Stacpoole,[31] the life and soul of our regiment, whom he addressed, telling them his object, and apprising them, that in addition to his having procured the recruits, he had a claim upon his country far beyond any other applicant, producing, at the same time, a long memorial that covered three sheets of paper, and stating, in detail, the numerous and irresistible claims his family had upon the government for services performed; and amongst other circumstances, that his ancestors had killed three hundred Romans, or Papists, after the battle of the Boyne.

Featherstone, who was bent upon mischief, told him, having first praised the contents of the memorial, that he had only one means of succeeding, and that by gaining the interest of the paymaster, who had great influence with the colonel, and, in order to obtain the paymaster's interposition, it was necessary to wait upon his wife, and pay her every attention.

The two officers even conducted the old gentleman to the door of our residence, and desired him, before they left him, to be most particular in impressing on the lady's mind all the good his family had done in destroying papists, and the utility of exterminating the remainder of them; 'and be sure,' said Featherstone, 'and read every single word of the memorial for her.' The old gentleman was announced and ushered up to the drawing-room; and, after the usual salutations were over, he told Mrs Harley his business, and commenced reading the memorial for her, according to his instructions, by an occasional observation to impress upon her mind the propriety – nay, absolute necessity, of destroying all the papists.

My wife, who was a rigid and rather bigotted Roman Catholic, saw at once that some deception had been used; and, perceiving that he was a good kind of old man, though foolishly prejudiced, promised she would use her influence for him, telling him they were praiseworthy acts his family had committed, and that she was sure government would no doubt reward them as they deserved.

He then took his leave in high glee with his prospect of success; and my wife, on my return home, related the whole circumstance, with a request, that as the old man had a large family, I should do all in my power to promote his wishes. I accordingly applied to the colonel, and showed him the memorial, which at first enraged him a good deal, but in the end amused him so much that he procured commissions for four of this worthy man's sons, who made excellent officers, and were a credit to our regiment.[32]

31 Featherstone had become a captain in April 1805; the other officer was Captain Hugh Stacpoole.

32 In 1810 the officers of the 47th Foot included Lieutenant Christopher Cochrane (who served in the Peninsula for two years) a Lieutenant James Cochrane (who only served in the Peninsula for a few months), along with Lieutenant Robert Cochrane (who also served in the Peninsula for two years) and an Ensign T.N. Cochrane (who never went to the Peninsula), all presumably his sons.

7

England

In 1807, we at length left Ireland, embarking at Dublin for Liverpool, under the orders of one of the most severe and tyrannical officers that ever commanded a regiment; among others by a certain colonel,[1] whose propensity for flogging his men was such, that it made him detested, not only by the soldiers, but by the inhabitants of every town in which we happened to be quartered, who, on one occasion interfered, and succeeded by force in preventing the flogging taking place. This occurred while we lay at Preston, in Lancashire. He ordered one of the recruits, a mere boy, to be brought out for some very trifling offence and flogged on the race-ground of Preston. However, on the regiment going out to escort him and witness the ceremony, it was attacked by a large body of women belonging to the cotton manufactories, with which that town and neighbourhood abounded, and actually forced back into the town. The numbers increasing from hundreds to thousands, the magistrates were obliged to interpose their authority, and only succeeded, after much difficulty, in dispersing the mob, having been compelled to read the riot act, and give an assurance that the boy should not be flogged.

I would beg leave to remark, as I am upon the subject, that the practice of flogging is, in my opinion, one of the greatest injuries to the British army; for, if a soldier receive even but ten lashes, he never can be a good soldier afterwards. His pride is wounded, his spirit is humbled, his person is debased, and he detests his profession, neglects his person and equipment, and becomes a useless member of the regiment.

This colonel did incalculable injury to the efficiency of the men, and consequently to the service, by his propensity for this mode of punishment – greater injury, indeed, than any other officer I have known or heard of. He delighted in courts martial, which he always ordered on the most trifling occasion. He usually read the sentence himself, a duty which is well known to belong to the adjutant, proceeding over it as quickly as possible, and then calling out, with an air of exultation, and with the feelings of a hero, the awful command 'strip! He stood by until

1 This refers to Lieutenant Colonel William Wardrobe.

A print from 1830 showing an Army flogging just as Harley would have witnessed. (Author's collection)

the sentence could be fulfilled to the letter, viewing the infliction of the punishment with brutal ecstasy, and never having been known in one solitary instance to remit one lash of the sentence that had been passed.

I sincerely hope, for the good of the British army, that an alteration in the Mutiny Act may do away with the practice of flogging altogether, as there are many modes of punishment less disgraceful, more efficacious, and more likely to bring the offender to a just sense of his crime, and of that duty he owes to his country; and, although it must be acknowledged that in the present high state of discipline and good conduct of the British army, it is a punishment not often resorted to, still it is a slur on the heads of free-born Britons; and its very continuance on the statute book, though from its infrequent use it may be considered almost a dead letter, occasions a painful feeling in the breasts of soldiers, not easily described.

No man can be a warmer or more sincere advocate for the strictest discipline and subordination than I am, yet I would wish to see the officers and soldiers on better terms, or, if I may be permitted to use the expression, more like brethren in arms: for, if the former were more bending and less tyrannical than I have known many of them, the latter would be more attached to their superiors, and more particular in attending to their duties.

I cannot leave this subject, so interesting to an old soldier, without stating, as proof of the justness of my remarks, one or two instances of those scenes of horror, of which, while in the army, I was myself an eye-witness. One of them, and there were many such, as I never can forget, was that of a soldier in Gibraltar, who, for a trifling offence, was sentenced to receive a thousand lashes. So strongly, indeed, is the circumstance imprinted upon my memory, that at this distant period I almost imagine I behold the wretched being writhing with agony on the triangles, his back and shoulders streaming with blood from every pore, and beaten into a complete jelly, while the surgeon, who was in attendance to dress his wounds, every now and then felt his pulse, to ascertain how far the degrading sentence and the horrid punishment could be carried into execution. It may appear to my readers to be incredible, but I can most faithfully assure them, that the unfortunate man in question received every lash of a thousand, and that, too, in the month of July, in the hot climate of Gibraltar.

Is it not, I will ask any candid reader, a cruel, a wanton thing, to leave a discretionary power in the hands of any commanding officer thus to torture a fellow-creature for some trifling offence, and unfit him for serving his king or country, after having spent the best years of his life in the service of both, as was the case with this poor fellow, who deserved a better fate, having fought bravely in the campaign of Egypt, and conducted himself for years without reproach, until he unfortunately at length came under the lash of a tyrant?

Another instance occurred while I was a subaltern, and in garrison in Winchester, to which, from a misunderstanding that I shall explain, I unwillingly became a party. We had a severe commanding officer at Winchester, who punished every offence, however trifling, by flogging. One of our blacks, a harmless poor fellow, who beat the big drum, happened to be one day about three minutes late at the evening parade; for this crime he was instantly tried on the parade-ground by a drum-head court martial, and sentenced to be flogged.

I was junior member of the court martial, and it was my duty to pronounce the sentence; and having been told by the other members, as I was then but a short time in the army, that if I pronounced a small number of lashes, he probably would receive them, but if a larger number, two or three hundred, he would not be punished at all – they, supposing that the whole proceeding was merely intended to frighten him and make him more attentive to his duty – a supposition which I regret to say the commanding officer himself led me to conclude was correct – I pronounced the sentence to be two hundred lashes; and, to my horror and dismay, saw the poor man immediately stripped and subjected, by the orders of our commanding officer, to the full number of lashes; the consequence of which was, that upon his recovery, he deserted, and we lost a most useful and well-conducted man. These and many similar scenes which I have witnessed disgusted me so much with the disgraceful and diabolical custom of flogging, that I often determined upon making my sentiments public against such an odious system; and I have no doubt but a large folio volume could be compiled of facts illustrative of the cruelty of the practice and its demoralising effects – exhibiting, too, the infamous practices connected with it, and the injury the British service has invariably sustained by it.

I am enabled by long experience to declare, with the strictest adherence to truth, that our army is composed of as fine and as orderly a body of men as any other in the world, nor is that state of discipline owing in the least degree to the inhuman practice that prevailed to such an extent till within the last few years. I would, therefore, abolish flogging altogether. I would erase such a word from our statutes, and no longer allow it to disgrace the Articles of War, or the Mutiny Act. When a soldier commits a crime, let him suffer confinement proportionate to it, or let him be transferred to foreign service for a limited number of years, or even for life, if the magnitude of his offence require a greater degree of punishment, or even death itself would be preferable to the system of flogging. In case such punishments failed in bringing the offender to a proper sense of conduct becoming a British soldier, I would discharge him altogether from the army; for, by this proceeding, the bad would in time be rooted out – the soldier would have a feeling of respect for his officer, and the latter would be more inclined to place confidence in the former as a faithful adherent who looked up to him for instruction and advice, and considered him less as a military leader than as a father and a friend.

In the autumn of 1807, the battalion marched to Chelmsford where it was completed by volunteers from the militia.

Shortly after that singular occurrence which took place in Preston, we got the route for Chelmsford, in Essex, where we remained for some time, and completed our full strength from the volunteers from the militia regiments. During our residence here, I had occasion to procure leave of absence to go to London on private business, where I met one of the most extraordinary characters that was ever in the British service, Lieutenant K[ennedy], of the 69th Regiment, a young man, who, notwithstanding his oddities, was universally esteemed and beloved by all who had the pleasure of his acquaintance.[2] He was extremely well educated; and, like many eccentric individuals, was possessed of considerable talent. In general, his demeanour was quiet and harmless, but he occasionally broke out into fits almost bordering on insanity, during which he was in the habit of saying and doing the most extraordinary things.

I shall never forget his following me about London, and his attack upon me in the Strand, in consequence of a supposed slight that I had shown him. He and I being both from Limerick, and distantly connected by some family ties, were always on the most-friendly terms, and, whenever we met, usually spent some time together. The day after I reached London from Chelmsford, I met him in St James's Street, in company with Sir John Moore, who was then vice-president of the court martial, sitting on the trial of General Whitelocke, at Chelsea.[3] As I

2 Lieutenant Marcus Kennedy of the 69th Foot. He exchanged to the 8th Foot on half pay in November 1805, he exchanged again to the 18th Foot in 1809 and to half pay in the Barrack Artificer Corps in August 1811.

3 The trial of General Whitelocke for his failure at Buenos Aries was held at Chelsea College from 28 January 1808. Sir John Moore,was one of the panel although he was not president.

was busily engaged conversing with General Backhouse at the moment,[4] I merely nodded with a smile to K[ennedy] as he passed, intending to call upon, if I could not overtake him, when I was disengaged. He, however, took it into his head that I had not taken sufficient notice of him, and that it must have been intended as a slight, and, accordingly, vowed vengeance against me to several of our mutual acquaintances whom he happened to meet. Having been informed of this, and advised not to come into collision, if possible, with such a strange character, I endeavoured carefully to avoid meeting with him while I remained in town, which was about a fortnight. I lodged at Hatchett's Hotel, Piccadilly; and, as I was to travel in a coach that left the Spread Eagle, Gracechurch Street,[5] I was obliged to employ a hackney coach the morning I was to leave town, to convey my portmanteau and several small parcels, having my name written legibly upon them, to the coach-office.

As I was passing through the Strand, I recollected having to make a call at a seal engraver's shop for an article I had left to be cut. While in the shop waiting to be attended, the coachman came to me in evident alarm, saying that a gentleman had forced his way into the coach, and was tumbling about all the parcels, reading the names on them, and seemingly in a great rage.

Upon my going to the door, I beheld, to my consternation and surprise, the identical K[ennedy] whom I had taken such pains to avoid. On seeing me, he immediately jumped out of the carriage, and, running over to the shop, accused me of having grossly insulted him some days previously, demanding, by way of satisfaction, an immediate meeting at Chalk Farm.[6] I was struck dumb, and did not know well what to say in reply to this demand. A gentleman, however, who accompanied poor K[ennedy], and whom I afterwards learned to be Captain Coates, of the 69th,[7] who was kind enough to follow him for his protection, relieved me from the dilemma and embarrassment in which I was placed, by suggesting, that, as I was not provided with a second or friend, it would be only proper to allow me three or four hours to procure pistols and make every necessary arrangement. With this understanding, K[ennedy] appeared satisfied: and, while he was telling the astonished shopkeeper and the frightened coachman the cause of the quarrel and the motives that induced him to demand honourable satisfaction, Captain Coates advised me to step into the coach and drive away, as he was apprehensive that something unpleasant might occur. Adopting his advice, I hinted my wishes to the coachman, who joined me in making a speedy retreat from the shop. No sooner did K[ennedy] perceive me do this than he rushed out after me, and made

4 Then Lieutenant Colonel Thomas Backhouse of the 47th Foot.

5 The Spread Eagle, built in 1637, stood at 84 Gracechurch Street until demolished in 1865.

6 Chalk Farm lies just north of Camden and was the name of a new development built in 1791, the village in the area previously having been known as Chalcot.

7 Major James Coates of the 69th Foot.

a desperate blow at me with a short bludgeon he had in his hand, and which was the principal object of Captain Coates' alarm. He, however, fortunately missed me, striking the roof of the coach such a blow as, had it descended on my head, must inevitably have fractured my skull. Before he had time to repeat the blow, or rather the attempt, the affrighted Jarvey drove off to Gracechurch Street,[8] in full gallop, leaving our pursuer far behind, and without taking time to close the coach-door, which was nearly torn off the hinges by the swinging motion against we got there.

When I had been set down, I explained to the poor coachman, who was really quite alarmed, a thing very unusual with gentlemen of his calling, that my friend K[ennedy] was not right in his mind at different periods, and told him how I had endeavoured to avoid meeting with him. He now became really astonished and panic-struck, on learning that K[ennedy] should have found me so strangely; so much so, indeed, that it was with evident reluctance he received his fare, being influenced probably by some superstition, taking his departure in as great haste as he had arrived, and in as bad a plight almost as K[ennedy] himself.

Among other singular occurrences in which K[ennedy] was a party, the following was related to me by Captain Coates, at a subsequent period when I had the pleasure of meeting him. During one of his insane moments he entered the house of that eminent firm, Messrs. Rundle and Bridges, silversmiths, Ludgate Hill, and ordered plate to a large amount, giving directions to have his crest engraven on them as speedily as possible, stating at the same time to Mr Rundle or Bridges that he was on the point of marriage with Miss Drummond, a daughter of one of the respectable firm of Drummonds, bankers, Charing Cross.[9] Unfortunately, he was alone and had no one to countermand the order, which, in consequence of his gentlemanly manners and appearance was immediately executed, without any delay, to the amount of £2,000; each article having his crest engraved on it.

The following day he called again, accompanied by Captain Coates, and selected some costly and elegant diamonds, necklaces, and other ornaments, stating that they were for his intended bride. On this occasion, Mr Rundle was in attendance at the counter, and congratulated him upon his being so soon united to so respectable and wealthy a family as the Drummonds. K[ennedy] hereupon entered into some particulars, as to the manner in which he first became acquainted with the lady – stated by whom he was introduced to her – and gave such strange and improbable details with regard to their courtship, that the old gentleman looked amazed, and shook his head. 'You look incredulous' observed K[ennedy], 'but were I to relate to you the many extraordinary things that have come to pass in the course of my own experience, you would find it still more difficult to give credence to them.' He

8 Jarvey: Irish for a hackney coach driver.

9 Messrs. Drummond was a private bank, founded in 1717 by the Goldsmith Andrew Drummond, based at 49 Charing Cross. Known clients included George III, Beau Brummell, Brunel, Gainsborough, Wedgwood and Capability Brown. The bank still exists as a private bank within RBS.

was then proceeding to describe some of his romantic adventures, when Coates, placing himself behind K[ennedy], looked significantly at one of the shop men, putting his finger to his forehead to intimate that all was not right with K[ennedy] in the upper storey. The hint was immediately taken, and conveyed to the heads of the establishment, who, though a good deal annoyed by the inconvenience to which they had been put, indulged K[ennedy] in receiving his orders, until his friend Coates at length prevailed upon him to accompany him out of the shop, on some frivolous pretence. Thus terminated his intended transactions with the house of Messrs. Rundle and Bridges.

Among the variety of scrapes into which poor K[ennedy]'s eccentricities led him continually, the following will give an idea of the fellow's liberality and good nature. Returning home one evening to his hotel, he came in contact with an Irish watchman, whom, after the interchange of a few warm words, he unceremoniously knocked down by a severe blow over the eye, in consequence of which he was taken to the watch-house, where he was detained during the night, and brought on the following morning before Sir Richard Birnie.[10]

When the case had been formally explained to that worthy and respected magistrate, K[ennedy] abruptly asked Sir Richard if he had ever heard of Godbold's Vegetable Balsam, or Dr Solomon's Drops;[11] a question which no doubt excited the astonishment of all in the justice-room; 'but Sir Richard,' said he, without giving the magistrate time to make any remark, 'do you not think I am a much better quack than either of those gentlemen, for I have an infallible remedy for curing sore eyes, the application of which is most simple?' Suiting the action to the word, and placing a guinea upon one of his eyes, and, at the same time, turning to the watchman with a significant look that he could not misunderstand.

It is needless to add that the remedy was as infallible as he described or intended it to be. The poor man took the guinea, with the magistrate's permission, and left the room highly satisfied with the result; while K[ennedy]'s serious manner on the occasion excited bursts of laughter from the bystanders. Sir Richard, with whom I had the pleasure of being intimately acquainted, has more than once mentioned the circumstances to me, inquiring at the same time in a particular and feeling manner after K[ennedy], for whom he felt much interested.

This singular character was once at a review of his regiment, which was held by one of the royal dukes, and at which he was with the other officers personally introduced to his Royal Highness. It is a well-known fact that the present

10 Sir Richard Birnie was a Scottish police magistrate, who worked in London, he later led a group of officers in arresting the Cato Street conspirators.

11 Godbold's Vegetable Balsam was a patent medicine concocted by Nathaniel Godbold in 1785 for the treatment of syphilis; he made a small fortune from it and purchased a country estate with the proceeds. He died in 1799, but his sons continued to sell it after his death. Solomon's Drops were sold by Trewman & Co. of Exeter 'For the cure of the scurvy, scrofula, leprosy, and all disorders originating in an impure state of the blood'.

royal family of Great Britain have a very strong recollection of any person whom they have previously seen. On this occasion, when K[ennedy] was introduced to the Duke, he stood perfectly erect, carrying his sword in the usual manner. The moment His Royal Highness saw him, he stopped and observed, 'I have seen you somewhere before this occasion, Lieutenant K[ennedy], but I really cannot at this moment bring the place to my recollection.' K[ennedy] was silent. 'Why,' said the Duke, 'I believe I have seen you at Dover?' to which K[ennedy] replied, without altering a muscle of his face, placing particular emphasis on each word, 'No! my Prince'. 'Then it was at Salisbury?' 'No! my Prince.' 'it was not at Portsmouth?' said the Duke, after a pause. 'No! my Prince,' was still his laconic reply. 'Then, could it have been at Plymouth?' 'No! my Prince.' 'Why, Lieutenant K[ennedy],' said the Duke, rather impatiently, 'I have certainly seen you before. Oh! I recollect now, it was at Chatham.' '*There* you have me, my Prince,' said K[ennedy], immediately dropping his sword, and retiring with a respectable bow, to the great amusement of His Royal Highness, who was not a little gratified at his own penetration, and of the colonel and his brother officers, to whom the circumstance afforded much mirth and diversion for some time afterwards in the mess-room.

Very shortly after this occurrence, he was stationed at Cork on recruiting service, a duty he was particularly fond of; and, among his numerous frolics, he was guilty of the following, perfectly innocent in itself, though it caused as much annoyance to some as it did amusement to others.

Mr Duragnes, a highly respectable merchant and banker in London, who had immense commercial transactions with nearly every house in the south of Ireland happened to be at that time residing in Barker's Hotel, Patrick Street, Cork, where his extensive dealings made him universally known.[12] As the Dublin mail arrives in Cork early in the morning, all the principal and wealthy merchants generally assemble at the news-room, at 9 o'clock, previously to their going to their counting houses, in order to hear the latest intelligence.

Here K[ennedy] made his appearance one morning at an early hour, the room being at the time crowded with the principle commercial gentlemen of the city. Having been asked by some acquaintance, had he any news, he replied, without hesitation, 'I have indeed news that may well astonish the world,' remarking at the same time with one of his most serious looks, and speaking sufficiently loud to attract the attention of every person in the room, that sudden death was an awful occurrence, and that nothing was more certain than the uncertainty of life; 'for instance,' said he, raising his voice, 'there is that good and wealthy man, Mr Duragnes, of London, who was but yesterday in the enjoyment of excellent health, and is now a breathless corpse, waiting the inquest of the coroner. On my way here, a few minutes ago, I learned with inexpressible regret, that he was found dead this morning in his bed; and, what is more distressing to morality, it has been

12 Despite intensive searches of banking records, it has so far proved impossible to identify this person.

discovered that one of those unfortunate women of the town had been with him all night, whom he smuggled up to his room in man's attire. But, gentlemen,' said K[ennedy], to his very attentive and astonished audience, who were not at this time acquainted with his oddities, 'this is but an additional proof of the wickedness and hypocrisy of the world; for I am sure he was the last person I should have thought capable of such disgraceful and abominable conduct; but now that he is no more, I shall only say, *requiescat in pace*.' With this observation, K[ennedy] took up his hat and left the room; while the principal merchants and traders laid down their papers which they had unconsciously retained in their paralysed hands, such being the effect the intelligence produce, and flocked down to the hotel, to inquire what time the awful event occurred, and what steps were to be taken to secure the woman who might probably have murdered him. Some of them were prompted by idle curiosity, and many by interest, especially such as were deeply concerned in commercial speculations.

Judge of their astonishment when, on entering the hall in a body, they observed the venerable old man descending the stairs to his breakfast, in perfect health and spirits, but quite at a loss to judge of the motives of his Cork friends in paying him such an early visit! On being informed of his suppose death, he could not avoid laughing heartily at the hoax that had been played on the merchants, though he did not altogether relish the charge of immorality that had been made against him.

While in Cork, K[ennedy] was generally a welcome guest to all the routes and tea parties which were at that time given almost every night. Amongst those whom he met most constantly, and for whom he conceived an utter and unaccountable dislike, was a Miss O'Shea, an old maid, who was never happy unless when at a card table, where she contrived to realize considerable profit, as she excelled in most games, but particularly in that of casino, then usually played.[13]

Such was K[ennedy]'s hatred of this lady, that he used to wait her appearance in the street, and would then follow her through the town, wherever chance or business might lead her, calling out aloud all the points of the game, such as 'cards and spades make four – little casino five,' &, much to her annoyance, and to the astonishment of such as might overhear him, while at the same time it afforded great amusement to the younger part of her own sex, and no little gratification to those whose money she generally pocketed at the card table.

At another time, while in this city, he would procure the uniform of a general officer, and, retiring to some outskirt of the town, he would equip himself, and mounting his horse, which would have the appearance of being fatigued, gallop speedily into town to the nearest guard-house. As soon as the sentinel on duty perceived him, there would be a lusty call for the guard to turn out to receive the general, who, on approaching, would inspect them; and, after asking them some

13 Casino is a card game which originated in Italy around 1797 and spread throughout Europe. The modern game has been heavily altered by American influences in the nineteenth century.

ludicrous questions, gallop off to some other military post, to repeat the same prank.

When General Champagne, the commander of the district,[14] was made acquainted with the circumstance, instead of being annoyed by such a breach of military discipline, he was highly amused at K[ennedy]'s eccentricities; but the matter would have been seriously noticed had any other officer but K[ennedy] been in question.

The last time I met the poor fellow was at the house of Charles Creed, Esq, in the county Limerick, a very wealthy and hospitable man, whose income was at least £8,000 per annum.[15] Of course, there were numerous guests, which was usually the case at his princely mansion.

I must premise that Mrs Creed was the daughter of a Mr John Norris, of Limerick, who had realised an immense property as a shopkeeper, and had lived to see all his daughters most respectably married and riding in their own carriages.[16] He was what was termed a near man; and it was a remark in the county Limerick that Mr Norris, in weighing a pound of raisins would, rather than give overweight, break a raisin in two.

My readers must be aware that those persons who are unfortunately subject to a slight casual insanity are generally very easily offended and displeased at any seeming inattention, howsoever trifling it might be. Such was, at least, K[ennedy]'s feeling, as instanced before in his attack upon me on the Strand. And on this day, as we sat at dinner, and while K[ennedy] was waiting to be helped to something our worthy hostess had before her, he fancied there was some inattention on her part, and bitterly observed, loud enough to be heard by everyone at the table, 'You are as precise and as long helping a person as your old father would be, when in his little grocer's shop, he would be biting the raisins in two, lest his customers should get half a raisin too much; what do you think of that, Madam?' Mr Creed, on hearing him, burst into a loud fit of laughter; and a facetious gentleman, Sir Richard Harte,[17] who was present, cried out, 'Bravo, K[ennedy], bravo, my hearty,' and contrived in a minute to turn the conversation.

The last account I heard of K[ennedy] was his having been sent to Coleraine, in the north of Ireland, with a recruiting party, when he shortly after died. His humorous propensities remained in him to the last; for a few days before his decease he procured several hundred copies of the celebrated ballad, 'Kitty of Coleraine,' which he sent in parcels of five or six, under cover, to all his numerous

14 Major General Forbes Champagne commanded the Western District of Ireland stationed at Bandon and with his headquarters at Cork.

15 Charles Creed owned flour mills at Kilmallock in Limerick, he died on 30 May 1814 whilst watching a horse race.

16 Charles Creed had married Catherine Norris.

17 Sir Richard Harte had twice been mayor of Limerick, the second time in 1806. He died in 1824 at Coolen.

friends and acquaintances, in different parts of the world.[18] I have never known a more eccentric character, nor have I ever met a worthier fellow than K[ennedy]; and unless at times, when he may be said to have been completely deranged, he was a safe and pleasant companion.

Writing of K[ennedy] and his adventures in Cork, brings to my recollection an anecdote of another man, not unlike K[ennedy] in character, but, however, never troubled like him by occasional fits of insanity. His name was McClure, or, as he was commonly called, Bob McClure. He had wasted a considerable property by extravagance, and being at last put, as they say in Ireland, to his wit's end, to obtain a livelihood, he prudently determined to prevail upon some old maid or widow, who had money enough, to marry him; and, as he was a fine looking and rather handsome young man, of which he was well aware, he had every prospect of succeeding.

Having made up his mind on the subject, and determined to make love in earnest, he urged his suit to several ladies of the description he required; but was, unfortunately, from one cause or another, dismissed by them in turn. But still he was not disheartened; and, as he was a young fellow that was very much liked and respected in Cork, he easily procured an introduction to a rich widow, who he learned had, in addition to a handsome jointure, very good expectations from an elderly relation. After a short acquaintance with her, during which he did everything in his power to get into her good graces, he made his proposal in due form, and with every hope of success; but, to his utter dismay and confusion, was rejected with great indignation, and forbidden to enter the house again.

Such a reception would have driven any man but Bob to despair, as this lady was a '*dernier resort*,' and, if he failed now, he had no further chance of succeeding; but he was too much accustomed to disappointments to be affected by them, and

18 The words to 'Kitty of Coleraine' are:

As beautiful Kitty one morning was tripping,
With a pitcher of milk from the fair of Coleraine,
When she saw him she stumbled, the pitcher it tumbled,
And all the sweet buttermilk watered the plain.
Oh! What shall I do now, 'twas looking at you now,
Sure, sure, such a pitcher I'll ne'er meet again.
'Twas the pride of my dairy, Oh, Barney McCleary,
You're sent as a plague on the girls of Coleraine.

He sat down beside her and gently did chide her,
That such a misfortune should give her such pain.
A kiss then he gave her, and before he did leave her,
She vowed for such pleasure, she'd break it again.
'Twas haymaking season, I can't tell the reason,
Misfortune will never come single 'tis plain,
For very soon after poor Kitty's disaster,
The divil a pitcher was whole in Coleraine.

merely determined to change his mode of operation, and instead of laying regular siege, as he had always done before, to gain his object by force or stratagem.

Having settled upon his plan of attack, he prevailed upon the widow's servant maid, with whom he contrived to be on pretty good terms, to admit him into the house at five o'clock on the following morning, without letting her know what his intentions were, for a good bribe silenced any enquiry upon her part. At the appointed hour, he gained admission, when he instantly stripped himself before the astonished girl of his coat, waistcoat, and hat; and, dressing himself in a morning gown and night cap, quietly entered the widow's bedroom, which looked into the street, and took his stand at the window, which he opened gently, the widow being at the time in a deep sleep, and the bed-curtains drawn closely round.

He had not been long in this situation when some of his acquaintances passed, who, seeing him in such a place, naturally thought that he had been married to the widow, and congratulated him on his good fortune, wishing him every joy and happiness; to which he replied, 'Thank you, my dear friends, thank you, I am much obliged to you, it is all settled.' And, if any person whom he knew happened to pass without noticing him, he attracted their attention by a cough, or by calling to them, and was congratulated by them in like manner; after which, they spread the news through the city that Bob had succeeded with the rich widow, and was actually married to her.

The lady about nine o'clock awoke; and, as she could not imagine what could make the room so cold, she drew the curtains aside, and, to her astonishment, beheld Master Bob at the window, just as if he had only just left his bed. Taking advantage of the surprise into which his presence in such a place threw her, and without giving her time to collect herself sufficiently to make a remark upon his strange conduct, he cried out, 'I entreat, my dear, that you will not be alarmed. I have been here these three hours, but not nearer your bed than the window. All the town now believe that we are married, and have been congratulating me, and wishing me joy the whole morning. You had better then take me in earnest, and I will make a good husband, you may depend on it. If you do not, my darling, your character and reputation, which I prize above everything in the world, will be lost for ever; and what will Miss Such-a-one say?' alluding to a censorious old maid, with whom the widow was not on good terms. 'She passed a moment ago, and looked devilish jealous when she saw me here; and, if you deny me now, she will think with the rest of the world that something improper has occurred, and never cease proclaiming you through the streets as the vilest of women.'

The widow being at a loss what to do or say, had recourse at last to her sex's weakness, and bursting into a flood of tears, at first upbraided him for his ungenerous conduct, but afterwards conjured him, if he had any regard for her, to leave her immediately.

Bob, however, being determined not to lose his vantage ground, persisted in endeavouring to reconcile her to her fate, and at length succeeded, after the use of some well-timed and well-applied flattery, swearing to her that she was dearer to him than any mortal breathing, in wringing from her a promise of being his. As soon as this object was gained, he lost no time in sending for a licence; and a friend, who, after partaking of a comfortable breakfast with them, accompanied them to St Barry's Cathedral,[19] where they were duly joined as man and wife, to the gratification of Bob's numerous acquaintances and well-wishers; and, before eleven o'clock, there was not an individual in Cork who had not heard of his good fortune.[20] The stratagem was then explained; and it was acknowledged by every person, that, putting his own merits out of the question, of which, however, all had a high opinion, Bob McClure richly deserved such a prize for the ingenuity he displayed in obtaining it. I have heard that an occurrence, almost similar in its character, took place in England at a later period. It is not unlikely but that someone may have borrowed a hint from Bob; if so, I trust that the result was in every way as favourable as in the case I have mentioned; for I can assure my readers that Bob McClure made an excellent husband, and that his wife never had cause to regret the singular occurrence.

Entreating my reader's pardon for this long digression, I will lead them back to Gracechurch Street, where, after my escape from poor K[ennedy], I took my seat in a coach for Chelmsford. The sole companions of my journey were a lady and a gentleman. In the course of conversation, having mentioned that I was going to Chelmsford, the lady asked me was I acquainted with any one there; to which I replied, that I was not, as I lived in the barracks; 'But, on recollection,' said I, 'I know a Mr J[ebb], a surly old magistrate, who refuses signing my accounts, unless I pay him one shilling upon each affidavit, although there is no allowance to us from government for that purpose; so uncouth a brute',[21] I continued, 'I never met with.' 'Indeed, sir,' said the lady, with great mildness, 'if you knew Mr J[ebb], you would not say so. The next time you have occasion to call, take my advice, and praise his pictures, for they are his hobby-horse; and I shall be greatly surprised if you do not meet with a good reception.'

When I arrived at Chelmsford, I was informed, to my confusion and astonishment, that it was Mrs J[ebb] with whom I had been conversing in the coach, and to whom I abused her husband in such unmeasured terms; not that I cared much for what I said of him, but I feared lest she might have supposed that I knew her, and therefore spoke harshly of her husband's conduct, of which no man pretending to respectability could be capable.

In a short time after my return from London, I had occasion to call on the same magistrate, to swear my accounts; and having been shown into a parlour hung

19 A nickname for St Finbarr's Cathedral which had stood on its present site since the 7th Century, although rebuilt in 1735.

20 This would appear to be the Robert McClure who married Martha Richmond at Cork in 1790.

21 Harley identifies Jebb later in this book, but a great deal of searching has failed to identify anything about this person.

with paintings, I was in the act of inspecting them with apparent interest and attention, when Mr J[ebb]; entered; I continued looking at the paintings, according to my instructions, without appearing to notice that anyone had entered the room. He did not speak for a minute or two; but then asked me with a smile of complacency, if I admired his paintings. I replied that I did, that they were very fine, and that in fact, since my return from Italy, I had seen nothing to be compared to them. The old gentleman's countenance brightened up with a great smile; and he said, 'I see, sir, that you are a connoisseur; if you will be good enough to accompany me upstairs, I will show you some works of the first masters; and, as those who are not good judges say they are not genuine, I should be glad to hear your opinion.'

He then ushered me into the drawing-room, at the door of which I met Mrs J[ebb], who, however, pretended not to recognise me, though I evidently saw her smile that she knew me well, and was conscious that I was making my first essay in the lesson in which she had instructed me. The paintings were certainly some of the most splendid I have ever seen, and had cost Mr J[ebb] immense sums of money – but I was no judge whatever of their value or genuineness. It was, therefore, really laughable to hear me, after minutely examining them, giving my opinion on their respective merits, and extolling them as the grandest collection – though not the largest, the most select at least, in Great Britain. In fact, I was almost afraid that I went too far; for I became, all at once, so intimately acquainted with that branch of the Fine Arts, that I made no hesitation in pronouncing *this* to be an Angelo, and *that* a Titian; *this* a Vandyke, and *that* a Reubens and another a Corregio – *this* of the Dutch school, and *that* of the Flemish, and those of the Italian, without once considering that Mr J[ebb] himself might have a knowledge of the authors of the respective works, and be thus able to detect and expose my ignorance. However, he was not; and I made such progress in the old man's good opinion, that he signed my accounts immediately, without asking me to swear to them; and made me stop to dinner, introducing me to Mrs J[ebb] as one of the best judges of paintings that had ever seen his collection.

I very often dined with him afterwards, and found him, upon acquaintance, just as Mrs J[ebb] described him – a well-disposed good-natured man. He was at that time extremely rich, being possessed of the enormous sum of £100,000 in ready cash – for so obstinate was he, he could not be prevailed upon to lodge it in any bank – and, such was his aversion to the income tax, that he would not put it in public funds. He died not very long after I became acquainted with him, leaving the greater part of his fortune to his widow, who, in the course of some time, married a Captain M, from whom, however, she was obliged to part, giving him one-half of the large fortune she had brought him.[22]

In March 1808, I went from Chelmsford to Marlow, having previously received a letter from General Harcourt on the subject of placing my son at the Royal

22 It has proved impossible to identify this officer with any certainty.

Military College:[23] I wished also to see an old acquaintance, Captain Otter, one of the captains of cadets, whom I had known formerly in the 28th Regiment.[24] On my coming to the College gate, I was stopped by the young sentry, who refused to allow me to enter with all the strictness of an old veteran, unless I had a pass. On sending in my card, I obtained admittance, and, in the course of the day, conversing with Captain Otter, the same young cadet, who had so strictly done his duty at the gate, made his appearance, and asked the captain for an hour's leave to go into town. The captain hesitated, and was very unwilling to comply with his request; when the little soldier looked at me, and said to Captain Otter, I hope this gentleman will be answerable for me, that I will return at the expiration of an hour if you grant me leave. This engagement I readily entered into for him, recollecting the strict manner in which he did his duty at the gate, and the captain then complied. I could not avoid asking who this fine youth was: when I was informed by Captain Otter, that he was son to the then Duke of Clarence, our late most gracious King. He returned ten minutes before the expiration of the hour, being as strict to his promise as he was to his military duty.[25]

There was a ball given during our stay at Chelmsford, by the officers of the 24th Regiment, on the occasion of their getting their new colours.[26] It was certainly a magnificent entertainment, and was attended by upwards of three hundred of the fashionables of the county of Essex; and amongst the company was Louis the XVIII of France, then an emigrant in this country, accompanied by his entire suite. He resided at the time near Chelmsford, at Gosfield Hall – a seat given to him by the Duke of Buckingham while he remained in this country.[27]

A ludicrous circumstance occurred while we were at Chelmsford by which one of our officers, Lieutenant Colonel B[land], was placed in a very awkward predicament, from which he was with no little difficulty released.[28] He was an extraordinary character, and so fond of the fair sex, that he never went into a town in which he did not pick up some female companion. At Preston, he had one residing with him; and when the regiment left that town she remained behind under the assurance that she should be sent for as soon as he was settled in his next quarters. The regiment remained at Manchester for three weeks, during which period he had another lady residing with him, to whom he made the fairest promises: and, on the regiment leaving that town, she continued in it under a similar assurance. In

23 General William Harcourt, the 3rd Earl Harcourt (1743-1830), was Governor of the Royal Military College at Great Marlow for its first nine years.

24 Captain John Otter was a Captain of the Gentlemen Cadets at Great Marlow from 1807, he had served in the 28th Foot in 1800.

25 This was George Fitzclarence, who became Earl of Munster, the first illegitimate son of King William IV and Mrs Jordan.

26 The 24th (Warkwickshire) Regiment of Foot.

27 The Marquis of Buckingham's house, was home to King Louis XVIII and his entourage from 1807-9.

28 Major Humphrey Dalrymple Bland in fact only became a lieutenant colonel in 1810.

Derby, he met another, and at Leicester a fourth, to each of whom he told the same story. And, on the very evening the regiment marched into Chelmsford, he formed an acquaintance with a female of that town, whom he took into his apartments in the barrack to reside with him.

After a few days had elapsed, he received several letters from his quondam friends, complaining of breach of promise, and saying they would join him as soon as possible. These letters he never answered, foolishly thinking that none of them would undertake the journey. But he was mistaken. He was scarcely a fortnight in Chelmsford when the lady from Preston arrived with all her luggage, and sent a message to him from the inn, informing him of the circumstance. As he could not bring her to his quarters in the barracks, which were already occupied, he was obliged to procure a lodging for her in the town and advance her some cash. In the course of another day or two, the Manchester dame arrived, for whom he had to provide another lodging. And lastly came the Leicester lady, who also required the like attention. Having then no less than four on his hands, he knew not how to act, and was in a state bordering on distraction. However, by sending Captain Featherstone and other friends to negotiate for him, the three ladies were, after much difficulty, prevailed upon to return to their respective homes; but not until they had been handsomely remunerated for their time, trouble, and travelling expenses.

B[land] was an unfortunate fellow. He had been originally intended for the bar – but having married early in life an accomplished young lady, the daughter of a music master, by whom he had one child, a daughter – and not liking his profession, which indeed did not suit him, he obtained a commission from his relative, General [Dalrymple], who was the colonel of the 47th Regiment.[29]

He joined his regiment in Halifax, leaving Mrs B[land] in Dublin, in a boarding house in the city, from which she eloped in a short time with a Captain [Richard King], whom she met lodging in the same house.[30]

On B[land]'s return with his regiment, he commenced an action against Captain [King], who was then residing with Mrs B[land] in the north of England. He had, however, in the meantime, formed an attachment himself while at Halifax, with a Mrs M[orley],[31] and made arrangements with her, that as soon as he had obtained a divorce from Mrs B[land], he would return and marry her.

29 Bland served at Lincoln's Inn until he joined the Army. He married Mary Graham at St James's Dublin on 2 June 1793. Mary ran a school after marriage. The couple actually had two children, one who died young, the daughter who survived was Helena Bland, who was sent away to school in 1804. William Dalrymple was Colonel of the 47th Foot from 1794-1807 and was presumably related to Major Humphrey Dalrymple Bland.

30 Captain the Honourable Richard King 96th Foot. Richard King was named as the other party accused of 'trespass, assault & criminal conversation' with Mrs Mary Bland in 1804.

31 This would appear to be a member of the Morley family of Halifax, but it has proven impossible to identify the exact person.

He then proceeded in his action against Captain [King], the damages laid being £10,000.[32] The cause came on for trial in Dublin – but, as so much neglect appeared upon his part, leaving her unprotected and seldom or never writing to her, the jury gave him £300.[33] This verdict, however small, entitled him to sue for a divorce; and accordingly, by the advice of his lawyer, he brought the matter into the House of Lords at a very great expense.[34] And so sure was he of succeeding in the divorce bill, and obtaining the hand of the rich widow, who had £13,000 in ready cash, that he made several preparations for their nuptials – ordering a handsome carriage to be built in Long Acre, and purchasing a pair of very fine coach horses at Tattersall's,[35] and many other things required for a splendid establishment. He also took his daughter from school, and placed her with her intended step-mother in Sloane Street, who, having sold all her property in Halifax, came to reside in London to wait the issue of the bill before the House of Lords.

B[land] called on me at my lodgings in Leicester Square, the evening that the fate of his bill was to be decided. He appeared in high spirits – and, remaining only a few minutes, hurried away to the house confident of success. General B[ackhouse] dined with me on that day, and shrewdly observed, as soon as B[land] had gone, 'Mark my words, Harley, and rely upon what I tell you. B[land] will be disappointed, in consequence of the irregular life he has led.' The general spoke but too truly, for the first news we read in the next morning's papers was, that B[land]'s divorce bill had been thrown out. On its being introduced, and the merits of it discussed, the Lord Chancellor remarked, that any person coming to their Lordship's house for redress, particularly in such a case as the present, should come with clean hands, which was not the case with Colonel B[land], as it had been proved by a gentleman who had recently been confined in the same room with him in the King's Bench Prison, that he had a female residing with him there, who even assumed his name. It is almost unnecessary to say, that in consequence of this statement, made by the highest legal authority of the country, the bill was thrown out by their Lordships without a dissentient voice – and B[land]'s fondest hopes were for ever dissipated.

He left London next day, and accompanied us to Jersey, where the regiment went soon after. We had been but a short time there when I received a letter from Mrs M[orley], requesting me to inform the colonel of her wish that his daughter should be sent for, which was of course immediately done; and she joined us at Jersey. Mrs M[orley], by way of consolation, I suppose, for the disappointment she had experienced, married in a short time a cornet of dragoons – who soon emptied her purse – while, on the other hand, poor B[land], who never recovered the shock

32 The aggrieved husband could seek damages from the wife's lover, the crime of adultery being referred to as 'Criminal Conversation'.

33 This is confirmed in the *Journal of the House of Lords* 48 GEO III, p.597.

34 A divorce at this time could only be passed by a special Bill in the House of Lords.

35 Tatersall's was an auctioneer of horses, founded in 1766, based then near Hyde Park Corner. Today Tatersalls (they have dropped the apostrophe) are the leading bloodstock auctioneer in Europe.

his feelings received, banished himself to India, where he died of a broken heart, leaving me a considerable loser by his death, as he had generally recourse to my purse in his necessities.[36]

36 Bland certainly died in 1816.

8

Jersey and Gibraltar

From Chelmsford, we proceeded to Jersey, where we arrived in the middle of May 1808.[1] The beauty of this small island is not half known. It was thickly planted with apple trees, which were then covered with blossoms, and gave the island the appearance of a large garden in full bloom. The people, from the lowest to the highest, we found uncommonly civil and obliging; and we were never more hospitably entertained. The climate, too, was delightful, and the necessaries of life were cheap and good. In fact, we considered it altogether such good quarters, that, although we remained in it for more than two years and a half, we left it with unfeigned regret.

I had almost forgotten to mention a ludicrous mistake that occurred at Blandford, where we stopped one night on our route to Jersey. The following morning, I rose at an early hour, as was my usual custom, and, on walking about the town, perceived placards announcing Miss Drake's benefit; which, however, had taken place the night before.

The name appeared familiar to me, and, after a few moments reflection, I recollected that, when quartered in Belfast in 1807, and when the theatre was opened under Mr Bellamy's management,[2] I became acquainted with two of his company – a Miss Hamilton and a Miss Drake – the former, whose real name was Cannon, being a daughter of Mr Cannon, a commissary at Athlone,[3] and sister to the wife of Mr Crampton, the Surgeon General of Dublin[4] – a remarkably fine and attractive looking girl – but neither a good actress nor singer. The latter, though low in stature and rather corpulent, was a most pleasing companion and a delightful

1 The battalion embarked for service in Jersey in May 1808 and then embarked from there for Gibraltar in October 1809. This move to Jersey is not shown in Wylly's history of the regiment but has been verified in the Army Returns at the National Archives.

2 Thomas Ludford Bellamy was a singer at Covent Garden, who became a theatre manager when he was bequeathed property from his grandfather in Ireland. He became the proprietor of Belfast, Londonderry and Newry theatres.

3 Patrick H. Cannon, Commissary of the Corps of Waggoners in Ireland on half pay.

4 Sir Philip Crampton, 1st Baronet, had married Selina Cannon on 11 May 1800.

singer. As she was the only support of her mother, I exerted myself successfully in procuring a full house for her at her benefit, for which her poor mother and herself felt truly grateful. I again met the same party in Newry and renewed the acquaintance, after which, I heard no more of her until I read the placards in Blandford. As I felt much interested for her, on account of the strong filial affection she displayed to her poor helpless mother, I determined upon paying her a visit before breakfast, as I had ordered the carriage for my family to proceed after the regiment at ten o'clock.

Having obtained her address from a hairdresser's boy, I proceeded to her lodgings, and, on inquiring of the woman of the house, I was informed that Miss Drake had not been long in bed, her benefit having taken place the night before; and, as she was of course much fatigued, she could not be disturbed at that early hour. I then assured the woman, that if the lady knew who wished to see her, she would come without hesitation, as I was her most particular friend. After a good deal of persuasion, I prevailed the woman to take my card, with a wish that I might see her immediately, as I was leaving town in a couple of hours. Miss Drake sent a message in reply, that she was then unable to rise from fatigue, but that, if I called about twelve o'clock, she would be happy to see me. As that hour did not suit my arrangements, I again persuaded the woman to inform her that I should leave town at ten o'clock, and should be sorry to go without seeing her; to which an answer came, that she could not possibly see me sooner than ten o'clock.

Being greatly annoyed at the reception I had experienced – so different from what I expected – I said, in an angry tone, that I would not see her then; and, muttering something about ingratitude, was about to depart – when the woman requested that I would stop for a moment, and she would go up to Miss Drake again. Having done so, she told me on her return, that the lady would see me in a few minutes. I, accordingly, walked into the parlour to wait for her; and, as I was anxiously expecting her appearance, the door opened – and behold, instead of my fair young friend, a figure presented itself to my view not unlike the ghost in Hamlet – only the lantern jaws were daubed with streaks of white and red paint! On seeing this tall, meagre looking, and raw-boned woman, between forty and fifty, enter the room, I started as if I had seen an apparition, and was really unable to speak – until, after surveying me for a moment from head to foot, in the most tragic style, she observed, with a tone of voice and sternness of manner that nearly made my blood run cold – 'I thought so.' Seeing that a storm was gathering, and that she was preparing to abuse me, I endeavoured to stammer out something of an apology for the unpleasant mistake. Interrupting me, she exclaimed, with the manner of a fury; 'this is not the first time that I have been annoyed by being mistaken for that little wretch that goes by my name; and you, sir,' said she, addressing herself more pointedly to me – I heard no more, for seeing a clear passage into the street, I darted out – ran off to the hotel – despatched my breakfast in a hurry – and, ordering the carriage to the door an hour earlier than intended, made a precipitate retreat from Blandford, happy at having escaped so well.

During our stay in Jersey, I was accosted one morning in the market by a lady, whom at first I did not recognise, but whom, on an explanation taking place, I found to be an old acquaintance of mine, a daughter of a Mr [Lowe], a respectable silversmith in Gloucester.[5] She informed me that she was no longer Miss [Lowe], having been lately married to a Lieutenant [Bailey], and that she had just arrived to join the 4th Garrison Battalion, the corps to which her husband belonged.[6] My family, of course, called on them; and when Mr and Mrs [Bailey] returned the visit, they were seen leaving our house by some of the officers of the garrison, who immediately inquired, was I aware who Mr [Bailey] was? On my reply in the negative, they told me he was the individual who had betrayed and hanged the unfortunate [Campbell], who were so much regretted; and that they had all determined to put him in Coventry, in consequence of his perfidious and ungenerous conduct.

After having been the bosom friend of the family, and become possessed of all their secrets, it must be admitted by every one of right feeling, that he was the last person in the world who should have denounced them.[7]

While we lay in jersey, a party of recruits arrived from Enniskillen, where we had a recruiting party; one of whom, on their appearing before the commanding officer, stepped forward, and, taking a dirty letter out of his waistcoat pocket, presented it to the colonel, saying, 'I brought a letter of *commendation* to you, colonel, your honour.' It purported to be from the late General Elrington, who was at that time colonel and inspecting field officer of the Enniskillen district;[8] and was as follows:

5 The only silversmith in Gloucester in the 1800's with the ability to add hall marks was George Lowe.

6 It has proven virtually impossible to identify this officer but it is likely that it refers to Lieutenant R. Bailey who had been in the 21st Foot and transferred to the 4th Garrison Battalion around January 1808. He resigned from the army on 25 July 1809.

7 There are very few incidents which seem to fit the few facts Harley mentions. The only one that does seem to fit, being the death of Captain Alexander Boyd of the 21st Foot in a duel with Major Alexander Campbell on 23 June 1808. Duel deaths were officially still murder but rarely seem to have led to court cases or indeed death sentences. However, in this case, due to the fact that the duel occurred immediately, without time for either side to cool down and reconsider and shake hands on it, the jury found the major guilty of murder and he was hanged. It is possible that Bailey alerted the authorities and was blamed by the other officers for meddling in a matter of honour.

8 Major General Thomas Gerard Elrington.

My dear Cornel,
This comes hoping you are well, as it laves me at present, thanks be to God for the same. The beror is a tenant's sun of mine; he will make you a fine soldier, be as kind as you can to him – for, say what you will Cornel, Pat Furlong, is the boy forever.
Your humble Servant,
Cornel
Pat Furlong

To Cornel Elrington
Commanding all Enniskillen
In Ireland.

Colonel W[ardrobe], who commanded the regiment, was a rough old Scotchman, and, having no patience in reading such a letter, instantly sent master Pat Furlong to the guard-room for the attempt to impose upon him.[9] From Furlong's appearance of simplicity and extraordinary epistle, I was induced to call upon him, and asked him what could have tempted him to practice such an imposition upon his commanding officer, as he had endeavoured to do. 'Why, then indeed, I will tell your honour the whole truth,' said he; 'I did get a letter from Colonel Elrington, and lost it on the march; and sure there was no harm to make another like it myself.' This, upon inquiry, was found to be the truth. And Colonel Elrington wrote a second time in his favour, on hearing of the circumstance. Furlong indeed fully justified the recommendation – for he made a smart good soldier.

From Jersey we went, in 1809, to Gibraltar,[10] stopping on the way for a few days at Falmouth, where we were when the jubilee took place on the 50th year of the reign of George the Third.[11] Gibraltar was then commanded by Lieutenant General Campbell, and was garrisoned by a strong force.[12] That celebrated heroine, commonly called the Maid of Zaragoza, although she had been married, resided in the town while we were there, and dined at our mess. I afterwards met her at the governor's ball, dressed in a blue uniform, with laced hat and feathers, and a small sword to her side. She appeared to be about twenty-four years of age, and was rather handsome. Her husband had been an officer in the Spanish Artillery, and was killed at the siege of Zaragoza. After he fell, she rushed to the batteries and displayed the most heroic personal courage – carrying the ammunition, pointing the guns, and encouraging her fellow soldiers both by precept and example. She

9 Lieutenant Colonel William Wardrobe, 47th Foot, he resigned from the army in May 1810 and died in Georgia in October 1812.

10 The battalion sailed for Gibraltar in October 1809.

11 George III's Golden Jubilee occurred on 25 October 1809.

12 Lieutenant General Sir Colin Campbell was Governor of Gibraltar from November 1809 to April 1814.

accompanied the garrison when they left Zaragoza and came to Gibraltar, from which she afterwards took the field again, vowing vengeance against the enemy, and animating the troops wherever she went, to fight against the French.[13]

We had not been long in Gibraltar when an expedition was undertaken to Malaga, consisting of large detachments of the 89th and 47th Regiments, under the command of Lord Blayney.[14] On arriving before Malaga, his lordship disembarked with the 89th Regiment; and, in consequence of a *ruse de guerre* practised by the French, who clothed themselves in Spanish uniforms, and whom his lordship naturally supposed to be a body of Spaniards, he and his detachment were taken prisoners, and sent to Verdun in France, a distance of between six and seven hundred miles – where they remained until the peace of 1814.[15] Among the number, was my cousin, Roger Sheehy, a lieutenant in the 89th, a wild volatile fellow, and well known in the military circles.[16]

While Sheehy was on his parole in Verdun, he suddenly left it, and reaching England safely, attended the first levee after his arrival by the late ever-to-be lamented Duke of York. Sheehy, in his usual gay manner, told His Royal Highness that he had just arrived from France, taking merit to himself for his ingenuity in escaping; but, to his great mortification, when the Duke, upon inquiring, found how he had escaped, and that he had been on parole at the time, he instantly ordered him back to France, saying, that no British officer should break his parole of honour.

Sheehy was of course obliged to obey the Duke's command, and retraced his steps; and, as I have been informed by some who were present, it was really laughable to see the governor of the fort of Verdun, and the officers of the 89th receiving him – each asking him what news from London – when he intended leaving them again – and to whom, or to what circumstance were they indebted for his re-appearance and agreeable society once more.

13 Agustina Raimunda Maria Saragossa Domenech, became a famous celebrity during the 1st and 2nd Sieges of Zaragoza in June 1808. Agustina is reputed to have been on the ramparts supplying apples to the soldiers when they retired before a French attack, she then supposedly loaded and fired a cannon, driving the French away. She later fought as a minor guerrilla leader during the Peninsular War, but it has been impossible to authenticate her presence at Gibraltar.

14 Major General Andrew, Lord Blaney, was an experienced officer, who had served in Flanders in 1794, the Irish Rebellion in 1798, Malta, Egypt, Hanover and South America. He was made a prisoner of war on 14 October 1810.

15 Blaney decided to make a surprise attack on Fuengirola where the garrison of Sohail Castle only amounted to 150 men and 11 dragoons with a few hundred more in nearby towns. He landed with the 2/89th Foot, the Spanish Toledo Regiment and some artillery totalling 1,700 men, later joined by the 1/82nd. Despite overwhelming force the attacks on the castle were driven off, the Poles then sallied out and drove the British force out of their batteries and turned their guns on them. Lord Blayney was captured and the troops re-embarked. It was not one of the British army's greatest hours. There is no record of the 47th Foot having landed. Harley's tale of the ruse de guerre is a fiction.

16 Lieutenant Roger Sheehy of the 89th Foot was captured at Fuengirola.

Although, by the laws of nations and customs of war, Sheehy deserved to be immediately put into close confinement for breaking his parole, yet the governor, who was a brave old soldier, and a generous foe, gave him the same liberty he enjoyed before his escape.

I have often thought how different this noble and honourable conduct of his late Royal Highness the Duke of York, in sending Sheehy back, I may say, to his prison, was from that of the French government at that time, in the case of General Philippon taken prisoner at Zafra by Lord Hill. Philippon, while a prisoner of war, and on his parole of honour in Derbyshire, contrived to make his escape from this country into France – and, instead of being reprimanded, was immediately employed. He was the governor of Badajoz when it surrendered to us – on which occasion, the brave Duke of Wellington, feeling, no doubt, that having broken his honour he was unworthy of being treated as a gentleman, or as a soldier, refused to grant him an audience, but generously sent him his horses.[17]

About the same period that the unsuccessful expedition to Malaga took place, the Marquess of [Sligo] and suite arrived at Gibraltar, being then on his travels.[18] He dined very frequently at our mess, and made himself extremely agreeable. He was particularly generous. He gave our band ten doubloons (£36 British), on St Patrick's Day, in order that they might enjoy themselves on the occasion. As such a sum of money enabled them to get drunk, morning, noon, and night, for three of four successive weeks after St Patrick's Day, our colonel was greatly annoyed, and attached all the blame to me, as he said that I countenanced the marquis's generosity – or I should have used some endeavours to prevent it. For a full month, it was impossible to tell what tunes the band played, as the men were in a state of continual inebriation.

It was at this time that the marquis, on proceeding up the Mediterranean, got into that unpleasant dispute with the Royal Navy, for which he was brought to trial and sentenced to a confinement in Newgate.[19] It was rather singular that this dispute gave rise to a marriage between the judge who presided at his trial, Sir

17 Harley has got the story mixed up a little. *Général de Division* Armand Philippon was the governor of the fortress of Badajoz during the bloody siege in 1812. When the fortress fell in April 1812, he retired into Fort St Christobal across the river, then surrendered. He was sent to England as a prisoner of war, staying at Oswestry on his parole. In July 1812, he escaped and was smuggled back to France, where Napoleon rewarded him immediately with the command of a division in the I Corps. Harley makes it appear that Philippon had been a prisoner of war before being governor of Badajoz, but this is not true.

18 Howe Peter Browne, 2nd Marquess of Sligo.

19 The Marquess went to Greece and met Lord Elgin there, he loaded his small ship the *Pylades* with ancient treasures. Having problems with his crew, he got a number of Royal Navy sailors drunk and got them on board his ship, where he persuaded them to stay with money and false papers. Pursued, he abandoned them on the Greek Island of Patmos, but the sailors then reported him and he was arrested at Malta and sent to England for trial. He was tried at the Old Bailey in December 1812 by Sir William Scott, who imprisoned him in Newgate for four months with a £5,000 fine. His mother married the judge the day after he was released.

William Scott, Chief Judge of the Admiralty, and the late Marchioness of [Sligo]. She called upon him to endeavour to prevail upon him to mitigate the sentence passed upon her son; and an acquaintance commenced between the parties which, in the course of some time, terminated in their union.[20]

While stationed in Gibraltar, in 1809, a trading vessel arrived from Cork, and brought us a new ensign, but not a young one, named David S[tapleton].[21] He was accompanied by his wife and nine children. To give my readers an adequate description of this cargo is impossible; but let my Irish reader from the south of Ireland figure to himself a poor man, his wife, and large family, following him from village to village. This was precisely the appearance of Ensign Davy S[tapleton], his wife Lucy, and his nine children, coming to inherit the enviable situation of ensign in his Majesty's 47th Regiment of Foot, on the splendid pay of 5*s*.3*d*. per day. Never was there a man so proud of his wife's family as David S[tapleton], she having married him contrary to the wishes of her friends, who had never seen her afterwards. S[tapleton] had been an excise officer, stationed in a distillery near her father's. His constant theme was his wife and her family. You could never offend him, unless you said that she did not belong to the most ancient blood in the south of Ireland. The lady's name was C[arden].[22] Poor S[tapleton]'s first inquiry was for the paymaster, as he had not been overburdened with cash on leaving Cork. He was conducted to my quarters, where he made his appearance, leading in Lucy and his large progeny. I instantly gave him in advance one hundred dollars, and asked him; 'what in the world could tempt you, Mr S[tapleton], to come out to Gibraltar with such a numerous family?' His answer was, 'Sure, sir, I will get plenty of rations for Lucy and the children.' Then, asking me, 'Don't you know Sir John C[raven] C[arden], one of the most distinguished persons in all Ireland, Lucy's brother?' – I said 'no.' Then, said he, 'Yerrow, sir, you know nothing of Ireland when you do not know Sir John C[raven] C[arden], the first family in it.'[23]

In a few days, we got the route for Cadiz, and every one endeavoured to avoid Davy and family, as we were so crowded, having five transports to take the troops. The one I embarked in was the one, unfortunately, that Davy was allotted to; but the moment the young officers saw them come on board, they resolved to remain on deck during the passage, so that Davy, Lucy, and the nine children, had the cabin to themselves, the officers spreading their mattresses on the quarter-deck. It was a small brig we sailed in, and the weather very hot; and, when night came

20 Louisa Catherine Howe, daughter of Lord Howe and widow of John Browne, 1st Marquess of Sligo married William Scott, 1st Baron Stowell.

21 Harley seems to be in slight error here, this was Lieutenant David Stapleton who joined from the 3rd Garrison Battalion in May 1810. Stapleton remained with the regiment until 1817, when he exchanged to half pay in the 41st Foot. He died at Portsea in 1847.

22 Lucinda Carden married David Stapleton at Templemore 3 September 1795.

23 Sir John Craven Carden 1st Bart. of Templemore (c 1758-1820). He was Colonel of the 30th Light Dragoons. Lucinda was not his sister, but a cousin.

on, we were highly amused by S[tapleton]'s account of himself and his marriage, which he was often made to repeat when the time for settling to rest arrived – Mrs S[tapleton] remaining below in full possession of the cabin. Davy had the children on deck with him. He commenced the task of children's maid, first stripping the youngest; and, not being accustomed to the vessel, or rather to save trouble, he made a short cut for himself, by holding a conversation with Lucy through the skylight, of which he raised the glass, and, to save himself trouble, he handed down the children one by one, by the leg or arms, calling out, 'Lucy, here's Paul! – here's Jim!' naming each as he handed them down. This scene afforded much amusement to the young wags on deck, who told Davy they never beheld so fine a family in the course of their lives; all of which Davy firmly believed. They encouraged him to strip the children one by one, but at length seeing him commence with a girl of thirteen or fourteen years of age, and fearing she was to undergo the same process of being put down by the leg or arm, I called him to desist, and begged he would send her down by the cabin door to her mother. I remonstrated with him, and said he ought to leave the management of his children to his wife. He told me, 'you know nothing at all about it, sir, for my wife is sister to Sir John C[raven] C[arden] one of the most distinguished persons in all Ireland; never left her drawing-room until she married me, and knows nothing of dressing or stripping children.

After arriving in Cadiz, the command of the regiment devolved on Colonel B[land], who, with all his faults, had good qualities, too, one of which was a feeling disposition. Upon our representing the state of poor S[tapleton] to him, with his large family, he excused him from regimental duty, and allowed him to act as quarter-master in place of Hagar, who had met with an accident, and was not able to do duty;[24] therefore, Davy S[tapleton] was put in orders as acting quarter-master; but a more unfit person could not have been appointed, for he knew nothing of accounts or returns; and, whether from design or not, drew rations for forty men more than were in the regiment, which surplus remained with himself. His barrack room was a curiosity at St Rock, in Cadiz,[25] hung up all round with pieces of salt pork and beef, and loaves of bread piled up. He took pleasure in showing to anyone his room, telling them, in his Irish accent, 'there is nothing like rations.' I mentioned to him seriously the consequence of drawing for more than we had, and that it was my duty to check his accounts. The sick quarter-master (Hagar) of his own regiment, as well as all the quarter-masters of the different regiments in Cadiz, were enraged; for S[tapleton]'s simplicity exposed the emoluments of their office, which, everyone knows, was one of the best situations in the army at that time. In plain speaking, it was peculation, for he blabbed out everything in the department. I remember, one night particularly, on the piquet

24 Quartermaster John Hagar or Hagger became a lieutenant in the 13th Royal Veteran Battalion in January 1813.

25 Actually San Roque or San Roch.

at Trocadero, outside Cadiz,[26] S[tapleton], urged on by the young officers to relate all his emoluments. They commenced by saying, 'Now, S[tapleton], tell us what you make as acting quarter-master.' He replied, 'Yerrow, Colonel Atchison,[27] it is the finest thing in the entire army; for I am only three months acting, and I have more money than all of yez put together, barring Harley, our pay-master.' 'Well, now S[tapleton], that is a good fellow, how do you make it?' 'Och, boys, ye'z don't understand at all; for sure, faith, it is very easy to add a few men to the return of rations for provisions, and then I have all that's left to myself; and faith, Colonel, honey, I do all this for Lucy and the childer.' To relate the anecdotes that occurred, connected with Davy S[tapleton], would fill a volume. The guards and many other officers, from his simple manner and large family, were very kind to him, and often ordered their rations to his barrack room. The subject and object nearest to his heart, were Lucy, the children, and rations. After one of the evenings spent in this way at the out-lying piquets, two of the young fellows went away before S[tapleton], but, having arranged their plan, they procured a bladder, and filled it either with shot or small stones, fastened it on the top of a long pole, and lay in wait under the porches of the bomb proof of the barracks of St Helena, where S[tapleton]'s quarters were.[28] He had not proceeded far under the bomb proof, when he was struck with the bladder on the head, not knowing what it was, nor one word from them, S[tapleton] crying out, 'What is this for? What can it mean?' A voice answered, in a hollow tone, 'I am a dead soldier, and you cheated me of my rations'. 'Oh, Lord!' ejaculated S[tapleton], while the bladder was rattling away at his head, his hat being knocked off. Let my readers figure to themselves a dreary passage not unlike the Thames tunnel,[29] without light – for the Spaniards neglected lighting it. S[tapleton], fully convinced that he was attacked by an apparition of one of the deceased men whom he had cheated of rations, again roared out, 'Oh! How long is this to last?' when Lieutenant Harper,[30] in a dark corner of the passage, and with a hollow voice (Captain Wainright still laying on with the bladder as quickly as possible),[31] exclaimed, 'one hour,' S[tapleton] called out, 'Och, poor Davy S[tapleton], you will be made mortar of!' The young fellows could stand it no longer, and made off. Davy returned to Lucy to relate his story, without his hat.

As soon as Mr Hagar recovered, he resumed his own department, and S[tapleton] was appointed acting paymaster to a corps of newly raised foreigners, who were

26 El Trocadero faces across the harbour from the City of Cadiz.

27 This would appear to be Ensign John Atherton, who became a lieutenant in June 1811. At Cadiz he was on command with the German recruits.

28 Santa Elena, Cadiz.

29 The Thames Tunnel from Wapping to Rotherhithe was built by Isambard Kingdom Brunel between 1828 and 1843.

30 The only Harper in the 47th was Surgeon William Harper.

31 Lieutenant Henry Wainright, 47th Foot.

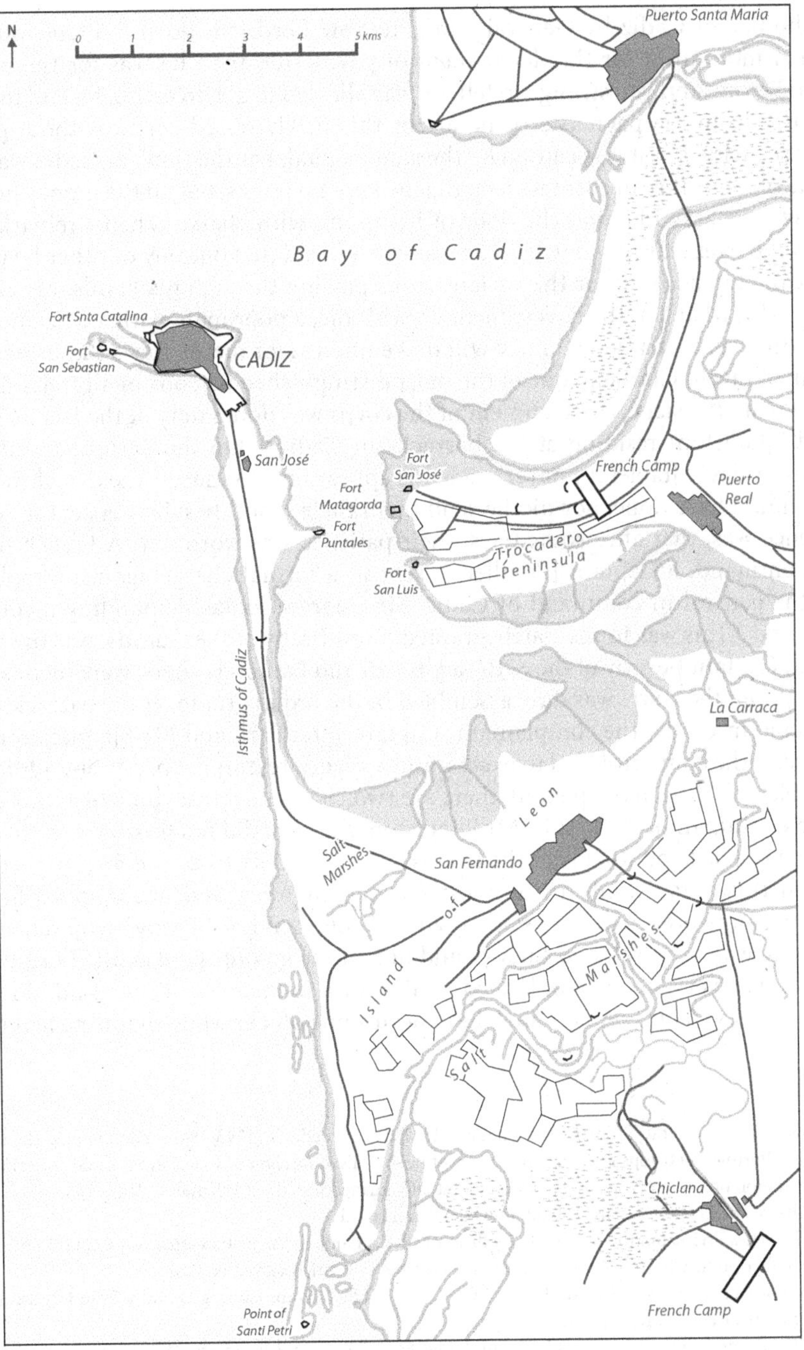

Map 4 Cadiz and environs during the siege. (George Anderson)

embodied at Cadiz by General Graham, now Lord Lynedoch.[32] S[tapleton] was much more unfit for the department of paymaster, than he was for the one he held before, and yet, strange to tell, he was allowed to act, to estimate, and to draw money from the paymaster-general, for this newly raised corps, without giving any security; but it was caused by the state of affairs at the time, as Cadiz was in a state of siege. It is an absolute fact, that he kept no books, but all the money he paid away he marked behind the door of his room, with chalk. When I remarked to him the irregular way in which he was acting, and that one day or other he would be called to account for the various sums passing through his hands, his answer was, 'Oh, what can the government do with me, a poor man, with a wife and nine children; and, at any rate, Lucy will make interest for me, as she is the sister to Sir John C[raven] C[arden], one of the most distinguished persons in all Ireland.'

During the siege, a detachment of the corps was doing duty at the Isla de Leon, and S[tapleton] residing at the barracks in Cadiz.[33] On the 24th of the month (muster day) S[tapleton] never made his appearance to muster the detachment as he should have done, nor did he send them their monthly subsistence; the consequence was, that after some days, their patience was worn out. A French officer in command, a Captain [Freuller],[34] sent in a formal charge against S[tapleton] to the general in command of Cadiz, Sir George Cooke, demanding a court of inquiry.[35] This was immediately granted: Lord Proby of the Guards, was the president, Captain Beverly of the 67th Regiment, and I among others, were members of it.[36] When the court was duly assembled in the orderly room, at the barracks of St Helena, in Cadiz, the complainant, Captain [Freuller], and Mr S[tapleton] being present, the court crowded to excess, and a silence reigning, Lord Proby addressed S[tapleton] 'Ensign S[tapleton], there are two charges against you which this court is to enquire into; the first is, Mr S[tapleton, that you did not go down on the 24th to the Isla de Leon to muster the troops (as is your duty to do) of foreign recruits.' Upon this, S[tapleton], in the most familiar manner, and unconscious he was guilty of any breach of duty said, 'I will tell you then Lord Proby – you remember the day was very wet, and Lucy would not let me go out there at all.' Lord Proby, who was a very stern man, looked at him for a moment, and then said, 'Pray sir who is Lucy?' conceiving it must have been some officer whose name he had made

32 Lieutenant General Thomas Graham, later 1st Baron Lynedoch (1748-1843), commanded the British and Portuguese troops at Cadiz. The 'corps of newly-raised foreigners' in question would appear to be a battalion of foreign deserters who were eventually formed into the 8th Battalion 60th Foot.

33 The Isla de Leon is the large island on which Cadiz stands.

34 He writes Freire, but the only French officer of such a name in the British army was Captain Fridolin de Freuller of the Chasseurs Britanniques, a detachment of which served on Cadiz.

35 Major General George Cooke, 1st Foot Guards, was officer commanding at Cadiz from July 1811- July 1813 in succession to Graham.

36 Lieutenant Colonel John, Lord Proby of the 1st Foot Guards and Paymaster William Beverley 67th Foot (who would be ranked as a captain in the Army).

use of, by way of subterfuge. S[tapleton] looked in his turn amazed, and replied, 'Why don't know Lord Proby, sure she is my wife, and sister to Sir John C[raven] C[arden], one of the most distinguished persons in all Ireland.' Lord Proby, who seldom laughed, could not refrain from smiling, and the members, as well as the bystanders, were convulsed with laughter; S[tapleton] was quite satisfied with himself, and convinced he gave a very satisfactory answer. The next charge against him was for not paying Captain [Freuller] and the detachment, and Lord Proby again addressed him. 'Mr S[tapleton], the second charge against you is a very serious one; what is the reason you did not pay Captain [Freuller] his own pay, or that of his detachment, when it became due on the 25th, but left them without subsistence for several days, although you had drawn it from the military chest, per your estimate?' S[tapleton] seemed much puzzled at this question, but soon recovered himself. He looked in a friendly manner at the president, and in a confidential tone replied, 'Yerren my dear Lord Proby, I will tell you the reason; there is no such thing as depending on these foreigners, and I was afraid he would run away with the money at night, and go over to his countrymen the French, that you know are over the other side of the bay, under that great general they call Soult, who they say is the greatest devil in the whole French army; don't you think this a good reason my Lord Proby, and faith and troth I know you do?' To picture the rage of Captain [Freuller] when his honour was doubted, would be impossible, for he was strict on that point. He stood up, but from passion and excited feelings, he could not utter one word. The court was highly amused at this scene, and Davy quite satisfied with himself that he had given an admirable answer. At this moment, I thought it better to interfere for him, for I saw the cloud gathering on the brow of Lord Proby, and feared the result for the unfortunate fellow; I begged of Captain [Freuller] to listen to what I had to propose, and hoped he would abide by it; I then offered that Captain Beverly and I, as two paymasters, should settle the abstract of accounts, and pay him and his detachment the arrears and usual subsistence that day, upon which Captain [Freuller] generously withdrew his charge, and we adjourned to my quarters, and soon made up the accounts and settled the matter.

This battalion was soon disbanded[37], and, as may be expected, Davy was a considerable defaulter; no wonder he should be, for when he brought home his estimate, he opened the bags of dollars, and flung them into a box without lock or key, saying 'who ever thought Davy S[tapleton] you would have so much money to look at?' there he left them to the mercy of children and servants.

Davy's appearance, on leaving Cadiz, was the most extraordinary; the wagon that moved his baggage, one of the largest size, drawn by eight mules, was loaded with monkeys, birds, dogs, and everything that he could meet with, for he indulged his children to excess, and gave them everything they fancied.

37 He talks here of this foreign battalion.

In 1815, at Chelmsford, in Essex, the second battalion was embodied temporarily.[38] S[tapleton] was with them, and, after the Battle of Waterloo he with many others, was placed on the half-pay. He came up to London, and nothing would convince him but that the agents Greenwood and Cox were in his debt, and owed him sixty pounds.[39] On applying to them, they repeatedly told S[tapleton] that there was no balance due, but that he was in their debt. He repaired to the Duke of York to the Horse Guards, and asked for an audience, which was granted; the duke no doubt was surprised at his singular appearance and manners. S[tapleton] commenced by telling the duke 'may it please your Royal Highness, I am come to make a complaint of them Greenwoods and Cox, who won't pay me £60 that they owe me.' The Duke replied to him that 'he was certain Messrs. Greenwood and Cox would act with justice, and pay him what was due to him.' On this, S[tapleton] returned to the office again, but this verbal message had no effect upon them, although he told them he came from their master. Back again he went, and, without ceremony, walked into the duke's apartments, and addressed him saying, 'I can get no good of them Greenwoods, but your Royal Highness, if you will give me a little bit of paper under your hand, they can't refuse me.' The good natured duke, in fits of laughter, gave him a bit of paper as Davy said, ordering him to be paid: with this he returned quickly to Greenwood and Cox's exulting, and instantly received the £60, which the poor fellow was robbed of that evening in passing up a crowded part of the Strand. What became of this extraordinary man afterwards, I could never learn.

Duelling was unfortunately very prevalent at Gibraltar when we were there. One took place at that period between Lieutenant Montfort of our regiment, who had but lately joined us, and a Lieutenant Heaviside of the 30th.[40] The quarrel originated in some very trifling dispute on the Land Port guard, which could have been easily settled to the satisfaction of both parties.[41] But the breach having been widened by a certain lieutenant whom we unluckily had in our regiment, nothing would satisfy unfortunate Montfort's mistaken ideas of honour but a hostile meeting, although he was unconsciously the aggressor.

He, accordingly, solicited a young ensign of the name of [Scott], an ignorant young man, who had just joined us, to be his friend on the occasion – a man totally inexperienced in such matters, which, if they must take place, require a person of prudence, courage, temper, and, above all, experience to conduct them.[42]

38 I can discover no evidence that the 2nd Battalion was officially ordered to reform in 1815, but a number of officers on half pay may well have been recalled and recruiting recommenced.

39 Greenwood, Cox & Hammersley, Army Agents, of Craig's Court, London.

40 Lieutenant Lewis Montfort exchanged into the 47th Foot and died before March 1810; the other party was Lieutenant Richard Heaviside of the 30th Foot.

41 The Land Port was the only land gate entrance into Gibraltar from Spain and was heavily guarded at all times.

42 Lieutenant William Scott of the 47th Foot, who responded at the eventual court martial 'I claim the protection of the court, I can't answer that question without committing myself'.

The result, as may be well supposed, when such a second was concerned, was fatal to one of the parties. They were allowed to fire five shots at each other; and, at the last discharge, poor Montfort fell, being killed upon the spot. As Heaviside was not to be blamed in the affair, he was honourably acquitted, after standing his trial; and I am convinced that no one could more sincerely regret that he should have become the unfortunate instrument of depriving a fellow-creature of his life.[43]

As we all knew that, though Heaviside was the instrument, Lieutenant [Rumley] was the cause of Montfort's death, the latter became the object of general aversion.[44] We were all, therefore, most anxious to get rid of him. An opportunity seeming to present itself in a short time after the fatal occurrence, the colonel who commanded the regiment, brought Lieutenant [Rumley] to a court martial for disobedience of orders, in wearing his hat contrary to the instructions of his commanding officer. Though this was a trifling deviation from military discipline, and one that would have been overlooked, had any other person been in question. The colonel persevered in bringing forward his charge, and, most unfortunately for himself; for, on the cross-examination of the witnesses, his character and conduct appeared in such a light, that he was obliged to retire from the service, in which he had spent above thirty years, and in consequence of which he fretted so much that he died soon after of a broken heart.[45] However, Lieutenant [Rumley] did not escape, as he was sentenced to be placed on the half-pay list.[46]

We left Gibraltar for Cadiz, in 1810 [1811],[47] where a most deplorable event occurred shortly after we reached it, which threw a general gloom over our society. Lieutenant Daniel of the 30th, with whom I was on intimate terms, left Cadiz with his wife, an amiable and interesting young woman, and five as fine children as I ever saw, with the intention of joining his regiment, then in Lisbon.[48] It unfortunately happened that, after sailing out of the bay of Cadiz, they were obliged to move out of one transport into another. Daniel preceded his family in a separate boat to prepare for their reception on board. The boat in which Mrs Daniel and her children left the transport was, in a sudden squall, upset, and, melancholy to relate, every person on board perished. Poor Daniel, on learning the fatal tidings, returned to Cadiz in a state of complete distraction at the grievous loss he had sustained, being devotedly attached to his family.

43 A Court Martial held on 20 December 1809 at Gibraltar heard that Heaviside had murdered Lieutenant Lewis Montfort in a duel at Fort Barbara in Spain. He was acquitted.

44 Lieutenant John Rumley 30th Foot likewise responded at the court martial 'I claim the protection of the court, I can't answer that question without committing myself'.

45 This must refer to Lieutenant Colonel William Wardrobe who retired on 3 May 1810 and died in October 1812.

46 Harley is wrong, he remained with the regiment.

47 Part of the battalion actually sailed to Cadiz in the summer of 1811 (Harley mistakes the year), the flank companies having been at Tarifa and then Barossa.

48 Ensign Robert Daniel became a lieutenant in July 1811.

He arrived at the barrack gate late in the night; and, as he was not of course expected, his sudden appearance at such an hour, surprised and alarmed us very much, although at the time we had no idea of the fatal event that caused his return. He was at first unable to answer our enquiries; and it was some time before we could learn from him the particulars of the distressing occurrence. We all did everything in our power to abate the violence of his grief, but in vain. He could not for a moment be persuaded to be reconciled to his affliction, and, after suffering agony of mind to which death would have been far preferable, he left us again, in a few days, on his way to join his regiment, but in such a state of despondency as made us apprehend that he could not long survive the loss of his family.

The plague now broke out in Cadiz with such extreme violence, that from one hundred and fifty to two hundred of the miserable inhabitants were interred daily. Nor did we escape – for we lost in two days a very fine young man, Lieutenant Clarke,[49] a sergeant-major, and ten of our best men. It pleased providence, however, to moderate the violence of the visitation in a short time, so that, in a few days, the mortality was considerable lessened.

In Cadiz, I had the pleasure of being acquainted with the late Sir James Duff, his Majesty's consul at the port – one of the most amiable men that ever lived.[50] During my stay in that city, I was frequently entertained at his hospitable table; and he was pleased to be, on all occasions, particularly kind and attentive to me.

I never can forget the first day I dined with him. When taking my leave that evening, he addressed me in the drawing room, and said, 'I have invited you to dine here to-day, but I will not do so in future – you will find dinner here on the table every day at four o'clock, and you shall have a hearty welcome; I shall, therefore, expect the pleasure of your company any day that you are disengaged, while you remain here.' As a proof of his hospitality, I need only mention, that he had covers laid, and chairs placed every day to the number of thirty, few of which I have seldom seen unoccupied.

At this time, he had been a resident in Spain upwards of forty years; during which period, on a war breaking out with England, he was preparing to leave it as a British subject and his majesty's consul; but the inhabitants, one and all, rich and poor, had such a regard for him, that they surrounded his house and would not allow him to depart, assuring him that they would all sooner lose their lives than that a hair of his head be injured. They even memorialised the Spanish government to entreat of him to remain – that the poor of the city might not be deprived of their father, nor the rich of their friend.

49 Lieutenant Samuel Clarke, 47th Foot, died at Cadiz in November 1810.

50 Sir James Duff 1st Baronet, Consul at Cadiz, died in 1815.

Sir James was a staunch royalist, and held the French in utter detestation. He was a zealous adherent of Ferdinand the Seventh, and his first toast after dinner every day, was the health of 'Fernando Septimo, and a downfall to his enemies.'[51]

I never saw his temper ruffled but once, and that was when an Englishman who was dining with us, a stranger, introduced by some friend, gave expression to some disrespectful sentiments against Ferdinand. He told him he wished to dispense with his company in future.

I well recollect the magnanimity of character and goodness of heart displayed by this kind old man on another occasion. Two young gentlemen arrived from England, and called at the consulate office to lodge their passports and pay their respects to the consul. As was his usual habit, he invited them to dinner – although they were perfect strangers to him. While taking our wine after dinner, Sir James conversed with his new guests in his wonted affable manner. Being again informed of their names, which in the hurry of business he had forgotten, in the morning, he inquired if they knew a person of that name in such a part of England: they replied that they did, and that he was their father. 'What,' said he, 'are you really sons of that gentleman?' They answered, 'indeed we are.' Sir James, then looking earnestly for a moment at the vice-consul, Mr Archdeacon, who sat at the foot of the table, turned to the young gentlemen, and said, 'you must both dine with me to-morrow again, and, if I can render you any service, you may command me freely.' When they had taken their departure, what was my surprise, when the vice-consul told me, that during the long life of Sir James Duff, who was then between seventy and eighty years of age, he had not an enemy except one, and that was the father of those young men – who had injured him in every possible way, and had unjustly deprived him, under the semblance of law, of property to the amount of several thousands!

While we were in Cadiz, the commissary who had charge of that station, was a Mr [O'Meara],[52] who manifested the most overbearing pride and extravagance – not deigning to entertain anyone under the rank of a field officer, though he was said to be the son of a person moving in a very humble station in life, and to have actually been a billiard marker, himself. But, having married into a respectable family, there was interest made to procure him a situation in the Commissariat department.

An Irishman residing in Cadiz, proposed to the commissary for a contract to supply the army with bread; and, having obtained a promise of a preference, he entered upon the necessary arrangements – purchasing flour, &c, but, after a few

51 King Ferdinand VII 'The Desired' was proclaimed King of Spain in 1808 but Napoleon forced him to abdicate so as to put his own brother Joseph on the throne. Spain rose in revolt and Ferdinand was reinstated at the end of the Peninsular War, ruling from 1813 until 1833.

52 Deputy Commissary General Matthew Delaval O'Meara.

days, learned to his astonishment, that the contract which had been promised to him, was given on the same terms to another person.

As the poor man had no redress in Cadiz for the expense and inconvenience to which he had been put, he adopted the following mode, at least, of revenge. He wrote to the Lords of the Treasury an account in the shape of an account current – on one side of which he enumerated the daily expenses of the commissary, and, on the other, his daily allowance – to show that his income was unable to support the extravagance in which he lived.

Commissary Debit	*£. s. d.*
To six mules and three carriages	2 5 0
To a country	0 10 0
To three servants	0 10 0
To – bottles of Champagne	7 10 0
To a house in Cadiz	1 0 0
To three Spanish ladies	7 0 0
Expenditure	**18 15 0**
Commissary Credit	
By Commissary's pay	2 0 0
By allowances	0 10 0
Income	2 10 0
Balance in favour of Expenses	**16 5 0**

'Query, my lords,' said the writer, 'how comes the difference, or what fund, may I ask, supplies the overplus in the daily expenses of the commissary, amounting to no less than £*16 5s.* per day more than his pay and allowance?' after the foregoing statement was sent to government, he was suspended; an investigation took place, and he was honourably acquitted. I mention this in justice to Mr [O'Meara]. It must be confessed that the contractor adopted a singular and ingenious mode of obtaining, if not redress, at least revenge, for the loss he had sustained by the commissary's breach of promise.

In 1810 [1811], the country between Cadiz and Malaga was infested by a numerous banditti, the commander of which was a well-known robber, and considered to be the cleverest fellow in his profession through the whole continent. I happened to dine about that time at a commercial house, in company with a Spanish merchant, Don Thomas Lopez, who informed us that on the following morning he intended travelling from Cadiz to Algeciras, on his journey to Malaga. The chances of his being robbed by some of the banditti, who were known to be constantly prowling about the different roads, were mentioned to him; but he said it was impossible, as he was well mounted and armed, and would have a good look out, and let no suspicious looking person approach him.

He left Cadiz early on the following morning on his intended journey. In the course of the day, as he travelled over the plain between Barossa and Tarifa, he overtook a peasant slowly limping before him, in a ragged and apparently destitute state. Upon Don Thomas bidding him good morning, he humbly returned his salute, asking him at the same time for alms. He then, pointing to a bush at the side of the road, said, in an under tone of voice, 'I see a fine hare, sir, under that bush;' and, on Don Thomas looking for it in vain, 'Oh, sir,' said he, 'there are two of them in it; you ought to take a shot at them; they are both sitting under the middle of the bush.' 'As you are on foot,' replied the merchant, 'you can kill them easier than I can, as I don't like the trouble of dismounting,' handing the peasant his firelock, which was loaded with two balls. No sooner had the fellow got it into his possession than he presented it at him, demanding his money, and telling him that he was the well-known commander of the banditti. True enough, upon his giving a whistle, some of his party came up and deprived him of horse, money, and arms, leaving Don Thomas Lopez to find the best of his way back to Cadiz on foot, heartily tired and quite ashamed of being so easily robbed.

We had an officer, a Lieutenant [Butler] of the 47th Regiment, who, I must confess, little merits the name of a British officer, and, I trust, for the honour of our service, there are not many like him in it; nay, I should hope not one. He joined us during the siege of Cadiz, and, from the moment he made his appearance there, he was most zealous in his carefulness of his own person. Whenever it came to his turn of night-piquets, he contrived to exchange his duty with some of the young officers, and, on the 47th embarking for Tarragona, where it was expected there would be some hard fighting, he managed so as to be left in charge of the baggage behind, until the return of the regiment once more to Cadiz. As a very great proof of his *modesty* at this time, he asked General Graham, the present Lord Lynedoch, to recommend him to be a captain of a troop of dragoons, a service he said he was very partial to; when the general, not a little surprised at his presumption at making the request, he being only a lieutenant in the 47th Foot, coolly answered him, and asked him 'Is that *all* you require, Mr [Butler]?' On the advance afterwards, to join the main army, he feigned illness at Talavera, where I found him in bed in his billet, covered up in his blankets, his servant telling me at the door, 'Sure enough, Captain Harley, the master is not sick at all; make him get up and go to his regiment.' I, accordingly, advised him to come and join. He pleaded illness, and it was in vain I urged the point with him, his servant entered the room, and I was not astonished, after what he had just said to me, to hear him saying he would 'no longer remain with him, but go forward and join his comrades in action, for sure enough you are not ill at all, master,' said he. He then put on his knapsack, took his fire-lock, and marched on and joined his regiment near Madrid. I therefore left Lieutenant [Butler] at Talavera, and the next account I heard of him was, his having got into a bullock-cart, with Sir Hugh

Gough[53] and some wounded officers going to the rear, and arriving at Santarem, where he took up his quarters, and remained until after the battle of Vitoria, and the siege of San Sabastian. He never joined until a little before the regiment was going to embark for England, the war being then over. This officer always took care to speak more of fighting than any other in the army. He made such a pitiful representation to the secretary of the Patriotic Fund at Lloyd's, that he succeeded in obtaining a sum of money in considerations of his wounds. Lieutenant Robert Cochrane and I called the next day,[54] in behalf of a poor sergeant's wife, at the office, and, on mentioning the regiment, 47th, the secretary, Mr Welsford,[55] told us of the poor wounded officer of that regiment, whom he had paid that morning. Upon this, Cochrane told Mr Welsford, 'more undeserved money you never paid, sir, as Mr [Butler] had never received a wound in a battle in his life.'[56]

We had another officer in our regiment, Lieutenant Thomas Shortt, a perfect contrast to [Butler]; this was indeed a brave fellow, and generally beloved. He got severely wounded at Vitoria, and had to go to the hospital. Never was I so astonished as at meeting him not cured of his wound, and limping along into Hernani.[57] I asked him for God's sake, what brought him out of the hospital, and begged he would return. He told me he was resolved to join his regiment then, in front of San Sebastian, and preparing to storm next morning. He congratulated himself that he had been up in time, and then said to me, 'Do you suppose, Harley, for a moment, from what you know of me, that I want to act like [Butler]?' I conveyed him that evening a little out of town; but fate decreed I should never see him more; for this brave fellow was blown up next morning in the same mine with Sir Richard Fletcher,[58] of the engineers. Lieutenant Shortt was brother to Surgeon Shortt, of the 79th Regiment.[59]

We were suddenly ordered from Cadiz at an hour's notice, in June 1810[1811], to the relief of Tarragona, then closely besieged by the French under General

53 Brevet Lieutenant Colonel Hugh Gough of the 87th Foot.

54 Lieutenant Robert Cochrane served in the Peninsula from January 1812 to January 1814 and became a Military Knight of Windsor 1864-78.

55 Mr J.P. Welsford was Secretary of the Patriotic Fund.

56 The only lieutenant to receive a pension for wounds from the 47th Foot in the '*Return of the Names of the Officers in the Army who receive pensions*' published in 1818 is Lieutenant Robert Butler, who exchanged from the 23rd Foot in June 1812 and therefore would fit the dates for Harley's story. He received a pension of £70 per annum from October 1814, for wounds received at the Bidassoa, although strangely, this is recorded as happening in 1812 not in 1813. The Challis list does record him as present at San Sebastian and Bidassoa, but the Casualty Return for the Bidassoa shows no officer casualties in the 47th Foot at all.

57 Four miles south of San Sebastian.

58 Lieutenant Colonel Richard Fletcher Royal Engineers was killed during the storming of San Sebastian on 31 July 1813.

59 Lieutenant Thomas Spunner Shortt was slightly wounded at Vitoria and was killed at San Sebastian. Assistant Surgeon John Shortt of the 47th Foot had become a local Staff Surgeon in the Peninsula and later joined the 79th Foot.

Suchet.[60] As the transports sailed with our regiments before I had time to embark, I should have been left behind, had I not fortunately obtained a passage on board the *Milford*, of 84 guns, commanded by Admiral Sir Richard Keats, the present venerable governor of Greenwich Hospital.[61] I found myself in a new world on board this magnificent ship, manned by 700 men, with her full proportion of marines. I own I was surprised at the regularity observed where there were so many human beings enclosed in a comparatively small place. The most perfect discipline appeared to prevail on board, and there was a ready obedience on the part of the men, exacted not by fear, but by respect for their officers, all of whom, including Captain Kittoe himself, were unremitting in their attention to me.[62]

It was now July, and my readers may form some idea of the pleasure of sailing up the Mediterranean at that season of the year, in fine weather, and in such a splendid ship. Proud as I have always been of my country, I had no idea of the glory of Britain until I beheld the ships of all nations paying the customary respect to the British flag, as they passed, and acknowledging us masters of the sea, while we sailed smoothly along scarcely deigning to notice them, the band playing the most enlivening airs, and the admiral's flag floating triumphantly in the breeze at the main mast head.

As we approached Cartagena, early in the morning, we gave the garrison a salute which was immediately returned with a discharge of twenty-one guns. The first shot from us was fired close to my head. As I was ignorant of the cause, I jumped out of the cot, in which I lay, in considerable alarm, to the great amusement of the blue jackets.

Captain Fothergill, who was now residing in Dublin, patriotically exerting himself for the good of his country, commanded the marines on board, and was particularly attentive to me, obtaining a cabin for me for my own exclusive use.[63]

Our expedition was unfortunately too late. The preparations for storming Tarragona were completed before our appearance, which only hastened the attack; and, before we could land a man, Suchet took the town by storm.

His cruelties were beyond description, and even his name was so dreaded in that country, that wherever he marched, the wretched, though peaceable inhabitants, fled with precipitation before him, through fear of falling into his hands.

At Tarragona, several of them made to the sea-shore, and, endeavouring to reach our ships by swimming, unfortunately perished in the attempt, though we sent boats out to pick them up.

60 *Général de Division* Louis Gabriel Suchet became a marshal following the siege of Tarragona.

61 Admiral Sir Richard Keats (1757-1834)

62 Captain Edward Kittoe, commanding HMS *Milford* (of 74 guns, not Harley's 84), which was stationed at Cadiz.

63 This refers to Captain Thomas Fothergill of the 10th Foot who had served on Jersey and Gibraltar in 1810. As to how Fothergill happened to be on board, it could only be as another passenger, if Harley has remembered correctly – there was no Marine officer of that name.

As we were too late to be of any service to the patriotic Spaniards who defended Tarragona so bravely, we returned to Cadiz, quite disappointed and out of temper with our fruitless expedition, and because we had no opportunity of assisting our friends and foiling the atrocious Suchet.

9

Cadiz and Tarifa[1]

On our return to Cadiz from Tarragona, I became acquainted with a singular character, Captain M[ellish] of the Royal Waggon Train, whose history is so remarkable, that I will give it to my readers.[2] Captain M[ellish] first entered into my life as a banker in London, but, as the firm to which he belonged either stopped payment or dissolved their partnership, he entered the army as an ensign, and, after some little time, obtained a company in the 1st or Royal Regiment of Foot. He was then an uncommonly handsome young fellow, and generally liked as he was generous to a fault. Unfortunately for himself, he was extremely attached to the fair sex, who were so captivated with his appearance, that they were seldom able to resist his importunities, for he did not hesitate to propose to unite himself to any girl to whom he took a fancy. He took care, however, to have every marriage a secret, and made some plausible excuse to each wife for not wishing her to join him at the regiment. Being sent with a detachment to Londonderry, in the north of Ireland, he fell in love with a young lady of respectable family and accomplished manners, whom he made his *fourth* wife, after a short acquaintance, having left three behind him in different parts of England.

In consequence of some unpleasant circumstance, he was obliged to leave the Royals, and, entering the Waggon-Train, or artillery-drivers, embarked with a detachment of his corps, for the peninsula. His sudden departure, and the manner in which he had taken leave of his Irish wife, exciting suspicion, prompt and particular inquiries were set on foot; and it was discovered by her family, that he had three other wives living; and, being determined not to submit tamely to such infamous conduct, they resolved to institute a prosecution against him the first opportunity. Accordingly, on his return to London, at the conclusion of the war, he was arrested while at dinner at Long's in Bond-Street,[3] tried by the Old Bailey, and sentenced to transportation.

1 This is the beginning of Volume 2 in the original.

2 Actually Lieutenant William Mellish of the Royal Waggon Train; he went on half pay in 1815.

3 Long's Hotel in Bond Street was still going at the turn of the twentieth century.

The only party who prosecuted him, was the brother of the Irish lady in Londonderry, who, before the trial commenced, addressing the judge and jury, told them, that though three English families were pleased to pass over Captain M[ellish]'s conduct, he should, in vindication of his sister, and in justice to his own honour, prosecute the offender to the utmost of his power.

As his term of transportation had long since expired, I was in some surprise at his not coming home, until I learned lately that he has a good situation in New South Wales, where he makes a conspicuous figure, and has, therefore, no wish to return.

Among M[ellish], faults, there was one completely derogatory to any person bearing the character of a gentleman, – he had a great propensity to draw the long bow, or, in plainer language, to tell *lies*. When he was in the Royals, His late Royal Highness the Duke of Kent, the colonel of the regiment, was particularly kind and partial to him, until he discovered, by the merest chance, that he did not always adhere to the truth. M[ellish], meeting an old general officer named Coghlan,[4] with whom he had been acquainted in London, invited him to dine with him at his residence in Burton-Street, Berkeley-Square, and treated him to some very superior Madeira at dinner. The general remarked that it was the finest wine of the description that he had ever tasted, and asked him from what merchant he had procured it. 'Oh!' said M[ellish], in his usual vain manner; 'it ought to be the best, for it is a present I have just received from my friend, the Duke of Kent, who is one of the most good-natured men in the world. I generally dine with him two or three days in the week at Kensington Palace; and having made a remark, the last evening I spent with him, on the excellence of his Madeira, judge of my surprise, on leaving the palace and entering my carriage, to find a large hamper of Madeira, which the butler had placed there, by the duke's orders.'

In a few days after, the general paid a visit to His Royal Highness, and was invited to dinner. The duke asked him in the course of the evening, as soon as the cloth was removed, what wine he would take. The general replied Madeira, as he had never tasted finer than some which His Royal Highness had made a present of to Captain M[ellish], on one occasion that he dined with him. 'What!' said the duke, 'M[ellish] of the Royals? *I* make a present of wine to *him, he dines with me.* He never tasted a drop of wine out of my cellar, nor has he ever sat at my table.' From that moment, the Duke never took the slightest notice of M[ellish], though he had been previously rather a favourite, so great was His Royal Highness' abhorrence of anything bordering on an untruth.

Some short time before I met M[ellish], he was ordered from Woolwich to Cadiz with a detachment of the Waggon-Train. The transport, in which he embarked with his men, being obliged to put into Portsmouth for a few days, in consequence of contrary winds, M[ellish], took advantage of the circumstance, and, although

4 Major General Roger Coghlan.

the only officer on board, went on shore to amuse himself, while the vessel was detained in the harbour.

As he was sitting alone after dinner at the George Inn,[5] where he intended remaining during his stay, a gentleman arrived, accompanied by several servants, and all the other *et ceteras* of a man of rank and fashion, and, addressing M[ellish], asked him if he knew any ship bound for the Peninsula, or any part of Spain, as he was most anxious to go there to see the theatre of war, many private gentlemen being at that time in the habit of going out as amateurs to witness the operations of the contending armies.

M[ellish] gave rather an evasive answer until he had enquired from the landlord who his new acquaintance might be, and found, to his agreeable surprise, that he was no other than Lord Hawke,[6] who was going to Spain with an abundance of supplies of every description for a twelve-month's absence, taking with him a splendid new curricle, and four beautiful horses, worth at least one hundred guineas; two livery servants and a groom; hampers of teas, sugars, hams, tongues, bottled porter, and even Devonshire cream. He had, in fact, every luxury to which he had been accustomed in this country, and which could not be easily procured in Spain; besides plenty of the best French wines; – such as champagne, Burgundy, &c.

As M[ellish] to use a vulgar phrase, had been run out of elbows in London, and was provided with a very slender stock, he saw at once that such a companion as Lord Hawke would be a great accommodation to him. Assuming, therefore, an air of great importance, he told his lordship, in course of conversation, that he commanded an ordnance ship then ready for sea, and bound to Cadiz; and that, from the pleasure he had already experienced in his society, he should feel most happy in giving his lordship a passage for himself and his suite free of any expense; but that they must prepare to embark immediately, adding, that he would go down and give the necessary orders.

Lord Hawke instantly accepted the offer made to him, returning thanks to Captain M[ellish] for his great kindness, while the latter hastened down to the ship, and, although only a passenger himself, prevailed upon the master of the ship not only to receive Lord Hawke, suite, and luggage, &c. on board without any charge, but also to allow M[ellish] himself to appear as the commander of the vessel; and so expeditious was M[ellish] in his arrangements, and so eager to secure such a valuable prize, that he contrived to have everything belonging to Lord Hawke shipped the same evening, including servants, curricle, horses, &c. &c.

The next morning, however, an order unexpectedly arrived from London for Lord Hawke, requiring his immediate attendance before the High Court of

5 The George Hotel in Queen Street Portsmouth was established in 1784 and still exists today.

6 This must be Edward Harvey-Hawke, 3rd Baron Hawke. The reason for his failing to sail might have been illness, as he died 22 August 1810. It cannot be his son Edward William, who succeeded him, as he was then only ten years old.

Chancery, on some very important business that was to be brought forward on the following day. He was, therefore, obliged to set off, at an hour's notice, stating that he would be back at Portsmouth within three days, and requesting M[ellish] to wait that time for him, with which of course, he promised to comply.

But as the wind changed in their favour, and a fair breeze sprung up in the evening, the master of the vessel weighed anchor, and set sail for Cadiz, before Lord Hawke had time to reach London; and M[ellish] thus found himself in possession of his lordship's servants, horses, carriages, baggage, and also about £100 worth of Spanish money, which Lord Hawke had given into his charge on the departure for London.

M[ellish]'s, predominant passion was vanity; and, as he had the materials now, he determined upon playing the great man, and to make such use of Lord Hawke's property, as would make every person think that he was himself the real proprietor; having, as a preliminary step, prevailed upon his lordship's servants, – no difficult matter where a douceur was in question,[7] – to call him master, and not to pretend to know that there was any such being in existence as Lord Hawke.

I shall never forget seeing M[ellish] in his lordship's curricle, with his two outriders, driving ladies about, paying and returning visits, and distributing cards of invitation. He frequently invited me to dinner, with many others of the garrison, and I must confess we certainly enjoyed, and did ample justice to the good things of old England, which were displayed upon his table in ridiculous profusion.

As M[ellish] was as hospitable a man as ever lived, and had many acquaintances in the army, whom he was fond of seeing at his table, the stock of provisions, abundant as it was, could not last very long. It had not, however, been many days exhausted, when we were ordered from Cadiz, on our leaving which, the curricle was detained for expenses, and also two of the horses, and the other two died on our route, in consequence of want of forage.

I subsequently met two of the servants at Truxillo in a very deplorable condition; the rainy season just setting in, and the poor fellows without a sole to their boots, following in the rear of the army. On recognizing them, I gave them such assistance as I could afford, and advised them to go to the nearest sea-port town and endeavour to obtain a passage to England, and pointing out to them the road to Bilbao and giving them a letter to the British Consul there, requesting him to procure the unfortunate men a passage home.

I met M[ellish] about the conclusion of the war, in the south of France, at St Jean de Luz, but very much altered, except in one particular. He had married another wife, a Spanish lady, and had some of her friends living with him, who were all ignorant of his numerous engagements; and he could have been but a very short time united to her, when he returned to London, and, as before mentioned, was

7 Douceur: a bribe.

prosecuted and sent beyond the seas, where in all probability, he has married again.[8]

From Cadiz, we proceeded to the Isla de Leon, about eight miles from it, where we were quartered for some time, and enjoyed much better health than when cooped up in Cadiz. The brigade of Foot Guards was also quartered there, and, being very near us, there was a social intercourse kept up between their officers and ours. One of them, Captain Hutchinson, now Lord Donoughmore, so well-known to the public, as having assisted Sir Robert Wilson in effecting the escape of Lavalette from prison in Paris, frequently dined in our mess.[9] I often sat next to him at dinner, and, from his free and affable manner, became intimately acquainted with him. Indeed, his conduct on all occasions was so generous and frank, and he seemed to have such a spirit of chivalry, that I often predicted his generosity would some time or other lead him into trouble.

My fears were, in some measure, realised by his interference in the instance to which I have alluded, as both he and Sir Robert Wilson were arrested in Paris, and tried for their heroic conduct in saving the life of a man they deemed guiltless, and assisting an amiable and attached wife in rescuing her husband from prison. The whole affair is so familiar to the public, that a repetition of it by me would be uninteresting – though nothing can be more amusing than the account of the trial, nor can anything be more praiseworthy, or more to be admired, than the firmness and manly conduct of Sir Robert and Captain Hutchinson upon this occasion.

While at the Isla de Leon we were surprised, one evening, after mess, by the sudden appearance of seven naked Frenchmen. At first, we were unable to conjecture the cause of their coming to us in such an unaccountable condition; but at length discovered, that, on deserting from the enemy, they had left their arms and clothes on the opposite bank of the river, and swam over to our side. As we did not want them, we caused them, as soon as they were provided with clothes, to be sent into Cadiz to join a newly raised battalion of foreigners.

The morning after the French raised the siege of Cadiz,[10] we crossed the Isla de Leon and took the large mortar which now stands in the park, opposite the Horse Guards.[11] It was taken near Santa Maria, opposite Cadiz, and had been spiked

8 A number of persons by the name of Mellish were sent out to New South Wales, but it has proved impossible to identify him specifically.

9 John Hely-Hutchinson, the future 3rd Earl of Donoughmore, was then an ensign in the 1st Foot Guards at Cadiz. As a captain in Paris in 1815 he became infamous for his part in helping the Comte de Lavalette, escape from prison. He was tried along with Sir Robert Wilson – who, after Egypt had served with the Loyal Lusitanian Legion in the Peninsula, before being attached to the Russian army in 1812 – and Michael Bruce; they were all found guilty and sentenced to three month's imprisonment.

10 The siege lasted from 5 February 1810 until it was abandoned on 24 August 1812.

11 This huge mortar was cast in Seville in 1811 and spiked and abandoned at the end of the siege. It was given by the Spanish regency to Rear Admiral Legge to commemorate the victory at Salamanca and put on display at Horseguards in 1816, where it remains to this day. The mortar could fire a shell over 3 miles

by the enemy previously to their retreat. The French had it cast in Seville by a Spaniard and it was the only piece of ordnance in their possession that was able to throw shot or shells that immense distance across the Bay of Cadiz into the city.

In 1811, our regiment, accompanied by the 87th, a part of the Rifle corps, and the Brigade of Guards, commanded by Lord Proby, were ordered from Isla de Leon to Tarifa, which was then threatened to be occupied by the French.[12] This place is situated in the Straits of Gibraltar. It is an old Moorish town, and is surrounded with a wall, but not sufficiently strong to stand a siege, having been built so long back as the Moorish wars, and being consequently in a state of decay. As it was not considered tenable, Colonel Skerrett, who commanded,[13] moved from Tarifa to Vehere,[14] a town situated on the top of a hill in form of a sugar-loaf, close to the Sancti Petri River, and about ten leagues distant from Tarifa, where he took up a tolerably strong position. Business detained me in the latter place for some days after the army had evacuated it, and, in the meantime, despatches having arrived from England and Cadiz, I determined on taking them with me to Colonel Skerrett to Vehere. As I had not horses, I was obliged to take my passage in an English gun-boat which was going to Cadiz, and could land me close to Vehere – being accompanied by one Spaniard who knew the country, and by a Mr Fraser, who acted as Vice-consul.

About four o'clock in the evening, we were put on shore at the nearest point of land to the town, and the gun-boat sailed for her destination. As we approached the town, we met a countrywoman and a boy coming towards us, who, as soon as they perceived us, hastily called out for us to stop and return as quickly as possible, if we did not wish to fall into the hands of the French, who had taken possession of the town with a great force, our army having fallen back in the morning on Tarifa. We, of course, hurried off to the landing-place where the gun-boat had left us – but it was unfortunately out of sight. While we were in considerable anxiety, consulting upon what steps we should take, we perceived a country vessel coasting along pretty close to us, which we hailed, entreating to be taken on board, and offering twenty dollars as a recompense. The master, however, refused to take us, telling us that he was afraid the French might hear of it, the consequence of which might be that his vessel would be seized and himself and his men imprisoned. Then hoisting more sail, he stood out to sea, leaving us in a state of mind not easily to be described.

It was now night, and we roamed about, not knowing what to do, or whither to bend our steps, until Fraser perceived a light in the wood at some distance,

and could therefore shell the city from the coast opposite. The bronze base was constructed in Britain and is not the original, the monster Geryon (representing Cadiz) is often mistaken for a Chinese dragon.

12 The battalion companies sailed from Cadiz in October 1811 to Tarifa where the entire battalion was now reunited.

13 Colonel John Skerrett of the 47th Foot, who was later killed at Bergen op Zoom in 1814.

14 He means Vejer de la Frontera.

towards which we instantly made, and, after several windings through the wood, frequently losing sight of the light, we came to a fire, before which were sitting two men and a boy, who were employed in herding cattle that were feeding close by.

They started on first seeing us; but Fraser, who spoke very good Spanish, soon quieted their alarm, describing our situation, and entreating of them to assist us. They seemed well inclined to do anything in their power, but expressed their fears of being hanged by the French if it were known that they harboured us, or gave us the least assistance; telling us there was no possibility of our escaping, as the French dragoons would be down in the wood to look for forage at an early hour in the morning. Nothing could equal the terror they were in of the French in that part of the country, and indeed in every part through which the French passed.

Having given us some bread and cheese, they were urging us to leave them, as they dreaded being seen in our company, when the boy remarked that we ought to cross the river in a boat, if it could be procured, for in that lay our only chance of escape; but both the men, one of whom was his father, denied that there was any boat near enough for the purpose, nor was there any possibility of obtaining one.

I told the boy, – taking out ten dollars, as I fortunately had money about me – that I would give them to him if he would procure one for me; suspecting that the observation the two men made, was only from fear. My suspicions turned out to be correct, as the boy instantly said that he knew where there was one under the bridge near the town, and that if we went with him, he would endeavour to procure it. We, accordingly, proceeded with the greatest caution, accompanied by the men with evident reluctance, who were, notwithstanding their fears, tempted by the offered reward, until we got under the bridge where the boat was fastened. Then, indeed, we felt no little anxiety on hearing the French cavalry horses trampling and pawing over our heads, and the men talking to each other so near us, that we could distinctly hear their conversation. The boy was as good as his word. He loosed the boat without any noise, and gently pulled it down the stream, holding the rope, and walking on the brink of the river. We walked slowly on before him that we might cross the river a good way below the bridge, fearing that daylight might appear, and that we should be seen. And, when we had proceeded a considerable distance down the river, we prepared to embark and venture across.

Giving the boy his well-earned ten dollars, we got into the boat, but found, to our dismay, that we had no oars. Our Spaniard then got out, and procured a young tree, which he cut into a shape resembling a pole, by means of which he contrived, with some difficulty, to shove the boat into the middle of the stream, resolving to take our chance and go with the current, since we were unable to reach the opposite side without oars.

As we approached the mouth of the river, which empties itself in to the straits, we had no doubt but that the current would have taken us out to sea, where, at the complete mercy of the waves, we must have inevitably perished, if not rescued by some vessel. Still we struggled on, and the poor Spaniard pulled and shoved as well as he possibly could with the pole, until at length he fortunately got us on a sand bank on the opposite side of the river, where the boat stuck fast, and then jumping up to his waist in the water, he took us, one after the other, on his back, with the bag containing the despatches and letters, and landed us safe on dry ground.

We now considered ourselves securer, as he informed us there was no obstruction between us and Tarifa, and set out to walk with fresh spirits and cheerfully, although the distance we should have to travel would be considerable, particularly after the fatigue and anxiety we has already endured. So great, indeed, was the fatigue that I had undergone the preceding day and night, that I actually dozed as I walked along, leaning on Mr Fraser's arm, who was a stout athletic man.

In the course of the day, we came to a few houses, at one which we called, where we found a poor woman and her daughter, who were much terrified at our appearance, exclaiming, in their fright, 'Ave-Maria! Ave-Maria!' until Fraser told them who we were, and how we came there, it being an unfrequented part of the country.

The poor woman informed us that she had no refreshment to give us, but said that one of her neighbours had killed a pig the day before, and that, as he was a respectable farmer, and a good generous man, she was sure he would give us as much as we required, and then sent her daughter to show us the house. We accordingly repaired there; our arrival caused as much alarm and affright as at the last house – they were so much in dread of the French.

At first, he denied that he had anything to give us, but, on our telling him who we were, he made us sit down, and, having spread a cloth on the table, went upstairs and returned in a short time with some steaks which he had cut off the pig, that he had hidden, lest the French might pay him a visit and take it from him. Having broiled them very nicely, he placed them before us, together with a large loaf of bread, a bottle of aguadente (bad brandy), and some spring water. It was the most delicious meal I ever ate; the sauce indeed made it so, for it was downright hunger. He then told us that he concealed his cattle and mules on the mountains, in a place where the French were unable to find them, who, although they came frequently to his house, could never obtain anything from him.

Without our making a request, or indeed any observation on the subject, he sent his man to the hiding-place where his cattle were concealed, from which he returned in an incredibly short space of time, with three excellent mules, with which he furnished us – sending a muleteer with us to bring them back. And, when he had shaken hands with us at parting, he gave the usual salute, 'Vive – vive.' We arrived the same night at Tarifa, where we found General [sic] Skerrett and the army. When we had delivered the despatches and letters, we were overwhelmed with enquiries, every one expressing his surprise at our fortunate escape, and telling us they had all concluded that we must have fallen into the hands of the enemy.

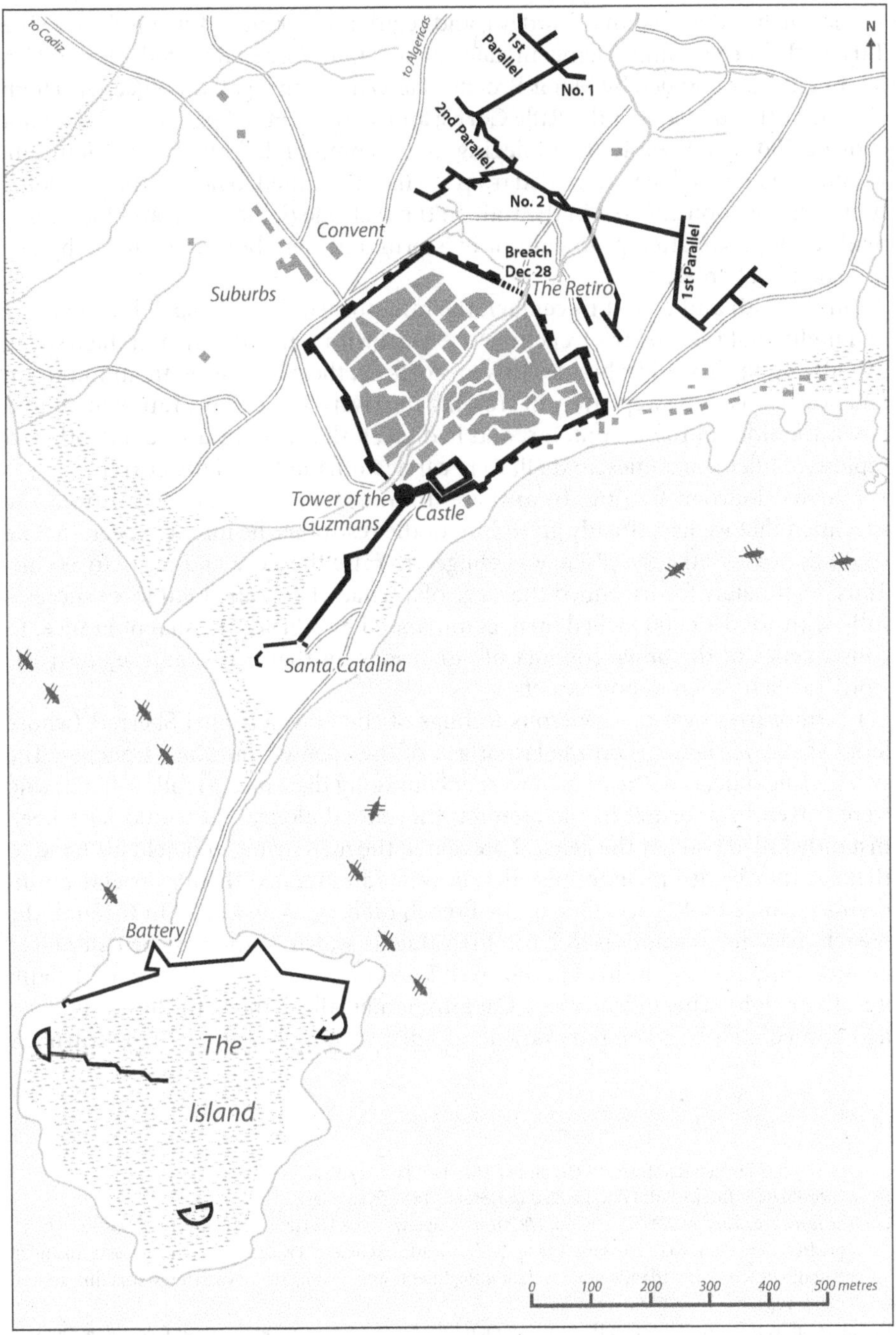

Map 5 The siege of Tarifa. (George Anderson)

The enemy advanced in a few days, and regularly entrenched themselves before Tarifa; the siege commencing in due form.[15] Our force consisted of the 47th Regiment, commanded by Major Broad;[16] the 87th, by that gallant officer Sir Hugh Gough, with a division of the Rifle Corps; and a regiment of Spaniards – in all not above 2,500 men;[17] while the besieging army, commanded by Marshal Jourdan, whom Marshal Soult had detached from Seville, amounted to no less than 10,000.[18] A breach was soon effected in the wall on the east side of the town, and the enemy made a desperate attempt to enter it by storm, but were bravely repulsed by our little band of heroes.

On the 30th and 31st of December, the rain poured down in such torrents, day and night, that the enemy's trenches were filled with water, the men in them being actually up to their hips; besides this misfortune, their convoy, with ammunition and provisions, was swept away in crossing the river, by the heavy rain that poured down the sides of the mountains, and had given the river an unusual depth and rapidity. Muleteers, mules, and all, were carried off and lost in the current.

Marshal Jourdan finding, from these untoward circumstances, and from the specimen that we had already given him of the resistance he might expect, that he could not easily take the place, was obliged to raise the siege and retire to Seville. Thus, fortunately for us, ended the siege of Tarifa, where our small force successfully withstood 10,000 picked men, commanded by a Field-Marshal of France. In consequence of the brave conduct of our troops on that occasion, they bear the word Tarifa on their appointments.

I cannot pass over the generous feelings of the brave Colonel Skerrett (whose loss I shall ever lament) on the last attack of the enemy from their trenches. The two leading officers of the French were encouraging their men to follow them, who were driven back or fell in the attempt; they stood alone, and would have been instantly killed had not the general prevented the men firing, and held his hand to them as they leaped in, extolling their bravery, and treated them as friends, until their exchange took place. One of the French officers, as he leaped in through the breach, had the precaution to hand his valuable watch to the first British officer he met, fully relying on his honour, well knowing that the soldiers would claim it as their right. This officer was a Captain Somersall, of the 87th Regiment, who had immediately to go on duty down to Cadiz, without having time to return the

15 The siege of Tarifa lasted from 19 December 1811 to 5 January 1812.

16 Major Richard Broad 47th Foot; he died in October 1812 from a fever.

17 The force consisted of 2/47th, 1/82nd, 2/87th, a company of the 1/11th, a company of the 95th and half a squadron of the 2nd KGL Hussars. The Spanish brigade of General Francisco Copons y Navia. included a battalion each of the Irlanda and Cantabria Regiments and a company of cazadores, totalling around 2,500 troops.

18 Marshal Jean Baptiste Jourdan did not command the French forces at Tarifa, it was *Général de Division* Jean Leval, who had about 8,000 troops with him.

The 87th Foot at Tarifa. (Royal Irish Rangers)

watch;[19] but, as soon as Colonel Skerrett had learned the circumstance from the French officer, and ascertaining that it must be Captain Somersall who received it in the confusion of the moment, requested of me, on going to Cadiz, to get the watch, which I did, and sent it to the colonel, who returned it to the owner, to his great surprise and gratification, it being the gift of a valued friend.

The losses of the 47th at Tarifa were Lieutenant Richard Hall and one man killed, Lieutenants George Hill, John de Burgh and two men wounded.

Leaving Tarifa to General Copons, to garrison it, we returned to Cadiz, at that time besieged and bombarded by the French from the opposite side. In consequence, however, of the victory obtained at Salamanca, Marshal Soult was obliged to raise the siege and retreat.[20]

Colonel Skerrett sailed with a force including the 47th Foot for Truxillo on 30 September and arrived there on 12 October. He then received orders to march to Talavera la Reina, which the troops reached on 18 October, having marched some two hundred and sixty miles in nineteen days.

19 Captain Anthony Somersall 87th Foot.

20 The Battle of Salamanca was fought on 22 July 1812 and was a huge victory for the allies, causing the French to retire from Madrid and forcing Soult to abandon the siege of Cadiz.

After this we moved on towards Seville, with a brigade of Foot-Guards, and the 87th Regiment.[21]

On approaching Seville, the western gate was closed, which caused us to prepare for a siege: and, on crossing the bridge, we were opposed by a formidable force, on which occasion Brigadier General Downie, an Irishman in the Spanish service, was desperately wounded.[22] The enemy had retreated through the eastern gates, leaving the city completely free. After a little pause, and the officers getting into their quarters, a French carriage stood in the street called 'Cabo Real,' entirely neglected, having been left behind by the enemy. While Captain Cadoux, of the Rifle Corps,[23] was dressing himself in his new quarters, a peasant seemed admiring the carriage; and, with his cuchillo, or Spanish knife, was ripping the lining, unperceived by any one, except an old shopkeeper on the opposite side of the street, who observing him taking out several articles of plate, told him that he was not entitled to them, and called on Captain Cadoux to come down and examine the carriage. The captain lost no time in doing so, and, with the assistance of his faithful sergeant, McLoughnan, soon got possession of all the concealed plate and money of the fugitive French general, which was secreted in the lining of the carriage. This was a common practice with the French generals throughout the campaign, who well knew the uncertainty of their tenure of the country. Cadoux (who was son to the paymaster of the corps)[24] knew if this fact became public, that it would go in common as booty among the army, very wisely sent his faithful sergeant that night off to Cadiz, with a mule laden with the treasure, who sold it in the city for cash. He then obtained bills on London for the amount (upwards of one thousand pounds); and, as soon as we had taken the city, which made a strong resistance, proceeded to join the Duke of Wellington, then at Madrid.

On leaving Seville, I was highly amused by a learned sergeant of the Foot Guards asking me had I read 'Gil Blas,' and quoting several passages for my information, particularly one –

> 'He that has not Seville seen,
> Never has a traveller been.'

But on our entering Zafra,[25] he was quite delighted, it being the place so much written of by his favourite author. This was the town that our brave general-in-

21 It also included two companies of the 95th, the 20th Portuguese Line, a squadron of KGL Hussars and two batteries of artillery.

22 Acting Assistant Commissary General John Downie raised a Spanish corps at his own expense and was made a Spanish general.

23 Captain Daniel Cadoux of the 95th Rifles; he was killed at the bridge of Vera in 1813.

24 Paymaster Matthew Cadoux of the 3/95th.

25 He incorrectly writes Jafra.

chief, Lord Hill, surprised, and where he caught Philippon, the French general, asleep.[26]

On passing over the Sierra Morena mountains, Major Livesay and I were joined by that excellent officer, Lord Saltoun, of the Grenadier Guards, who travelled all day with us under a scorching sun.[27] The gallant conduct of Lord Saltoun is so well known at the siege of Bayonne, and at the memorable battle of Waterloo, that any mention of it, by so humble an individual as myself, is unnecessary, particularly after having been so ably described by Colonel Mackinnon.[28]

On arriving at Truxillo, the birth-place of the celebrated Pizarro,[29] Major Broad, of our regiment, fell ill of a violent fever, and died in the very house in which, it is said, Pizarro had lived and died. There was an extraordinary circumstance attending his death. On his first entering this house, having tripped against a board, which occasioned him to stumble, he exclaimed, though by no means superstitious, 'I hope that board may not be my coffin!' It is a fact, that the very same board was used in making the poor fellow's coffin a very short time after the occurrence.

As I had a high esteem for Major Broad, I obtained permission to remain with him, and attend him after the regiment left Truxillo. A few evenings before his death, he communicated to me, as I stood by his bed-side, (the servant having been previously sent out of the room) some curious details connected with his family and friends, but of so private and delicate a nature, that, in justice to the memory of my gallant friend, I do not consider myself justified in making them public. He went on to say that he had been brought up in his father's house, had received a good education, and was led to expect that he was to be well provided for; but his father dying suddenly, without having time to make a will, not only the title and estates, but the personal property, went into another family, and he was consequently left totally destitute.

The person who came down to take possession of the estate offered him ten pounds, which he rejected with distain. A person connected in some way or other with the 6th Regiment of Foot, calling about the same time to see his mother, and representing to him the pleasures of a military life, he was induced to enlist; and accompanying him to London, called on the late Duke of Gloucester, who was then colonel of the 6th Regiment, for the purpose of entering the service under him.[30]

26 This is an error, Philippon was taken at Badajoz as previously noted. Harley seems to have confused things with Hill's action at Arroyo dos Molinos on 28 November 1811, where the Prince d'Aremberg was captured.

27 Captain Charles Livesay, 47th Foot, who was to be severely wounded at San Sebastian and died of his wounds on 15 September 1813; Lieutenant and Captain Alexander, Lord Saltoun 1st Foot Guards, who was to become famous at Waterloo.

28 Lieutenant and Captain Daniel Mackinnon of the Coldstream Guards wrote a history of the regiment.

29 Francisco Pizzaro, the conqueror of Peru, was born at Trujillo c1474.

30 Prince William Henry, Duke of Gloucester, brother of King George III.

Map 6 A map of Spain and Portugal dated 1812. (Author's collection)

FRANCE
Bayonne
Bilbao
the Pyrenees
Perpignan
Tudela
Saragossa
Borja
Lerida
Gerona
Mataro
Barcelona
Villa Franca
Calatayud
Tarragona
Daroca
Alcaniz
Montalban
Tortosa
Ebro R.
Siguenza
Mont Real
Albarrazin
Teruel
Cuenca
Segorbe
Valencia
Requena
Jorquera
Albacete
Almanza
Chinchilla
S.Felipe
Villena
Xixona
Alicante
Jumilla
Elche
Ziezar
Murcia
Lorca
Carthagena
Almeria
Vera
Aguilas
K.m OF MURCIA
K.m OF VALENCIA
BALEARIC ISLES
Minorca
MAJORCA
Palma
Iviza
Colombretes
SEA
MEDITERRANEAN
Algiers
Tenez
Magrowah
Mostigan
Arzeu
Oran
AFRICA
Leagues
Degree

The good Duke having heard of his situation, and being informed of the prospects with which he had been brought up, attempted, in the kindest manner, to dissuade him from it; but when Broad told his Royal Highness that if he did not receive him into his corps, he would try some other regiment, the Duke gave him a guinea, and a strong letter of recommendation to the commanding officer, Colonel Campbell, afterwards General Campbell, who was then with his regiment in Kilkenny,[31] whither Broad immediately proceeded by way of Bristol. As he was very young and delicate, the load of his knapsack, together with the heat of the weather, so overcame him on his journey, that he fainted on the road. 'I never shall forget,' said he, 'the kindness of a poor Irish woman to me on that occasion. When I came to myself, out of the swoon, I found the poor creature leaning over me in the tenderest manner, pouring milk into my mouth, and, at the same time, exclaiming, 'It's little, poor young man, your mother, that reared you tenderly, knows how you are now stretched on the common road, and no one to heed you but one more unfortunate than yourself.'

As soon as he had joined his regiment, he kept entirely to himself, never associating with any of the soldiers, and observing the strictest attention to his military duties. This was soon taken notice of by his captain and other officers, one of whom, on seeing how fond he was of retirement, conceived him to be some respectable individual who had been obliged to enlist from misfortunes; and therefore pitying his condition, was in a habit of frequently conversing with him, and giving him instructive and entertaining books to read during his leisure hours.

He had not been long in the army, when his good conduct obtaining promotion for him; he was made sergeant, and the officers at the time having, by some means or other, but not through him, learned the whole of his history; and knowing that the gentleman who succeeded his father was Sir J[ohn] M[orshead] of Cornwall, who was then raising the regiment called the Cornish Miners, they wrote to him, recommending Broad in the strongest manner, and, by their exertions, he was appointed ensign and adjutant in the [Royal Cornwall and Devon Miners] Regiment, which he joined in Winchester, where I first met him in 1800.[32] From this regiment he was promoted to a lieutenancy in the 85th Regiment, where he had not been long when the late Duke of Kent meeting him, and admiring his military appearance, appointed him his equerry, and gave him a company in his own regiment, the Royals, from which he was afterwards promoted to a majority in the 47th Regiment.[33]

31 Lieutenant General Colin Campbell commanded the 6th Foot from 1795-8.

32 Sir John Morshead of Trenant Park in Cornwall (1747-1813) was Colonel of the Royal Cornwall and Devon Miners. This corps was raised in 1798 and disbanded in 1802, before being raised again in 1803. The militia battalion was trained as light infantrymen and Broad joined the regiment in 1799.

33 Broad was transferred to the 85th Foot as Ensign and Adjutant and went on half pay; he was then transferred to the 83rd Foot as Lieutenant and Adjutant in October 1802 and promoted as a lieutenant in September 1803. He transferred to the 43rd Foot as a lieutenant in September 1804. He then became a

'Harley,' said he, 'I relate my history to you, as various reports, have, at different times, got into circulation respecting me, that in case of my death you may be able to clear up any points to my brother-officers; for I conceive it is due to them to know the particulars which I have now communicated to you; from the period of our first acquaintance, I have always held you in the highest regard. I only ask you, if I had not conducted myself through life like a gentleman, should I now be what, thank God, I am?'

The poor fellow died in a few days after this statement, although, at the time he made it, we had no idea of his illness terminating fatally. In the course of my experience, it was my lot to meet with few persons whom I had so much reason to respect, on various accounts, as my friend the major. It was natural, therefore, that I should feel his loss deeply.

I met a Captain Williams of the 9th [11th] Regiment at Truxillo, but had known him some years before in Kilkenny.[34] At that time, the great rage for banking commenced, and, as Williams had married a Miss Finn of that city, whose brother, Michael Finn, was then a banker, he sold out of a troop of dragoons, and joined his brother-in-law in the banking business, opening establishments in several of the principal towns of Ireland.[35] But the firm did not continue more than two years.

Williams, like most military men who have left the army, longed to return to it again; he obtained a cornetcy in his old regiment, the 9th [11th], and accompanied them to Spain, leaving all his family in Dublin, except one little boy, whom he foolishly took abroad, being too fond of him to part from him. The poor child, who was only nine years of age at the time, went through all the campaigns with his father, until at length, Williams, while on an outlying picquet in Portugal, being unfortunately surprised by the enemy, was mortally wounded, and died on the following day. The dear child clung to his dying father, endeavouring to raise his spirits by the most affectionate endearments; and, after his decease, was, with the utmost difficulty, removed from his corpse, and not indeed until force was obliged to be resorted to.

As the army had to retreat about the same time, the poor boy's sufferings were increased, although all the officers of his father's regiment did everything in their power to alleviate them. It was, however, a satisfaction afterwards, to all who were acquainted with the circumstances, to know that young Williams obtained a commission. He well deserved it, for he endured as much fatigue on the retreat as any of the officers.

captain in the 1st Foot in December 1804. He became a major in the 10th Foot in February 1811 and transferred the same day to the 47th Foot.

34 It has proven virtually impossible to identify this officer with any certainty as Harley had muddled the story. However, he most likely refers to Cornet William Williams of the 11th Light Dragoons, who was severely wounded at Salamanca on 18 July 1812 and died the same day. It is recorded that he was married and 'His son received his effects he being with at his decease'.

35 Michael Finn then owned Archers Grove, Kilkenny.

10

Prisoner

I now proceeded to join my regiment, after having witnessed poor Broad's interment, and having met with a Major Todd of the Staff Corps,[1] and a Lieutenant Keough of the 57th Regiment,[2] we agreed to travel together, as they were also anxious to join the army. Nothing particular occurred until we arrived at a place called Navelcarnero, six leagues from Madrid, where we stopped to breakfast, and learned that Lord Wellington had retreated from Madrid, and that Marshal Soult had entered it with a large force; the English army taking up an encampment near the Escorial, a palace or country seat belonging to the King of Spain, about twelve leagues off.[3] On gaining this important intelligence, we determined, as the safest course, to endeavour to reach the main body of our troops by crossing the country, and accordingly took the road to the left, leaving Madrid upon our right.

On our approaching the village of Las Rozas,[4] we observed some dragoons at the entrance, and a vidette stationed on an eminence outside the town, whom, although they were in blue uniform, and therefore bore the appearance of the English troops, I shrewdly suspected were some of the French outposts; an opinion in which Major Todd, who was at this time suffering under a severe attack of ague, perfectly agreed; but Lieutenant Keough, insisting that they were some of our light cavalry, urged us to proceed, which we did. The vidette stationed on the hill beckoned with his sword to the dragoons at the entrance, the moment he perceived us and they as quickly disappeared.

This again exciting our suspicious, we stopped, and were deliberating what course we should pursue; my servant endeavouring to persuade me to turn back before it was too late, when the French dragoons, galloping round the hill, surrounded us, and made us prisoners.

1 Actually Captain Alexander Todd, Royal Staff Corps who became a brevet major in August 1813. He was taken prisoner of war in December 1812 as stated by Harley.

2 Lieutenant Francis Gethings Keough 57th Foot, was made a prisoner of war in December 1812 but escaped in April 1813 as described by Harley.

3 The Site of San Lorenzo de El Escorial built by Philip II of Spain.

4 Las Rozas is just north of Madrid on the road towards El Escorial.

The French officer behaved with the greatest politeness, and told us that we were extremely unfortunate in coming at the time we did, for had we come an hour earlier, we should have met our own party, or an hour later, and we should have escaped them, as they were only a reconnoitring party and had merely come into the village by chance. He offered us such refreshments as he had; after partaking of which, we accompanied him to headquarters, about three miles further, where the advanced guard of the French army was stationed, under the command of General Soult, nephew to the marshal of the same name.[5]

The general received us very politely in the Praca, or Market-place, and, having called his interpreter and aide-de-camp, took down our names and rank, and then entered into conversation with us. He asked me if the bridge across the Tagus was destroyed. I informed him that it was; after which he inquired was there not a convoy of money at hand intended for the British troops. I replied in the negative, stating that there had been a number of mules laden with dollars on their way to us, but in consequence of our army leaving Madrid, orders were given to return the money into Portugal, to avoid its falling into the hands of the French. He then took off his hat in the most courteous manner, and bade us good evening; and, at the same time, several French officers came up and invited us to dinner. We, of course, accepted their invitation, and accompanied them to their mess-room, which considering their army was continually in motion, was wonderfully well furnished. They did everything in their power to make us as comfortable as our situation would permit, and gave us a good dinner, with abundance of excellent wine.

The next morning one of the dragoons who took us prisoners called me out and showed me the fires of our army, offering to assist me in escaping that night if I chose to avail myself of the opportunity; but I was so overcome with fatigue, that I found myself incapable of the effort, were I ever so inclined to profit by the soldier's offer; and besides, I could not, in justice to my feelings and sense of honour, think of leaving my comrades in durance, and therefore declined the proposal in the most delicate way I could, being resolved to stay with them and abide their fate, let that be what it might.

The following day we were sent into Madrid with several other prisoners, under a strong escort of gendarmes, and, on passing over the great plain near Madrid, we met Marshal Soult, accompanied by his entire staff, and the main body of the French army. I never beheld a more magnificent sight. It consisted of 14,000 cavalry well mounted and clothed, with 44,000 infantry, all in the highest spirits and order, and about seventy pieces of cannon. It was then the 4th of November, and the morning was extremely fine; and, as we were approaching Madrid, they passed us on the beautiful and level plain, as if they were marching in review upon some favourite gala day. At any other time, or upon any other occasion, I must

5 *Général de Brigade* Pierre Benoit Soult (1770-1843) brother of Marshal Soult.

have enjoyed the grand and imposing spectacle which their splendid appearance presented to the eye; but when I recollected that they were about to engage in hostile combat with our army, composed of my own countrymen, and in which I had a son and two nephews,[6] I felt a sudden pang that made my spirits sink within me. It was not that I doubted that the issue of the contest would be favourable to our side, if the numbers were nearly equal, but feelings, in which a soldier can seldom indulge, possessed me for the moment, on seeing Marshal Soult's fine army going out to battle; and I involuntarily shuddered, when I reflected on the thousands who were doomed to fall so soon on the field of blood – who were buoyant with life and hope, anxious to take part in the dreadful struggle, and yet unconscious of the awful fate that awaited them.

I happened to be more fortunate than my brother officers, from the circumstance of my having met a French dragoon who had been a prisoner of war some months before at Cadiz, and who, having made himself useful to my family, had been treated by them with great kindness. I was surprised on hearing my name called out by a dragoon, as we were passing the French army, but took no notice of it until he rode up to me, and saluting me, cried out, 'How are you, Captain? I hope your family are well. Don't you remember Jack, the Frenchman, who was a prisoner of war at Cadiz, and escaped? I will now endeavour to repay the kindness I received from your family. You shall have a horse to ride, and plenty of the best provisions that can be procured; and I will manage to be with you myself.' He then rode off, and, returning in a few minutes, told me that he had obtained an order to be placed on duty with the guard that escorted us, that he might have an opportunity of doing something for me.

We now arrived at Madrid, having met at the entrance King Joseph and his suite, who saluted us respectfully; and had we been differently situated, I should have been rejoiced to visit this celebrated and splendid city. The Retiro, which was the State-prison or citadel, something similar to our Tower in London,[7] having been blown up by our army on leaving Madrid, the officer of the guard informed us, that he was under the unpleasant necessity of placing us in the Casa de Ville, or city prison, where we were accordingly taken and confined, all three of us, together with my servant, in a small room at the top of the building.

We had been locked up about an hour before the turnkey brought us a small pitcher of water, and four small loaves of brown bread, which, he informed us, was the prison allowance; but we had neither bed nor bedclothes, nothing in fact, but a small bench, upon which we could scarcely sit. We continued in this state until about six o'clock in the evening, when a female came to the door, and demanded

6 His son, John Harley, was a lieutenant in the 47th Foot. Lieutenants John and George Hill of the 47th Foot were his nephews.

7 The Royal Retiro park at Madrid had a large China Manufactory set up in it in 1760, which was converted into a citadel by the French and was captured by the allies in 1812.

admittance. The little turnkey, instantly obeying her, opened the door, and ushered her in. The moment she saw us huddled up in one corner of the room, she exclaimed, in Spanish, 'Poor English! I pity you!' and then adding 'Have patience for a little, and I will return,' She left us, and returned in less than half an hour, accompanied by three other women, two of whom brought us mattresses, blankets, and pillows; and the third, a comfortable supper of soup, rice, and boiled mutton, with one pint of wine for each; and also a supply of chocolate and bread for our breakfast the next morning, telling us, on taking her departure, that she would visit us again the next day.

On enquiring of the turnkey, after she had gone, we learned that this excellent creature whom we justly named our guardian angel, was the Madrio Prisonero, that is, the mother of prisoners, and a Sister of Charity, from a neighbouring convent.

Our first night was spent in great misery, Major Todd being very ill with ague, and I scolding our companion, Lieutenant Keough, the whole of the night, for his obstinacy in persisting that the French dragoons were some of our light cavalry, by which mistake we were unfortunately captured. The following day, however, we were more cheerful and reconciled to our fate – our worthy friend again visited us; and, while she was making preparations for our dinner, what was my astonishment, when, in the person of another prisoner, who was put into our small room with us, I recognised a lieutenant colonel of the Spanish army, a young man about twenty-seven years of age, with whom I had been for some time living, near Cadiz, on the most intimate terms, each of us having conceived a more than common regard for the other. His filial affection having induced him to risk everything, he came to Madrid in disguise to see his family, and had scarcely entered it when he was unfortunately captured. He had not been more than one hour with us, when a lovely and interesting young lady, his sister, called on him, to whom he introduced me as an old friend and companion of his in Spain. On hearing this, the poor creature paid me nearly as much attention as her brother, making room for me to sit near her at dinner, helping me equally with him, and promising that we should want for nothing. As the Sister of Charity abated nothing in her attentions, notwithstanding the assistance we had from our new friend and ally, we had a profusion of everything we could require.

We had been just a week in close confinement, when a French colonel called on us very early one morning, and informed us, in the most gentlemanly manner, expressing his regret in being obliged to tell us of it, that we must prepare to go off, with all the other prisoners in Madrid, in the course of two hours, at which period the escort would be ready to attend us. Shortly after the appointed hour, the escort drew up in front of the prison, and about 200 English soldiers who had been taken prisoners at different periods of the war, were placed with us, in the centre of the guard. We were about to march, when a French general riding up, reprimanded the officer of the guard in very severe terms, for having placed British officers in common with their men, directing that the men should be placed in front, and

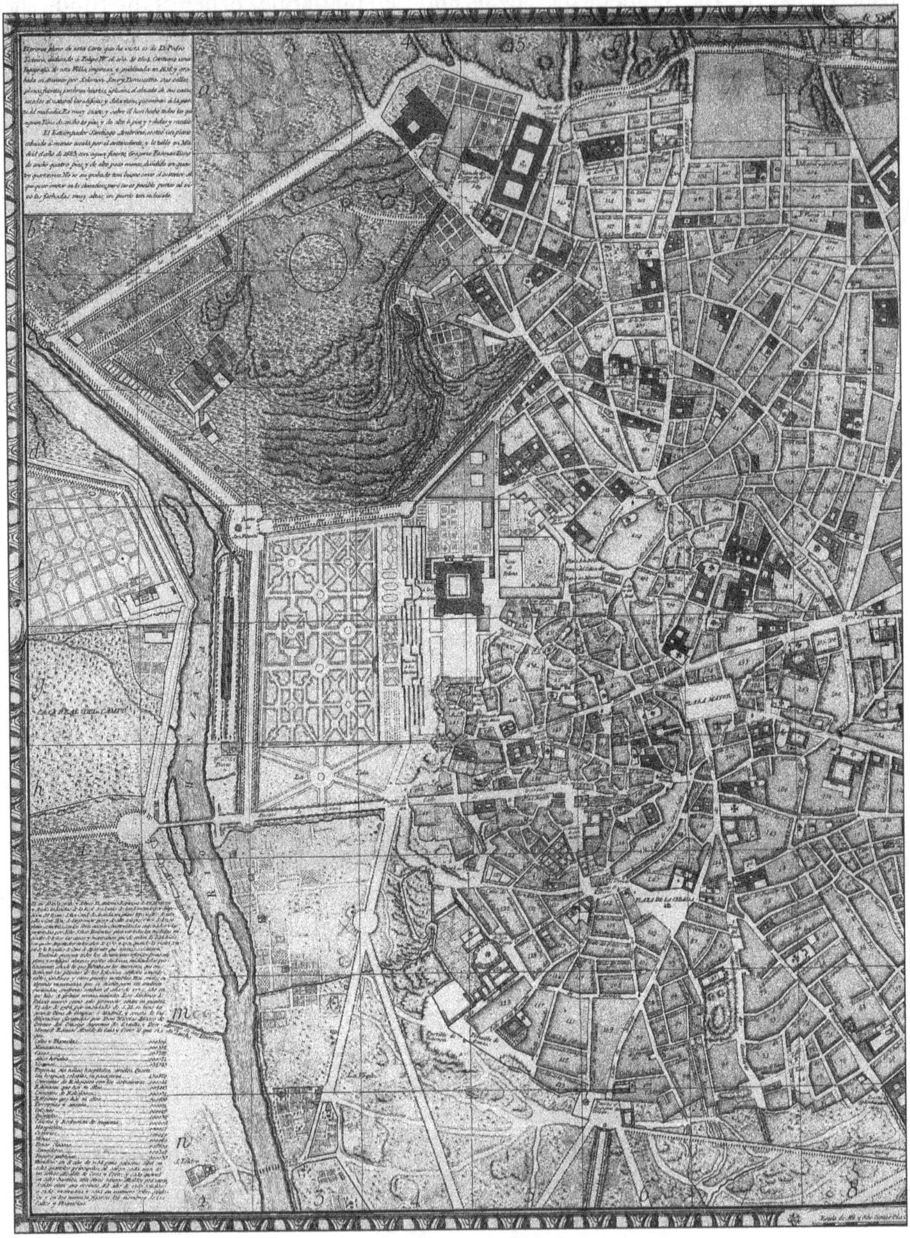

Map 7 Map of Madrid circa 1785. (Author's collection)

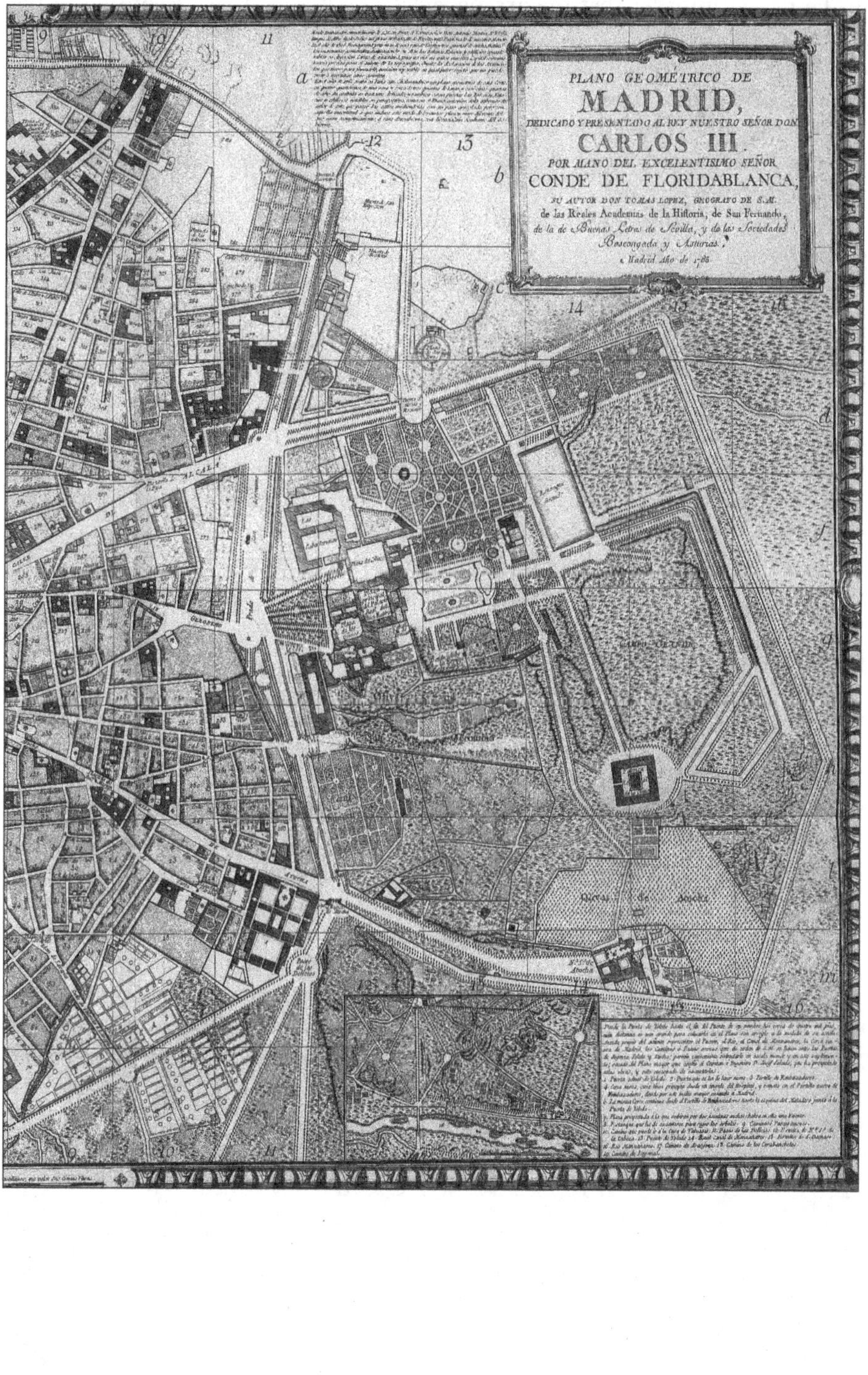
PLANO GEOMETRICO DE
MADRID,
DEDICADO Y PRESENTADO AL REY NUESTRO SEÑOR DON
CARLOS III.
POR MANO DEL EXCELENTISIMO SEÑOR
CONDE DE FLORIDABLANCA,
SU AUTOR DON TOMAS LOPEZ, GEOGRAFO DE S.M.
de las Reales Academias de la Historia, de San Fernando,
de la de Buenas Letras de Sevilla, y de las Sociedades
Bascongada y Asturias.

the officers allowed to follow in the rear. In consequence of this order, we returned to the prison in order that the arrangement might take place, according to the general's wishes, and to wait the arrival of another guard, who were destined to escort us, instead of the former one. As I was going with the rest into the prison, a young lady rushed forward, and thrusting a large muslin handkerchief into my hand, with a dollar rolled up in it, quickly disappeared, before I could sufficiently recover the surprise into which the incident threw me, to ascertain who the individual could be.

After about half-an-hour's delay, we were ordered down stairs again, the other guard having arrived. When we had descended, we met our friend the Sister of Charity at the foot of the staircase, who, seeing the attention of the two French grenadiers who were with us, withdrawn for a moment, seized the favourable opportunity, and pulling me suddenly by the arm, shoved me into a small dark apartment, but faintly lighted by a loop-hole facing the street, where I concealed myself without detection, as the new guard knew neither the persons nor the number of their prisoners at the time. And, what is really singular, she succeeded in securing the escape of my servant Pat Dolan, also, whom she contrived to secrete in the neighbourhood of the convent, until we were both enabled to venture out, when the remainder of the French had evacuated the city.

I remained in concealment during the day, keeping, according to her directions, from the light which the narrow casement but very partially admitted, that there might be no possibility of my being seen. She informed me that I might consider myself safe, as the governor and turnkey were her friends, whom she had persuaded to favour my escape, seeing the miserable state of my mind, and hearing that I had a family. At nine o'clock, she brought me refreshments, and during the night my ears were assailed by the noise of cannon and military stores, passing by the prison on their way to join the French army. She appeared again in the morning, brought me breakfast, and cheerfully told me she hoped she would set me at liberty in the evening, as the French were evacuating Madrid. 'I must be well satisfied,' said she, 'that they are all gone before I can allow you to appear in the streets during the day.' She then visited every public place, and, amongst others, the navieros, or coffee-houses, to ascertain if any of the French army yet remained in the city;[8] and, on her being fully satisfied that they were all gone, she returned to me at four o'clock, accompanied by two Spanish gentlemen, whom I understood to be merchants. The head turnkey immediately opened the door, the governor took off his hat and shook hands with me, the little turnkey himself bowed most graciously, and I was quickly released from confinement, and ushered into the street with this truly worthy person and her friends.

Here I was awkwardly situated, not being sufficiently acquainted with the Spanish language to comprehend their meaning, as each of the gentlemen, on

8 The term 'navieros' actually translates as a shipper.

saying something, pulled me by the arm, one wishing to take me one direction, and the other in another. While in this situation, I began to entertain unjust suspicions of my friends, and my mind became miserable, fearing that I was betrayed, and again about to be plunged into prison. Meeting, however, at this juncture, with a Spanish nobleman, who spoke good English, and to whom I expressed my fears, he smiled, and told me not to be alarmed, saying, 'those gentlemen were contending with each other, to know which of them you are to dine and remain with while you are in Madrid. Decide now, sir, that I may tell your friends your determination.' I replied that I felt equal gratitude to both, but that as the smaller person of the two, had been the first that had taken me by the hand, I decided to go with him. This the nobleman told them and wished me good evening.

We now proceeded to the house of Don Diego Collina, such being the name of my host, who seemed much pleased at the preference given him, and gave us a very good dinner, treating us with some very fine wine of La Mancha.

On Sunday morning, I went to prayers, and on my return met my good friend the Sister of Charity, who, with my host, accompanied me to the town hall, to introduce me to the alcalde or mayor, who was sitting with the public authorities of Madrid. He received me kindly and embraced me, offering me any service in his power, inquiring if I wanted any money; of which, my female friend immediately told him, I stood in no need. We had not exchanged many more words, when an express arrived that the French general, Suchet, with an army of 12,000 men, were coming up from Valencia, and would enter Madrid the next day.[9] This sudden and unexpected news threw the alcalde and council into confusion; some flew off, others remained, the alcalde turned to me, and asked me what I wished to do; and my female friend again replied for me, that it was necessary that I should leave Madrid immediately, and that all I required from him was an animal to convey me away. He instantly ordered one of his officers to go into the street and press one for me, who returned in the course of a few minutes with a mule and muleteer. When the alcalde had cordially wished me every success, I left the town hall; my friends, Collina and the good nun being still with me. As she would not allow me to make any delay, hastily furnishing me with twenty dollars and two shirts, she brought me immediately to the place where my servant Pat was concealed, to whom she gave one shirt and two dollars. Being now fully prepared for my journey, I was about to take leave of them, when she told me that I must not proceed for a moment, as she had a charge to give me, leading out, in the course of a few minutes, six English soldiers who had been severely wounded at the Battle of Aranjuez, near Madrid,[10] one of whom, a private of the 14th Regiment of Light Dragoons, received a most dreadful wound, the sabre passing under his shoulder blade and through his body.

9 Marshal Louis Gabriel Suchet (1770-1826).

10 General Rowland Hill's rearguard of 4,000 men held up the French advance at the bridge of Aranjuez the day before the British abandoned Madrid on 31 October 1812, allowing them time for an orderly retreat.

This good woman, assisted by the ladies of the convent, had dressed the wounds of those poor fellows, fed and concealed them from the enemy, until she gave them up to my care.

The Sister of Charity, and the good little Collina then accompanied us through the gate of Madrid, expressing their fears that my red coat would attract notice, the sun not having yet set.

The terror of Suchet, who had committed such enormities and cruelties in Tarragona, made her so anxious for our safety, that she entreated of me not to stop that night, but to proceed on without delay, until I got beyond the possibility of falling in with any of the advance picquets of Suchet's army. On bidding an affectionate farewell to my friends, I discharged the mule and muleteer, being determined to walk with my poor soldiers and my servant. What was my surprise when my Spanish friend, Collina, stripped off his coat, a little brown one, such as the shopkeepers of Madrid wear, and put it on me, as well to hide my regimentals, as to make me more comfortable for the night.

I left Madrid that evening by the gate called the Puerto de Carreno, and, after being kindly embraced (according to the Spanish custom) by my friends, and beholding them offering up a prayer for our safety, we continued walking all night. The following morning, we arrived at a village, and were well received by the alcalde; who gave us rations, and told me that he had information of my escape from the French, and was instructed to afford me all the assistance in his power. After leaving this good man, the following morning, I fell in with a party of the guerrillas or banditti, who wore a kind of uniform, and were well mounted, and had come down from the Castile Mountains in the hopes of meeting some of the stragglers of the French army. On finding that we were English, the captain or chief of the party spoke kindly to us, and conducted us to a place of retreat, a cave, where he gave us bread, and wine, and dried fruit, and then sent some of his men to put us on the high road to Talavera.

After parting with the guerrillas, and proceeding about a league, we fell in with a Spanish lady on horseback, who, stopping, asked how far we had come, and having, on inquiry, learned every particular of our escape, took out her purse and offered me money, which I of course refused. The next day we reached Talavera, where we rested two days. The Spanish commandant there then was Don Carlos de España, who spoke excellent English; the same individual who is now so distinguished a character in Spain.[11] He gave me refreshments, and offered me conveyance of letters to our army, of which gladly availing myself, I wrote to Lord Wellington, apprising him of my being taken by the enemy, and telling him of my escape, and the strength of the French army, which I had seen on the plains near

11 General Roger Bernard Charles Espagnac de Ramefort (1775-1839) commanded Spanish troops at the Siege of Badajoz, Battles of Salamanca and Vitoria. He was consistently referred to as Don Carlos Espagna by Wellington.

Madrid, while a prisoner of war. I also informed him that the bridge across the Tagus, at Almaraz, was blown up.

While I was waiting for Don Carlos to prepare his own letters and despatches, I felt a curiosity to visit the field – the celebrated field – where, a few months before, the Battle of Talavera had been fought.[12] The plain, where this dreadful conflict took place, is situated about half an English mile north of the town. I walked to it, accompanied by a Spanish peasant, who was well acquainted with all that occurred; for in those days the Spanish peasantry were so accustomed to warfare, that any one of them could describe the positions of the two contending armies as well as some of the most experienced generals. My guide brought me into the centre of the field. Then, indeed, I beheld a scene which even a soldier cannot contemplate without his feelings being harrowed up – the bones of horses and men lying close together; the rider and his steed, and the skeletons, in rank, just as the poor fellows fell on that memorable day. My guide being an intelligent fellow, I asked his opinion of the scene and the contest that had taken place; he said it was a drawn battle, both English and French claiming it. When I remarked the numerous skeletons that covered the plain, he told me the cause of their remaining there was, when the British and French armies retreated, the dead bodies were left on the field; and that there being no one to inter them, the vultures, therefore, had fed on the bodies. Even then the birds were hovering over this recent scene of carnage, seeking fresh prey. I paused – all was silent. It was then evening – I reflected with feelings of real pain, how that many of the poor fellows, whose skeletons were now before me, I had often met, in health and spirits at the mess table. I know not how long I might have remained here, if my guide, observing the melancholy mood in which I was indulging, had not hurried me away. Indeed, so much was I affected, that Don Carlos, on my return, when he was taking leave of me, remarked, 'Signor Captain, I see you feel the spectacle you have been witnessing.'

The next day, I proceeded by the mountain, en route, to Badajoz, and arrived at Santacruz [de la Sierra].[13] On my going to the alcalde's house, his wife and daughter welcomed me, he not being at home; but, on his arrival, I related to him my escape, and requested rations and billets for my party. Sending for his secretary, he had them instantly made out, with the exception of one for myself. Upon my asking for it, he gruffly replied, 'that he would not give me one; for that his house, altering his manner, was my billet, and his table at my service.' He then took me for a walk, telling his wife we should return to dinner, where, to my surprise, neither his wife nor daughter was permitted to sit, but stood and attended us during the repast. In the evening, we were joined by his son-in-law, who was the doctor of the village. He told me I must remain at Santacruz [de la Sierra] for three or four days, and said

12 Hardly a few months before! The Battle of Talavera had occurred on 28 July 1809 over three years previously.

13 On the road between Trujillo and Merida.

he had given directions for the party to that effect, who should be well provided for. He then showed me my bed, where I was to sleep, and said it was the same in which Charles Fox slept, when he travelled through Spain some years since.[14] The tapestry consisted of rich crimson silk, bound with deep gold lace; and the quilt was a green satin, bound with silver lace, – affording a great contrast, indeed, to my late habitation in Madrid. I spent three or four days very happily with this good man and his family, and, soon as my party and I were completely refreshed, we proceeded on our journey.

On entering the village of Alcala, a French dragoon came galloping down to meet us. We thought we had again fallen into the hands of the enemy, when he informed us in Spanish that he had deserted with seven infantry[men] from the French, – that they were in a house surrounded by the peasantry, who threatened to kill them. He, therefore, begged of us to go with him to their relief; we did so, but our interference would have been in vain, were it not, that, at the moment, a Spanish commissary came from Cadiz with an escort, who soon succeeded in persuading the peasantry not to molest them, advising me to take them with me, as it would not be safe to leave them behind us; and, accordingly, they were joined to our party. We were now a motley crew, and continued our journey until the French dragoon insisted on pressing a horse for me to ride, which circumstance nearly lost us our lives, as the owner of the horse followed us to the next village, and raised a party of banditti against us, who lay in wait outside the village with the intention of firing on us when we should appear, as they were all armed. However, a Spanish colonel, who was on his way to join the army, hearing the circumstances from his servant, lost not a moment in coming to me to inform me of the intended attack, entreating me to return the horse to them, as otherwise our lives would in all probability be forfeited, as he could not protect us, having no troops with him.

As we were in a desperate part of the country I complied without hesitation, and at day-light the horse was given up; the colonel at the same time coming to me, pointed out the party of banditti crossing the country, which seemed to consist of from forty to fifty persons; therefore, not one of us would have escaped but for the colonel. This imminent danger being avoided, we continued our journey from day to day until we arrived at Badajoz. On coming to the gate, the officer on duty refused us admittance, until he should have apprised the governor. Our appearance, in fact, seemed so singular – a French dragoon fully mounted and armed – I walking after him unarmed, followed by the Frenchmen and our English soldiers – that they knew not what to make of us. After some delay, I was sent for by the governor, to whom I explained our situation, and the cause of our mixed party. He laughed heartily at my escape, and congratulating me, ordered rations and billets for the men, keeping me to dine with him.

14 Charles Fox, the renowned Whig politician (1749-1806).

The appearance which Badajoz presented after the late siege was truly miserable – houses unroofed in every direction, and walls threatening to fall on the unwary passengers. I lodged here in a habitation which now appeared almost shattered to pieces, although it was once splendid. The lady of the house informed me that her family had fled to Lisbon during the siege, but that she remained to preserve as much of their property as she could. She assured me, that, during the time of the plunder of the English, she was frequently placed on her knees with a loaded pistol to her breast to extort a confession from her where her treasures lay, while she constantly persisted in saying that she had no more than they had taken. At first, she seemed distant and reserved to me; but when I related my escape from Madrid, and mentioned the name of my good friend Collina, who had given me his coat, she informed me that she was a relation of his, and throwing off her reserve, entertained me elegantly, producing her plate and valuables. She mentioned that notwithstanding all she had suffered, and the frequent attempts made on her life by the soldiers, she still preserved all that was valuable of her property for her family. From Badajoz, we proceeded to Elvas, which is on the frontiers of Portugal, where we were well received by Mr Wood from Limerick, who was one of our commissaries.[15]

Here I parted from my French deserters, sending them to Lisbon. They regretted leaving me; and it was with much difficulty they would be persuaded to believe they were not to be enrolled in the 47th Regiment. The other soldiers I sent to their respective regiments. I now, lest my first letter to Lord Wellington should have miscarried, wrote an official letter to the Adjutant-General Pakenham,[16] at headquarters, and proceeded with my servant, in the best direction I could, to join my own regiment on the banks of the Douro, being accompanied on the route by a Mr Howell, a commissary, a good and pleasant fellow.[17] As we proceeded, our provisions became very short, and, notwithstanding my having the provider of necessaries with me, we could not procure any. This deficiency, however, my servant, Pat Dolan, whenever he could, made up for us, by picking up whatever came in his way. In fact, he never allowed us to want, always keeping some distance behind us, and never coming into any place where we stopped, without bringing a fowl or a young pig. At one time, we were in the greatest distress for a dinner, and had no hope of procuring anything, when Pat made his appearance with a large turkey, saying, 'That Portuguese farmer, sir, whose house you passed this morning, sent his compliments to you with this turkey.' At another time, he used to appear with

15 Deputy Assistant Commissary General John Wood.

16 Major General Edward Pakenham, Adjutant General, was later killed leading the attack on New Orleans in 1815.

17 Probably Lieutenant Jonathan Howells of the 77th Foot, who had until recently (June 1811) been a 1st Lieutenant Commissary in the Royal Artillery Drivers.

fowls, with some other person's compliments, when in fact, we well knew that Master Pat had helped himself without the farmer's consent.

It was laughable, one morning, to see Pat industriously driving out an old sow, before the inhabitants of the village were up. On his being asked his reason for so doing, he said it was the only plan to catch the young ones; 'For,' said he, 'they will soon follow the old one.' As usual, in the evening, Pat made his appearance with a sucking pig or two in his haversack. Thus Pat was a useful and faithful servant, – never allowing us to want.

At length, I joined my regiment at Lamego, on the 24th December, on the banks of the Douro, where it was cantoned in a valley near Lamego. Sometimes indeed, my conscience upbraided me for partaking of Pat's supplies, as I well knew they were taken from the poor inhabitants unfairly; but necessity had no law, and we could not starve. One day, on my remonstrating with Pat, and telling him, if Lord Wellington knew how he obtained the fowls, pigs, &c., I feared he would punish him severely; his reply was, 'Sir, neither you, nor Lord Wellington understand it right; for,' said he, 'sure *our* king, sir, is fighting for *their* king, and to put Ferdinand back on his throne; and sure, sir, all that can be done is to charge what I take to our King.' 'Why Pat,' said I, 'you seem to think there is an account between the two monarchs, and that your plundering can be settled in that way.' 'Certainly, sir,' replied Pat; 'it is the only plan, in my opinion.'

On my return from Madrid, a second time I entered the ancient and famed city of Truxillo. I called on Captain Gibson of the 31st Regiment of Foot,[18] who was stationed there as commandant, and found before me the baggage of my deceased friend, Major Broad, with his horses and servants. I communicated to Captain Gibson the retreat of Lord Wellington's army from Madrid, and he, apprehending a surprise, proposed starting the next morning with me, on my way to Badajoz, or, rather for the first English port I could meet with.

We therefore, set off next morning, escorted by twenty Portuguese dragoons, which he, as commandant, had attached to him. Our first day's march went off pleasantly enough, were it not for parting with our friends; and the second day proved tremendously wet. Captain Gibson and I were a good way on before our party, and in deep conversation, when we were suddenly called to by a Spanish boy herding sheep: 'A qui, a qui, Yngleses, estan ladrones!' that is, in English, 'Here, here, English, are the robbers!' and, upon turning our heads, we observed five or six ill-looking ruffians rushing from the wood at the bottom of the plain, and coming towards us, no doubt with a certainty of good prey, as we were well mounted. They had arrived very close to us, their leader calling us to halt; and, before we could make any reply, they saw at the turn of the road our Portuguese escort of dragoons and party, who then made their appearance. It was now our

18 Actually Lieutenant William Joseph Gibson, 31st Foot, who actually served in the Peninsula from 1808 to 1814 but only saw action at the battles of Talavera and Bussaco.

turn to exult at our fortunate escape, and it was laughable to see those fellows return to the wood at the sight of our dragoons. We proceeded forward, and in the evening arrived at the village. On sitting down to refresh ourselves at our billet, we were astonished by the arrival of four men naked, robbed of their money, horses and clothes. They proved to be two British officers, an English sutler, and his clerk, who were travelling to the rear, and were attacked on the same spot by the robbers, soon after we had passed, the same who had so unsuccessfully made the attempt on us: we did all we could for them, assisted by a Spanish priest.

The retreat from Burgos, which occurred about the time I was taken prisoner, though little described or written on, was very disastrous, and attended with privations almost incredible, – the rain coming down in torrents – the men enjoying little or no sleep, and having nothing to eat, as the commissaries were unable to procure any reasonable supply for the army, in consequence of the country having been already drained of nearly all kinds of provisions, so that it frequently happened, that our officers fed one day on rotten biscuit, and on another on meat alone; and latterly, barley, acorns, and small beans, called calavancas, were resorted to, for subsistence.

The French cavalry, too, harassed our rear constantly, which obliged us to leave the main roads and get into the woods, and ploughed fields, and sometimes to join into squares for our protection. Indeed, the retreat was so harassing, that we were often compelled, before our meat was half cooked, to leave it behind us, and proceed as well as we could – some of our poor men leaving their shoes behind them, and others dropping down dead from fatigue. Sir Edward Paget was taken on this retreat at the corner of a wood. He might have escaped. It was his brave conduct and anxiety to cover the retreat that occasioned his capture.[19]

As the Fifth Division of the army retreated, they perceived the horses and mules lying dead on the road, and occasionally observed that pieces had been cut out of the thighs of the horses, and eaten by the Portuguese soldiers. When a weak man was unable to march, his comrade was left behind to mind him. Rather than let him fall into the hands of the French, the Portuguese soldier would, on such occasions, shoot his companion; as it was well known the French gave them no quarter; but the English prisoners were treated well; for when taken, they were only required to break their firelocks, and then were sent to the rear. During the retreat, the army marched all day, when they took a short and uncomfortable rest, and at day-light the enemy commenced firing shot and shells, particularly when our men were crossing rivers, at which time they annoyed the columns very much, and we frequently lost numbers of our stoutest and best soldiers. The army, at length, got to Ciudad Rodrigo, and, encamping under the protection of the guns,

19 Lieutenant General Sir Edward Paget, previously encountered in this narrative as colonel of the 28th Foot in Egypt, was captured near San Marcial on 17 November 1812 and remained a prisoner of war until the end of the war in 1814.

forced the enemy to retire and give up the pursuit, from which position they shortly after broke up and went into winter quarters in Portugal, the Fifth Division being cantoned in the Province of Lamego, on the banks of the Douro, where I joined it after my escape.[20]

There were three brothers, very fine young men, as honourable as they were brave, of the name of Ireland, in the 87th Regiment, on the retreat from Burgos – one of whom being severely wounded, and another seized with that dreadful complaint, dysentery, they were both placed, writhing with agony, by a friend of mine, in a hospital waggon, with the wife of an assistant surgeon, who was in her *accouchement*, and sent to the rear. The poor fellows died before morning, sincerely and deservedly regretted by all who knew them.[21]

Government gave a liberal allowance to their mother; but what sum could compensate for the loss of two such young men?

Among the many and various scenes that occurred during this retreat, the following distressing circumstance took place in our regiment, the 47th. An excellent woman, our mess cook, and wife of one of our sergeants, Cowell, followed the regiment from Cadiz, although repeatedly advised to remain behind, in consequence of the situation she was in, being near her confinement. Notwithstanding every remonstrance, she persevered in going, and joining the regiment, which was then encamped near Madrid; she was, on the night of her arrival, delivered of twins.

As the regiment had no tents, this poor creature was obliged to lie under a tree; the soldiers, indeed, like men, taking off their coats to cover her. Two days after the entire army moved; and this poor woman, with her twins, unaccountable as it may appear, travelled with her infants in her arms, or on her back, during the retreat from day to day, under incessant rain and hail, which falls much heavier there than in England. Though she frequently had to pass over two or three rivers in the day, up to her knees in water, the enemy pressing us in the rear, and the shot and shells constantly falling about her, yet she escaped, and arrived safe at Ciudad Rodrigo, and proceeded to Lisbon, where she embarked for England, which she reached in safety with her children, after losing her poor husband, Sergeant Cowell, who was killed at the storming of St Sebastian. The occurrence I have just related has reminded me of a similar instance, but in a different rank of life, which strongly exhibits the noble conduct of a faithful wife.

There were at least 800 ladies in Lisbon, enjoying comparative ease, while their husbands were enduring all the horrors and chances of war. Among the latter was a lady, the wife of a captain, whose attachment for her husband was so great, that she determined on going to the army and braving the terrors of war.

20 After the retreat from Burgos, the 2/47th Foot were allocated to the 2nd Brigade of the 5th Division.

21 Ensigns William and De Courcey Ireland of the 87th Foot died on the retreat from Madrid, their brother was Lieutenant Stanley Ireland, of the same regiment, who survived the war.

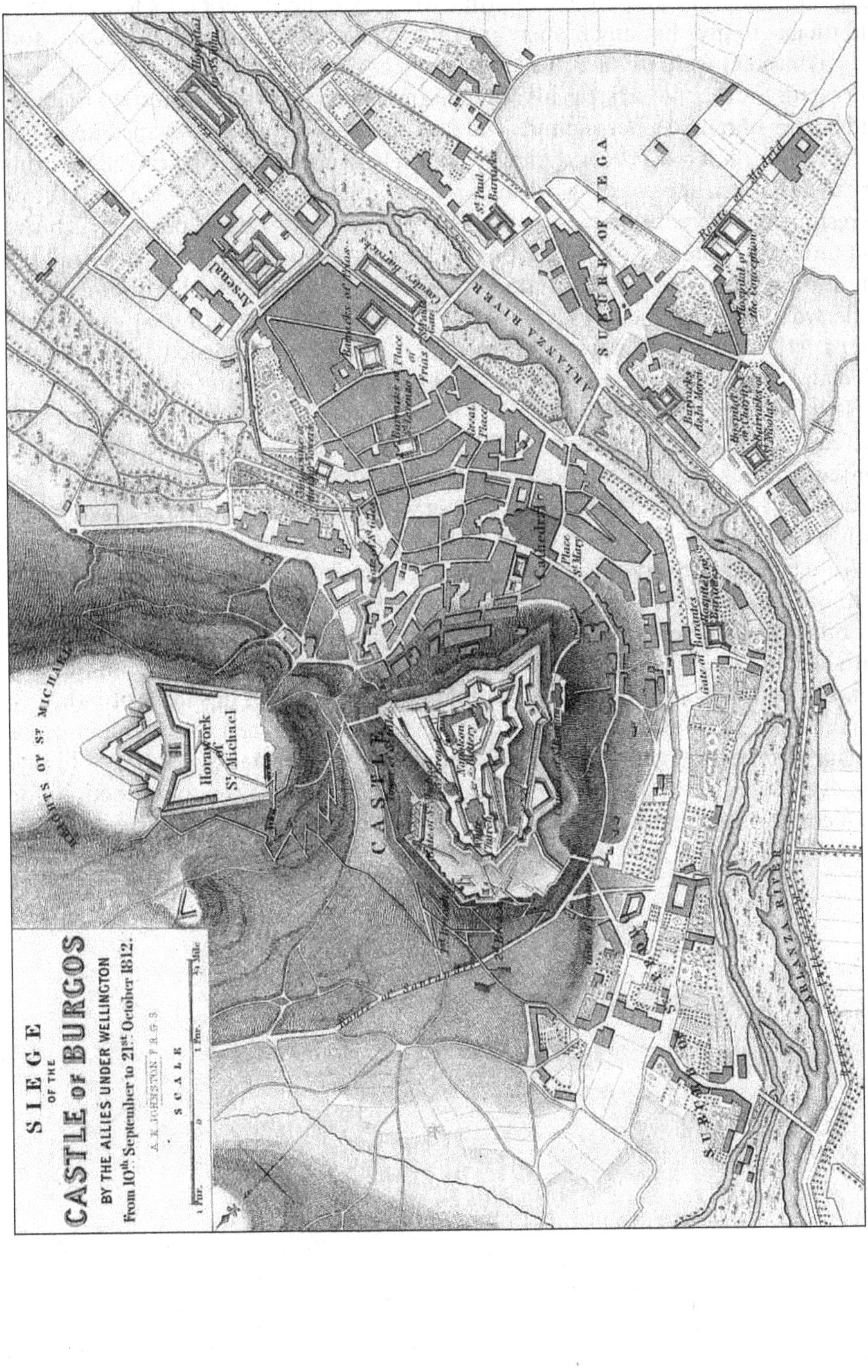

Map 8 Map of the Siege of Burgos 1812, published by Alison. (Public Domain).

On her arrival, the army was entrenched before Burgos; her situation became deplorable, her husband not having time to speak to her except for a few minutes, and unable to give her any money, as the army had little or none with them, and the paymasters were frequently some distance in the rear. However, he collected among his brother officers, for his amiable and deserving wife, about sixty pounds, and having obtained a horse, mule, and Portuguese boy for her, prevailed upon her to leave him, but with great difficulty, and return to Lisbon. She travelled, from day to day, until, after passing through a wood, she arrived at a posada, or place of refreshment, where, to her inexpressible horror, she missed her purse, which she had unluckily fastened every morning on setting out, on the crutch of her saddle. On finding the loss she had sustained, supposing it to have caught in some of the underwood, she returned in search of her treasure, and, after minutely examining the path through the wood, but unfortunately in vain, she returned to the posada, tired and miserable, where she was lodged that night free of any expense.

Next morning, she re-commenced her journey, having, from the time she parted from her husband, nearly 300 miles to travel, almost broken-hearted in consequence of her loss; but, alas! Her misfortunes were not to end here, for the next night, her Portuguese boy fled, taking with him her horse and his own mule, with all the clothes she had brought for her journey. Judge, now, her situation, a delicate female in a strange country, subject to insult, and enduring every privation! But hers was not a common mind: instead of giving way under the weight of her misfortunes, she now prosecuted her journey on foot, and continued walking, until her shoes were worn off her feet. At length, the army retreating from Burgos, came up with her, and were struck with horror at seeing her in such a situation.

I shall not attempt to picture her husband's feelings, when his regiment came up; nor the meeting which took place under such circumstances. Suffice it to say, that everyone vied in paying her all the attention in his power, and procured for her a comfortable mode of travelling during the remainder of the journey.

11

Vitoria to Toulouse

After the retreat from Burgos, while we were at Lamego, Colonel Skerrett having been appointed on the staff,[1] different officers were anxious to become his aides-de-camp, and applied to him on the subject; but he was undecided, from habitual indifference. Captain Fane, of the 87th Regiment, was one of those who were ambitious for the appointment.[2] As soon as it became known to us, we had it communicated to him, that he had succeeded in his application, although he was at a distance of sixty miles, when he immediately travelled up, supposing it to be the fact, which, however, it was not; as Colonel Skerrett then had not the least idea of appointing any one in particular. We were standing together the evening of his arrival, in the market-place, some enjoying the idea of his being disappointed, and others beginning to regret the extent to which the joke had been carried – when Colonel Skerrett, who was present, understanding the trick that had been played on Captain Fane, turned about to him, and said – 'I do appoint you, Captain Fane, to be my aide-de-camp, and you may now, in your turn, laugh at those gentlemen who have had their laugh at you.' Thus, what was intended as a mere jest, turned out a fortunate circumstance for him.

While at Lamego, I was sent for a few days to Portalegre, on duty, accompanied by Lieutenant Lyne.[3] When we had come to a certain part of the road, we heard moaning on all sides, as we rode quietly along. We immediately dismounted, and, on looking around us, perceived a sergeant lying on the ground, fastened by his leg to a mule, and a good deal bruised. On asking him what occasioned the disastrous state in which we found him, he related that he, with two soldiers and a Portuguese, had been coming up from Lisbon to join the army, each leading his mule laden with baggage; that the two soldiers were jawing, as he termed it, along the road, but were not able to come to blows, as they could not let go their

1 Colonel Skerrett was given command of the 2nd Brigade of the 4th Division in November 1812.

2 Captain Thomas Fane of the 87th Foot became an aide de camp to General Skerrett from August 1813 when Skerrett had taken over a brigade in the Light Division.

3 Lieutenant Michael Lyne of the 47th Foot.

mules, or they would have run away; and that at length, he, the sergeant, had determined on bringing them up the hill, and letting them fight it out across their firelocks, as was the custom in Ireland to fight across a stick or garter. Having, accordingly, fastened the mules to their legs, the sergeant took one end of the firelock, and the Portuguese the other, the butt end; and, as the combatants commenced fighting, the Portuguese unknowingly touched the trigger, upon which the gun, being loaded, went off: the report startled the mules, which fled in different directions, each dragging his leader with him to the bottom of the hill, where they lay cut by the rocks and torn by the briers in their descent. We extricated them as speedily as possible, unfastening the ropes, and enabling them to proceed on their journey. The two combatants were pretty well cooled by the disaster, and the sergeant was truly grateful for having escaped being shot by the awkwardness of the Portuguese.

After our return to Lamego, a dreadful fever broke out in the army, from eight to twelve of our men dying in a day. A remarkably fine fellow, a grenadier of the name of Randle Bannister, was attacked by it, and held out thirty-five days,. to the astonishment of Dr Forbes, who was physician to the division,[4] but died on the thirty-sixth day. In him, we lost as brave a soldier as any in the army. The chaplain of the 5th Division, the Reverend Mr Browne, an excellent young man, also caught it from his close attention, in the course of his religious duties, to the poor patients. After suffering a few days, he followed the poor Bannister, to the sincere regret of all who knew him. I attended his funeral. He was buried in an open field, on the very spot where he had so often heard the drums beat for the service to be read – and the men, Protestants as well as Catholics, shed tears over his grave.[5]

While the regiment was stationed here, I went down to Oporto, a distance of fourteen leagues, being accompanied by my son, my nephew, and my faithful servant, Pat; and stopped at the Amarante, about half way. I should have rested there that night at the Casa de Pasta, or inn, but the vigilance of Pat found better quarters for me. He ascertained that there was a convent in the neighbourhood, where it was customary to entertain strangers; we accordingly repaired to the gates, where, on ringing the bell, one of the friars admitted us, pointing to the stable to put up our horses – and, having conducted us to an apartment, was going to give directions to prepare dinner for us, when my careful Pat, ever on the look-out, pried into the kitchen, where there was a noble dinner getting ready for the friars, seventy in number, and, hastening back, told me not to give Padre Louis any farther trouble; 'For,' said he, 'master, I have inspected the kitchen, and advise you to eat your dinner with them, in preference to getting it in your own apartment, for they will only give you the leavings.' Agreeing with Pat, we went into the Sal,

4 Charles Fergusson Forbes, Physician to the 5th Division from May-August 1813.
5 The Reverend Frederick Harvey Browne, Chaplain to the 5th Division, died 24 January 1813.

or dining hall, and took our seats at the table, the friars by our side. The dinner was excellent, and while we partook of it there was one of those religious men in a pulpit, reading prayers. There had been a plentiful supply of wine placed on the table at first, but Padre Louis, knowing our habits, nodded to us to remain. As soon, therefore, as the other friars had left the room, he gave us a dessert, and plenty of additional wine. Pat was not forgotten in the kitchen, but was well provided for by the lay brothers, whom he amused highly with his travels. We got good beds that night, and our horses were taken every care of; in the morning we were furnished with an excellent breakfast, Pat suggested, that as we were in no hurry, and were so well provided for, we might as well stay for two or three days longer, but it was out of our power to remain more than another day. The second day we were introduced to the Prior, who was a fine, venerable looking man, and expressed a hope that we were made comfortable – telling us not to be ashamed to call for anything that we might want while in the convent.

The same day the Prince of Orange came, and remained that night, and was pleased to be very familiar with us.[6] Leaving the good brothers, we proceeded to Oporto on the morning of the third day. The English merchants were particularly polite to us. We returned, in a few days, to Lamego, just in time to accompany the army, which got into motion on the 14th of May, and advanced into Spain.

I had almost forgotten to mention, that while we were quartered in Lamego and cantoned in the valley of the Douro, our sergeant attended a house on the road to take orders. While assembled there one day, a Portuguese muleteer with a litter (a sedan chair suspended between two mules, as carriages cannot travel through that part of Portugal) stopped for some minutes on the road, near the house. The novelty of this mode of conveyance attracted the attention of one of our men, Sergeant Sheridan, and he, from curiosity, while the muleteer rested, opened and looked into it. This harmless act enraged the fellow so much, that when the poor sergeant returned and took his seat among his companions, the muleteer followed very quietly, and placing himself on the bench by the side of Sheridan, secretly drew a long clasp-knife from his pocket, and, unperceived, plunged it into poor Sheridan's side, up to the handle, who had only time to repeat, 'I am a dead man!' when he expired. The instant the muleteer committed the act he rushed out of the house, and, throwing the knife outside of the door, ran across the road, and jumped into the fields. He was followed by the sergeants, with their swords drawn, but they could not come up with him, and he would have escaped, had not some of the officers' servants, who were out airing their masters' horses, prevented him from reaching the mountains. With their assistance the sergeants had nearly come up with the murderer, whom they would have cut into pieces but General Robinson, who commanded the brigade, rode up, and had him handed over to

6 Colonel the Prince William of Orange, extra aide de camp to the Duke of Wellington.

The Battle of Vitoria 1813 by James Beadle. (Nuneaton Museum)

the civil authorities at Lamego;[7] however, he was never punished. We understood, afterwards, that he took refuge in the church, and became a monk. Poor Sheridan was buried in the cathedral of Lamego, and his funeral was attended by the bishop and all the clergymen, as he was a Roman Catholic.

Leaving Lamego, I followed the army, having been detained by business, and, on approaching Vitoria, met General Andrew Hay,[8] who had a son, a captain in the Royals, an excellent and deserving young man.[9] We both felt much anxiety about our sons, who were very young men, his being but twenty-one, and mine, a lieutenant in the 47th Regiment, only nineteen years of age. I had also my nephew, Lieutenant Hill, a fine lad of seventeen, in the same regiment. I passed over the field after the battle, on the evening of the 23rd of June, the enemy retreating, and our army pursuing them. At that time, I little knew the wretchedness that awaited me, my then only son having been killed, together with my nephew, Hill, on that fatal day.[10] As the melancholy intelligence was abruptly communicated to

7 Major General Frederick Robinson commanded the 2nd Brigade of the 5th Division.

8 Major General Andrew Hay commanded the 1st Brigade in the 5th Division.

9 Captain George Hay, 1st Foot, served as aide de camp to General Hay. He was killed at the Battle of Vitoria on 21 June 1813.

10 Harley missed the Battle of Vitoria, fought on 21 June 1813, but the regiment was fully involved in the attack on Gamarra Major and took heavy casualties. His son, Lieutenant John Harley, and nephew

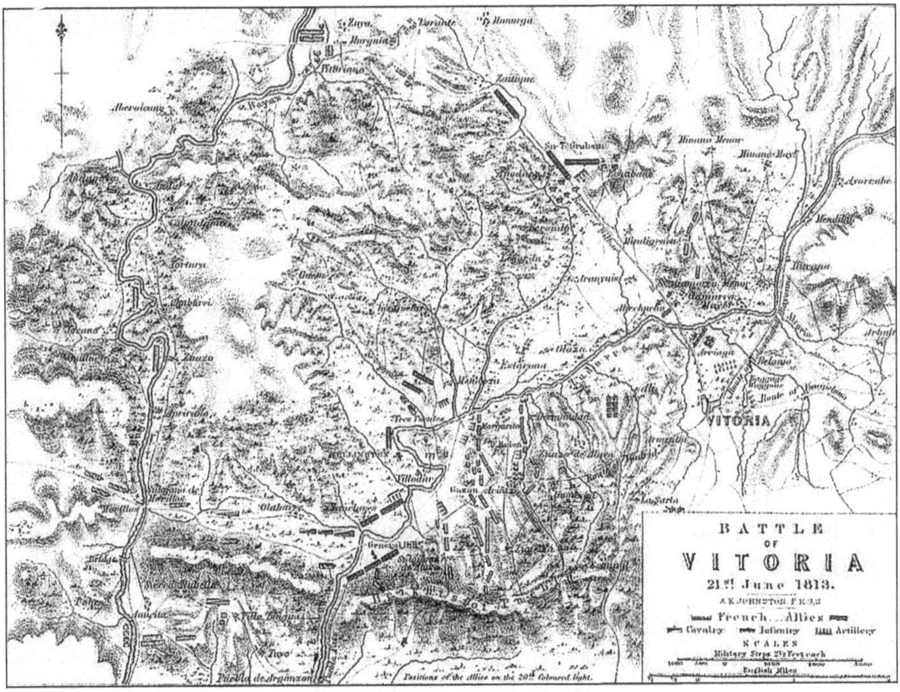

Map 9 Map of the Battle of Vitoria by A. Johnston. (Author's collection)

me by our Adjutant, Drew,[11] whom I was surprised to find in the rear, it very nearly proved fatal to me, nor can I now tell what became of me for some time after. The general [Hay], also, lost his son on the same day.

Colonel O'Halloran, of the 4th Foot,[12] prevailed on me to accompany him from the field, and we proceeded together, until we arrived at the village of Hernani, near San Sebastian, where I found the regiment encamped with the 5th Division of the army, the regiment being then commanded by Major Robert Kelly;[13] and, about the same period, I received a letter from Colonel Skerrett, condoling with me on the loss I had sustained. It was the letter of a sincere friend, which he had always been to me. We now remained at Hernani, close to where the siege was going on, and furnished the working parties to cut the line of entrenchment, which was carried through the brow of the hill in front of San Sebastian, where the

Lieutenant George Hill, were killed along with eighteen men; Captains William Hodges, Henry Parsons, and William Yates, Lieutenant Thomas Shortt, and eighty-eight men wounded.

11 Harley's memory has failed him here, there was no officer named Drew in the regiment, nor anything similar. The adjutant of the 47th at the time was actually Lieutenant Johnston Burrows.

12 Actually Major George O'Halloran 4th Foot.

13 Major Robert Kelly, 47th Foot, was killed at San Sebastian.

convent was situated. Our miners had to cut through the burying ground of the convent, and here was presented a melancholy spectacle as the soldiers proceeded in their work. Coffins and bodies appeared in every stage of decay; some recently interred, and becoming decomposed, others already mouldering into clay. From the miners being under the level of the burying ground, I myself saw two coffins tumble down, and the bodies roll out. They must have been persons of distinction, as they were dressed in black velvet, and could not, from their appearance, have been long in the ground. During these scenes, every heart became callous, even the coffins were broken up and made fuel of.

A breach was nearly effected in San Sebastian, when the town was stormed; but, unfortunately, the attack failed, and we suffered a severe loss – many a brave officer and man fell.[14] I saw that morning, that excellent officer, General Sir Thomas Graham, now Lord Lynedoch. In his countenance was depicted the greatest anxiety and distress, occasioned by the repulse he had met with, and which was not his fault. We were now obliged to wait for heavy artillery, before we could make a second attempt on the town; at length, in the middle of August, the heavy cannon arrived, and being soon mounted, a considerable breach was effected.

At this time, I had occasion to go to Lesaca, in the Pyrenees, which was then our head-quarters, and where the military chest was kept. I slept at the house where Captain Murray of the Guards was stationed, at the rising of the hills.[15] I arose early, and, on ascending the Pyrenees, I met Lord Wellington coming from Lesaca on his way to San Sebastian. Before I left Captain Murray's quarters, I could plainly see that the heavy guns, which we had planted near the convent, had made a very considerable breach, and were yet firing with increased effect. Lord Wellington asked me whence I came, and if the heavy batteries had opened on San Sebastian; I replied, that I came from San Sebastian, where the batteries had opened a fire with such effect that a large breach was made. He seemed surprised at this, and said, 'If you left San Sebastian this morning, how could you be here now?' but I informed him that I slept at Captain Murray's quarters, at the foot of the hills, and on ascending them early in the morning, I could see every shot from our guns take effect. 'Oh! That,' said he, 'is explaining it.' He then wished me good morning, and rode off. His Lordship was only attended by a single dragoon. I proceeded, and, in about an hour after, met his Staff, who hastily inquired if I had seen Lord Wellington. On my telling them the direction he had taken, they galloped after him. On parting with Lord Wellington, I recollected where I had first seen his Lordship. It was in the city of Cork, where he was then Lieutenant Colonel Wellesley, commanding the 33rd Regiment. My cousin, Captain McMahon, of the Irish Brigade in the French service, who had emigrated, as before stated, had the

14 The first storm of San Sebastian was made on 25 July 1813 and ended in failure with the loss of 693 killed and wounded and 316 captured.

15 Lieutenant and Captain Archibald Murray of the 3rd Foot Guards.

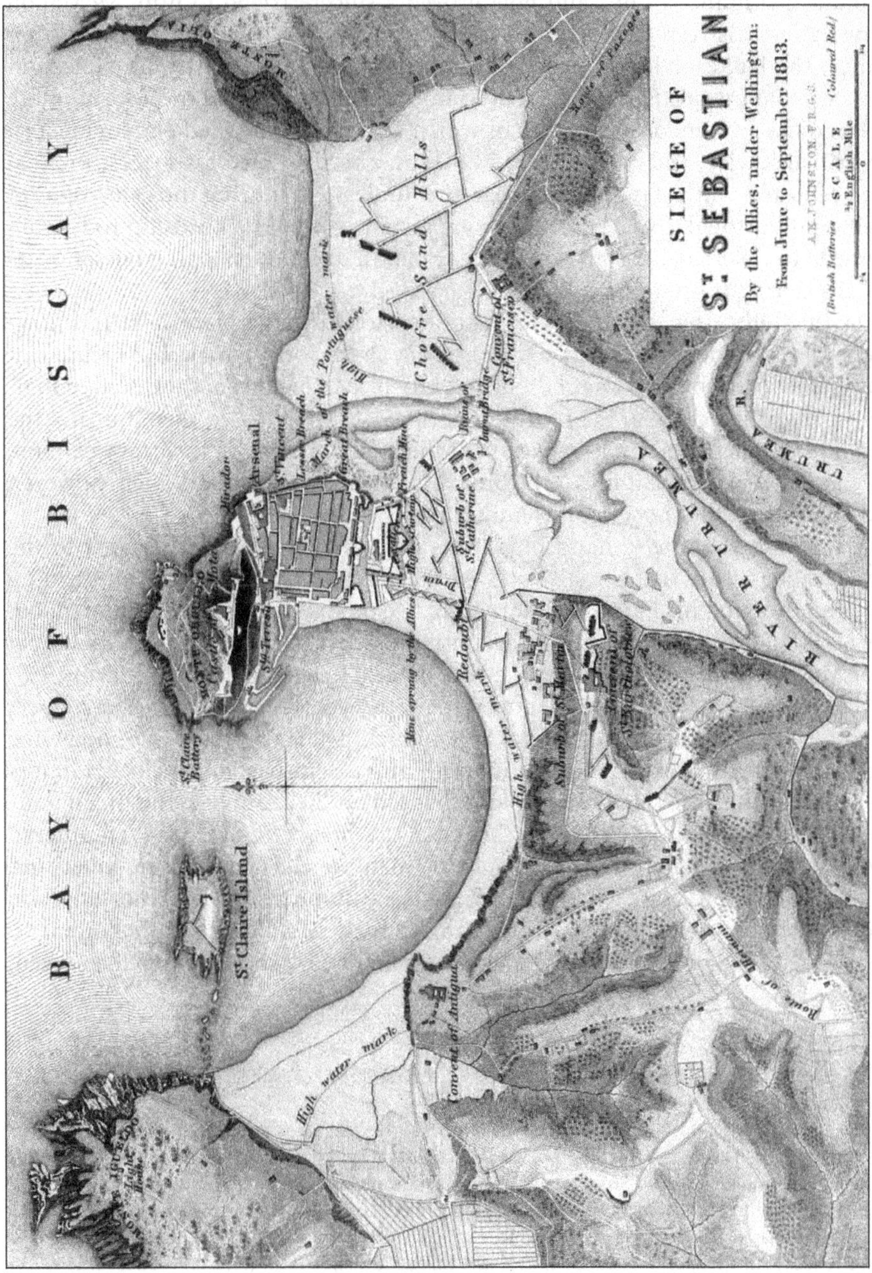

Map 10 Map of the Siege of San Sebastian published by Alison. (Public Domain)

honour of being intimate, after his return, with Colonel Wellesley, who had been an old acquaintance of his, and now proved a sincere friend to him. McMahon being in very distressed circumstances, and unemployed when he returned from France, the Duke invited him to his residence, and gave him letters of recommendation to his brother, the present Marquis Wellesley, then Lord Mornington, and in office in London; by means of which McMahon obtained employment in the British service, and to which afterwards may be attributed his success in life. I often reflected on the fatigue this great man underwent, during the campaigns of Spain and Portugal. I well remember one instance of it. His Lordship rode from Freineda to Celerico, a distance of eighty miles in one day, changing horses occasionally during the journey.[16]

On the 30th, preparations were made for storming the place next morning. There were a number of candidates for leading on the forlorn hope, but Lieutenant Maguire, of the 4th Foot, was chosen, and fifty picked men from the different regiments. At eight o'clock in the morning of the 31st, Maguire led them on, and the men in the trenches began to move out of them, under cover of the heavy cannon, which kept up a constant fire at the breach and walls; our artillery-men, however, taking care that the shots went over our men's heads.

I saw poor Maguire, a handsome, fine young fellow, lead on his men to the breach, under a fire that actually mowed them down, and observed him turning about and waving his hat to the remaining five or six, and encouraging them on. The poor fellows dropped, one by one, until the whole party were killed, including poor Maguire himself, who fell at the very breach, in sight of the whole army.[17]

Major Robert Kelly, who commanded the 47th, accosted me about seven o'clock, when he was going down to the trenches, and saying, 'Harley, that was good wine you got for me,' requested I would dine with him at half-past four o'clock; humorously remarking, 'provided I live so long.' He led on the regiment, and, in an hour after, was killed between the trenches and the breach. Our regiment suffered severely. Out of twenty-two officers and 500 men, we had eight officers killed and nine wounded, and 200 men killed.[18] Among the number wounded mortally, was Major Livesay, who received a wound through the shoulder, exactly similar to that of the late gallant Nelson. He was an officer of long standing, having served,

16 By modern roads the distance is about 42 miles, by the less direct roads then, it may have been 50 or 60 miles.

17 Lieutenant Francis Maguire 4th Foot led the Forlorn Hope at San Sebastian and was killed.

18 Harley's figure is correct except there were only eight wounded officers according to the records. His statement of the men killed probably meant killed and wounded; as the official numbers of dead were 108 rank & file and 117 wounded. Officer casualties consisted of Major Robert Kelly, Captain William Hodges, Charles Livesay (died of wounds later), Lieutenants Thomas Shortt, George Norris, Ensigns J. Bakewell, John Campbell, Thomas Bennett, and Ensign Alexander Hall (died of wounds later) killed; Captain Henry Oglander, Lieutenants Thomas Power, William Kendall, William Johnson, John Nason, Edward Agar, and Stephen Burke wounded.

Siege of San Sebastian by Edward Orme. (Public Domain)

A contemporary print of the Siege of San Sebastian. (Anne S.K. Brown Collection)

since he had been a very young man, in the 47th Regiment. He possessed every good quality which could endear him to his brother officers, who all regretted him deeply. He fell, bravely leading the light company through the breach, being shot from the top of a wall by a French rifleman.[19] Major Livesay had two brothers, one of them a general in the Spanish service.[20]

At twelve o'clock, our troops had full possession of the town, and the French garrison retired into the citadel, situated on a hill, which was near the town. I went, in the evening, through the breach, which was filled with dead bodies, so that I could scarcely get over them. The scene that presented itself to me was horrifying – the dead lying in heaps in the streets – the French and British lying side by side; and not unfrequently a drunken soldier of ours was seen amongst them fast asleep; plundering parties, too, women as well as men, were very active in every direction; breaking, not only into private houses, but into the churches and theatres. It was laughable, notwithstanding the melancholy scenes around us, to see those thoughtless fellows coming out of the theatre dressed in the costume of the players, and others leaving the churches in the robes of the clergy-man, and singing through the streets. I cannot give an adequate description of the horrible scenes that occurred during that night and the next day.

The following morning, I was conversing with General Hay (near the great church) and Captain Stewart, of the Royals – the enemy's riflemen at the time keeping up a brisk fire from the citadel, wherever they could discover a red coat. Captain Stewart was very curious to see them, and though often admonished by the general not to expose himself near the church, his curiosity was so great that the unfortunate fellow stooped down in order to have a peep at them, at the same time holding a firelock in his hand, to have a shot at them; but the sharp sight of the French was such, that the moment he showed the top of his head over the wall, having first taken off his cap, they fired, before he could raise his eye to the wall, and shot him through the forehead. He fell flat on his back, near us, gave one convulsive struggle, and in a moment was quite dead. Captain Stewart was as fine a young man as there was in the British army. He had gone through all the campaigns, fighting bravely in every action, and thus foolishly lost his life by his curiosity. This poor fellow was contributing to the support of his mother and two sisters at the time of his death.[21]

During the siege, the enemy sprung a mine near the breach, by which Colonel Sir Robert Fletcher, of the Engineers,[22] Captain Hodges and Shortt, of the 47th

19 Captain Charles Livesay led the storming party after Major Kelly was killed. He was mortally wounded and died of his wounds on 15 September 1813.

20 William Livesay served in the Spanish army, he had been in the Hibernia Regiment in 1808.

21 Harley must have assumed he was killed outright. In fact, Captain James Stewart, 1st Foot, was severely wounded on 25 July 1813 and died of his wounds on 4 September 1813.

22 Lieutenant Colonel Richard Fletcher, Royal Engineers, was killed at San Sebastian on 31 August 1813.

The ruins of San Sebastian as drawn by Thomas Driver in February 1814. (National Museum of Bermuda)

Regiment, were blown up.[23] Lieutenant Lyne, of the 47th, bravely rushed from the trenches and went in through the breach, for which he was afterwards put under arrest by General Hay, for being too forward, or rather, going without leave, though it was a courageous act of the poor fellow. He was brother to the present C[ornelius] Lyne, Esq of Hance Street Dublin. We were in possession of the town for some days before the French, in the citadel, capitulated.[24] They were summoned to surrender two or three times, but still held out, in hopes of relief – but that was impossible, as they could only receive it by sea, which was prevented by our men-of-war, that were cruising about. As, therefore, no force could get in, we hemming them in on the land side, and their provisions becoming nearly exhausted, they were at last compelled to hoist a flag of truce, and accept of the terms offered; which were, to march to the Praca, in the town, or grand square, with the honours of war, and then to lay down their arms and be sent to England. After the surrender of the citadel, about nine o'clock next morning, accompanied by an engineer officer, I walked up with an intention of going to the citadel, but meeting General Rey and his staff, at a small guard-house, we stopped.[25] The general politely asked us in, and, as they were at breakfast, pressed us to take some refreshment. It appeared

23 Captain William Hodges and Lieutenant Thomas Shortt were killed on 31 August 1813.
24 The citadel of La Mota Castle stood on the promontory of Monte Orgullo, it fell on 8 September.
25 *Général de Brigade* Louis Emmanuel Rey had commanded the French garrison in San Sebastian.

The first known photograph taken of San Sebastian, with the defences appearing much as they would have done in 1813. (Author's collection)

that they were waiting until the hour should arrive when they were to go into the town.

A respectable elderly lady, and two younger ones, were with them, whom General Rey requested I would be good enough to see safe down the hill, and through the town. I accordingly took charge of them, and, on account of the rain which fell the night before, we found the descent very unpleasant. When I got them safe to the bottom of the hill, I met a Mr McKenzie, a very excellent man, one of our assistant commissary generals, and being anxious to return up the hill, in order to see the citadel, I requested him to pay attention to the ladies, and protect them until they got through the town, after which he might procure a lodging for them, on the other side. They were the widow and two daughters of a commissary general, who had died a short time before, in the citadel. McKenzie was so pleased with them that he was married to one of the daughters of this lady in less than two months after.[26]

At twelve o'clock, the ceremony of surrendering the citadel took place. The brave General Rey and his garrison having marched down, I witnessed his handing his

26 Assistant Commissary General John McKenzie.

sword to General Oswald,[27] and the French soldiers grounding their arms. They were then marched out of the town, immediately after which the general and his staff went on board a man-of-war, and the soldiers sailed for England in transports.

During the time of plundering, the soldier's wives were some of the most active. I have gone into a church, and found three or four of them seated together, dividing watches and jewellery, and, on my speaking to them, they asked me did I want to interfere with them, and desired me to go off about my business.

The Spanish families were entirely stripped and plundered of their apparel, and I saw, in the course of a few days after, ladies purchasing their own silk stockings, and other articles, from the soldiers' wives on the roads. The second day of plundering, my servant, Pat, was most anxious to get permission to go into the town; I had always refused him, well knowing his *honourable* propensity, but, at last, finding I was absent, he went into the town for an hour. On my return I missed him, and on inquiry, learned that he had provided himself with a sack out of the stable, and whistling very merrily, had gone off, no doubt anticipating the prospect of his golden treasure. Pat, as he afterwards told me himself, carefully examined the remote parts of the city, where no plunderers had gone, it being near the citadel, and where he was confident they had not ventured. From his own account, he entered a very respectable house, the family of which had all fled to the upper apartments; but no sooner had Pat made his appearance, than a young lady, one of the family, came down and said, 'Signor, you are come for plunder, come with me, and you shall have all we have to give.' She descended with Pat, to the ground floor, and with her hands removed some earth, and produced china cups and saucers, which she desired him to take, but this did not satisfy Pat, and he began very industriously to remove the earth in every part of the floor, and at length came to the family plate, in great abundance. 'Accordingly,' said Pat, 'I filled the corn sack with coffee-pots, tea-pots, spoons, forks, and everything of plate I could carry, and proceeded by a private way to get to the gate which led to my way home.' I must remark, that the Portuguese never plundered, themselves, but they invariably took it from our soldiers, whenever they met them singly. Pat, in a lonely place, and before he got to the gate, met some of those fellows, who soon disburthened him of his sack-load of plate, and gave him a good drubbing into the bargain. He returned home that night, with his face all cut and bruised, vowing vengeance against the entire Portuguese nation.

Two or three days before the citadel fell, Lord Wellington came down from his headquarters, Lesaca, about seven leagues from San Sebastian, to witness the siege. I was standing near him, when the enemy's magazine blew up, in consequence of a shell from us falling on it, and took particular notice how cool this brave man was under the circumstance, though we were all a good deal excited at the occurrence. I observed his lordship attentively viewing around him how everything was going on.

27 Major General John Oswald, commanding the 5th Division, was slightly wounded on 31 August 1813.

One glance of his penetrating eye was sufficient, and we all read in his countenance that he was satisfied the place must fall in a few days. After conversing with some of the officers familiarly, and remaining about an hour, he rode off again. No general in the British service knew better the French mode of fighting than Lord Wellington. He was perfectly acquainted with their system, and it was that which made his lordship more than a match for them. I well remember one day, near Bayonne, when the enemy showed an extended line in front of us, and appeared in order of battle, he smiled, and said, 'Now they are going to retreat.' His lordship's words were true, for in the morning not one of them was to be seen. They had all retreated during the night.

Several scenes, revolting to any man of feeling, came under my view during this dreadful siege, some of which I could not commit to paper. I will, however, relate one, told me by Lieutenant Power, of our regiment, who, in consequence of his bravery, was afterwards promoted to a company in the 60th Regiment, at the recommendation of Major General Robinson.[28] He was passing along the streets, when he was addressed by an old servant woman from a window, who cried out, in Spanish, 'Aqui tiene toda que quieres guards vos nosotros;' which is, in English, 'Here is everything you want, – protect us.' Lieutenant Power went upstairs, and, on entering a splendid room, beheld a lovely young Spanish lady. Her father and mother had gone away during the siege, through dread of the English, and left her and the old lady in care of the house. They pulled out various drawers, showing Power a quantity of money, plate, and jewellery, proposing him to take all, but entreating that he would remain and protect them. No officer in the army would be more willing to do so than Power, but his time was not his own. While he was in the room, and considering how he could serve this interesting female, a drunken soldier of the plundering party proceeded upstairs, and unceremoniously entered the drawing room. Power remonstrated with him, and advised him to go away, but the man refused, and was inclined to be sulky, as, during this dreadful scene of plundering, soldiers had little or no respect for their officers. The stairs, in this part of Spain, are quite straight, from the entrance of the front door to the room, being without any landing-place. This fellow had his firelock in his hand, and Power, finding all argument unavailing, and that he was determined on violence, seized the firelock from him, and pitched him down the stairs to the bottom. As he had thus gained possession of the loaded firelock, the fellow had no redress, and skulked away. Power was, however, unfortunately called off to the trenches, and put on duty for the night, which prevented him from remaining and protecting these unfortunate females. His first object in the morning, as soon as he got off duty, was to fly to the house, to see how they had got on during the night. On entering it, he was horror struck on witnessing the scene before him – the poor woman lying on the floor, not able to speak or move – the young lady reclining on a sofa, with her hair hanging loosely over her neck, and her garments torn to

28 Lieutenant Thomas Power, 47th Foot, was promoted a captain in the 60th Foot for his bravery.

pieces. She covered her face, on seeing him, and, when she could be understood for her cries, she begged that Power would have compassion on her, and shoot her. 'I often,' said she, 'heard that the English were brave and generous, prove it now, deprive me of that life which is now hateful to me.' She told Power, when she got a little quieted, that, after he had left her the day before, the soldier whom he had thrown down the stairs returned, with many others, and took everything they possessed, committing all the violence they could, and remained there during the night. Power felt as a man for this lovely and interesting female, but he, unfortunately, could give her no redress. He left her with regret, quite miserable at her wretched fate. This is only one instance out of many similar occurrences which took place after the storming of San Sebastian.

From San Sebastian we advanced, and crossed the Bidassoa River, which divides France from Spain, our brigade being led on by General Robinson.[29] Our men were up to their knees in water, and, for the first time, we encamped in the South of France. After some day's halt, the division moved on, and took possession of St Jean de Luz, without much resistance. The scenery was grand; the lofty Pyrenees appearing nearly to hang over us: nothing, indeed, could equal the beauty of the surrounding country. My billet, after a few days, not pleasing me, I wished to change it, and therefore told my sergeant to look for a better one for me, which he did, and I removed my baggage, accordingly. It was a linen-draper's shop, near the market-place. I arrived, at four o'clock, at the house, and, going into the room, I was told by an old man, in broken English, that I could not be there. He gave me no further explanation, but again repeated, 'You cannot remain here, Sir.'

While I was arguing with him, and giving directions to my servant respecting my luggage, and the necessary preparations for the night, a gentlemanly man came out of the next room (in this house there were only two rooms) and politely assured me, that if there was accommodation for me I should be very welcome to remain, but that he had scarcely a place for himself. My answer was, (being irritated at the time,) that I did not care, that I was entitled to my billet as I was an English officer. He then quietly said he had got his billet from the Quarter-Master-General, Sir George Murray,[30] and told me he was sorry he had not room for me, adding, that he had only arrived two or three days before from England. It was the Duke d'Angoulęme.[31] My astonishment may easily be conceived. I immediately asked pardon, bowed and ordered my baggage off as quickly as I could, assuring him that had I known the quarters were his, I should not have intruded on him. He politely came to the room-door, saying he regretted he could not accommodate me, and that he would be happy to see me at any time I might call.

29 The brigade took part in the crossing of the River Bidassoa into France on 7 October 1813. The 47th suffered only five men wounded during this operation.

30 Major General Sir George Murray, Quarter Master General.

31 Louis Antoine of de France, Duc d'Angoulême, nephew of Louis XVIII.

On entering St Jean de Luz, a genteel looking elderly lady, a native of France, came up to me, and laying hold of the bridle of my horse, entreated of me to come to her house, near the foot of the bridge, and lodge with her; saying, she would make me as comfortable as she could. At her urgent request, I went and found a most excellent house and splendidly furnished. There was every attention paid to me; and, when the lady of the house heard I was pay-master, and was satisfied to remain with her, she begged of me to have a sentry placed at the door for the preservation of my money, books, and papers, with which I complied, though I well knew that she had her own motives in making the request. She was a very rich woman, and dreaded being plundered on account of her wealth; but she well knew that, by having a British officer lodging with her, it would be a protection to her, so that there would then be no fear of her being plundered.

Finding I was quiet, and easy to be imposed upon, she told me she would be ever grateful to me if I sent for her two daughters, who, on the approach of our army, had fled to Bayonne; telling me, that she had interest enough with the French general, to have them conducted through the French lines, if I could get them taken through the English camp with safety. Wishing to oblige her, I sent my sergeant and my horses in the morning; and, according to her arrangement, the young ladies were safely conducted through our army. Having been first left at the out-post of the French army, and delivered over to their mother by my sergeant. Every little kindness it was in my power to show this French family, I did; such as procuring for them tea, English ham, porter, &c; but the old lady finding she had got me to accomplish all she wished – her daughters safely at home, and no chance of her house being plundered – while I was out one day, she had all my baggage removed into the hall, telling my servant that she had no longer any quarters for the English. So much for the gratitude of this French woman! I soon discovered that she had made acquaintance with a colonel in the Guards, a gentlemanly elegant fellow, whom she introduced into my quarters, but who had no wish to have me turned out.

In the advance towards Bayonne, the 5th Division formed the left flank, advancing towards Biaritz. In the subsequent battle of the Nive from 10-13 December, the 2/47th lost twelve men killed, with Lieutenant Anthony Mahon, Ensign James Ewing and fifty men wounded and with Lieutenant Randolph McDonnell and fifty men missing.

We left St Jean de Luz for Bayonne. On my riding along the road leading to the latter place, four very fine ducks started out of a house and proceeded before me. I instantly dismounted, and, with the aid of a woman, I caught them; tied them by the legs two and two, threw them across my saddle, and continued my journey. I have often thought since, what a ludicrous figure I cut; I knew well that I did not escape the laughter and merriment of the officers and soldiers, as we moved along; but I had the best of the joke, for the ducks proved useful, and

Contemporary print of the sortie at Bayonne by Thomas Sutherland. (Public Domain)

furnished Captain Murray of the Guards and myself, that day and the next, with a good dinner.[32]

I was billeted with a very sensible and clever lady, at Hernani, within three miles of San Sebastian, who remarked to me that we were strange allies to the Spaniards. 'You come from England,' said she, 'to assist them; you take a Spanish town from the French, (meaning San Sebastian,) a brave and meritorious act; but why have you plundered it?' I must confess I could make her no other reply, but that it was impossible to restrain an enraged army, who had lost so many men. The French soldiers never plundered or sacked a town which fell into their hands, but they laid a contribution on the inhabitants, which was paid in preference to their being subjected to plunder.

We now encamped in the fine wood near Bayonne, close on the banks of the River Adour. My respected friend, General Andrew Hay, called on me one morning, stating that his family had just arrived from Lisbon to join him, and that he wanted money to pay the muleteers that drove their carriage, and requesting that I would lend him 200 dollars for that purpose; which, of course, I instantly gave him. He, however, turned back in two or three minutes, saying, 'I must give you a written acknowledgement for this,' which I refused; but he persisted, saying

32 Lieutenant & Captain Sir Archibald John Murray, 3rd Foot Guards.

in a pleasant manner to me, 'I am crossing the river to-morrow, Harley, to attack the enemy at the other side of Bayonne; and how do you know what may happen? – perhaps I may not return.' It was too true for he was killed the next day in a sortie made at that side of Bayonne, in which also Sir John Hope was severely wounded.[33] I was indeed grieved to hear of the fall of the general. In a few days after, Mrs Hay honourably repaid me the 200 dollars I had lent him.

Here, my good servant, Pat Dolan, again proved his propensity for *making his fortune*, as he termed it. Being one of the foremost, on our approaching Bayonne, he entered a mansion in search of valuable articles; and, as he delayed too long examining the splendid house, his party retreated without him. Immediately after, a party of French dragoons surrounded the house, and Pat was found counting over the plate and other valuables, no doubt thinking his long-wished fortune was made. He was not a little surprised, when he was taken prisoner and conveyed through France, from south to north, until he at last rested at Valenciennes. Here he remained till the peace was declared, when he joined us at Chichester in Sussex. Having obtained leave of absence from Bayonne to Toulouse, in the south of France. I arrived there just as the battle was over, (which was generally considered a very unnecessary one.) I met again my cousin, Colonel McMahon, here. He had been a prisoner of war for many years; but, on the taking of Toulouse by Lord Wellington, he appointed him commandant of the town. I spent a few days pleasantly there, and admired the country and the distant view of that side of the Pyrenees, the summits of which are covered with snow throughout the year, though the climate at the foot is quite warm. Toulouse is a fine rich city, and full of wealthy inhabitants.

Leaving it in a few days, I travelled by the banks of the Garonne to Bordeaux, my road lying through immense fields of wheat and vineyards for one hundred miles. It was then the latter end of June; – the country appeared delightful, and was in full bloom. I was highly pleased with Bordeaux, which is a splendid city, and a place of great commerce and riches. From Bordeaux, I went to Mont [de] Marsan, and returned to Bayonne, where I joined my regiment.

The battalion sailed for England in August, landing at Portsmouth and marched to Chichester. In October the battalion marched to Liverpool where it arrived on 10 October. On 24 October the 2nd Battalion was disbanded with most of the men fit for service sailing to join the first battalion in India. The 2nd Battalion was ordered to reform at Chelmsford on 4 May 1815, but was disbanded again in January 1816.

33 In the sortie of Bayonne on 14 April 1814 the 2/47th lost three men killed and Lieutenants John de Burgh, William Kendall and eleven men wounded with another ten men missing. As Harley records, Major General Sir Andrew Hay was killed and Lieutenant General Sir John Hope, later Earl of Hopetoun, was wounded and became a prisoner of war.

On the 24th of August, 1814, we embarked for England; and, having landed at Portsmouth, marched immediately to Chichester in Sussex, where the different men of our regiment, who had been prisoners of war in France, joined us; and, among the rest, my old servant Pat. On going from the barracks to the town, I met him; and seeing some fine sheep and fowls by the road side, I asked him if he would take some of them; but Pat, looking very serious, replied, 'No, no, sir, not here; for the English are too particular in these matters: I would rather not touch them, but leave them quietly where they are, sir.'

In September, we left Chichester, and marched to Liverpool, where the Second Battalion of the 47th Regiment was disbanded on the 24th October, 1814, and I retired on the half pay. My health requiring it, I went to the Hotwells of Bristol,[34] where I remained until the spring, when I returned to London; and, having some business to transact at Bordeaux, set out through Brighton, and crossed over to Dieppe. There was a passenger in the packet who also travelled with me to Paris, and we put up together at the 'Hotel de Prusse,' in the Rue St Honoré. As this person occupied the same room with me, I observed that he had his boot-trees fastened on his portmanteau, and remarked to him that it was extraordinary he should bring them from London, as he could get his boots as well polished in Paris as in any part of the world. In the morning he went out, and returning in a short time with another man, to my no small astonishment, he opened the boot-trees, which were hollow, and filled with English needles, very difficult to be had in Paris at that time. He assured me he had cleared £80 by this mode of smuggling.

I joined two gentlemen in travelling to Bordeaux in the diligence;[35] and on the road to Tours, a French officer came into the coach, being on his way to Elba, where Bonaparte then was. When he understood that I was in the army, he was very attentive and polite to me. He stopped at one place on the road to visit a venerable old gentleman, whom I subsequently learned was his father.

At an inn where we halted to obtain some refreshment, the female servant was extremely rude to me, and refused giving me any attendance. When the officer heard of it, he sent for her to the room, and reprimanded her; and, on her saying that she disliked the English, he remarked: 'You have not half the reason to dislike them as I have; but recollect we should be always polite in our own country.' At parting near Bordeaux, he shook hands with me, and wished me a safe return to my country. I inquired his name of the conductor, who paid him great respect. He informed me, that he was General Bertrand, who was going out to Elba. I am

34 An area of Bristol under the Clifton Suspension Bridge where hot springs bubble up. The Pump room built in 1696 was demolished and a new Hotwells House was built in 1816.

35 A large four wheeled enclosed carriage for long journeys carrying up to sixteen travellers.

now positive he was then returning from Paris, after organizing the people for Bonaparte's return.[36]

Having finished my business in Bordeaux, I returned to London, passing on my way through Paris, where I remained for a few days.

36 *Général de Division* Henri Gratien, Comte Bertrand, Grand Marshal of the Palace, eventually went to St Helena with Napoleon.

12

Travels in the Low Country and Germany

After my arrival in London, my old and respected friend, Captain Rose, of the 59th Regiment,[1] called on me one morning, and requested me to accompany him to the King's Road, Chelsea, where we waited on a lady whom he introduced to me as Mrs C[larke]. On her table lay the cards of several persons of rank and fashion; and, while we were there, her servant came to the drawing room, to know what time the carriage should be ready, which we afterwards learned was done to impose upon us, and made us think that she was a person of consequence. She informed Captain Rose that she had got the appointment for his grandson, which she had promised him. Rose was of course delighted, and we took our leave, – the poor fellow quite pleased at the prospect in view for his favourite child, – which was a cadetship – that Mrs C[larke] said she had obtained for him in the Honourable East India Company's Service.[2]

In a few days after, Captain Rose and I, calling on the lady, found that she had fled, and no trace of her was to be found. It was only then my friend informed me, that he was afraid he was duped; for that he had given her £100. His surmise was too true, as he neither got the cadetship, nor his money. This lady afterwards became notorious, and was prosecuted for a similar act, by some person in the city, from whom she had obtained £300. for an ordnance appointment in Guernsey. I know not what became of her afterwards, but she obtained a great deal of money in this way, – duping many credulous people who were unfortunate enough to trust her. One morning Lieutenant Nixon,[3] on the H[alf] P[ay] called on me at Kennington, where I then resided. On leaving my house, after paying his visit, a lady passed him whom he had never seen before. Going up to her, he asked her if she would be so kind as to direct him to Gloucester-Street, well knowing that there was no such place on that side of the water; and then continued walking

1 Paymaster Hickman Rose, 59th Foot.

2 The Honourable East India Company at this time maintaining a private army.

3 This must refer to Lieutenant John William Nixon of the 48th Foot, who went on half pay in 1814.

and conversing with her until they arrived at her own door – her house being on Kensington Common.

She was returning thanks for his having escorted her, and bidding him a good morning, when he said: 'Faith, my dear madam, if I was in my dear native country, Ireland, I would be invited in.' She then said: 'Pray walk in, sir;' and ordered cake and wine. He asked her to whom he was indebted for all this kindness. She replied that her name was Edwards. He then said he should be happy to see Mr Edwards; when she informed him that he was dead. This Nixon was not sorry to hear, as he saw everything about him very comfortable. He took his leave, asking permission to call the next day. This was on Tuesday. I met him on Friday; and he told me he was to be married on Saturday; and that he was then ordering a wedding cake. I laughed heartily, for I could not believe he was serious; however, on Sunday morning curiosity took me up to the Common; and on enquiring next door to Mrs Edward's about eight o'clock, I was informed by the maid servant that the widow was married the day before.[4] Just as the girl had informed me of this, Nixon threw up the window of the bedchamber, and, appearing like Bob McClure in his nightcap, bade me good morning.

I returned home, not a little surprised; and at twelve Nixon came with two or three pounds of wedding cake to my family, at the same time inviting me to dine with him at five. I accepted his invitation, and spent the day very pleasantly, staying until a late hour, and making rather too free with the bride and bridegroom's good wine. On going home, it was raining very heavily, and the night was extremely dark; and, although I had not far to go, I called a watchman to assist me. From the effects of the wine, I imagined myself a wealthy man; and when I arrived at my own door, I requested that the watchman would be very careful of my house that night, as I had a great deal of money in it – upwards of £40,000 in specie, which I had brought from foreign countries.[5] The poor man appeared greatly surprised, and told me that he would take care to protect it, advising me to send it to the Bank of England the next day. I went to bed and thought no more of it, until the next morning, when I was informed that a watchman waited in the hall to be paid for the great charge he had he had all night, as he had watched the house, fearing I should lose my treasure.

My wife was naturally astonished at this, as she did not know to what he was alluding; the watchman declaring at the same time, that he ought to be liberally paid for his trouble, as he had never stirred from the door all night; but had remained under showers of hail and rain, watching the money. She at last demanded: 'What money, man?' 'Bless my heart and soul, madam,' said he; 'you cannot be a stranger to the £40,000 the master told me he had in the house.' 'Good heavens!' she exclaimed: 'What can this man mean? for we have only one pound

4 John Nixon married Margaret Edwards at St James in Piccadilly on 4 November 1816.

5 This would equate to about £2 million today.

fifteen [shillings] of the last half-pay in the house,[6] and that must bring us to the next pay day.' She then said: 'I now know how it is; – the effects of wine have caused this folly.'

It was with much difficulty we got rid of the watchman, by giving him five shillings, as he wanted one pound for his trouble, and said he could take no less. The loss of the five shillings was not my only grievance. I deserved a good lecture, and got it. Having a claim upon a gentleman whom I expected to meet in Brussels, I set off for the purpose of seeing him; and having landed at Ostend, proceeded to Bruges; from whence I travelled in a canal boat to Ghent – the charges being most reasonable. The distance is thirty miles, and I was furnished with an excellent dinner, a bottle of wine, and a passage, for eight francs, about six [shillings] and eight-pence.[7]

Here I dined with the 32nd Regiment,[8] and proceeded the next day to Brussels. I was delighted with this beautiful city. The park is extremely handsome, and is a promenade much frequented by fashionable people. The more wealthy inhabitants generally ride in the evening in carriages on the *Allée verte.* I here met several old acquaintances; among the rest Mr Mahoney, whose first wife was niece to my mother, with whom I spent a week very pleasantly. Two of our party, Mrs Mahoney, and another lady, a Mrs Mullins, otherwise Lady Ventry,[9] were famous for card-playing. They understood whist, piquet, and loo very well.[10] Mrs Mahoney requested of me one morning to get her change of an English note for £100, desiring me to be particular in procuring the highest rate of exchange. I tried, and could only obtain twenty-three francs, where she expected twenty-four and a half. As she and her friend had gone to a large party that evening, I did not see her on my return; but the next day when I called, she asked me if I had exchanged the note. I replied in the negative. She said she was much pleased I had not, as she did not then want it. I understood she and her friend had won £400 each the night before. Many a young officer's was made to ache, for the loss of his money, at this period, in Brussels.

Not finding the gentleman I wished to see, I proceeded to Antwerp, which was lately the bone of contention between the Kings of Holland and Belgium.[11] I visited the citadel, which is wonderfully strong, and went all over it, with Captain Crawford, of our artillery, with whom I spent the day.[12] From thence, I went to Bergen-op-Zoom, one of the most remarkable fortresses in the world. I traversed

6 About £100 today.

7 About £20 today.

8 The 32nd (Cornwall) Regiment of Foot.

9 Mary Mullins (nee Rowan) was the wife of Thomas Mullins 1st Baron Ventry.

10 Piquet is first mentioned in 1535 and loo around 1650.

11 He refers to the Belgian Revolution of 1830, when the Dutch held the citadel and bombarded the town. The rising led to the split of Belgium from Holland and King Leopold becoming the King of Belgium.

12 Captain George Crawford of the Royal Artillery.

the fortifications of this place, and was astonished at its construction and strength. Although I am well acquainted with Gibraltar and Malta, it is doubtful to me whether Bergen-op-zoom is not as strong as either of them. It appeared to me to be impregnable; and I verily believe it would be impossible to take it, were it fully garrisoned and provisioned. It was here that my respected friend General Skerrett fell, in 1814; a short time previously to which he had called on me, and, in his usual manner, asked me for pen, ink, paper, and, observing that life was uncertain, and that he wished to leave his property to his mother, who then lived separate from his father, he wrote the following will:

> In case of my death, I leave all I possess in the world to my mother.
>
> (Signed) J.B. Skerrett
>
> Witnessed by John Harley,
> Jos. Featherstone

As soon as he had written it, poor Skerrett handed the will to me, to keep, which was as good in law as if all the lawyers in Lincoln's Inn had been employed to draw it up. There is a monument erected to the memory of this brave officer, on the left hand side as you enter St Paul's the inscription is as follows:-

> Erected, at the public expense, to the memory of Major General Arthur Gore, and John Byne Skerrett, leading the troops to the assault of the fortress of Bergen-op-zoom, in the nights of the 8th and 9th March, 1814.

Leaving Bergen-op-Zoom, I visited the Hague, and Haarlem, the gardens of which were most delightful; and from thence proceeded to Rotterdam, and visited the fair, at which I was much entertained. The canals, with the shipping in the several streets – the loading and unloading of vessels at the doors of the different merchants, surprised me much. The effect was, indeed, extremely pleasing, as both sides of the canal were beautifully planted. A stranger cannot but be astonished to see the masts of ships, trees, and tops of houses, all intermixed. I here noticed the cleanliness of the Dutch in their houses: I had always considered England superior to any country in that respect, but, in justice and truth, I must acknowledge that we cannot compare with the Dutch, in the interior cleanliness of their houses.

I next proceeded to Amsterdam, and passed a few days there, during which I went to see some splendid paintings, in the Town House, which reminded me strongly of my old friend Judd, of Chelmsford. Crossing the Zuyder-zee, I proceeded to Oldenburg, and from thence to Bremen, where I stopped five days, and procured a conveyance to Hamburg.

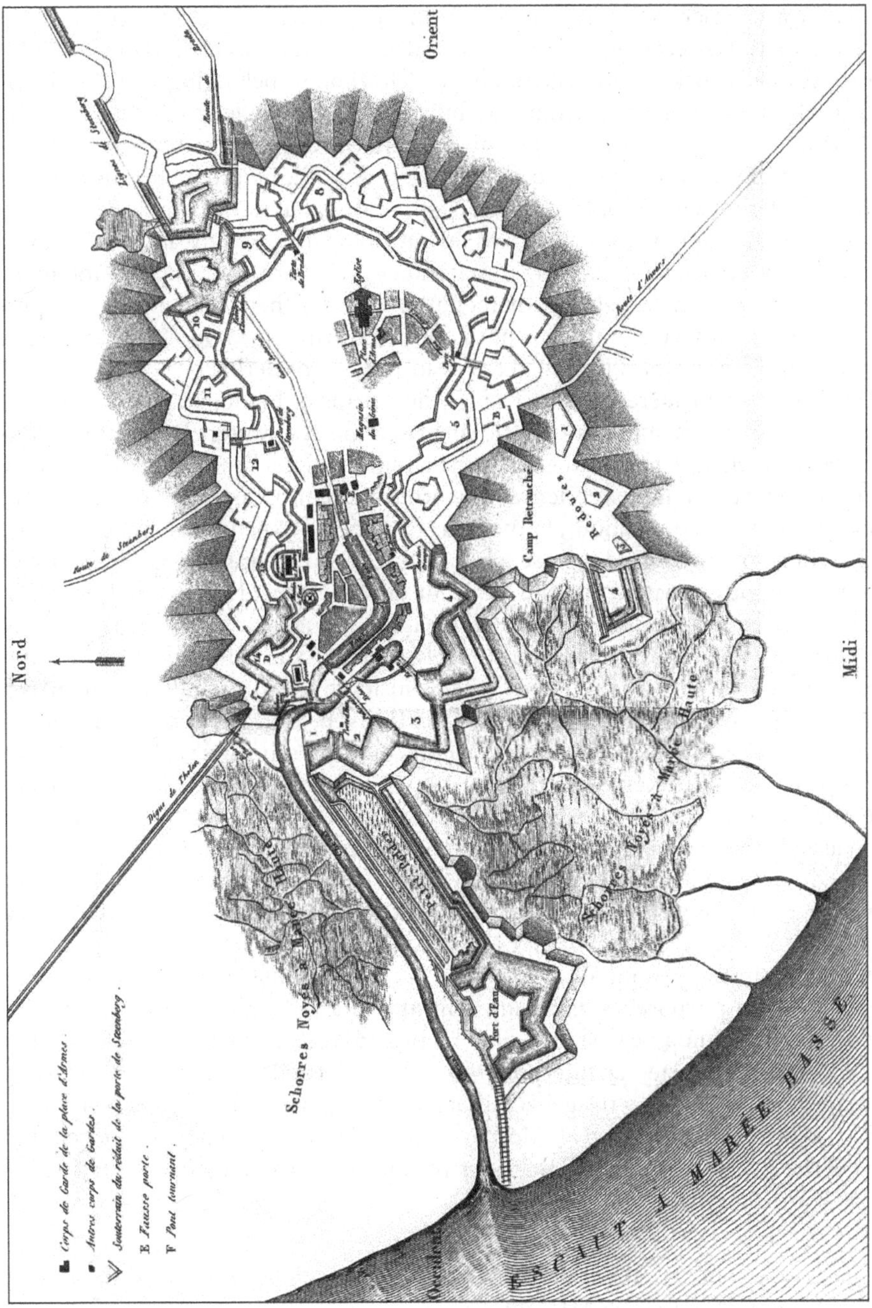

Map 11 A French plan of Bergen op Zoom circa 1814. (Author's collection)

This is a fine city, and renowned for its commerce. I was highly gratified by seeing the environs, which are extremely handsome. Here I had the pleasure of meeting an old acquaintance, General Montague Mathew, brother to the Earl of Llandaff.[13] From Altona, which I also visited, and which, though belonging to the King of Denmark, is about one mile from Hamburg, I thence travelled to Berlin. This was the most disagreeable journey I ever took, from the deepness of the sand and the badness of the road, which passes through a forest of lofty pines. To this must be added, the tedious mode of travelling, in a stool waggon: we only proceeded about three miles an hour. My situation was no enviable one; I was dreadfully annoyed by my fellow-passengers, six or eight in number, who were smoking, day and night continually. I remonstrated with them, but in vain, for they still continued to puff their smoke in my face, until at length, after enduring, for two nights and days, every kind of annoyance, I reached the beautiful city of Berlin.

As I always considered the best hotel the cheapest, I stopped at the Hotel de Sol. The style of this house not a little surprised me, the waiters being in splendid liveries of green and gold, and everything about the hotel bearing the appearance of a princely mansion. I experienced the utmost attention and comfort here, and, notwithstanding its splendour, found it far from being expensive. During my stay, Prince Rostopchin arrived, whose name will reach to future generations.[14] It will never be forgotten that he was the governor of Moscow and set that noble city on fire; in consequence of which decisive measure, Bonaparte and his grand army were obliged to retreat, and were ultimately destroyed, and Europe rescued from the despotic sway of a tyrant. I had great curiosity to see this remarkable man, but could not devise any plan, to have a peep at him even, as he never left the hotel. He had an American servant with him, to whom, on expressing my wish to see Prince Rostopchin, he assured me he was very easy of access, and particularly partial to the English, and that, as I was a British officer, he would be pleased to see me. He then asked me for my card, to present to the prince, which I gladly gave him.

The following morning, at six o'clock, I was disturbed by the servant to whom I had been speaking, who came to my bed-side, and informed me that the Prince expected to see me. I got up, and accompanied him as quickly as I could. He received me in the parlour, on the ground floor at the hotel, which answered him for the double purpose of drawing-room and sitting-room, for this great man lay on the floor, on a bear-skin, which he preferred to any bed in the hotel. The American servant acted as interpreter. I said, it afforded me singular pleasure to have the honour of seeing the general that had saved Europe. He replied, 'Of course you have heard that I burned all Moscow, but I did not,' said he, 'I only caused that part of the city near the French to be destroyed, which was a work of necessity.' He

13 The acquaintance was Lieutenant General Montague James Mathew (1773-1819); his brother was Francis James Mathew 2nd Earl of Llandaff (1766-1833).

14 Count Fyodor Vasilyevich Rostopchin (1763-1826).

asked me many questions; how long I had served, and in what parts of the world. He said he did not intend to join the army again; that he was getting old; that he had a regiment, and that his son, who was a colonel, was actively employed;[15] and that he was then on his way to the warm-baths in Germany. After I had partaken of coffee with him, he wished me every happiness, and I left him, greatly pleased that I had an interview with this celebrated man.

One morning, while in Berlin, I was addressed by a man who offered to show me all the civility in his power; stating he was a native of Ireland, had been unfortunate in different parts of England, in business, and lost a great deal of money, and at length determined on going to Berlin, where he had been now nearly four years. He accompanied me, or, I should rather say, led me to every place worth seeing, after which he invited me to dinner. His novel mode of earning bread surprised me; he adopted the profession of teaching English, and his method was very uncommon. He visited the houses of his pupils, making a charge, at each place, for the time he remained. He used neither book, pen, ink, nor paper; he merely pronounced the word, and made his pupil repeat it after him. Singular as this may appear, it gained him a livelihood; it is needless to add that his pupils made but little progress in the English language. This good-natured man, becoming extremely anxious for my welfare, and not knowing that I was a married man, came early to my bed-side one morning, and told me that he had made an arrangement which was very much for my benefit; that among his acquaintances there was a lady, who had 100,000 Prussian crowns, to whom he wished me to be married, as he knew she would make a good wife, adding, that he had mentioned the circumstances the day before to the lady, and it met her approbation, and that she had appointed twelve o'clock the next day for our interview.

I then told him that I was a married man; but he said, that as his word was pledged, I should at all events go, and my own curiosity led me to do so. She received us more than politely. Her appearance was rather that of an Italian than a Prussian; her house was splendid, and she entertained us in a sumptuous manner. During our conversation, she expressed a great wish to see England, particularly London, and proposed, after our marriage, (for she thought that was fixed on) to take her brother with us, and leave him at school in Germany, on our way to London. I left her, without any explanation, and saw her no more.

I had been six weeks in Berlin, during which time I made several excursions into the country, and visited every place worth seeing, going to Potsdam and Magdeburg, the place where Baron Trenck suffered so much in a dungeon.[16] I

15 Count Sergei Fyodorovich Rostopchin.

16 Friedrich Freiherr von der Trenck (1726-1794) was a Prussian officer who had been imprisoned in 1745 by Frederick the Great when rumours circulated that Trenck was a spy. He escaped a year later and served in Russia but was captured again in 1753 when he attended the funeral of his mother. He was manacled in prison by his hands, feet and body, but eventually released in 1763 after the intervention of Empress

left this city with reluctance; but, as I was anxious to return to England, I was obliged to set out; and, travelling by a different route, came to Hanover, where I waited on His Royal Highness the Duke of Cambridge (as a British subject) at the palace; and was received by him with the greatest politeness.[17] I crossed the Rhine at Dusseldorf, visiting Cologne, and Aix-la-Chapelle; and passing through Liege, once noted for a remarkable Roman Catholic college, but which is now established at Stony-Hurst, in Lancashire. I arrived at Brussels, from whence I proceeded to London, and re-joined my family at Kennington.

In 1816, shortly after my return, I dined one evening with a party of officers of the 87th and 47th, at the Northumberland Coffee-house;[18] and having been induced, by the pleasure of meeting my old companions, who had gone through so many scenes with me in Spain and Portugal, to drink rather too freely, I got a little out of order, and, on going home, instead of proceeding direct over Westminster Bridge, I turned down to the House of Commons, and, influenced by the effects of wine, madly walked into the body of the house; an act, which I should never have been guilty of in my proper senses. It was the very night that an important question was brought forward, and upon which the House was about to divide.

On the question being put, amongst others, but rather more boisterously, I called out, 'No,no' when instantly one of the attendants, or deputy sergeants-at-arms, came up, and looking at me, said, 'You are no member, sir' and then taking me into custody, removed me into the lobby, where, most fortunately, a Captain M[acalpine], of the 81st Regiment, interfered for me with the sergeant-at-arms, who was, with difficulty, prevailed upon to allow me to return home. Were it not for his care of me, I should unquestionably have been sent off to Newgate, for such a flagrant breach of privilege.[19]

The gentleman with whom I formerly travelled to Paris, and who so ingeniously concealed the needles in his boot-trees, called on me one morning, in 1817, and informed me, after conversing with me for some time, that he had an exceeding good plan whereby to realize £2,000 a-year; £1,000 for himself, and another for me, with little or no trouble or expense. As he appeared anxious to communicate with me, apart from my wife, he suggested my retiring with him to the back drawing-room; he held a bundle of papers in his hand – and I took him upstairs. My wife, who suspected something wrong, followed us closely. He then revealed his plan to me; which was to open a lunatic asylum in Kennington. He had

Maria Theresa. He was later sent to Paris by the Austrians to observe the French Revolution, but was accused of spying and was executed by guillotine.

17 Prince Adolphus, the seventh son of George III became Viceroy of Hanover, but when Victoria came to the British throne, Hanover separated, retaining Salic law. The Duke of Cumberland, his elder brother, became King Ernest August I of Hanover and the Duke of Cambridge returned home.

18 The Northumberland Coffee House was on the west side of Chequer Court, which was later cleared to form Trafalgar Square.

19 Captain Archibald Macalpine 81st Foot was on half pay from 1814.

prepared a prospectus, which was to receive twenty-five patients at £100 a-year, each – amounting, altogether to, £2,500 per annum. House-rent, servants' wages, and all expenses, would be about *£500* a year; leaving a surplus of £2,000 a-year, to be divided between us both. He also said that, in order to commence it immediately, he would take an active part on himself, and arrange everything; but that he should require of me an advance of £300 or £400; in fact, he would begin on £200 to set the business going. 'There would be no difficulty,' said he, 'in getting patients; for I have already three or four, and surely you must know some others.' Upon this, my wife, who had been a silent and unobserved witness, replied, 'I know one that should be put in it first, sir, if he has anything to do with you and this scheme, – and that is my husband.' On hearing this, he went away much disappointed, and I never saw him afterwards. This is one of the numerous schemes practised every day in London, to take in the unthinking and unwary.

Lieutenant Laiff, or Lahiff, of the 54th Regiment, whom I met in London in 1818, was certainly one of the most unfortunate officers I ever met with.[20] He had served in the American war, and was second sergeant-major under that celebrated political writer, Mr William Cobbett, who was then first sergeant-major in the 54th.[21] Lahiff told me many anecdotes of Cobbett: he said he was a most temperate man in his habits, and strict and correct in his military duties; and, when not engaged in the orderly room, or on parade, he employed himself in reading in his barrack-room; by which means he obtained much useful knowledge. Lahiff also told me, that he imputed much of the republican principles of the unfortunate Lord [Edward Fitzgerald],[22] who was major of the 54th, to Cobbett; for though the latter was a non-commissioned officer, yet his major had such a regard for him, that he used him frequently to send for him at night to his barrack-room; and Lahiff often assured me, that it was on such occasions, that the seeds of rebellion were implanted in the ill-fated Lord [Edward Fitzgerald].

After many years of faithful services, Lahiff arrived at the rank of Lieutenant and adjutant of the 54th Regiment, then commanded by Colonel G. Strutt, and of which Colonel Darby was then major.[23] The regiment was stationed in Holland; where a smart young man, a German Jew, named Lewis, who had been in the Prussian service, got acquainted with the colonel and the major. Being very assiduous in his attentions, and of a military appearance, those officers became anxious to get him into the regiment, thinking that his Prussian tactics would be of most essential service, and cause the 54th to excel all other regiments of the line. The plan then was to make him adjutant; but how were they to get him in, and Lahiff

20 Lieutenant Dennis Lahiff was in the 54th Foot before the Peace of Amiens and went on half pay. At the time referred to, he was retired on full pay as a lieutenant in the 2nd Royal Veteran Battalion.

21 William Cobbett the radical politician, had previously served in the 54th Foot as a sergeant major in Canada between 1783 and 1791.

22 The famous Irish rebel leader Lord Edward Fitzgerald had served as a lieutenant in the 54th Foot.

23 Lieutenant Colonel William Gooday Strutt and Lieutenant Colonel Christopher Darby.

out? It was proposed to Lahiff to resign, with a promise, that on his doing so, he should be recommended to the War Office for promotion, and get leave to return from Holland.

Poor Lahiff, having a wife and child, agreed to this; and being an old lieutenant and adjutant, of course looked forward to a company, in some other corps. He arrived in London; but judge his disappointment, when, on taking up the Gazette, he saw himself named to a lieutenancy in a West India regiment; and, on waiting on the then military secretary, and describing to him his disappointment and grievance, the only consolation he received was, to be ordered out directly to the West Indies. Having, therefore, no alternative, he, his poor wife, and child, sailed for that detestable climate; and, by the unfortunate step he was induced to take, he lost his seniority and rank in the 54th Regiment, where he must have been, in the course of his promotion, a captain. When he arrived in the West Indies, the Black Regiment, to which he was appointed, was disbanded, and poor Lahiff was thrown on his half-pay. He returned to London, and resolved never more to enter a profession, where he had been so very unfortunate. He rented a small house in Lambeth; contrived to exist on his half-pay, which was then the old rate of two shillings and four pence, per day. Thus, poor Lahiff dragged on a miserable existence, until the month of May, 1800, when the 54th, then in Winchester, formed a second battalion, and he was requested, by Colonel Layard,[24] to come into full pay as lieutenant; and that he would soon obtain his object, and get a company; and that he, Colonel Layard, would recommend him for the adjutancy.

In this he was also disappointed; and this circumstance annoyed the colonel very much, who was indeed a good man and kind hearted. He was brother to Dr Layard, Dean of Bristol and nephew to the Duchess of Ancaster.[25] Poor Lahiff, after that, accompanied the regiment to Egypt. I shall never forget, one evening, as we were sitting in the front of our tents, before Alexandria, there came news of a ship arriving from England. We were all naturally anxious to hear from our families and friends, and read our letters with interest Lahiff opened his letter; he looked at me, and could not speak. It was from his wife at Lambeth, acquainting him that a fire had taken place next door, which communicated with his house, and unfortunately, as poor Mrs Lahiff termed it, *their all* was consumed in the devouring conflagration, consisting of beds, chairs, and tables, &c, leaving her without a house to cover her. The feelings of poor Lahiff may be better imagined than described. We all felt for him, and endeavoured to reconcile him; but he told us that it was not for himself, but for his wife and child he felt.

He then passed much of his time with me; and soon getting ill, from anxiety of mind, he got leave of absence to England; but, as dame fortune seemed to frown upon him, the peace of 1802 taking place, poor Lahiff was once more thrown on

24 Lieutenant Colonel John Thomas Layard.
25 Mary Bertie, Duchess of Ancaster, died in 1793.

the half-pay. Never was there a more deserving, or more unfortunate officer; for though many years in the army, and much in active service, he never arrived at the rank of captain. When I last heard from him, he was living at Plymouth.[26]

26 Sergeant Major Denis Lahiff became Adjutant of the 54th in 1793, he transferred to Colonel Howe's Regiment in 1795 which became the 5th West India Regiment in 1798. Lahiff returned to Britain and joined the militia before joining the 54th and going on half pay in 1802. He was appointed, as a lieutenant, to the 60th Foot on 19 April 1803 and a week later he transferred to the 2nd Royal Garrison Battalion and had become the senior lieutenant before the battalion was disbanded in 1814 and he went on half pay.

13

Difficult Times

I was living at Kennington, quiet and happy, when the late John Nestor proposed to me to assist him in an Army Agency Establishment, in Craven-street, in the Strand.[1] I foolishly and unfortunately joined him, which I have ever since had reason to regret, as I lost by it not only my time, but the remnant of what I had saved. The business consisted of being agent for half-pay officer's and widow's pensions. It is evident that no persons but those in distress, who resided in London, would employ us; but we did not consider this in time; we were eternally employed in making advances to such people, so that our funds soon became exhausted, and then the half-pay officers, after leaving us minus, employed other agents. I shall never forget, that in making up the widow's list I found four that had not brought in their certificates; I therefore went to the Pay-office, and found them in the act of drawing their pensions themselves. Upon my appearing and bidding them good morning, they left me, and went down the back stairs. I went round the front stairs, and when they saw me they returned again. We thus continued chasing each other, up one stair and down another, to the great amusement of the gentlemen in the office. At length, I got my widows in a corner, in the Cashiers' room, and they surrendered on the following terms. They gave up their certificates, and I paid them the half of their pensions, but, as I never saw them afterwards, we lost the balance due to us. To sum up my misfortunes, Mr Nestor went off to Ireland, leaving me to all the demands and annoyances of the creditors, until we at length dropped the agency with a loss of £300.

After leaving the unfortunate pursuit of half-pay agent, in Craven-Street, I went to reside in Sloane-Street; and here I renewed an acquaintance with the Reverend Mr Weld, now Cardinal Weld, of Rome.[2] He is the proprietor of Stonyhurst College, in

1 There were the offices of three army agents in Craven Street. Brookshank & Bernard at no. 19, George Parys at no. 33 and Bruere & Webb at no. 40.

2 Cardinal Thomas Weld (1773-1837).

Lancashire,[3] and possesses, besides, extensive estates in England. A few years previously, Mr Weld had resided in the next house to me, at Clifton,[4] with his amiable wife and daughter, who employed the whole of their time in relieving the wants of the poor. He there lost his wife,[5] and having married his daughter to the Hon. W. de Clifford, son to Lord de Clifford,[6] giving her the chief part of his property, and reserving about £4,000 a-year, to be disposed of in charity, he took holy orders; and acted as Roman Catholic Priest, in Sloane-Street Chapel, Chelsea. I have known this worthy man to draw his accounts so close, at Mr Wright's, his banker, of Covent-Garden,[7] as to leave scarcely anything in hand: he dispensed liberally among the poor of all religious persuasions, never asking to what sect they belonged. This I frequently witnessed at Chelsea. At this time my half-pay was suspended, in consequence of errors in my accounts, which occurred in Spain. Indeed, by the melancholy event of losing my son, at Vitoria, I was rendered, for a time, totally incapable of managing my affairs, and was therefore obliged to leave them to my sergeant, who made double payments, and committed many errors, which now came against me. Misfortunes seldom come singly; my baggage, which was on board the *Ceres* transport, consisting of many valuable things belonging to myself and family, were all lost, the *Ceres* having been wrecked on the coast of France, near Bayonne.[8] The next misfortune, I learned two months after, on taking up an English paper at Bordeaux. This was, the failure of Messrs. Whitehead and Howard, my bankers in London,[9] by which I lost considerably, and became involved in inextricable difficulties. The Reverend Mr Weld coming to the knowledge of my situation, entirely unknown to me, called one morning, and put a letter into my hand, which he bade me read at my leisure, and then went off, without a moment's delay. On my opening it, I found it contained £40, with the *following words:*

My dear Sir,
It will be full time to return the enclosed, when I apply to you for it.
Yours, truly,
Thomas Weld

3 Stonyhurst was a Jesuit College, first established at St Omer in 1593, it moved to Bruges and Liege, before finally moving to Lancashire in 1794.

4 The Weld family owned a property at Clifton between 1810 and 1818. It is still a Catholic school.

5 Mary Weld (nee Clifford) died on 1 June 1815.

6 Harley is in error here. Mary Lucy Weld actually married Hugh Charles Clifford, 7th Baron Clifford of Chudleigh on 8 February 1819. The Lords de Clifford were a different family branch altogether.

7 Mr John Wright, banker at Covent Garden, his business collapsed on his death in 1840.

8 The only ship named *Ceres* which was lost in 1814 on the French coast was lost on 20 January at Cap Breton which surely would be too early.

9 The bank of Whitehead, Howard and Haddock and Co. was declared bankrupt on 16 November 1814, however Harley, like all investors, got most of his money back. It is recorded in the *Morning Post* of 11 December 1835, that six payments had been made to investors over the years eventually totalling reimbursement of 16s 10½d in the pound.

I leave my readers to judge what the heart of that man must be, who could act in this generous and delicate manner, so considerate to the feelings of an old officer. Soon after this, I went to Spain, and never had the happiness of seeing my benevolent friend since. He was, shortly after, made Bishop of Canada, and since that, has been appointed a Cardinal of Rome, where he now resides.[10] Cardinal Weld is the proprietor of Lulworth castle, one of the most beautiful seats in England,[11] where his venerable father usually resided, and who was a great favourite with the late George III. The good king, every season, on visiting Weymouth, never failed to spend two or three days with his old and esteemed friend, Mr Weld. It was the Cardinal's father that brought over the monks of La Trappe, who were persecuted in France at the time of the Revolution, and to whom he generously gave an asylum, on his ground at Lulworth castle, which these men enjoy to this day.[12]

While walking up the Strand, I met a person whom I thought I recollected. He saluted me very respectfully, and I immediately called to my remembrance that he was Sergeant Williamson, of the 30th Regiment, whom I had known abroad.[13] He was very well dressed, and had quite a respectable appearance. On my expressing my satisfaction at seeing him apparently so comfortable, he thanked me, and told me, without hesitation, that he was now very independent; stating, that on his being discharged from the army, he got a pension of one shilling a day, and, from being well recommended, had also obtained a situation of a guinea-and-half per week, in Sir Richard Carr Glynn's banking-house, as out-door messenger.[14] He also told me of his marrying, under the following extraordinary circumstances. Having been advised, by a person in his own situation in life, to advertise for a wife, he took the hint, and put the following advertisement in one of the newspapers, which he repeated to me word for word.

> 'A respectable man, who has travelled, and who has seen a good deal of the world, thirty years of age, possessing a small income from government, and holding a situation of one guinea-and-half a week, in a banking-house in the city, would be happy to meet a female, whom he would study to make comfortable; but, to enable him to do so, she must have £500.'

10 The Cardinal died on 10 April 1837, Harley added a note -since deceased.

11 Lulworth Castle was owned by the Welds for centuries, it was largely destroyed by a fire in 1929, but has been partially restored by English Heritage.

12 Cardinal Weld's father, Thomas Weld of Lulworth gave the Stonyhurst Estate to the Jesuits and he founded a Trappist monastery at Lulworth, which has since moved to Mount Mellaray in Ireland.

13 Sergeant John Williamson 30th Foot became Quartermaster in October 1814.

14 Sir Richard Carr Glyn (1755-1838) was a partner in Halifax, Mills, Glyn & Mitton Bank from 1773. He became the senior partner in 1789 in the renamed Glyn, Mills & Mitton until his death in 1838.

He told me he put this advertisement in the Morning Herald, on a Friday, and by Wednesday he had eleven letters.[15] When he and his friends had carefully looked over these letters, they fixed their attention on one in particular, the address of which was, 24 Spitalfields. He accordingly set out, after the hours of business, to search for the house, and, on arriving at the number, he found it to be a pawnbroker's-shop. Williamson, who thought there might be some mistake, looked at the direction again, and asked a boy, in the shop, if there was any other number 24 in the same place, to which the boy replied in the negative. He was then about leaving the shop, without making any further inquiry, when the parlour door opened, and a lady asked him what he wanted. He told her that he had received a letter, holding it in his hand, in answer to an advertisement of his, and apparently dated from that house, but he feared there was some mistake. 'None, whatever,' said she, 'pray walk in, and rest yourself.' He obeyed, and, after a few words in explanation, he told her how he was circumstanced in life, and produced some very strong testimonials of his good and regular conduct while in the army. She then made him stop to tea, and asked him to call the next evening.

In the course of one or two other interviews, as they became more familiar, she observed, 'You have advertised for a wife, and named £500 as the required portion;' and, at the same moment going to the desk, and taking out £800, she continued, 'I have this much in ready cash, besides all the pledges in the shop, the amount of which I am unable to tell; the house and furniture are my own, and I have no child; and, from your manner and behaviour, I must say that I have no objection to become your wife.' 'We were accordingly married,' said he, 'in a few days.' I went to their house, and was much pleased with her. He retained his situation at the bank, she her pawning-office; and by this time they have no doubt realised, if not a handsome, at least an independent fortune. This is proof that a man can procure a wife with money, by advertising; a circumstance which I could never believe before.

The celebrated General Devereux was introduced to me this year, by a gentleman of my acquaintance.[16] He was then preparing to go out to South America, to join Bolivar. I dined with him, at the Piazza Coffee-house, where he gave us a most splendid entertainment.[17] I heard no more of General Devereux for two years, when I accidently met him in Liverpool, and travelled with him to London. It was an extraordinary turn this gentleman took. In his early life, in 1798, he joined the rebels in Ireland, and was at the battle of Vinegar Hill, from whence he was fortu-

15 The *Morning Herald* was a daily newspaper which had begun in 1780 by the Reverend Sir Henry Bate Dudley.

16 John Devereux (1778-1854), became a recruiter for the Irish Legion in the army of Simón José Antonio de la Santísima Trinidad Bolívar y Palacios (1783-1830), the Venezuelan military and political leader, and was made a major general by Bolivar. He was paid $175 per soldier recruited for Venezuela.

17 The Piazza Coffee House stood on the north side of Covent Garden and was a favourite of Charles Dickens.

nate enough to make his escape; but, as he told me, he was then an inconsiderate lad of sixteen years of age, or he should not have joined them. He escaped from the coast of Wexford, without one shilling in his pocket, got to the neighbourhood of Bristol, and from thence worked his passage on board an American, and got to Baltimore, where he was employed as a clerk, in the house of Oliver and Co.[18] He remained some years in their employment, and was sent by that house to South America, as supercargo; and there he met Bolivar, with whom he got acquainted, and who authorised him to go to Ireland, to raise men; thus, at once, the supercargo became a general. His recruiting system, in Dublin, is well known, and the greatest part of the poor fellows that followed him had to regret it. Devereux, after much travelling, got to Bogota, the capital of South America, and settled all his accounts with Bolivar. After his return to London, he showed me a Spanish bond, amounting, at the exchange of the day, to £90,000, being his entire charge for transports, men, provisions, and clothing; thus an accidental meeting with Bolivar, made the fortune of Devereux.

A gentleman, whom I had known from a boy, used often to come out and take an early dinner with me at Kennington, before he went to the House of Commons, of which he was a member, being one of the representatives of the county of Limerick for the period of twenty-one years.[19] He had been originally put in by the late Earl of C[lare], during the minority of his son, for whom he was keeping the county of Limerick;[20] but at length my friend, losing the representation, wrote to me to purchase a borough for him, as boroughs were then on sale in London, almost as common as horses at Tattersall's. I was not then aware that to be a negotiator in such a case was illegal, and, in accordance with his wishes, I applied to several persons, on the subject. At length, a gentleman, as I then thought, waited upon me, and informed me that the price of a borough was 6,000 guineas. This I let my friend know, who instructed to offer £1,000 a-year for every year he held it, stating to me that as Lord Castlereagh, who was then in office, and his friend, promised him a situation, it was of the utmost importance that he should get into parliament, where he could support his Lordship, whenever he had occasion for his vote.[21] I made the proposal to the agent, who, after some conversation, told me that he would communicate with the principal; and the next day, he waited on me, and said that the gentleman had agreed to my offer; and that all that now remained to be done, was to give him the name of my friend, and a cheque for the amount; adding that although my friend was not in the country, it made no difference. To this I replied, that as I was acting for another person, I wished to have an interview

18 A merchant house.

19 This would appear to be William Odell who was actually a Member of Parliament for the County of Limerick for seventeen years from 1801-18.

20 John Fitzgibbon 1st Earl of Clare, who died in 1802.

21 Robert Stewart, Viscount Castlereagh (1769-1822), the Foreign Secretary.

with the principal, or owner of the borough, previously to which I could take no further step. After much reluctance, the agent consented to introduce me to him, informing me that he was a man of the greatest importance, I must not be too particular with him; but pay him at once, should he require it. He then conducted me to a house on Ludgate Hill, where he introduced me to a venerable, old-looking gentleman, who was seated in an arm-chair, with a great quantity of papers before him; and many letters opened and unopened.

On our first entrance, he seemed immersed in business, and took no notice of us, until the agent observed to him that I was the gentleman that came about the borough. He instantly said; 'Sir, you have been very fortunate, for I have had two or three offers for it; but as my agent spoke to you first, I have reserved it for your friend.' I then again mentioned the terms, £1,000 a-year, in order that there might not be any misunderstanding, while my friend should be in parliament; with which he declared himself perfectly satisfied. 'But,' said I 'my friend is not in London.' 'Oh! That,' said he, 'makes no difference. I will have him returned if you go down and represent him, or be his proxy.' I then required to know the name of the borough. After some hesitation, he informed me it was A[rundel]. On hearing this, I own I was a good deal astonished, as I had always understood that A[rundel] was the property of the Duke of [Norfolk].[22] He stated that it would be necessary for me to go down in two or three days; at the same time, taking down the Christian name of my friend; and commencing a letter, which he said was to be sent off by that night's post, to prepare my friends for my reception. He added, that the only part of the money that would be required, until my friend was safely seated for twenty days in the house, and beyond any possibility of a petition militating against him, would be about £200; the remaining £800 might remain for the present, until our perfect convenience, as he was aware that he was acting with men of honour.

He further said, that I should go down, and give a dinner to the electors, which would cost from sixty to eighty pounds; and, politely bowing me to the door, wished me success. I must confess I felt delighted at the idea of getting a borough for my friend on such reasonable terms. As candid truth is best, it was the intention of my friend to make me his deputy, if he got a situation at home or abroad, should he succeed in getting a seat in Parliament, and resuming his old situation under the command of Castlereagh.

I wrote to him that night the pleasing intelligence, which I had scarcely done, when I read a polite note from the proprietor (as I thought) requiring £100 on account, by bearer; and that the other £100 would answer on my return from A[rundel]. I then began to reflect that the residence of this person was not the most respectable; and this sudden application also raising some doubts in my mind, I told the messenger verbally, that I would attend to it next day. On calling at Messrs

22 Bernard Howard, 12th Duke of Norfolk (1765-1842)

[Adlington] and [Shepherd], the respectable solicitors of John Street, Bedford Row, I was informed that the member for the borough of A[rundel] had been elected, and that they were the solicitors employed on the occasion.[23] This at once threw open the scheme to me. Still I had another and another letter from this fellow on Ludgate Hill, requesting fifty pounds, – nay, thirty pounds, on account. I then found out he was nothing more nor less than a resident of the rules of the Fleet Prison. The last visit I had from his messenger, I told him to inform his employer that I would prosecute him, if he tormented me any longer; and thus ended my negotiation for a borough.

After my friend had, as I before remarked, been twenty-one years member for the county of L[imerick], when he stood a candidate in the election of 1820, he was thrown out; and failed also in the purchase of a borough; not but there were several in the market, which he could have got, particularly T[rim] and D[unwich];[24] for both of which he was negotiating; for he showed me the correspondence with the parties, who had the sale of those and other boroughs; but he wanted to be returned and firmly seated in Parliament, before he would part with a shilling of the purchase-money – terms to which the owners of those rotten boroughs would not agree; well knowing, that if he was once elected, they could not legally demand payment; and having no reliance on his honour and punctuality.

In the first regiment in which I served, I had a brother officer and countryman, Lieutenant Wilkinson;[25] who had married a wealthy lady in Gloucester, a Miss Mild.

Wilkinson arrived in London, in 1831, in a wretched state of health, and immediately sent for me to come and see him. Fearing that he was in imminent danger, I lost not a moment in procuring for him the best medical aid; but it was all in vain; he declined daily. I then had him removed to my own neighbourhood, and constantly visited him four or five times in the day.

When the hour of his death at length drew nigh, poor Wilkinson said to me, while his lips quivered with emotion, and told that the hand of the spoiler was upon him: 'I know, Harley, I am dying; and I have but one request to make of you, which I know you will not refuse. Let me be put into a leaden coffin, and sent to county Limerick, to be interred with the rest of the family.' Upon my promising, as well as his wife, who had been called into the room, he seemed reconciled and perfectly resigned to his fate. In about an hour after I had left him, and was seated at my dinner, his servant came in great haste, saying that his master wished to see me without a moment's delay. I immediately went to him, when he said to me, 'I have been reflecting, Harley, that the rebels would take up my coffin if I were buried in a leaden one, and melt it into balls; I entreat, therefore, that you will purchase an

23 Thomas Adlington and Charles Shepherd had offices at 4 John Street, Bedford Row from 1794.

24 These constituencies are the most likely, both being Rotten Boroughs.

25 Lieutenant Francis Wilkinson, of the Royal Tarbert Fencibles.

iron one for me, for I would wish my poor skeleton to remain undisturbed.' The poor fellow died in about an hour after this, and I went to Goswell Street;[26] and having been shown a variety of coffins, purchased a good strong one for seven guineas. The coffin-maker, who was an adept at recommending his goods, wished me to buy another for myself, which he offered to me for six guineas, showing me one of the same description that a gentleman, who had purchased it, had got painted, with a lock and key put to it; telling me that he often visited it in the stores. However, I declined such an extraordinary purchase; observing, that it was hard to tell where I might drop; and it was too cumbersome an article to carry about with me, or to send any distance.

As soon as the undertaker had everything arranged for my departed friend, agreeably to his last request, I had him enclosed in his iron coffin; and, having procured a cover for it, made in the shape of a harpsichord case, to deceive the sailors, who are well known to be superstitious, I had him put on board a ship bound for Limerick, where he arrived without detection, and was interred in the family vault at Caherly, in the County Limerick.

In 1822, a Mr E[dmund] B[ourke], from Limerick,[27] called on me in London, and as countrymen, particularly Irish, freely communicate their affairs to each other, he informed me of his great disappointment, on coming to his uncle, who was a partner in one of the first houses in London, of the firm of B[aker] and M[orsheads] Broad-Street, to find the house had unfortunately failed, and, consequently, that any pecuniary aid from that quarter could not be expected.[28] His uncle, however, gave him a few pounds out of the wreck, to enable him to return home; which, indeed, though insufficient, was all the poor man could spare. When B[ourke] got as far as Birmingham, his finances were exhausted, and he was of course obliged to remain there. He knew not what to do, or what would become of him; but the old saying, 'Necessity is the mother of invention,' was soon verified in his case. Being a very well educated man, and finding that the people with whom he lodged were of some dissenting sect, for which they were very zealous, he hit on the plan of becoming one of the preachers of this sect, and, though he was a good and firm Roman Catholic, in his own country, he was determined, now that he was in distress, to endeavour to make a livelihood in this way; and succeeded to his utmost wishes, being well entertained, and well paid for his trouble.

About this time, an ironmonger of Limerick arrived in Birmingham, to lay in his usual supply of goods; and the person with whom he dealt invited him to dine. After dinner, they mentioned to him that a very popular preacher officiated in their chapel. From what country he had come they knew not, but on the night he preached he brought vast crowds. Asking Mr Harrison to go with them to hear

26 Goswell Street, Islington.

27 The only gentleman with these initials recorded living at Limerick was Mr Edmund Bourke.

28 Baker and Morsheads was a firm of accountants at 3 Pinner's Court, Broad Street.

him, he accompanied them, took his seat in their pew, and, when the preacher had ascended the pulpit, what was his astonishment, to behold Ned B[ourke], his townsman, who had, a short time before, left Limerick for London. To be more fully convinced that it was no other than B[ourke], he left his seat and got nearer to him, constantly looking at him, until he caught his eye. B[ourke] shook his head significantly, and Harrison remained quiet. After the sermon, he excused himself to the company he had come with, and remained outside of the door until the reverend preacher came out, who took him to his residence, and entertained him; telling him to keep his own counsel, and assuring him that he had lived well during the short time he was in Birmingham, and had saved £160 from presents made to him by the congregation. This extraordinary fellow imprudently left Birmingham and his followers, and returned to Ireland, where he soon spent his money, and was then as badly off as ever. I afterwards learned that he turned quack doctor, in some village in the county of Tipperary, and incautiously bled an old woman to death, for which he was prosecuted; but what became of him afterwards I know not.

A very worthy man, an old acquaintance of mine, whose circumstances became much embarrassed, from his having a large family, determined on leaving London, and going to some village in the country, where he could exist on the remnant of his fortune. He had nearly disposed of his furniture, and was on the eve of taking his departure, when an old faithful servant, who had lived with him in his prosperity, called on him, and, on hearing the plan that had been formed, requested that he would remain in town for a few days, as she had something to communicate to him. To this he consented, having a great regard for her. It appeared that this servant lived with a widow, of seventy years of age, possessing a large fortune, whose husband had treated her very ill. When he was dying, he was attended by a Methodist clergyman, who impressed upon his mind, in order to make atonement for his cruelties, and to appease the wrath of the Almighty, the necessity of leaving to his injured wife all his property in houses, money in the funds, plate, furniture, carriage, horses, &c; the pious Methodist clergyman having, at the same time, every idea of marrying the lady, as soon as the old man was laid in his grave. Poor faithful Mary immediately thought of her old master, and as often as the Reverend Methodist lover called to pay a visit, after the old man's decease, so often did Mary tell him that her mistress was unwell, or out, or engaged in business, which prevented his having an interview with her. Seeing that no time was to be lost, she came to her old master again, and informed him of her plan; saying, 'You must come over, Sir, to-morrow evening, and inquire for me – I will manage the rest' Mr S.[29] went, according to agreement; when Mary took him in front of the house, on the lawn, where she conversed with him for some time, so that her mistress might have a full view of him, as she was sitting in the drawing- room. On Mary's return to the house, she inquired who the gentleman was that had been speaking to her.

29 Not enough information is provided by Harley to identify this Mr S.

Mary said, 'My old master, Ma'am'. 'Is he religious, Mary?' said the old lady. 'He is, mistress,' replied Mary, 'very religious, indeed;' and she then held forth largely on the many good qualities and religious habits of Mr S., saying that he constantly read the bible, and attended divine service.

Old Mrs _ then consulted with her servant, and it was settled that Mr S. should be invited to the house. Mary flew to her master, and instructed him how to act. On his first visit, he read prayers to the lady, and was everything she could wish: suffice it to say that in ten days, he became, through Mary's assistance, the husband of Mrs _, and all the property she possessed, and in seven months after, she died. When I was last in London, I saw Mr S. well and happy. Thus did the faithful old Mary provide for her master and his family, whom she had known in better days, and succeeded in rescuing them from that state of poverty, into which they had unfortunately fallen.

The first time I saw Mr O'Connell was in Dublin, in 1822, after my return from London; at which time I was introduced to him by Charles O'Connor, Esq of Merrion Square. Mr O'Connell was then working for Catholic emancipation. I remarked to him that I thought he never could bring it about; his reply was, 'No matter, we will persevere, and no doubt but we shall one day or other carry it.' His determined manner and appearance struck me forcibly, and I could not help thinking that it was a pity he was not brought up as a military man, for he would have made an able general officer. His zeal for his country, and his exertions in favour of civil and religious liberty, will hand his name down to posterity; while his private character, which is so exemplary, as a husband, a father, and a friend, endear him to the recollection of all who have the pleasure of being acquainted with him in his domestic circle.[30]

30 Daniel O'Connell (1775-1847) – 'The Emancipator' – was born at no. 30 and lived at no. 58 Merrion Square in Dublin.

14

The Spanish Revolt

Only six years after the end of the Peninsular War, Spain and Portugal were again in uproar. In Spain, troops under the command of General Rafael del Riego revolted at Cadiz in 1820, forcing King Ferdinand VII, who had returned in 1814 as an absolute ruler, to accept the Constitution of 1812, which guaranteed universal male suffrage and freedom of the press.

Ferdinand was effectively a prisoner of the Cortes and when a counter-revolution failed in 1822, Ferdinand appealed to the other monarchs of Europe for help. Initially France was not keen to intervene and Britain took a stance of neutrality on the issue. Eventually a French army of sixty thousand men commanded by the Duc d'Angouleme invaded Spain in 1823: the French intervention was decisive and the liberals were defeated. All went quiet in Spain until the Carlist wars erupted in the 1830s.

Sir Robert Wilson fought on the side of the Cortes and sought British mercenaries to fight with him. Harley, and may other Peninsular War veterans, became involved.

In consequence of arrangements that my much respected friend, Sir John Milley Doyle, had made with the Spanish and Portuguese governments, he purchased the *Royal George*, steam-vessel, at an expense of £10,000[1], and, influenced by the most patriotic motives, fitted her out at considerable expense, with an intention that she should ply between England and Spain, and thereby open a more regular communication between Madrid and London than had hitherto existed.[2] As I had served with Sir John in Egypt, Spain, and Portugal, and was an old brother-officer, he requested me to accompany him to Spain. On the 6th of June, 1823, I left London in the mail for Falmouth, accompanied by Mr George Holmes, from

1 About half a million pounds today.

2 Sir John Milley Doyle (1781-1856) had risen to command a Portuguese brigade in the Peninsular War. He chartered the *Royal George* in 1823 to take despatches to Cadiz for Don Pedro but was captured in 1828 by Dom Miguel and imprisoned for four months.

the foreign office, who had charge of despatches from the Spanish ambassador then at the court of London, and residing in Portland-Place. The instructions to me were very particular, that I should forward the despatches to the Cortes then sitting in Madrid. I had under my charge a large supply of arms and accoutrements, furnished by the patriotic Spanish committee, who held their meetings at the Crown and Anchor in the Strand,[3] of which the indefatigable Member of Parliament, Joseph Hume, Esq was the chairman.[4]

I embarked in the *Royal George* steam-packet, which came round from Blackwall, and met us at Falmouth, having the arms and accoutrements on board, with fifty passengers from London, very pleasant, agreeable fellows; among the number was Sir John Doyle, his brother, the Reverend Mr Doyle, and his son, who did all in their power to add to our happiness and comfort.[5] I need not mention Sir John's good disposition, for all who have the pleasure of knowing him, are sensible of his extreme worth. I have been an eye witness to his generous conduct to several young gentlemen who were going out with us to seek their fortunes; and who, having but small means, could hardly afford to pay even for their passage, the fare being eighteen guineas. He nobly directed that they should be free of all expenses, and ordered a good table to be kept for them.

Having laid in coals, and made every necessary arrangement, we left Falmouth on the 12th of June, – the weather being very fine, and the Bay of Biscay remarkably smooth; and, after an agreeable passage of three days, arrived at Corunna, in Spain; ours being the first steam-vessel that had ever sailed through the Bay of Biscay. The approach to this part of the coast of Spain is beautiful; the view of the mountains of Galicia, covered with vineyards and cottages, is splendid beyond description. As we entered the harbour at five in the morning, leaving Ferrol on our left, it brought to my remembrance the ridiculous expedition under Sir James Pulteney, in 1800, in which I served in the 54th Regiment, as mentioned in the commencement of this narrative. On our approach, we perceived the inhabitants on shore running backward and forward in the greatest confusion – never having seen or heard of a steam-vessel before. The Spaniards, being very superstitious, on observing the great smoke, but no sails, supposed us from the infernal regions, and were certain that we came to burn their town and shipping; upon which they fired some heavy shots at us from the batteries.

Fortunately, they did not strike the vessel, although they passed very close to it; and Sir John Doyle immediately ordered Captain Bissett, who commanded the steamer, to anchor, and hoist English colours. He then ordered the boat, and going

3 The Crown and Anchor in the Strand was a very palatial tavern with fine meeting rooms, it burnt down in 1857.

4 Joseph Hume was a Scottish doctor and radical MP (1777-1855).

5 The Reverend Nicholas Milley Doyle and his son, the later Colonel Sir John Milley Doyle.

ashore, waited on the Governor, General Vigo,[6] and informed him that we had come as friends to the Cortes and constitution of Spain, that we had on board several volunteers, arms, and accoutrements, for the cause of liberty, and a supply from the Spanish committee in London; and that more in a few days would follow. The governor was delighted, and embraced Sir John, ordering the officer of artillery at the battery to be put under arrest; but Sir John begged that he might be released and pardoned.

The steam-packet, having entered the inner harbour, and anchored there, was in a short time crowded with the inhabitants, who all vied with each other in paying us every possible attention; and crowds of boats, filled with handsome ladies and musicians, surrounded the vessel till twelve o'clock at night. At six o'clock the following morning, they recommenced visiting us, numbers having arrived from all parts of the country to see the wonderful ship, which they call in Spanish 'Barco de Vapor' or ship of smoke. There were balls and entertainments given us in the town every night; and we in return gave a ball on board to the inhabitants, at which the governor, his lady and family, and all the generals and staff of the garrison were present; and the beautiful and interesting Madame Mina, wife of the celebrated General Mina, who was then in Catalonia, fighting for the freedom of his country.[7]

After delivering the arms and accoutrements to the governor, the *Royal George* sailed from Vigo to Lisbon, and thence to Cadiz. It is impossible for me to give a description of the entertainments and amusements that took place during the week the *Royal George* remained at Vigo; the place resembled fairy-land, everyone trying who could make us most happy.

I had despatches for Sir Robert Wilson, from the committee of London; also from the Spanish ambassador, which were to be delivered immediately to him. Learning that he was then at Vigo, I determined to return there; and accordingly hired the *Tartar* cutter, then lying in the bay, for 500 dollars, to go round to Vigo. After being there three days at sea, we had a violent storm off Cape Finisterre, which carried away our boom and topmast. We were nearly wrecked on the coast of Galicia, and with much difficulty reached the harbour of Corunna. The next day I determined to go by land to Vigo, a distance of ninety miles, and set out at six in the morning, accompanied by a Spanish captain, named Barco. He was aid-de-camp to General Quiroga, who was then Captain-General of the provinces of Galicia and Asturias.[8] We were furnished with a guard of sixty soldiers to protect us, as it was most dangerous to pass the mountain roads between Corunna and Santiago, which were infested with banditti, several of whom we could perceive

6 Actually Field Marshal Rafael del Riego (1784-1823) the Captain General of Galicia.

7 Lieutenant Général Francisco Espoz y Mina's (1781-1836) forces were obliged to capitulate in November 1823 and Mina was allowed to flee to Britain.

8 General Antonio Quiroga (1784-1841) commanded the troops in Galicia against the royalists.

at a distance, as we pursued our journey; but they allowed us to proceed without molestation.

The first day we arrived at the ancient city of Santiago, about forty miles from Corunna. This place is the see of an archbishop, whose revenue is very large. The inhabitants assured me his income amounted to a doubloon, or an ounce of gold per hour. Value £4 British, making about £40,000 sterling, per annum. It is a fine old city, has a most splendid cathedral, and is crowded with convents and nunneries. There is one very superb nunnery, for the daughters of grandees, the others are for the lower classes of society. There has been formerly a building of the Inquisition here, which I have seen myself, having gone all over it; and the scene it exhibited, when torn down a few months since, by a party of constitutionalists, headed by an Irishman, named Captain Matthews, was horrible indeed. He informed me, that on their breaking into the dungeons, they found numberless skeletons, some old men, worn out with long confinement, the most miserable objects that can be imagined. They were unable to inform him on what account, or for what crimes, they had suffered such imprisonment. On the place being attacked, the inquisitors fled, and thus escaped that punishment their guilt so justly deserved. Such was the state of bigotry in this country a few years back, that, for the most trifling word against the church, or the monks and friars, the unfortunate victim would be seized in the dead of the night, thrown into a damp cell, and probably never more be heard of. This Captain Matthews was the gentleman that was afterwards taken prisoner,[9] with the unfortunate General Riego, and confined in the same prison with him in Madrid. He was, however, released and sent to England, through the exertions of the late Mr Canning.[10]

The innkeeper, Don Martin and his wife, were very kind, and furnished us with a good supper of roast fowls, and excellent wine. The country from Santiago to Vigo is beautifully rich, and highly cultivated; the scenery most magnificent, and the vineyards were then in full bloom, and the extensive fields of wheat nearly ripe. The people, in fact, appeared to want nothing, and there was not a single beggar to be seen. I arrived at Vigo on the 24th of June, without the occurrence of anything worth notice; and immediately waited on Sir Robert Wilson. I delivered my despatches to him, and was received most warmly by that brave and excellent soldier. When I had been four days at Vigo, Sir Robert set out for Corunna, in order to defend that place, which was threatened with an immediate attack by the French, who, we learned, had marched a division of troops in that direction. We

9 It has been impossible to identify Captain Matthews with any certainty. Later Harley states that he was a commissary during the Peninsular War. The only man with a similar name who could fit is 1st Lieutenant Commissary Alexander Matheson of the Royal Artillery Drivers, who served in Spain from January 1813 to the end of the war in April 1814.

10 George Canning (1770-1827) was Foreign Secretary, and later became Prime Minister.

were accompanied by Colonel Light, and Lieutenant Elliot.[11] The garrison fired a salute for Sir Robert, at his departure, and sent with us a troop of dragoons, as an escort to Corunna.

We slept, the first night, at a village called Caldas, famous for its hot-baths; the water of which is so hot, that, in many places, it would boil an egg.[12] We set out the next morning, and, after a quiet march of a few hours, stopped to dine in a small pleasant village, called Padron, situated at the foot of one of the Galician mountains.[13] As soon as our horses had been put up at the posada, or inn, I left Sir Robert and the party, and walked about to view the place. Having seen a monastery, a fine, ancient looking building, beautifully situated, above the village, curiosity led me to see the interior. I accordingly went up, and knocked at the front gate. A monk, or friar, opened it, and asked me what I wanted; on my replying that I was a traveller, who was anxious to see the convent, he immediately invited me to come in; saying, 'Entra, Signor.'

He first conducted me to the great chapel, and showed me some very fine paintings, and everything that was curious there; and told me the history of the convent, from its foundation. The order was the Capuchins. He led me upstairs, through a long gallery, at each side of which were the cells of the different friars. Several of them, opening their doors, came out to look at me, made a salutation, and then retired within their cells. When we got near the end of the gallery, a fat, jolly, good-looking friar made his appearance, and, from the respect I saw my guide pay to him, I judged he was the president, or superior of the order. I was not mistaken; for my conductor called him, 'Padre Prior,' and bowed to him. The prior saluted me in a very friendly manner, and asked me to what country I belonged. I answered, Ireland; he replied, in Spanish, 'Good country, good Christian.' He then turned to my conductor, and said to him, 'It is much better for this gentleman to have his dinner, than to be looking at these places; therefore, conduct him to the dining-hall, and give him the best wine'. It was then past five o'clock, and two lay brothers were sent to cook for me, and, in a short time, placed a comfortable dinner before me, – soup, fish, and fowls broiled, with a dessert of fruit. The friars had dined at twelve o'clock. The prior walked up and down, near the table, conversing with me, and pressing me to eat and drink. The wine, which was excellent, was placed before me in a white china basin, which held more than a pint; it being contrary to the rules of their order to make use of glass to drink out of. Having eaten a hearty dinner, with a keen appetite, I soon emptied the bowl of its delicious contents. The prior observing it, asked me would I like another, to which

11 Lieutenant Colonel William Light had served in the Peninsular War in the 4th Dragoons, but had now joined the Spanish army. According to Thomas Steele (see footnote 24, below), it seems that Elliot had tried to pass himself off as an aide de camp of Sir Robert Wilson.

12 Caldas de Reyes.

13 Padron is eight miles south-west of Santiago de Compostela.

I replied in the affirmative. He laughed, and ordered it immediately, and said, if I lived near them, I should always be welcome to their wine. I then walked with him and my guide through the rich and highly cultivated gardens of the convent. He asked me several questions about my native country, and told me that they had once an Irishman, a friar, in the convent, whom they all liked very much, but he died some years ago. As the evening was now advancing, I was obliged reluctantly to take my leave. The prior then, and not till then, asked whence I came; I said, from Vigo. He then enquired where I was going, and whether I was a negotiant, or merchant. I replied, I was proceeding to Corunna, and that my profession was military. He wished to know who my friends, at the inn, were. I informed him, General Sir Robert Wilson, and his staff.

At the mention of his name, he looked at the other friar, and both repeated the name, General Wilson; seemed alarmed, and repeated it again, in evident anxiety; fearing, from his well-known liberal principles, that he might be the means of suppressing the convents in Spain. Notwithstanding this, they shook hands with me warmly, said, no matter who was of my party, and requested that if I came that way again, I would not stop at the posada, or inn, but come direct to the convent, with my servant and horses, where I might remain as long as I liked, as I had a hearty welcome.

How often through life have I since regretted that I did not enrol myself amongst those happy and comfortable men, and give up all worldly pursuits! In truth, I should have made as good a friar as any of them. When I arrived at the inn, my friends, who had dined during my absence, were quite at a loss to know what had become of me, not having returned to dinner, and were highly amused when I related to them the reception I had met with. We immediately proceeded on our journey, and reached Santiago once more, at a late hour. Here it was that Marshal Massena, on his celebrated retreat out of Spain, plundered the church plate, and took the cloak and covering of the titular saint from the altar.[14] The inhabitants informed me that it was of incalculable value; being made of velvet, thickly studded with diamonds, which had been the gifts and donations of ages.

At an early hour the next morning, we took our departure for Corunna. The sky was clear, and brought to my mind the climate of Italy, which Spain, in all its various and numerous beauties, so much resembles. We were met on the road by crowds of people from Corunna; and, at the entrance of the city, a carriage was in readiness, in which Sir Robert Wilson was placed by the inhabitants, and drawn to the grand plaza, or square; the adjacent streets being lined with the troops of the garrison. On our arrival, a crown of laurels was held over the general's head by two lovely Spanish girls, dressed in white, a mark of great respect in this country,

14 The church plate and the remains of Saint James were taken by French forces under Marshal Ney in 1809. The saint's remains were discovered in a cistern a century later, but rumours of the burial of the church plate still cause treasure hunters to seek it out to this day.

as black is their usual costume. A dinner was given at the town-hall to Sir Robert Wilson and his staff.

Everything was now going on well at Corunna. General Morillo was at Lugo with a large Spanish army, and in a strong position covering Corunna.[15] The garrison consisted of 3,000 regular troops, besides the city volunteers and militia, – a very large force. The place was commanded by the well-known General Quiroga, who was Captain-General of the province. Morillo, however, joined the French, and left Corunna unprotected. But what else could be expected from such a man? He had been originally a corporal of marines;[16] but having in the last war distinguished himself at the pass of Pontevedra, near Vigo, where he defeated a considerable French force; he was in consequence promoted to the rank of an officer. Since the peace of 1814, Morillo had been employed in South America, where, by his cruelty and extortions practised on the wretched natives, he amassed a large fortune. I knew him well in 1813, having been billeted with him in the same house, in St Jean de Luz, in the south of France.

On the 15th of July, the French advanced guard reached the village of Betanzos, four leagues from Corunna, of which the garrison were totally ignorant; and, on the 16th of July, at two o'clock in the afternoon, the most favourable and well-judged time for attack, – as the Spaniards are well known to take their siesta or sleep at that hour, – General Count Bourke,[17] with 4,000 regular troops, approached Corunna, and attacked the outposts. General Sir Robert Wilson instantly mounted his horse, and, heading the Spanish regular army, repaired to the heights, where our ever-to-be-lamented Sir John Moore fell; and bravely checked the advance of the enemy, retaking two pieces of cannon. As at that time no Spanish generals had joined the engagement, I went to the palace, and found General Quiroga taking his sleep, and rousing him from his comfortable nap, urged him to go out and join Sir Robert, who kept the enemy at bay, and disputed the heights till four o'clock in the evening. The Spanish troops, at length, after very hard fighting, gave way and fell back on the town. Sir Robert, however, rallied them, and gallantly led them on to the heights again; but when about half-way to the windmill-hills, he unfortunately received a musket ball through his thigh, near the groin – a severe and dangerous wound. I was standing on the battery, near the Almeda, when a Spanish peasant called out: 'Sir Robert Wilson is severely wounded.'[18]

With feelings of deep regret, I immediately repaired to him, and had him removed to the inner town, and laid in bed at his quarters; and, as we had no English medical attendant, I procured for him a Spanish doctor. On the enemy

15 General Pablo Morillo (1775-1837).

16 Morillo had fought at Trafalgar as a Spanish marine and was captured.

17 *Lieutenant Général* Jean-Raymond Bourke (1772-1847), originally of Irish descent, he had made a career in the French army.

18 Sir Robert Wilson was wounded in the lower thigh, but not seriously.

seeing Sir Robert fall, they immediately drove the Spaniards back to the town – the gates of which were instantly closed, and the siege commenced. The firing now became very heavy. The enemy's shot and shells reached the town, and struck several houses. As it was generally supposed that they would storm the place the following morning, I went in the evening to the palace of the Commander-in-Chief, Quiroga, and suggested to him, that as the French had that day marched upwards of four leagues, and had been fighting all day, they must be consequently much fatigued; and, being flushed with the success of the morning, were probably then enjoying themselves in repose; and as his troops were fresh, and he could muster a large force, it was the best plan to make his sortie after dark, and attack the French, when he would probably rout and destroy them. I also pointed out to him, that if he waited till the next day, it would be too late, as they would then be refreshed, and would have time to entrench themselves. The general seemed inclined to adopt my plan; but one of his staff, a German, who had great influence over him, prevented it, proposing to defer the sortie for some days; but it was then too late, – the opportunity was lost – perhaps for the better, as it could not possibly have saved Spain, and must have been attended with the loss of a number of lives. Colonel Light, an excellent officer, was severely wounded this day. He received a grape shot in the right hip: it passed entirely through, carrying part of his pantaloons into the wound, which caused him great pain, until it was extracted. Colonel Light fought as became a British soldier. He was greatly beloved by the Spaniards, and indeed by all who had the pleasure of his acquaintance. He was first aid-de-camp to Sir Robert Wilson.

17th July – A courier arrived, with despatches from the Cortes, then sitting at Cadiz, appointing Sir Robert Wilson a general in the Constitutional Spanish army, and Commander-in-Chief, in the north of Spain, with letters of service to raise a legion, to consist of 10,000 men, to be recruited in England and Ireland. He was to have the appointment of all commissions in the first instance; and the vacancies were afterwards to be filled up by the Cortes. The officers, after the war, were to be placed on the same half-pay as officers of the same rank in the British service; or, in lieu of the half-pay, were to get some of the church lands to be divided amongst them; which were the finest in the country, particularly those in the provinces of Castile and Valencia. Sir Robert signed a commission for Colonel Light, as colonel and Quarter-Master-General, and another for myself as captain and Paymaster-General of the Legion.

18th July – I was by Sir Robert Wilson's bed-side when the British consul-general, Richard Bartlett, Esq came into the room; and, being very much alarmed for the safety of himself and wife, said, he was determined to go off and leave Corunna; asking me if I would accept the situation of vice-consul, Mr Bartlett being at the time consul-general of the provinces of Galicia and Asturias. By the advice of Sir Robert Wilson, I accepted the situation; which was duly notified to the intendante, or collector, of the custom-house. My appointment having been signed, as will appear at the end of this work, Mr Bartlett and family sailed the next day, for Ferrol, and I commenced acting in my new situation, as vice-consul, and representative of the British government in Corunna.

July 26th – This morning, I received the annexed letter from the vice-consul of Vigo :-

John Harley, Esq Corunna.
Vigo, 23rd July, 1823.

When I received your esteemed favour, of the 7th instant, I was obliged to keep my bed, as I was then labouring under a very strong attack of gout; but I desired Mr Walton to acquaint you with the receipt of the favour of yours, and that everything brought by the Baposa reached this place, and was delivered to the authorities of this city.

By the letter you addressed to Mr Walton, we were acquainted how things were at Corunna; but we heard, with the deepest concern, the wounds received by the brave Sir Robert Wilson, and my good friend Light; please to have the goodness to make my compliments to them, and that I long with anxiety to hear they are recovered, or at least doing well. Mr Walton left this place, on the 19th, by the packet Kent; and here afterwards the mails are to be consigned to me. The Kent, brought a despatch from Mr Bartlett, which I do not attempt to forward by this conveyance; not thinking it a very safe one, as there are French cruisers off your place. Please to have the goodness to write to Mr Bartlett on the subject, and request that he will give me his directions where I am to send to him the despatches.

Morillo arrived, on the 19th, at Pontevedros; and preparations were immediately made to receive him here. The people showed the best patriotism; and the volunteers garrisoned the forts, &c. Had Morillo advanced the next day, Vigo, perhaps, would not have been able to stand long; but now, on the contrary, because there are in the town about 2,000 men, composed of corps of the line, guerrillas, volunteers, &c; everyone is obliged to bear arms. Thus Morillo will want a very strong force to attack this place; and it is intended that tomorrow there shall set off 10,000 troops, in combination with those at Corunna, to attack him; and we expect that this expedition will be crowned with success. All the people round this place have risen, 'en masse,' against Morillo. I have seen newspapers as late as the 10th instant; they bring nothing particular, but that there was an anonymous subscription to the cause of the Spaniards, of £5,000. Many reports are afloat about the state of Corunna; but I believe none of them.

I hope that when you may have the goodness to write to me, you will inform me of everything; and I will do the same by every opportunity.

With best remembrances to all friends, I am, most sincerely, dear sir, your most obedient servant, Leopold Menendez.

I hope W. Dilton and his companion are with you before this.

General Sir Robert Wilson was now a good deal recovered; I begged of him to leave the garrison, dreading, and indeed sure, that the place must be soon taken by the French. He at last consented; and I hired a vessel for 200 dollars, to take him round to Vigo; Captain Matthews, and a Spanish medical officer, accompanying him. The sloop sailed in the evening, with a fair wind. Captain Matthews served in the English Commissariat, in Spain, during the late Peninsular war; by which means he acquired a perfect knowledge of the Spanish language. He had been residing, for the last three years, at Corunna, where he was much beloved by the inhabitants, for his obliging disposition. He headed a party of the constitutionalists, and marched from Corunna to Santiago, where he attacked and demolished the Inquisition, as before stated, and let the few surviving prisoners free. He was in the battle of the 16th of July, outside the walls, and fought well; rendering great service to the cause.

Sir Robert Wilson's object in going to Vigo, was to raise a force in that neighbourhood, to attack the besieging French army in the rear; and, by that means, relieve the city of Corunna; but he was not able to accomplish this plan, in consequence of the behaviour of General Morillo, who had joined the enemy.

Captain Mathews proceeded from Vigo to Cadiz and Gibraltar, and joined General Riego, as aide-de-camp, in Catalonia; and, after poor Riego was deserted by his troops, Mathews was the only officer who remained with him, which he generously did, although he could have escaped at the time.

Being both betrayed by the peasantry, they were made prisoners, and dragged from prison to prison, until they were conveyed to Madrid, where the ill-fated General Riego was executed, and Mathews confined in a dungeon.

After some time had elapsed, the British Government interfered, and had him set at liberty; but he was then nearly famished with hunger and cold, having frequently been two days without food, and seldom allowed any fuel.

28th of July – I received a letter from Sir Robert Wilson, this morning, as follows:-

To Captain John Harley, Corunna
Vigo, 27th July,1823

Dear Harley, –

A rough but quick passage of twenty hours, all sick and miserable, but the speed was fortunate. We arrived in time to repair mischief and effect good – all will now go on well, and we shall be able to give you good aid very soon; but I expect to hear the English mediation has prevailed, and an armistice named; for certain negotiations are far advanced; and this may account for the enemy not having regularly besieged you. Bristow[19], and about twenty officers, are here. Everything is going on as well as possible. At Cadiz, General Ballesteros[20] was menacing the enemy's left flank with 15,000 men. Send Colonel Light to England – I hope the Frenchmen are gone – give my despatches to Doyle – send Mathews' coat – let me have the cutter, if she arrives at Corunna, but make her as useful in any way as you can to the good people, I have special service for her – my wound is getting better – horses quite well – write to Colonel Grant – keep your journal regularly. – A ship will go to you with rice for the garrison and inhabitants.

Yours, with indelible memory of your affectionate and useful services,
R.T.Wilson

The Frenchmen, that Sir Robert mentions, were an old colonel and ninety men, veteran soldiers of Bonaparte's army, that came from France, and, joining the Constitutionalists at Corunna, fought in the battle of the sixteenth, carrying a tri-coloured flag with them. Sir Robert was uneasy lest they might fall into the hands of the besieging French army; but I had sent them away on board an American vessel, bound to Cadiz.

Little did the good and generous Sir Robert Wilson know, that at the moment he wrote the foregoing letter, the Spanish Generals, Morillo and others, had turned over and joined the French. From that moment, the Spanish patriotic cause was at an end. I had foreseen this for some time, as I knew well that no reliance could be placed on General Morillo.

31st July – Another letter this morning, by a fishing boat, by which it will be seen that Sir Robert had still hopes of success.

Vigo, 30th July, 1823.

Dear Harley,

Despatches to Mr Canning by an American. If possible an English ship will be sent to the British Vice-Consul from Vigo. My telegraph to you at Corunna will be a flag of truce; and be sure to send to the Spanish ambassador, via Canning. – Attention to Light, and embarkation – remembrances to Bartlett and wife.

Yours ever,
R.T.Wilson

19 Major Henry Bristow previously of the 11th Foot.

20 Francisco Ballesteros was a Spanish general in the Peninsular War, but was imprisoned at Ceuta in 1812, having refused to accept the Duke of Wellington as Commander in Chief of the Spanish army. In 1820 he commanded a force that surrounded the royal palace to get King Ferdinand VII to accept the Constitution of 1812. He fought the French army of the Duc d'Angouleme in 1823 but was forced to capitulate at Caporla.

'Episode of the French intervention in Spain 1823' by Hippolyte Lecomte. (Public Domain)

The town, after a siege of some days, had been summoned to surrender on the 23rd instant. The following copies of the summons, and of the governor's answer:-

> Army of the Pyrenees – 1st Corps, 2nd Division,
> Camp before Corunna,
> 23rd July, 1823
>
> Signor Governor,
> After having crossed all the windings of Spain, always victorious in all the oppositions I met with from your troops, I have arrived at the extremity of Spain, and before the city of Corunna, under your excellency's command. You are not ignorant, that since the entry of the French army into the Spanish soil, it has not suffered any disappointments; and you also know, that the whole nation repels the Constitution that you defend vainly.
>
> I write to you, then, Signor Governor, in the name of humanity, and in order to prevent any effusion of blood without necessity; that you give up the town of Corunna, as a deposit to the French army, commanded by his Royal Highness the Duke d'Angoulême; that it may be returned to your king the moment he is restored to his liberty. I must observe, that a denial

will expose the garrison and inhabitants to all the rigours that war allows in a town taken by force.

In order that you should determine better, I am authorised to tell you, in the name of His Royal Highness, the Duke d'Angoulęme, that he does not wish to have any character in Spain than that of pacificator; and all the military men, that submit voluntarily to His majesty the King of Spain, will preserve their ranks and situations, as His Royal Highness guarantees. They will be paid by the French army. Those who do not wish to serve,. such as the National Guards, or Provincial Volunteers of Bilboa, &c. will be at liberty to return to their homes. They are not to be molested for their opinions before our entry into the town; for such is the wish, so well manifested, of His Royal Highness the Duke d'Angoulęme.

Signor Governor, your Excellency will see we wish for the happiness of Spain, and to free her from the internal contest that consumes her; we lay our arms open to you; will you be your own enemy by not embracing us? I have the honour to be, Signor Governor, your humble servant, Bourke, Lieutenant-General.

Answer:

Corunna, 23rd July, 1823
By what your Excellency states in your summons, which I have received, at five o'clock this afternoon, I perceive your Excellency to be before the town under my command, and announcing yourself victorious in the operations you had with our troops. I do not know of any other engagement than that of the 16th instant, before this town; and I do not believe we are of the same opinion, on which side was the victory. Your Excellency has experienced it, therefore you well know, it is not yet the whole nation that depreciates the Constitution, which it defends here, as in many other parts of Spain, by a sacred duty, bound and contracted by a solemn oath, and the Spanish military honour. It is not, therefore, possible for me to accede to your proposals, whose effects your Excellency could prevent, by withdrawing your troops from the front of the town. Humanity should make you desirous to spare the blood that would be shed; and to preserve to the peaceable inhabitants of Corunna their liberty.

If your Excellency wishes, as likewise His Royal Highness the Duke d'Angoulęme, the happiness of Spain, let the dissensions vanish, which, a short time ago, we knew not here. The mode of realising it effectually will be to leave us in the tranquillity we once enjoyed. It began to disappear the moment in which your Excellency came to hostilities with us. God preserve your Excellency many years!

Antonia Quiroga

1st Aug. 1823 –The *Royal George*, steam-packet, having received a supply of coals at Ferrol, yesterday, sailed this morning at two o'clock for Portsmouth, having General Quiroga and staff on board, and forty-three other passengers. The general goes to London, for the purpose of making arrangements there, and from thence to Cadiz, where the Cortes are now sitting; I fear it is an unwise step. His sudden departure has damped the spirits of the people here, with whom he was a great favourite. The night of his departure was a fine moonlight one. The servants of the palace were in the utmost grief at parting. He could not take his horses with him; he therefore made a sham sale of them to me, and gave me s receipt to show, in case they were demanded, as follows:

> Corunna; July 30th, 1823
> Received, from the English Vice-consul, payment for my horses.
> Antonia Quiroga

The above was written in Spanish, with his own hand, which document I have at present in my own possession. I gave his horses up some time afterwards, to his brother, when all was quiet.

A very smart firing of musketry this morning, at daylight, between the enemy's advanced post, and the Spanish soldiers on the works.

A report has just come, that General Morillo is dead; it is said that he died at Santiago, of wounds.[21] A woman has come in, she states, that the French General, Bourke, was wounded yesterday, by a splinter of a shell, and that he is very ill, in the French camp on the hills.

The following is the French force in front of the town, of which a deserter, that came in this morning, informed me, viz.

> 7th Regiment of the line,
> 15th Infantry,
> 22nd Ditto,
> 37th Ditto,
> 38th Ditto,
> 1st Regiment of Hussars,
> 1st Regiment of Light Dragoons,
> 8 Pieces of cannon (six pounders).

In consequence of the governor having gone to Vigo, and General Quiroga to England, the command of the garrison has this day devolved on General Novella, a very experienced artillery officer, in whom the people repose great confidence.

21 The rumour was false.

The enemy are very quiet this day, and have not fired a shot since morning, but I perceived, with a glass, they are busily constructing works.[22]

This evening, the schooner, *Nassau*, arrived from London, with arms and accoutrements, together with a large quantity of ammunition, which, however, are of no use here, without men.

I have just delivered over to General Novella, 500 stand of arms; 500 sets of accoutrements; and 20,000 flints; brought by the *Nassau*. The general very properly remarked, that 500 men would render more service to the Spanish cause than all the arms, and accoutrements, and ammunition in the Tower of London; that they had plenty of military stores in their own arsenal – all they wanted, was a good body of men to assist the Spaniards, and to fight by their side. There came out, by this ship, a Mr Llewellyn, and three or four gentlemen, who wished to be officers. The general laughed, and said that all the arrivals from England were officers, but no soldiers. I certainly coincided in his remark, for it was truly ridiculous to see the crowds of young men coming out, all expecting commissions; never considering that there was no army formed, to which they could be attached. Indeed, in this respect, a very great mistake, or misunderstanding, appears to prevail; for all the young gentlemen from England, are coming out to be officers, while the people in Spain are daily expecting hundreds of soldiers, to fight for them in the cause of liberty.

Were it not for the penalties, which make the crime misdemeanour, under the Foreign Enlistment Bill,[23] and which prevent any of his British Majesty's subjects entering into the service of any foreign power. I am convinced that an army of 50,000 men could be raised in a few weeks, in England and Ireland, at this time; which would make a great alteration in the political government of Spain.

A French frigate is at anchor at the entrance of the harbour of Ferrol. The *Nassau* has left the harbour of Corunna, and has passed close under the stern of the frigate, but she has taken no notice of her.

The French have, this day, sent all their cavalry from Ferrol, with 1,300 infantry, to join the force before Corunna.

2nd. A grand review took place this day, at four o'clock, in the great square. The troops were in excellent health and spirits and, at the conclusion of the review, the soldiers gave three cheers for the Constitution and called out, 'Viva Ingleterra!'

3rd. Two Spanish vessels arrived this morning from Vigo, bringing despatches for the governor here, and provisions for the garrison.

A very heavy firing this morning. A captain of Spanish artillery, walking in the Calle de St Andero, has just been killed, by a musket-ball from the enemy. A poor girl, bringing a pail of water from the fountain, and two children, who ventured

22 General Francisco Novella Azabal Perez y Sicardo.

23 The Foreign Enlistment Bill was passed in 1819 in an attempt to stop British subjects signing up to fight in the wars of independence in South America and any future conflicts. It failed signally.

into the street, have been also killed; and an engineer, looking through his glass, has this moment been shot through the head, on the battery next the Almeida.

A brig arrived from London this day, laden with arms, accoutrements, and clothing; all sent out by the Spanish Committee of London, purchased out of the fund that is subscribed in England for the aid of the Spanish constitutional cause. The subscriptions amount now to £35,000 before the vessel sailed, one lady, it is said, gave £4,000 to the fund. This cargo is come out in charge of Mr Dixon, as supercargo, and he is accompanied by Mr Steele, and others.[24] Mr Steele informs me, that he is a member of the Spanish Committee of London, and a native of Ireland. There being no want of arms at Corunna, the vessel, with her cargo, sailed for Gibraltar.

An inhabitant, a carpenter, was discovered early this morning making his escape to the enemy, and, some papers having been found about his person, offering to point out to them the weakest part to enter, he was brought into the great square, immediately tried by a court martial, and shot, at four o'clock, on the ramparts, in view of the French camp.

4th. Provisions have now become very dear; meat has risen three reals per pound; bread, also, very dear; no vegetables to be had; as the enemy have cut off all communication with the country. Water is beginning to be very difficult to be procured, as they have also destroyed the aqueduct that supplied the town; and, the weather being very hot, the want of water is very much felt.

On this day a waggon, drawn by six mules, and laden with forty barrels of gunpowder, was blown up, nearly opposite the main guard. The explosion was tremendous, having shattered all the houses in the neighbourhood, killed the mules, and killed and wounded several of the guard. This accident was caused by the careless conduct of the Spanish sergeant, who had charge of the powder; for, although he was only conveying the ammunition from the magazine to one of the batteries, yet he was so lazy that he sat on the waggon, and smoked a cigar, a spark from which fell among the barrels of powder, and caused the dreadful accident. He was blown to pieces.

This morning, Mr Dillon and several other gentlemen, as volunteers, arrived from England to join the patriotic cause; but, as it was now too late, and all the fighting nearly over, I judged it best to send them to England again, which I did the next day.

The greatest want of firewood now prevails. The people are obliged to burn their furniture in order to cook their meals; and in a few weeks more, if some wood does not arrive, the people will be without the means of making fires.

24 Mr Thomas Steele. He wrote a book entitled *Notes of the war in Spain; detailing occurrences military and political, in Galicia, and at Gibraltar and Cadiz, from the fall of Corunna to the occupation of Cadiz by the French.* Published London 1824.

5th. This morning, the French frigate that went into Ferrol is come out, and has brought with her a brig of war. They are now at anchor outside the harbour of Ferrol.

The French are quite silent today; and have ceased firing; and very few of them are to be seen in their lines. They have succeeded in getting four guns, twenty-four pounders, round from Ferrol: they are busy endeavouring to mount them on the battery, which they have erected on the hill of Santa Margaretta, near the windmills.

All the French troops at Ferrol have left it, and joined General Bourke before Corunna, which makes his force very formidable. A small vessel arrived this morning from St Antonia; she brings the melancholy intelligence that the place is besieged, and in a state of starvation.

15

Corunna & Return to Britain

6th. This day, at two o'clock, the enemy sent in a flag of truce, and summons: the following are the copies of it, and the governor's answer:-

> Army of Spain – 1st Corps, 2nd Division.
> Camp in front of Corunna,
> 6th of August, 1823
>
> Signor Governor,
> I will not repeat to your Excellency the advantageous proposals which I directed to your predecessor, in the name of His Royal Highness the Duke d'Angoulęme; I cannot do less than assure your Excellency on my word and honour, that they will be executed, if you accept them. Compare them, then, with the inevitable events of a place by force.
>
> I offer to your Excellency security for the future for the whole garrison. Would you, then prefer captivity, and all the horrors of a siege? My frankness is well known. Never have I made use of treachery or deceit. All Galicia has submitted to obedience under Ferdinand VII; and my troops, with those of General Morillo, have entered Vigo. In the first place, your means of defence are diminished, as those of the besiegers are augmented. You have seen the French cruisers in the bay; and you cannot be ignorant that my artillery is mounted, and ready to destroy a town that I wish to save. I assure you on my word and honour, that I am sincere. I conjure you, then, Signor Governor, to submit to his Royal Highness the Duke d'Angoulęme, whose person I represent. The town of Corunna will remain in deposit, to be delivered to the King of Spain, when he ceases to be captive. It is then to you, Signor, and to Spain itself, that your Excellency would surrender it. On the contrary, your Excellency will be responsible to all the military of the garrison for the loss of their commissions, and to the inhabitants for all the misfortunes which are the consequences of a town taken by assault. I suppose, Signor Governor, you have an affection for your King, and that you do not wish to deprive His Majesty of those

officers who would serve him well. I believe your Excellency humane; and can you then behold, without horror, all the misfortunes of a population reduced to the worst and last calamity? I hope, Signor Governor, you will not hesitate in accepting these propositions, that do not in the least tarnish or stain your honour. The means of restoring peace and felicity to your country rest with your Excellency. I transmit a copy of my former propositions, in case your predecessor should not have judged proper to communicate them to you.

I have the honour to be, Signor Governor, with the highest consideration, your Excellency's obedient servant,

Bourke, Lieutenant-General.

Answer:

Most Excellent Signor,

I am prepared, and, with the garrison of this place, decided to maintain it at all events, as our oaths, and honour, and fidelity to the Constitutional King, demand it, whom we by no means consider a captive, as the most recent news informs us, – and particularly His Majesty having lately had the goodness to name me Internal Commandant of this district, and consequently General-in-Chief and Governor of this city. Would it, then, correspond with his confidence in me, if I delivered up the place to your Excellency, who present yourself as his enemy, and the enemy of the Spanish nation? Those same horrors, with which your Excellency now threatens us, and the innocent people of this town, – they indeed move my humanity; but they have not diminished my resolution to defend the place. All the evils which the inhabitants suffer, are promoted by your Excellency; and, since the means of avoiding those evils rests with those whom your Excellency names as friends of King Fernando Septimo, why should you destroy a place defended by his subjects, who consider him at full liberty? The latest news from Vigo, and the other provinces of Galicia, do not agree with those sent by your Excellency to me, and I am certain that all this meritorious garrison will convince your Excellency of it very soon.

God preserve your Excellency many years!

Francisco Novella,

Governor of Corunna

This answer was delivered by the chief of the staff, to the officer who came with the flag of truce, and ten minutes were allowed him to depart; at the expiration of which, the firing commenced on both sides, with cannon and musketry. At the same time, two French frigates, two brigs of war, and two gun-boats, came into the bay, and stood in, near that part of the city called Orzan; but, in consequence of a heavy firing from the batteries, they were soon obliged to desist, and stand off to sea.

The enemy had constructed four batteries on the hills of the Mills, and on the Pallosa. They kept up a heavy fire on the town, without intermission, throwing in shells, grenades, and cannon shot. They directed their fire chiefly to that part of the town called Pescaderia the finest and richest part of the town, where the wealthiest merchants resided, and particularly the Canton de Lacy, and the streets of St Andrew, Nichola, and Cordelina. In the evening, several houses were on fire in those streets. The French, perceiving the poor inhabitants bringing water, to put out the flames, fired grape-shot tremendously on those poor innocent people, killing and wounding several men, women, and children.

7th. The firing was kept up all last night, by the French, and did not cease till six o'clock this morning. Lieutenant Colonel Don Pedro Barca, a good artillery officer, was killed, about nine o'clock at night;[1] also, Lieutenant Jose Muñez, and several artillerymen. Every man in the town, old and young, is now under arms. The women are busily employed, carrying sandbags to the batteries, which they do most cheerfully, though nearly fainting with fatigue. They think no trouble or hazard too great, when their husbands and children are in danger.

The firing having ceased this morning, the French have not shown many of their men in front.

8th. The French seem moving in different directions. A report is in circulation, having been communicated by a deserter just come in, that they have withdrawn their artillery on the road to Santiago, as they dreaded an attack in their rear, by a supposed force that was reported to be on the march from Oranzee and Vigo, under General Sir Robert Wilson.

9th. All is perfectly silent in the enemy's lines this day, and very few of them to be seen.

10th. A boat, with a flag of truce, arrived from Ferrol, and brought Colonel Cuesta, who had accompanied the governor to Vigo. He states that Morillo had entered on the 3rd instant; and that Sir Robert Wilson had embarked from thence for England or Cadiz. In consequence of the arrival of Colonel Cuesta, the Junta assembled and remained in conference all night, deliberating on the despatches he has brought, and the information he has communicated.

11th. The enemy seemed very busy this morning in erecting new batteries on the opposite side of the bay, in front of the Canton de Lacy. They keep up the fire of musketry from the hills near the windmills which command the town.

A Danish ship sailed this day from Corunna for Hamburg. She has taken a bag of letters for England, which the captain promises me to put on shore as he passes up the British channel. I have sent despatches by her to the committee in London.

1 Colonel Don Pedro del Barca, commanding the artillery.

In consequence of the intelligence brought by Colonel Cuesta, and after a long conference between the governor and Junta, at two o'clock this day a flag of truce was sent out from the city, demanding a cessation of arms, until some intelligence arrived from Cadiz. This was agreed to, and all is perfectly quiet now. The French soldiers came down to the gates and conversed with the Spanish soldiers.

12th. Two French officers were sent in this day; and two Spanish officers have gone out as hostages, until all the terms of the capitulation are finally agreed on.

13th. Nothing particular occurred this day. The greatest anxiety prevailed among the inhabitants respecting the negotiations that are going on; and various reports are in circulation respecting the terms.

14th. An English cutter appeared this evening at six o'clock, and attempted to enter the harbour, but was prevented by one of the brigs of war that is blocking us. The cutter has sailed to the southward, – I suppose for Cadiz or Gibraltar.

15th. Colonel Campilo set out at two o'clock this day to the headquarters of General Morillo, at Vigo, in order to finally arrange the capitulation of this place.[2] It is said the French are not to enter Corunna; but all the French in Spain are to retire beyond the Ebro, until all differences are settled. However, they still occupy the heights opposite Corunna. Their working parties are still employed, and they seem to be raising redoubts.

16th. All quiet this day.

17th The markets begin now to be plentifully supplied; and, although the gates are not yet open, the country people are allowed to send in provisions over the wall.

18th. This morning, the governor General Novella issued a proclamation; the purport of which was to desire the inhabitants to remain quiet, and that negotiations are going on.

19th. Nothing extraordinary this day.

20th. This evening, an aid-de-camp of General Morillo came in, and took up his quarters at the same house, in the Grand Plaza, in the inner city, that Sir Robert Wilson formerly occupied; it being the same house, as before remarked, in which Sir John Moore expired. It is the principal house in the city, is opposite the palace, and is the property of Madame Sangrave, who is absent, being no friend to the constitutional party.

21st This morning all was anxiety among the inhabitants. At ten o'clock General Morillo entered by the great gate of St Andrew's, preceded by an advanced guard, and followed by a numerous staff, with an escort of 100 cavalry. He proceeded through the Calle de St Andero to the palace in the city. On his way he was not taken the slightest notice of, nor did any person salute him, which mortified him much. General Bourke entered at the head of 1,000 infantry, and was met by Morillo, who accompanied him to the Plaza, in the city, where General Bourke

2 Colonel Don Juan Lopez Campillo, commanded a brigade at Corunna.

made a short speech to his troops; after which he and Morillo embraced. About two o'clock the 35th and 38th French Regiments entered, 1,000 men each, with four small field-pieces of artillery, six-pounders; and at four o'clock the French military chest, and the commissariat arrived, and the town was ordered to be illuminated; an order that was but partially complied with. In the evening, a Spanish regiment marched out, and was saluted by the French Guards on duty at the gates. All is now tranquil; I cannot avoid remarking the orderly, good conduct of the French soldiers. They have not been known to commit one act of impropriety, but are polite to a degree to the inhabitants.

The following are the articles of capitulation this day published:-

> TRANSLATION OF THE ARTICLES OF CAPITULATION.
> Head-quarters, Vigo, 17th August, 1823
>
> Article 1. The city and garrison of Corunna will recognize the authority of the Regency of Spain and the Indias, installed in Madrid during the absence of the King.
>
> Article 2. No Inhabitant of Corunna, or the neighbourhood, can be molested or persecuted for the opinions he has held, or political conduct he may have observed up to the present time.
>
> Persons and property will be most scrupulously respected.
>
> Article 3. Corunna will be garrisoned by as many French troops as the Count de Bourke may deem convenient; and there will be also in the garrison, Spanish troops under the orders of the Count of Cartagena.[3]
>
> Article 4. To the National Militia, not belonging to Corunna, will be furnished passports to their respective towns, or other places, that may best suit them, and they will be furnished with every necessary aid; and in no manner are they to be molested, or persecuted, for the opinions they have manifested, nor for the political conduct which they may have observed as private persons, or as national militia.
>
> The National Militia of Corunna are comprehended in the second article, and in as much of this as may correspond with them.

3 General Pablo Morillo was made Count of Cartagena.

Article 5. The garrison of Corunna, that has for a time been separated from the army, will return to incorporate with it, and to be considered with the rest of the troops that compose it.

Generals, chiefs, and officers, will retain their employments, ranks, and destinations, and the troops will continue serving as hitherto.

Passports will be furnished to the generals, chiefs, and officers, whom it may not suit to incorporate with the army; or, if they do not accept those terms, they will remain prisoners of war.

(Signed) The Count Cartagena

Camp in front of Corunna, 20th August, 1823

The Most Excellent Lieutenant-General, commanding the troops of His Majesty the King of France, accedes to all the conditions mentioned in the foregoing articles.

(Signed) J.Bourke

22nd. Nothing particular this day; crowds of the country people coming in with provisions and supplies to the city, and everything is becoming cheap. Abundance of game of all descriptions, and particularly the red-legged partridge, as large as our common hen, which sell at eight-pence per pair. It is singular that all game is brought to the market alive.

23rd. This morning, the four French frigates and two brigs of war, that have been blockading the place, entered the harbour and anchored before the city. Corunna now resembles a French town, the streets being crowded with French soldiers and sailors. This evening the last of the Spanish troops marched out in perfect silence.

24th. Nothing has occurred this day worth remarking.

25th. This being the birth-day of Louis XVIII, or feast of St Louis, at six o'clock this morning the French frigates fired a salute; and at twelve o'clock the French troops, having been drawn up in front of the Custom-house, on the Grand Canton or Quay, fired several volleys. They were inspected by Generals Morillo and Bourke. The French frigates fired twenty-one guns each. General Bourke gave a grand entertainment at his quarters to the French military and naval officers. The stone which was placed in the great square by the liberal party, with the word 'Constitution' on it, was this evening pulled down, and the inhabitants were ordered to illuminate their houses at night, which was very reluctantly complied with.

26th. I paid a visit this day to General Count Bourke: he received me very politely, and conversed with me in English, and talked a great deal about Sir Robert Wilson; he asked me particularly about his wound, and hoped he was recovering; said he was a brave officer, and that he was very happy that he was not taken prisoner.

Colonel Campillo, Colonel Van Hallen,[4] and a number of the Spanish officers, rather than acknowledge the Regency in Madrid, have, this morning, embarked

4 Antonio Van Hallen was Chief of Staff.

on board a French frigate, and gone prisoners of war to France. They are to be landed at Rochefort.

27th. Another of the French frigates has left the harbour, and there only remains now two frigates and one brig of war.

The post from Vigo has arrived, and a great number of the English letters are missing, having been taken out from the mail by Morillo on the road. He has acknowledged this act to Colonel Conolly, an Irishman, who is a Colonel in the Spanish service.[5]

28th. General Bourke sent for me this morning, and asked where Colonel Light resided. Perceiving me hesitate in answering him, he quickly mentioned to me, that he had no motive but to render him a service; that if he wished to do him an injury, he would readily find him out by the police of the city; but, on the contrary, that if he wanted money or medical aid he should have it. He then advised me, as soon as Colonel Light's wound was better, to send him to England, as he was not safe here, the Spaniards being a treacherous people. This morning, I received the annexed letter from Mr Bartlett, the Colonel, from Ferrol.

> Ferrol, August 26th, 1823.
>
> My Dear Sir,
> I am surprised to learn by your letter that a French officer has been sent to my house. The enclosed is a protest against such a proceeding: pray let it be sent immediately to the President of the Ayuntamiento. I shall leave this on Thursday morning for Corunna, if the weather will admit. We had a grand ball here last night, and I was invited, I thought it would appear marked if I did not stay to attend. This circumstance, and letters which I expected from Santander, have detained me here a day or two longer than I wished for. Always very truly yours, Richard Bartlett
>
> Of course, if the Ayuntamiento give you any reply about the billing, you will decline giving any opinion until my arrival.

There were seventy prisoners of the Royalists confined by the Constitutionalists in the castle, partly friars, partly civilians. When the town was likely to be taken, the governors and authorities judged proper to send them away: they were accordingly put on board a Spanish brig, and sent off in the night, with a guard of the volunteers; but, horrid to relate, after they had got into the bay, and passed Ferrol, they tied the unfortunate men together back to back, and stabbed them with knives and bayonets, and then threw them overboard. It was supposed in the town that they were banished to the Canary Islands, as exiles for life. The quick return, however, of the vessel in two days created surprise and suspicion, which was confirmed by

5 Lieutenant Colonel James Connolly, ex-26th Foot.

several of the bodies of the victims being washed on shore. Seven men of the guard secreted themselves in the neighbourhood of Corunna, among their friends, for some weeks, waiting an opportunity to get away, there being an English brig, the *Hebe*, then lying at anchor, and ready to sail.

The principal custom-house officer applied to me, as British vice-consul, to visit some English ships in the harbour, under pretence of searching for smuggled goods. When we boarded the *Hebe*, on going into the hold, to my great surprise, the officer found the seven men of the guard, who had stabbed the people on board the Spanish brig, and thrown them overboard. It seemed as if providence directed that they should not escape, for the *Hebe* had put to sea the evening before with these men on board, and had a fine breeze; but after being nearly out of the harbour, she was forced back by a strong swell of the sea. The return of the vessel much surprised the people on shore. The seven men were immediately made prisoners and brought before Morillo, who had them searched, and several documents were found on them, which implicated the Lieutenant Governor, also the Teniente del Rey, or King's Lieutenant, and many others, who were all taken up that night, and thrown into prison, and afterwards banished. The seven wretched men were hanged in Corunna: and as they were related to the first families in the city, it presented a melancholy spectacle, all the shops being closed on that day.

A Spanish execution is most barbarous; for the executioner, or hangman, jumps upon the shoulders of the culprit, immediately after he is turned off, and presses on him with all his weight. You see the wretched culprit suspended in the air, and the hangman standing on his shoulders till he is dead.

10th. Nothing has occurred since the 28th ultimo; everything quiet and tranquil in Corunna, and commerce seems again to revive a little, but several of the merchants and principal people having gone away, very little business is doing. Colonel Light, being a good deal recovered, I thought it best to send him to England, and therefore, I this day had him put on board a small sloop, bound to Plymouth. I also procured a passage for a Mr McKenzie, a Scotch gentleman, who had been residing here, and going on board with them myself, saw them safe out of the harbour.

15th. A ship laden with provisions came in this day from London, from the Spanish committee. The captain brought me a letter from the secretary, saying he was directed by the committee to inform me, that I was requested to divide the provisions among the garrison, and that soon as they heard from me, another ship with arms would be sent out if I required it; but the garrison having been taken, and the place being then in the possession of the French army, I wrote immediately to inform the committee of the circumstance, and sold the whole of the cargo of provisions, which consisted of beef, pork, and salt fish, with biscuits and potatoes; but the potatoes, of which there were twenty tons, I distributed among the poor of Corunna, and the produce of the other provisions I remitted to the committee by a bill from Mr Santos, of Corunna, on his banker in London, which was duly honoured.

At this time I received a letter from Colonel Grant, by which I was informed of the death of Lady Wilson, who died in consequence of hearing suddenly that Sir Robert was dangerously wounded. The alarming intelligence was incautiously communicated to Lady Wilson, at a time, when she was rather unwell; and thus the melancholy event, which was universally regretted, was the unhappy consequence.[6]

I became acquainted in Corunna about this period (October, 1823), with the French General Tisson, who commanded the 37th Regiment of the line:[7] when he found that I was an old Egyptian, he expressed his happiness in meeting me, having served there himself under General Menou,[8] being at the time only Lieutenant of infantry. As the brave and lamented Sir John Moore's tomb was in a dilapidated state on the ramparts, I was going one morning to get it repaired, accompanied by Spanish masons and workmen, when I met the general, who inquired of me what I was engaged in; when I informed him, he looked at me steadfastly; and then said: 'No, these fellows shall never have that honour, myself and regiment will go, and be proud to repair the tomb of that hero,' I of course refused his noble offer, as my orders were to have it done by the workmen I had with me. I am sorry to say it was discreditable to England, that it should ever be in the state in which I found it, and situated as it then was, I much fear the tomb of that gallant officer is, by this time, completely dilapidated.

An English gentleman, a Mr Hampson, a most respectable merchant, from Gijon, in the Asturias, arrived at Corunna at this time, after having suffered privations of the most severe description, from the base conduct and persecution of a Spaniard, bigoted to a degree, named Uergo, who was then holding the same situation as British vice-consul at Gijon that I held at Corunna. I was informed by Mr Hampson, that he had suffered the greatest cruelties: he was threatened with imprisonment on account of his constitutional principles and liberal ideas. He was therefore obliged to quit the country, at the loss of £12,000, or £13,000, from the underhand dealing of Uergo, who, it was said, was a friar, as well as vice-consul, and who also detained his wife and child for a period of two years, as she was a Spanish woman, until at length, after much fatigue and trouble, and being compelled to travel by night to get safely out of the country, she arrived in England and joined her husband, at Liverpool, where they now reside, upon the remnant of their property, much respected.

As the proof of the patriotic feelings by which Mr Hampson was actuated, I would subjoin the following letter from him (written to Colonel Light, who was wounded outside the gates of Corunna, the same day as Sir Robert Wilson), which

6 Jemima Wilson died on 12 August 1823.

7 General Jean Marie Tissot.

8 Jacques Francois de Boussay Menou, who commanded the French army in Egypt after Napoleon left in 1800 and his successor, Kléber, was assassinated.

will also give my readers a tolerably accurate idea of the state of the country at that period.

Gijon, Asturias, 28th Sept.1825

My Ever Esteemed Colonel,
Admiring the noble order of your patriotism in favour of a people, who, individually, are so little deserving of the personal talent and exertions you have so generously and heroically displayed to extricate them from an unprovoked, unjust usurpation of conspiring despots, induced me to pay you a complimentary visit in Corunna, where I found you excruciatingly suffering from a wound received in one of the most arduous and dangerous exploits under the walls of that city, and at the same time experiencing (in my opinion) little attention or show of gratitude from those for whom you had hazarded and endured so much.

Notwithstanding the pungent twinges that accompanied each movement of the body, these individual pains, together with the provoking apathy of an ingrate torpid few, were cast into oblivion, the moment the grand cause of suffering liberty and independence were touched upon. With honest heart elate, and energetic voice, you exclaimed, 'The cause is not yet lost' This exclamation, ejaculated without the least tincture of sordid control, made such an impression on my constitutional feelings, that it has never ceased to vibrate upon my thrilling tongue, especially upon the following occasions: wherever I turn, my country, and political sentiments are soon discovered to be free passport to patriots of all classes, and in return, their cheerful countenances and confident garrulity, bring to mind, my dear colonel, that you are right; and I instinctively repeat, 'The cause is not lost'

When I see the town and village walls plastered over with complaints of corporation poverty, accompanied with threats of military execution, to levy the public contributions and taxes, which, from their frequent repetition, the people look upon with sneering contempt, can I say other than, 'come, come, colonel, you were right – the cause is not lost'

When I daily hear complaints of the rapacious usurpation of the friars, seizing upon the monastic property heretofore sold for the benefit of the nation, and they, not content with the improvements made thereon, attempting to levy excessive fines upon the purchasers, thereby not only provoking said purchasers, but all who conceive they have a collateral or relative expectation in the said property, then, I say this will eventually prove the colonel right – the cause is not lost

When I see men of classical learning and sound judgement deprived of their magisterial office, walking the streets in pensive careless lounge, replaced by frowning sullen pretenders, to what their round heads can never possibly attain, I readily recur to the idea of the colonel, that the cause is not lost When I see the languid countenances of experienced officers of customs and other public affairs, discarded to make room for ignorant audacious upstarts, without credit or character, the families of the latter not content with only supplanting, but personally ill-treating the families of the former, – then I exclaim, go on my boys, this is the way to confirm the colonel, that the cause is not lost When I see the creditable, well-instructed youth of the province spurn with disdain the traitorous call of the self-elected usurpers for their aid to enslave their still more loyal, dutiful neighbours, then I am convinced, the cause is not lost When I see an armed peasantry commanded by disreputable officers of the meanest estimation inadequate to urge subordination, and without pay, individually taking upon themselves to dictate and execute their own system of police, violently dispersing merchants from their accustomed place of resort for communication of business, dragging others from their beds, thrusting them into loathsome prisons, and there detaining them without trial or cause assigned for their capture and detention, I am led to think that those who depend on this class of protectors, will shortly express themselves happy, that the cause is not lost When I see throughout the province, men of the lowest order in society, despicable in their manners and character, thrust into the highest civic offices, exposing their imbecility and dangerous power by executing their personal resentments on their more refined, peaceable neighbours, under the feigned guise of political security, I think I see the curtain move and bringing to view, the cause is not lost.

When I hear the more honourable and respectable families forbid the practice of their ancient custom (allowed even in the despotic days of arbitrary monarchs) of entertaining, in their own houses, their social evening parties, I hear the eager inquiry of disappointed dames of, 'Will no one attempt to bring back the strayed cause – I say all is not lost'

When I see families of education and property, who, for the sake of private interest, heretofore opposed the cause, now ashamed to avow their former actions, opinions, and company of their present rulers, I feel the good cause has not reduced the number of her friends. When I hear the householder and husbandman begin to state their pecuniary differences, on account of the late violent, traitorous, and unnatural change of the political system, together with the never-ceasing, intolerable importunities, and threats, of the collector of tithes and taxes, attending them whilst in the act of scraping together to pay their ill-timed disbursements, their muttering discontent shows with what rapturous felicity they would receive back the wandering cause?

When I hear the infidel friars preaching up their impious doctrines of passive obedience and non-resistance to their rapacious usurpations and juggling deceptions, to accumulate temporal property, barter away the evangelic gospel of our blessed Saviour to fill up Judas' traitorous bag of worldly pelf, and defile the pulpit- oratorical denunciations of extermination of such of their fellow-creatures who have the temerity not to admit their consciences to be placed under the despotic control of these unbelievers of the very doctrine they teach. Then I say, it is a duty incumbent upon all good Christians to join in the holy cause of redeeming the church from the irreligious grasp of these sons of Belial.

When I see flying edicts, advertisements and gazettes filled with fulsome, abominable, invented untruths of succumbing armies, and yielding fortresses before their moth-like ephemerical minions of impotency, it exhibits their fears, exposes a weakness reduced to a dependence on falsehood, and shows that something is going on in favour of the cause of suffering humanity. When I see the adult strength of the country deprived of their youthful sports, and all reunion of innocent devotions suppressed by the threat of that grand engine of priest-craft, the Holy Inquisition, too much to be patiently borne by those who have had but a slight taste of rational liberty, breaks out into thrilling mummery, afterwards hurries into a rushing violence, then comes into glorious view – the cause, though missing for a time, was never lost But when I see the military patriot, who, by his prowess, experience, or length of service, has raised himself in the ranks of his compatriots, and on which is his sole dependence, because his honour and conscience will not allow him to truckle with the usurpers of his legal government and the rights of mankind, he is turned adrift, un-provided for, by an uncharitable world, reduced to want –hungered –spiritless-and debilitated -when the time of reaction should be seized upon with an ardent enthusiasm and energy that commands success. This, this is, where, in my opinion, the cause is losing ground.

The military officer of honour and experience, whilst he is decently fed and supported, is always in action, never loses sight of the main object to which he is directed; knows the material necessary for the enterprise; and to maintain his honour and establish his credit, seeks them with anxious, persevering diligence; and, by his own contentment and hilarity, enlivens the scene, and rouses to action wherever he presents himself. How many ardent spirits are now laid dormant, perishing in rust for want of timely, friendly, assistance in this storm of adversity! Who ought to be in sleekness burnished up, and rendered useful to the very cause their honest heart-strings vibrating the sounds of freedom's triumph, are on the stretch to embrace her earliest call, and whose patriot zeal flashes sparks of rapture, at the bare mention of her name.

How many thousand of budding heroes could a comparative well chosen few of these sons of Mars reunite and stimulate with military constitutional ardour? The expense would be but trifling in maintaining and giving life to the cause, through the means of officers of this class. If I had means I would put it in practice before I would trouble myself to mention it to a third person. There is no scarcity of youthful force in this best populated province in the peninsula. Not such a want of public spirit in support of the King and Constitution, as of public-spirited leaders. Gentlemen of independent property are not inclined to hazard their estates in the first instance, though they might be inclined to render every assistance possible, after they see a fair beginning, or materials for it; the past errors are well known, as well as the principles and persons of all parties now discovered, whilst, heretofore, 'twas only suspicion.

For the present, Colonel, farewell, and believe me, yours very faithfully,
J.M. Hampson

We have now (October) learned that King Ferdinand has returned to Madrid, so that all the bright prospects of Spain are over, and one of the finest countries in the world is again plunged into superstition and slavery.

Corunna, which was lately such a scene of gaiety and happiness, is now become wretched and miserable. The people have no confidence in each other; nothing but arrests every day, by Ferdinand's enemies. The people, lately so happy and united, are again divided into parties. Trade and commerce at a stand – no business going on – and the people beginning to feel every want, as the principal and richest inhabitants are quitting Corunna and going to different parts of the world. Some fly to Gibraltar – some to Cadiz – but the greater number to England, that land of civil and religious liberty; to many of them I have given letters of introduction to friends of the cause in London. The poor, for want of employment, are in great distress; numbers actually starving; it is heartrending to see their suffering; but, at present, there is no possibility of giving them relief.

I now (20th December) left Corunna myself for England, as I could be of no further service there, accompanied by the young Marquis of Santa Cruz and his preceptor, taking letters with me for General Mina, from his wife Madame Mina, who was a native of Corunna, and daughter to the Intendante, or collector, of the Custom-house. When we arrived at Dartmouth, I proceeded without delay to Bristol, being anxious to deliver the letters to General Mina, who I heard was then residing at Clifton Hot-Wells.

In removing our trunks at the coach-office in Bristol, a very zealous Methodist, named Thomas Wood, and also a very rich man, paid great attention to my speaking Spanish to my companions, the Marquis and his preceptor, who also wished to see General Mina.[9] An Irishman, a very humorous fellow, an acquaintance of mine, who was present, perceiving it, assured Mr Wood that nothing could

9 Thomas Wood served as a Methodist Minister from 1787-1826.

equal the influence I had with the Spaniards; for that I could convert the entire Spanish nation into Wesleyan Methodists if I pleased.

I could not at the time account for the great attention paid me by Mr Wood, in the removing of my baggage and other matters, until five days after my return to London, when a letter came during my absence, one morning, by the two-penny post, signed by the secretary of the Wesleyan Methodist Missionary Society, and requesting my attendance at their house in Hatton-Garden, on the following day, for the purpose of considering the best mode of converting the Spaniards. This letter was written to me in consequence of a communication from Mr Wood of Bristol, who informed them it was in my power to accomplish that long-wished-for event, for that benighted nation.

As it was received in my absence by my first wife, who was strict, and, as before remarked, rather bigoted, in the Roman Catholic religion, her surprise may well be imagined, supposing, as she was silly enough to do, that I had repudiated the faith of my fathers, and become a Wesleyan Methodist

On my return to dinner, I was handed the note; and had a good lecture read to me for having anything to do with such business, or with such people. In vain I assured her that it was all a mistake, brought about by my good Irish friend and fellow Catholic, Mr O'Mealy, who had, by way of a joke, recommended me to the notice of the Methodist Missionary Society.

I gave the matter no further consideration, allowing it to pass off, as it was intended by O'Mealy, as a merry joke, until, in two or three days after, a man called with a polite note, dated from No.7, Bedford Square, requesting to see me on particular business, and signed 'Joseph Butterworth.'[10]

Not knowing who Mr Butterworth was, I was at a loss to know who so wished so much to see me, until I met a gentleman on my way there, who laughed heartily upon learning my intended visit, and asked me what I could have to do with the Methodist member of Parliament for Dover.

I, however, proceeded, and received a polite reception from Mr Butterworth, who, after some preface, mentioned that he was anxious to have an interview with me, and cultivate my future acquaintance, as he had understood, through Mr Wood of Bristol, and from the Society at Hatton-Garden, that I could convert the good people of Spain to the true faith, and make them followers of John Wesley.

At this period, I had every intention of returning to Spain, of which I happened to inform Mr Butterworth; at the same time telling him, that I dared not attempt anything of the kind, as the friars and monks would have me immediately put into the Inquisition, from which I might find a difficulty in getting out. It was in vain I tried to convince Mr Butterworth that it would be impossible, or at least dangerous, to attempt anything of the kind; for he still persevered in proposing his plans; and, in the hope that I would at length accede to his wishes, invited me

10 Joseph Butterworth (1770-1826) Member of Parliament, became a Wesleyan Methodist in the 1790's.

to breakfast with him next day, proposing to send out a missionary with me, who should be entirely under my guidance.

So intent, was this good old gentleman on his plans, that he had given orders for both Bibles and Prayer-books to be printed in Spanish, one of which he showed me; offering me, at the same time, £300 or £500 per annum, if necessary, to defray the expenses of the intended conversion of the Spanish nation; an offer which many of my friends blamed me for not accepting.

About this time, I was obliged to leave London for the Hot-wells of Bristol, for the restoration of my health, which was now considerably impaired. When Mr Butterworth heard that I had left town, supposing it was for Spain, he caused 1,000 Bibles and 1,000 Testaments to be shipped and directed to me to Corunna, where, upon their arrival, they were seized by the officers of the Custom-house, where they probably now lie; nor would they be allowed to be re-shipped from thence to any other place, without security to a large amount being given, that they would not be landed in any other part of Spain.

These circumstances show the lengths to which the dissenting sects proceed to gain proselytes. I have been told since, that nothing could equal the exclamations of the Spaniards, when the cases containing the books were opened at the Custom-house of Corunna, as they considered me, from my attention to my religious duties during my residence amongst them, as a strict Roman Catholic, and one whose faith could not be easily shaken.

As, after my return from Spain, in 1824, I resided in Sloane-Square, in the neighbourhood of which several of the unfortunate Spanish emigrants lodged, and, amongst the rest, General Quiroga, and Madame Riego, wife to poor General Riego – I called to visit her and her sister, their brother being then with them. He had been a canon of the church of Oviedo, in Asturias. I found the unfortunate lady in a very distressed state of mind, owing to her anxiety respecting the uncertain fate of her husband.

While I was endeavouring to console her with the hope that his life was not in danger, Captain Matthews, whom I have before mentioned in this narrative, as the companion and fellow-prisoner of General Riego, unexpectedly arrived from Spain, and, calling to see Madame Riego, very incautiously told her of poor Riego's having been executed at Madrid; presenting her, at the same time, with a bird which the general had with him in prison, and also a handkerchief which he had worn on the day of his execution.[11] This was too much for poor Madame Riego. She sank under it; and, being a most sensitive and delicate lady, survived the melancholy intelligence but one day.[12] I was at the funeral, which was attended by Mr Hume, Alderman Wood, a Mr McDonnell, the Irish Roman Catholic agent in London, General Devereux, and many others of high respectability. She was

11 Rafael Riego was hanged on 7 November 1823.

12 Rafael Riego's wife, Maria Teresa del Riego died of grief one year later.

buried in the vaults under the Roman Catholic chapel in Moorfields;[13] and it is but just to remark, that the carriage of His Royal Highness the Duke of Sussex was in attendance, as the last tribute of respect for the unfortunate victim of patriotism.[14]

A few days after Madame Riego's interment, having occasion to go down to Chelmsford in Essex, on business, I took my seat on the out-side of a stage-coach at the Bull in Aldgate,[15] where I was scarcely seated, when the coachman drove off at a most furious rate, quickly passing another coach, that had been a short distance before him, and then redoubling his speed. I remonstrated with him on his conduct, but in vain; for he continued to whip and cut his horses in a desperate manner. I spoke to him at each stage where we changed horses, expostulating with him, but he paid no attention to what I said; and the last ten or twelve miles he drove even at a more rapid pace than before. A fellow-traveller, who sat beside me, a London attorney, who had a bag full of deeds and law-papers, trembled dreadfully, and was so frightened, that he actually was deprived of speech for some time.

My readers may judge the rate at which we travelled, when I tell them we were only two hours and a half on the road, going a distance of thirty miles. I was, of course, in a great rage with the driver, who seemed to care very little about me; but, when I came off the coach at the Black-Boy in Chelmsford,[16] I thought of a mode of bringing him to his senses, and asked him, did he know who I was? He replied, no; nor did he care. I then told him I would make him know who I was, – that I was Mr Richard Martin, Member of Parliament, the terror of all the coachmen in London; and that I would punish him for furious driving and cruelty to the animals.[17] He seemed immediately thunder-struck by this intelligence, turned deadly pale, and, taking off his hat, followed me about the streets, calling me 'Good Mr Martin,' and praying me to forgive him, telling me that it was not his fault, for that his mistress had strictly ordered him, even if he killed the horses, not to allow the other coach to pass him, which belonged to her sister, as they ran in opposition'.

From this, it appeared that those ladies spared no expense to injure each other. It was truly laughable to see how the mention of Mr Martin's name humbled the fellow, who was a few minutes before so saucy, but who would not now leave me until I partly promised not to be too severe upon him.

On my return to London, I told Mr Martin how I frightened a coachman, and gave him a description of the scene; but so zealous was he in his endeavours to protect dumb animals from cruelty, that he wanted me to prosecute the man, which, however, I begged leave to decline.

13 St Mary Moorfields in Eldon Street, London.

14 Prince Augustus Frederick, Duke of Sussex, the 6th son of King George III, (1773-1843).

15 The Bull Inn, of Bull Inn Yard, 25 Aldgate High Street, was demolished in 1902.

16 The Black Boy public house, on Springfield Road, Chelmsford, was demolished in 1857.

17 Colonel Richard Martin, MP (1754-1834), brought in Martin's Act in 1822, banning the ill treatment of cattle, and helped found the Society for the Prevention of Cruelty to Animals in 1824.

16

Back to Ireland

A circumstance occurred to me about this period that annoyed me very much: a friend of mine was intimately acquainted with a gentleman who held a respectable situation in the Treasury, and obtained for me a frank to cover some letters to the County Limerick. No sooner had the frank reached Limerick with the treasury-seal on it, but a report was spread far and near that I was in a grand situation in London – in fact, that I was no less than a Lord of the Treasury:[1] the consequence of which was, that I had not a relative or friend, or even an acquaintance, in the whole country, but wrote to me for situations and employments. Fathers and mothers on behalf of their sons, and uncles and aunts for their nephews; and, so numerous did my correspondence become, that I had in one day to pay eleven shillings for postage. I was surprised one morning by the appearance of a young man at the gate: on asking him his business, he said that his brother had sent him to me from Bruff, in the County Limerick,[2] to get him a clerkship in the treasury. As I could not blame the poor lad, I kept him for some weeks, and then got him a commission in the patriot service with General England,[3] fitting him out for it, at some little cost to myself, but unfortunately he was drowned in crossing a river soon after.

The circumstance of Mr Wakefield's carrying off Miss Turner must be still fresh in the minds of the public.[4] Soon after the lady's return home to her father

1 He probably means a Lord Commissioner of the Treasury, of which there were six appointed at any one time.

2 Bruff lies ten miles south of Limerick.

3 Major General Richard England.

4 Mr Edward Gibbon Wakefield of Cheshire carried off Miss Ellen Turner, a very beautiful young lady aged only 15 years old who was at school in Liverpool, to Gretna Green in March 1827. A coach was sent for her with a letter claiming that her father was dangerously ill. On arriving at Manchester she was taken on by Mr Wakefield and his brother, who convinced Miss Turner to marry to save her father, whose business had purportedly collapsed. The couple went immediately to France but her uncle caught up with them and she returned home. The Wakefield brothers were arrested on their return to the UK (for child abduction – the marriage was legal) and after a trial they were both sent to gaol for three years. The following day a bill was introduced in the House of Lords to annul the marriage and was passed with ease. Miss

and friends in Cheshire, Mr Wardle, son to the celebrated Colonel Wardle,[5] and a nephew to my former wife, named O'B[rien], a wild unthinking young fellow, suggested the idea that one of them should propose for the rich heiress. Wardle was the one selected for the suitor, for which purpose he sold the reversion of a property, and, being thus in cash, purchased an elegant curricle and a pair of horses, and, not wishing to trust his secret to any servant, bought a splendid suit of livery, to be worn by his friend O'B[rien]. They travelled from London by easy stages, until they arrived at Manchester, and, going to the same inn where Wakefield had stopped, made the waiter shew them the room which Miss Turner had occupied. Wardle was so full of his matrimonial scheme and imaginary love for Miss Turner, that no chair would serve him but the very one in which Miss Turner had sat during her stay there.

As soon as they had ascertained the part of the country where Mr Turner's mansion lay, they proceeded to the nearest inn in the neighbourhood; O'B[rien] most alertly performing all the duties of valet to his respected master, and omitting no opportunity of praising him among the servants. Next day, Wardle sent his valet with a letter on the subject of marriage to Mr Turner, stating his family, connections, and expectations.

To this letter, of course, there was no reply, and, after waiting in vain for two or three days, the valet became impatient, and not having a change of clothes, and finding the scheme had failed, sat down with his master to dinner. This astonished the innkeeper and his family, who frequently stole to the door to take a peep into the parlour, exclaiming, on their return, that they never saw anything like the conduct of that master and servant, in associating with each other on friendly terms.

They returned to London, and, as they travelled along the road, the valet was frequently told, there was a place for him among the servants of the inn, a hint to which he turned a deaf ear, and continued travelling, breakfasting and dining with his master, until they arrived, vexed and disappointed, in London. Thus ended Mr W[illiam] Gwynne Wardle's scheme for a rich wife, after the loss of a considerable sum of money.

The occurrence I have just related brings to my recollection of that thoughtless man O'B[rien], who was brought up in the navy, and possessed a property that soon went through his hands. About three years ago, he lodged at the house of a widow, in Frith-Street, Soho-Square, who became much attached to him. Whenever he was out of pocket, he contrived to devise, with the aid of his friend

Turner married Thomas Legh of Lyme Park two years later and had a daughter, but in 1831 she died in childbirth.

5 William Gwynne Wardle, son of Lt. Colonel Gwillym Lloyd Wardle (1761-1833). It was Colonel Gwillym Wardle who had brought the notorious case against Mrs Mary Anne Clarke, a former mistress of the Duke of York, for selling commissions, which forced the Duke to resign his office.

Wardle, one stratagem or another by which he succeeded in obtaining a supply of money from the widow, who was very wealthy.

At one time, he would send to her, to say that he was in the watch-house, in Marlborough-Street, for a riot, and that the trifling sum of two or three pounds would release him. This she would immediately send him; while he, at the same time, was waiting for the return of the messenger in some neighbouring house. In the evening, O'B[rien] would return to her house, and his appearance would dispel all her anxiety, and occasion the greatest joy. At another time, he would date his letter from a lock-up-house, in Chancery-Lane, where he would prevail on the sheriff's officer to allow him to remain, stating to her that his debt was £30, but that he could compound or compromise it, and get his liberty for £10, which sum she would instantly send him. The last plan he hit on to move her compassion, was to employ a man named David Dodd, a journeyman tailor, and a fellow quite equal to any scheme entrusted to him to execute.

After O'B[rien] and Mr Wardle, and this Dodd, had seriously consulted together, it was resolved to send Dodd to the widow in the dress of an undertaker, for which his appearance was well calculated. Dodd was a plausible fellow, and, when equipped in his long black coat, was, in every respect, fitted for the character. He accordingly waited on Mrs_,[6] and, after a long preface on the many good qualities of Mr, O'B[rien], at length informed her, apparently with great reluctance, that he was dead, having died only two days before.

On hearing this intelligence, she ran about the room quite frantic, while Dodd endeavoured to appease her with all the gravity of his assumed profession, but in vain; he could not quiet her for a long time. He then told her that the last word the poor dear gentleman uttered was her name. Upon asking where the corpse lay, and being told that it was near the Regent's Park, she said she would go to see him, and have a last look at him before he was interred: but the pretended undertaker, who did not relish the intended visit, informed her that he was nailed up in a shell, and it would not be fit to have it opened, nor would it be allowed by law, unless with the consent of the parish authorities, which would be attended with great expense.

After some further remarks, he at length came to the point, and told her, that he was the undertaker employed, and that though others of his profession would charge £30, he would bury him genteelly for £13 10*s*, in consequence of the friendship he had for the poor deceased gentleman when he was alive, adding that he wanted no profit for himself by the job, handing her, at the same time, an estimate amounting to £13 10s, which he immediately required from her, so as to have him buried that day. She, in the utmost grief, got up, and going to the desk, was actually giving the money, when her maid servant, who had been out on a message, returned, and, seeing her mistress in tears, inquired the cause. She told her that Mr O'B[rien] was dead.

6 It has proven impossible to identify the lady.

Mary, who was an Irish servant, and knew nothing of the scheme, immediately said, 'Oh! Dear mistress, do not be crying, for I saw Mr Wardle and Mr O'B[rien] at the corner of the street, laughing heartily, and I never saw them looking so well.' The surprise and joy of Mrs_ were as ridiculous as her grief had been previously, while the pretended undertaker, taking advantage of the confusion of the moment, stole off, without saying one word, telling O'B[rien] and Wardle, when he joined them, that they had ruined the plan, by their coming so near the house. Since this strange occurrence, I have heard nothing either of the widow or O'B[rien].

I now determined to return to my native country, for the purpose of spending the remainder of my life, which, in the course of nature, could be but short, in domestic retirement, enjoying at the same time the society of some of my old companions in arms, and a few select friends; and, accordingly, took up my residence in Dublin, removing from thence to the sea-coast during the summer months, for the benefit of sea-bathing.

About two years ago, while at Carysfort Avenue, near the Black Rock,[7] in the bathing season, a circumstance occurred, which annoyed me at the time, though it amused all my friends a good deal.

I was one day in a hurry to have a letter on important business put in the post-office, and was particularly anxious that it should be post-paid. As my servant was out at market, I gave the letter and money to an eccentric character living near me, who was considered steady and knowing, and strictly honest, of the name of Monks, requesting him to take it to the office, and desiring him, above all things, to be particular in paying the postage. On returning, he said all was right, and that he had paid for the letter, which of course satisfied me.

In a few days, however, I found that the letter had not been post-paid, and calling on this extraordinary fellow to know why he had not done as I requested of him, he solemnly assured me that he had: 'Why, captain,' said he, looking at me steadfastly, and at the same time reproachfully, 'sure, sir, your Honour don't suspect me of keeping the money you gave to me for the letter?' I told him I did not. 'Sure enough,' said he, 'I post-paid the letter: first, sir, I put the letter into the little hole in the box, and then I put the money after it, so I cannot be mistaken that I post-paid the letter.'

Annoyed as I was at the mistake, as the letter was for a gentleman who abhorred the very idea of paying for letters, I could not avoid laughing at this new mode which Monks had adopted. Although I explained to him the manner in which he should have done it, he seemed quite annoyed at the postmaster's conduct, as he termed it, in not knowing what the money was for, when he found it in the box, and insisted upon my accompanying him to demand it. We, accordingly, went to the office, and found the money lying in the bottom of the box, a circumstance which occasioned great joy to Monks, who was apprehensive that if the money was not forthcoming, his honesty would be impugned, and his character lost.

7 Black Rock, near Dublin.

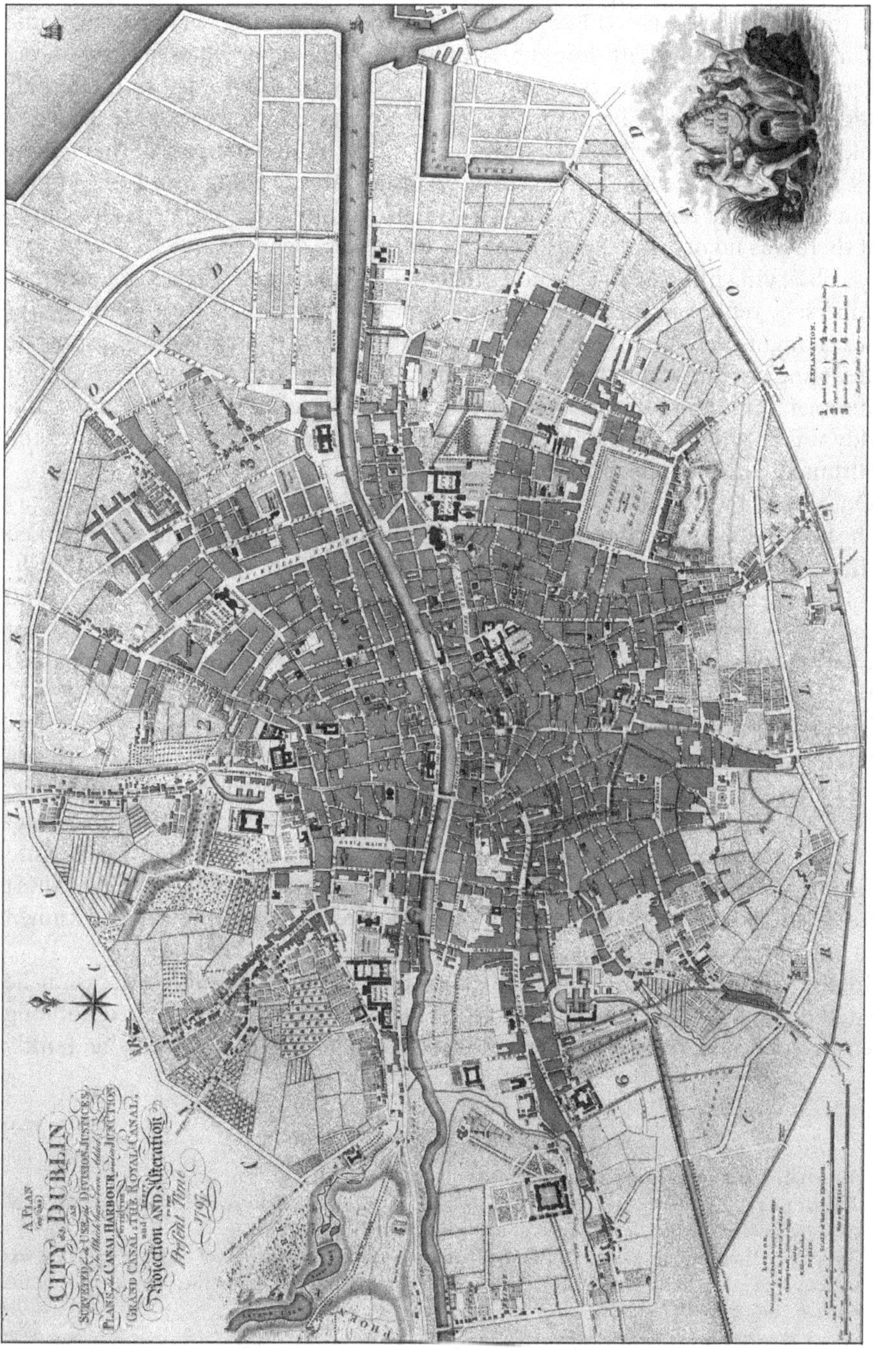

Map 12 Map of Dublin dated 1797. (Author's collection)

Previously to my leaving Ireland, which I did in some time afterwards, I directed that any bank-notes sent to Liverpool for me by post, should be cut in two for security, meaning that one half should be sent first, and the other when the first halves were acknowledged. Some time after this, I received a letter enclosing two half notes, which the person mentioned he had cut for security. I went to Mr Barnett's Bank, in Lord-Street,[8] without examining them, to try and get part of the money, until I received, as I thought, the corresponding halves, telling him I would give him a respectable reference, as I was a stranger to him. He told me with a smile that there was no occasion, as he knew the notes were genuine.

On observing him putting the notes together, I asked him were they not different numbers; he replied in the negative, and laughed immoderately on my telling him that I thought there were forty pounds instead of twenty pounds. The idea of the notes being cut and the halves put into the same letter for security, caused much amusement among the gentlemen of the bank, who told me they did not think Paddy was so silly; while I walked home quite disappointed in the amount of the remittance, which happened to be but twenty instead of forty pounds.

One day, as I was walking through Black Rock, I met some convicts on their way to the hulk at Kingstown,[9] from which they were to be sent to Cork, to be embarked in the regular convict ship, and perceived among them, to my great astonishment, a respectable gentleman, with whom I had been acquainted some years, and whose name must be familiar to many of my readers, Staunton Daveron. I was not allowed to speak to the unfortunate fellow, as he was hurried by; but there passed between us a look of mutual but melancholy recognition.[10]

The first time I met this celebrated character was in London, some years ago, when he had just, to use the fashionable phrase, entered into life. He was then a very handsome young man, and apparently free from every bad quality – one, indeed, whose society was generally cultivated, and who was regarded with esteem by all his acquaintance. He soon after, however, got into dissipated habits, into which he was seduced, like many others, by bad example, and became, in a short time, so altered a man, that no person would have recognized him who had known him in former years.

In the year 1826 or 1827, I met him again in Dublin, on which occasion he invited me to his house, and introduced me to his wife, to whom he had not long been married.[11] Her maiden name was Stanton; she was of a respectable family

8 Barnett, Hoare & co. which eventually merged into Lloyds Bank.

9 The harbour at Kingstown was completed in 1820 and in 1824 HMS *Essex* (ex-USS *Essex*) arrived to be converted as a prison hulk for prisoners awaiting transportation.

10 Patrick Staunton Daveron of Ennis, County Clare was a preventive surveyor of excise in 1821. He was tried in Dublin on 30 August 1831 and sentenced to 7 years; he was transported to Australia on the *Captain Cook*, arriving in 1832.

11 Patrick Daveron married in Dublin in 1825

and had a good fortune; and it was evident she was not aware of his embarrassed circumstances, from the expensive manner in which she lived.

From this period, I had not seen him until 1831, when I, by chance, met him on Stephen's Green. He was then, indeed, the most altered man I have ever met; nor should I have known him, had he not stopped me in a hurried manner, telling me he wished to see me the next day, on particular business. Fortunately, I declined going, on pretence of business; but in reality, I was far from wishing to be seen in his society, as his character had by this time begun to suffer materially. The first news I heard, on the following day, was, that he had hired a house in Dublin, and had been detected in some swindling transactions, for which he and others were committed to prison. He was tried and sentenced to transportation. Though we must acknowledge that his crime deserved such punishment, I could not but regret that he did not meet a better fate, for he was talented and clever; nor was there ever a man more generous, or one more alive to the feelings of humanity. He was, in fact, left a beggar, from assisting others in distress. While he had a sixpence in his house, no one ever applied to him in vain.

After remaining some time in Ireland, I came with my family over to England, and then took up my quarters in Liverpool, where I determined to finish the narrative of my life. Among the many whom I have met in Liverpool, with whom I had been formerly acquainted, I cannot forbear mentioning one, my respected friend and old brother officer, Colonel Allen Kelly, of the 54th Regiment.[12] Having ascertained that I was in Liverpool, he kindly called on me at my residence, invited me to his house, where I dined with him, and was introduced to his amiable wife and daughter. Mrs Kelly is a lady of the most prepossessing manners, of a highly respectable family, and had a large fortune.

Though it was delightful to behold the brave warrior reposing beneath his laurels, in the bosom of his family, in the full enjoyment of domestic happiness, it was with regret that I saw Colonel Kelly's health visibly declining, unobserved, too, by his family, it having been much impaired during his residence in the Burmese country. He joined the 54th Regiment when he was quite a lad, not more than fourteen of fifteen years of age, thirty-six years ago, and served in Egypt, and afterwards in the East and West Indies, and at Waterloo: never having been, during that long period, absent a day from his regiment. When his health obliged him at length to retire from the service, he carried with him the best wishes of his brother officers for his future welfare, who could not but regret his departure, as in Colonel Kelly they had possessed a brother and a friend, whose constant object was to promote the comfort of all under his command, and whose gentleness of manners endeared him equally to both officers and men.

A ludicrous circumstance of recent occurrence, and noticed by the London newspapers, has just brought to my recollection some anecdotes of one of those

12 Major Allan Kelly joined the 54th Foot in 1811 and he became a lieutenant colonel in 1819.

singular characters occasionally to be met with in every rank of life. Among the numerous recruits that were sent from London, while the regiment was quartered at Colchester, was a man of the name of Freeman, who, without exception, was the most strange and unaccountable character I ever met with. On arriving at Colchester, he was brought to my quarters to receive his bounty, &c, where, observing the regimental tailor cutting out a coat for me, he remarked that it would never do, as it was not properly cut; but, said he, 'let me fashion one out for you, and, my life, sir, but you will be pleased,' After a while, I consented; and, on my asking him if he could also make it, he replied, no, that he did not understand that part of the business. To my agreeable surprise, when the coat was made, nothing could fit or look better. He soon afterwards began to display his abilities in music; and, through my recommendation, was placed in the band. He played on every wind-instrument, but excelled on the clarionet. On the regiment removing to Kilkenny, he got me to intercede for him, with the commanding officer, to allow him to play at a private theatrical performance at the house of a Mr Loughnan, a banker of the city,[13] where he delighted the friends of that gentleman, and became deeply enamoured of one of his daughters, who had lately returned from the county Clare, and to whom he addressed some poetical lines, expressive of the warmth of his passion and the sincerity of his attachment. This poetical effusion caused much mirth in Kilkenny, and excited so much interest, that every lady in the town had a copy.

Freeman, however, not thinking himself sufficiently known, and wishing to increase his fame as a clever fellow, commenced miniature-painting, at which he appeared a perfect master.

In a few days, he had all the young ladies in and near the town calling on him; and, as he made no charge, but left it to themselves to give him what recompense they thought proper, ha had not lack of business, particularly as at that time the professed miniature painters would not take a likeness under five or six guineas. Shortly afterwards, he deserted, and was not heard for a long time, until one morning information was given that Freeman was taken up. The moment it was known in the town, we had intercessions from all the principal ladies and families of distinction to prevent his being flogged; for which, however, there was no occasion, as it proved to be a false report; nor did we ever hear anything more of Freeman. When I sum up his qualifications, I can safely say, that he was an excellent tailor, an experienced musician a capital miniature painter – an inimitable dancer, and a first-rate theatrical performer; in addition to which he possessed a ready fund of wit, which he well knew *when* and *where* to apply. When he chose, too, he could also do his duty very well as a soldier; but it was evident he never intended to remain in the profession, as he might have been promoted to the rank of sergeant, had he wished; but he never coveted the honour.

13 Mr Connell Loughnan.

While in the army, I unfortunately had dealings with commercial men, by which I lost all my hard-earned savings, and the consequences of which I feel even at this moment. The persons in whom I trusted, though acquaintances of long-standing, and professional friends, basely plundered me of my property, and reduced me from a state of independence to one of comparative want. As others may be induced, when placed in a like situation, to engage in similar transactions, I shall relate the circumstances as they occurred, adding one or two others that came within my own knowledge, and sufficiently mark the characters of the persons with whom I was so unfortunate as to have any dealings. As they have now gone to render their last account, I should, in accordance with the maxim, 'Nil de mortuis nisi bonum,'[14] be inclined to be silent on the subject, did I not think that my fate may serve as a warning to others, and prevent their falling into the power of unprincipled men.

While absent from England with my regiment, I was very frequently solicited for orders by many houses in London and Ireland, and to allow them to forward me various descriptions of articles for the use of the army, to which I seldom replied. At length, when I was stationed at Cadiz, some of the soldiers being in great want of shirts and shoes, I was induced to give an order to a house in Ireland, upon whom I fancied I could rely (having known the senior partner since I was a schoolboy), for a large quantity of shirts and shoes, which, on arriving, gave much satisfaction to all parties.

John Harley goes on to describe here how he was scammed in late 1813, being supplied with poor quality goods and thus put into financial difficulties. He then spends a great deal of time blaming a Mr Venables for a number of crimes, some of which would appear to have some basis in truth, but at the end of the day, this is only Harley's version of events.

It so happens that records show that documents supplied to the Lords Commissioners of the Treasury by Charles Aylmer, Deputy Commissary General, in 1820 in his own defence show that Harley had in 1818 gone to the Comptrollers of Army Accounts, stating that Aylmer owed him money. Aylmer claimed that Harley had pretended to have left the army and was then in partnership with Messrs Venables & co., which would agree with Harley's account. On leaving Spain, Harley had loaned Aylmer £1,500 privately for three years, however he had written to Aylmer from Bristol in September 1815 stating that he needed the loan repaid as he was in financial difficulties and was then in Bristol gaol, but Aylmer was unable to do so. Whilst at Lisbon in 1816 Aylmer received a letter demanding the sum. On his return to Britain Aylmer claims that he paid his loan off with interest and also paid a further charge for £1,900 although he questioned its entire

14 'Of the dead, nothing else good' i.e. do not speak ill of the dead.

validity – a strange thing to do, having to take another loan out to meet it. It seems however, that Harley took him to the comptrollers for non-payment of debts in 1820 and Aylmer had his half-pay stopped and was dismissed the service in 1819. Aylmer includes affidavits from Mr Venables, Captain Edward Templeton of the 47th (not mentioned at all in Harley's memoirs) who claimed that he had been swindled by Harley with usurious loans, and Lieutenant John de Burgh of the 47th (also not mentioned) who stated that he had knowledge that Harley had been under arrest a number of times. It is now very difficult to be certain who was in the wrong, although Aylmer failed in his efforts to be reinstated. One is inclined to suspect that they may well all have been as bad as each other, but it does put some question to Harley's claims that he was very much the innocent party.

On the regiment marching to the Pyrenees in 1813, the men had destroyed nearly all their shoes and linen; and, as I was so well and punctually attended to in my former order, I sent another to a much larger amount, and anxiously looked for its arrival. I had particularly stated in my letters, to let every article be of the best quality, and all full-sized, for which I was willing to pay a fair price. The firm was not long in executing the order, and, to the joy of the whole regiment, I received early one morning the invoices, and bills of lading; and, not having the least idea but that the goods would turn out as well as the former order, I wrote back without any delay, acknowledging the receipt of them, and enclosing an order on my bankers, Messrs. Whitehead and Howard, for the full amount of their demand. The goods accordingly arrived, and the poor soldiers entreated me not to delay distributing them; some jocularly saying that they might as well be killed with a good shirt on their back as a bad one; and a poor Irishman, who was killed in the next action, remarked, – 'if we have dirty shirts on, the Frenchmen will think us very poor, and as badly off as themselves; and bad luck to them!' I therefore lost no time; and had the different bales arranged out according to the invoice; but, just before we had opened them, the Duke of Wellington rode up, and inquired what they were, and, on being informed, was much pleased, and said I deserved great credit in running the risk I had done, for it really was a hazardous undertaking. On opening the bales one after the other, judge my astonishment on finding the shirts scarcely run together, and the shoes made of sheep-skin, untanned and pasted together, and then blackened! The shirts were so small, they would not fit the drum-boys, and of course were entirely useless; as for the shoes, they were no better, for as soon as they were wet the soles came from the uppers, and, until I explained to the army the imposition that had been practised on me, and the loss I consequently sustained, I firmly believe that they privately thought I had intended to defraud the poor privates, and enrich myself by the transaction. But quite the contrary were my intentions; for I was always a friend to the soldier; and, at the present day, I am often respectfully and affectionately accosted by men who have entirely escaped my recollection, and who are anxious to show that they have not forgotten the different kindnesses which I might occasionally have shown them.

The following is a copy of the letter I received from my unprincipled friend; and, when we consider the circumstance, it must be acknowledged an inimitable production:-

> My dear little John,
> Our holy religion teaches us to do as we would be done by – send me a cheque on your banker, and you will see what I have done for you. There never went to the peninsula such a supply as I have sent you – 5,000 shirts, and 5,000 pair of shoes.
> Yours affectionately [Hugh Venables].

Feelings of high respect for persons connected with the gentleman I am now writing of, induce me to withhold his name from the public.

This hypocritical man was the head of the firm of Messrs. [Venables] and Co; and, under the garb of religion, was committing the most infamous frauds that I ever heard of. He was a Roman Catholic; and knowing that I had been brought up in that faith, he used it as a cloak to cover all his imposition.

While the different packages were opened, a Mr R[edden] was present, a highly respectable merchant, who was much astonished at the unjust transaction. My first loss with this knavish firm, or, rather the knavish head of it, was considerable, for which I had no redress, having paid for the goods on their arriving. A short time after this, Mr [Venables] thought proper to ship another lot of these slops, which I refused to take, to the amount of £1,400 and, on my arrival in England, took law proceedings against me, by which I was, to save myself enormous law expenses, compelled to pay him a small sum. His infamous conduct, however, was soon brought to light by subsequent transactions; and, as I am writing of him, I shall mention some of the circumstances, which, as I said before, came under my own observation.

A Mr [Keen], from the country of [Ireland], who at first rented a mill, which was burned down, being obliged to seek employment in Lisbon, got something to do about the commissariat department, and, after a short time, became a sutler to the army, and subsequently a contractor for the supply of provisions. From his knowledge of the nature of commissary supplies, and having friends in that department, he in two years actually accumulated the enormous sum of £35,000. When the peace took place in 1814, he returned to his native county, where his fortune was soon magnified to be ten times the amount it really was. Mr [Venables] got introduced to him, invited him to dinner, was most attentive to him, and advised him to be careful of his money, which [Keen] had placed, by mine and Captain M[oore]'s advice, of the Guards,[15] in the three per cent consols, in London. After

15 This is most likely to be Lieutenant and Captain the Honourable Robert Moore, Coldstream Guards.

staying a few weeks in the country among his relations and friends, he determined to go to Paris to spend some months, and called on me at Clifton and breakfasted with me.

He then proceeded to Paris, where, unfortunately, he got into an intrigue with a French woman; the consequence of which was, that as he was standing one evening on the Boulevards conversing with a number of gentlemen, he was suddenly run through the body with a stiletto, by some assassin, who contrived to effect his escape. It was generally supposed to have been done by some man connected with the French woman with whom [Keen] was carrying on the intrigue.[16] Poor [Keen] was carried to his lodgings, where he immediately made his will, and bequeathed his property between his two brothers and sisters; and, that there might be no disputes between them, and, as he said, to have it regularly divided, he appointed Mr [Clugston?] his executor,[17] which circumstance was scarcely known in Ireland, when one of [Clugston]'s brothers got a wife and fortune on the strength of his proportion of the large sum. At this period, Mr [Venables] was, what is termed in business, going down the hill, and having a number of bills to meet, and being overdrawn on his London bankers, to the amount of £40,000, he took out letters of administration under [Keen]'s will, as executor, and sent over his power of attorney to sell out poor [Keen]'s consols, expecting that the bankers would allow him to draw on them as usual; but they, doubting his solvency, placed the £35,000 to Mr [Keen]'s credit in their books, and refused to have any more dealings with him. Thus, poor [Keen]'s hard-earned fortune went at once to pay Mr [Venable]'s debt to his bankers, and the poor family never got one shilling of it; and, to add to their loss, some persons advised them to go to law, which they did, and were cast with cost. They have, as well as myself, sufficient reason to remember the firm of Messrs [Venables] and Co.

I shall add two other circumstances highly illustrative of the want of feeling and principle, and the dishonest, as well as dishonourable, practices of Mr [Venables].

A certain poor shoe-maker, who supported himself and a large family by his trade, had a brother in India who realised a large fortune, and, dying very suddenly, left him the sum of £6,000, which to him was a princely fortune. The poor fellow lost no time in disposing, at any price, of his stock in trade, which was but trifling, and removing to a better habitation, where he was scarcely settled, when he was called on by the wary Mr [Venables], who thus addressed him; 'Well, Tom, what brings you here? I am happy to see you.' 'I thank you, sir, a thousand times' said poor Tom, 'for your kindness in calling on me – of course you have heard, sir, of

16 The *Annual Register* of 1815 records on 6 September that Mr Keen was walking the boulevards when he got into a very petty confrontation with a Frenchman for accidentally standing on his foot. The Frenchman stabbed him with a sword stick and he died. The assailant was not captured.

17 Keen apparently only had a Mr Clugston with him when mortally wounded in Paris, who presumably was made an executor.

my good fortune.' 'I have,' said Mr [Venables]; 'but take my advice Tom, and be careful of your money, for there is no security scarcely now; but if you like to come down to my counting-house to-morrow morning, I will advise with you what is best to be done.'

Poor Tom was very grateful, and, at parting, heaped blessings on the head of his supposed benefactor. Mr [Venables] the next morning, being well aware that Tom would lose no time in coming, took the following way to throw him off his guard: on his desk he spread ten parcels of notes, placing one to a large amount at the top of each, with small ones underneath. On Tom's arriving, he was obliged to wait a long time, during which Mr [Venables] appeared to be very busy; but, after some time, turning round, he said, 'Ah, Tom, glad to see you; I cannot say anything to-day, as I am very hurried, as you may see. Here are, £30,000,' pointing to the parcels of notes, 'which I have to invest, but cannot get more than three per cent for them – but call to-morrow, Tom, and I will do something for you.'

The poor fellow left him, after thanking his disinterested and religious friend, for all the trouble he was taking for him. The next day Mr [Venables] said, 'Well, Tom, I have been consulting with my partner, and we think that as you are a man we can rely on, we will allow you six per cent, which is five per cent English money.' The poor fellow extolled their kindness to the skies, and immediately gave an order to draw the full amount out of the Bank of Ireland; Mr [Venables] at the same time saying, that to save Tom all the trouble he could, he might draw his interest weekly.

For three weeks, all was very well; but, on Tom's calling the fourth time, he found the house shut up; and, knocking loudly for admittance, was accosted by a gentleman, who informed him that Messrs. [Venables] and Co. were bankrupts, and that the counting-house was closed. The poor creature left the place in a state of mind bordering on insanity, and was shortly afterwards begging about the streets.

Mr [Venables] was a man, as I said before, that made religion a cloak for hiding all his dishonest transactions, and his assumed nicety induced many of the poor tradesmen and weavers in the neighbourhood to intrust their little capital in his hands, supposing him to be the safest and most honourable man in the town. I will give another instance of his avarice and unfeeling conduct:-

A gentleman, a merchant in the town, was persuaded by him to speculate very largely, and then made out an account of £7,000 against him, a sum which was entirely out of his power to pay, and from which he never reaped one shilling benefit. The next step Mr [Venables] took was to make him a bankrupt, getting himself made sole assignee. He then procured an insurance on _'s life for £8,000 to cover all expenses, which he pretended had been insured: when all the creditors had signed the certificate, Mr [Venables] refused, alleging the following reason to his confidential friends: 'Mr _ is a weak man, has a large family, and is of very delicate habits, and, if his certificate is not given to him, he will soon die, and I shall receive the £8,000 from the insurance company.'

In this supposition, however, he was wrong, for I afterwards had the pleasure of dining with Mr __, at his seat near the city of Cork, and often heard him mention the villainy practised on him by Mr [Venables], who, on the contrary, was like one of his own victims, reduced to begging, in which situation I met him in the streets of Dublin; and I was solicited for alms by the very man who had ruined so many.

The transaction with Messrs. [Venables] and Co. was not the only one in which I sustained a loss in my dealings with mercantile men.

When encamped near Bayonne, in 1814, I entered into a speculation, and purchased a thousand barrels of flour, under the impression that it was of the best quality, and had come direct from Ireland. In this, however, we were deceived; as Mr [Codd] brought it from Plymouth,[18] where he purchased it at a very low rate. As we were on the eve of leaving the country, we directed Mr Bishop, our principal agent, and partner, an excellent young man (who is now a merchant of high respectability in the Minories) to go into the town of Bayonne, and sell it there. He, accordingly, disposed of it to a baker, and who, being a contractor for the French garrison at Bayonne, had bread made of it, for the use of the soldiers. It was, however, so very bad, that it was found impossible to make use of it; the garrison naturally refused to take it, and the baker was called to account for furnishing such bread to the army.

As he was conscious of not having used any adulteration himself, he had the flour analysed by the chemists, who soon discovered that there was a large quantity of white clay in the centre, with a little flour on the top and at the bottom of each barrel. The uproar it occasioned among the French garrison it would be impossible to describe, as it was supposed that it was purchased from the English, with the intention of poisoning them. Every old woman who had been ill for three months before, attributed her illness to our flour, and every death that occurred was placed to our account.[19]

As the magistrates decided that the barrels should be returned to England, we applied to have the flour surveyed and destroyed, so that we might be entitled to recover the amount, which was upwards of £1,500; but this request was made in vain – they would not allow it to be done, insisting upon having it re-shipped and sent back to England. Mr Bishop, with much difficulty, escaped from the garrison and mob of Bayonne, who were by no means friendly to any English person, in consequence of our success in the latter of the war. We discovered afterwards, that those barrels sold to us as flour were nothing but China clay, dug out of some pits near Plymouth. Never was there a more infamous cheat practised, or a crime

18 From the papers supplied to the hearings by Commissary Aylmer, it is clear that Harley was then working with a Mr Codd.

19 The *Annual Register* states on 16 May 1814 that two millers of Truro named John Rowe and Henry Rundle were proved to have mixed pulverised clay with their flour. Forty sacks of this flour were found on a ship at Plymouth. They were fined the maximum for the offence – 10 shillings! It would seem that Harley had received a larger shipment of this flour before they were discovered.

that called for more severe punishment; but we were unfortunately unable either to discover the perpetrator of it, or to obtain any compensation. The entire money was lost to us (£1,500) for we found it impossible to recover it, Mr [Codd] having no document to produce.

Nearly about the same period, when I was stationed at St Jean de Luz, in the south of France, the two Mr __'s, from Cork,[20] who were more fortunate in their speculations, arrived with a cargo of provisions for the army, it being then a common speculation from all the ports of Ireland – but those gentlemen came too late, the war being then over, and Bonaparte gone to Elba. One of those gentlemen solicited Mr Venables to introduce them to me, that I might assist them in procuring a sale for the provisions. I cannot describe the close manner in which I was besieged by those brothers, until I obtained for them a sale, with a vast deal of trouble to myself, by which they realized a sum of £60,000, and saved their house in Cork, which was then in a tottering state, in consequence of a well-known speculation in sugar from Hamburg. Through my exertions, their house was saved, and I must say they were in return anything but grateful for the kindnesses shown to them.

As I am writing about these gentlemen, I will give my readers the commencement of the fortune of their father, who indeed was a very good kind of man; as it shows the extraordinary turns the wheel of fortune will sometimes take.

He kept a public-house, the sign of the Red Cow, at Watergrass Hill, near Cork,[21] but had been previously employed as porter, in the ancient house of Shea and Sons, on the Sand Quay in Cork,[22] who considered him a very honest, prudent man; and were willing to guarantee any small transactions that he might undertake.

On one occasion, it occurred to him, as hoops for beef barrels were then in demand, that he could make a few pounds by ordering some; and, accordingly, he wrote a letter to the London correspondents of the house of Shea and Sons, to ship him immediately a small cargo. As he was awaiting their arrival with great anxiety, having made arrangements for the sale of them with coopers in the city, judge his astonishment, when a brig arrived much larger than he ordered, and heavily laden with the best Kentish *hops!* He started, when he got the bill of lading, supposing himself destroyed. It proved a fortunate mistake for him. They were shipped at five pounds ten shillings, in the early part of the season, but having risen in a short time up to fifteen pounds, and from that to twenty pounds per hogshead, he gained three hundred per cent on a most valuable cargo. This lucky mistake, which arose from the poor man's not understanding orthography, (having written hops instead of hoops,) laid the foundation of the subsequent prosperity of the family.

20 It has proven impossible to identify these two gentlemen with any certainty.

21 Watergrass Hill is a small village about twelve miles north of Cork. The Red Cow no longer exists.

22 There are two John O'Sheas, merchants at Sand Quay, Cork in the 1787 Directory, father and son. The father died in 1789 and his son in 1797.

Among the many singular characters with whom I have been acquainted, and the different remarkable circumstances that came within my knowledge, the following are some which I have omitted to notice in their place.

I have been acquainted many years with C[ornelius] Lyne, Esq a barrister in Dublin, a most gentlemanly good fellow, who lives in Hume Street, and entertains hospitably and in good style.[23] He was in the habit of receiving at his house many persons of the highest respectability in the city, by whom he is of course entertained in return.

Some years ago, another barrister of the name of O'Regan, of Killaloo, near Limerick, then residing in Dublin, wrote the life of the late John Philpot Curran; but, unfortunately, he was unable to dispose of one volume. It so happened that the countenance of Mr O'Regan was distinguished by a peculiarly ruddy hue.[24]

Being, from pique or otherwise, annoyed by the constant invitations which Lyne received, he wrote the following lines, and had them left where he would find them:

> 'Where'er you go to dine,
> You're sure to meet the great C[ornelius] Lyne.'

Lyne, on reading them, laughed, and wrote instantly, with his pencil, under them as follows:

> 'O'Regan's face, unlike his book, is *red*.'

I was informed that Judge Jebb, some time after observed, that the reply by Lyne was admirable, and that had he added one word more he would have spoiled it.

I first met the good and humorous fellow, Doctor Maurice Quill, in Enniskillen, in 1806.[25] He came to join the ninth garrison battalion then forming there. I dined at their mess the first day he joined, and sat near him. While the glass was merrily going round, he seriously proposed to me to leap over the table, which, to our great surprise, he performed, sitting in a moment at the other side. We then little knew the droll fellow we had in Doctor Maurice Quill. He had a fund of humour and good nature.

Being afterwards promoted to the 31st Regiment, then in Portugal, he proceeded to join, and landed at Lisbon, his regiment being in the neighbourhood of Elvas; Quill, however, was in no hurry to get to his destination, finding Commissary Wood's table so very agreeable.[26]

23 Cornelius Lyne is recorded to have been in Cork as a barrister in 1824.

24 William O'Regan, barrister, was still practising in 1849. The subject of the book was John Philpot Curran (1750-1817), Master of the Rolls in Ireland.

25 Assistant Surgeon Maurice Quill 31st Foot served most of the Peninsular War in Spain until April 1813.

26 Deputy Assistant Commissary General John Wood served at Cadiz from April to November 1812.

He had been about a week there, where I again met him, when his commanding officer came to the town, and, seeing an officer in the uniform of the regiment, rode up to him, and asked him his name. He replied that he was Maurice Quill, going to join his regiment; a reply which, being expressed with his natural brogue, and simple, careless manner, rather displeased the commanding officer, who, after commenting on his remaining so long away, and delaying so long on the road, asked him how, or why he came to the 31st Regiment.

'Why, then, indeed, sir,' said Quill, 'my reason was, I had a little brother in the 32nd Regiment, and I liked to be near him, and faith, that is the reason that I came to the 31st Regiment:' at the same time, (as if he had been a fool,) looking close to his commanding officer's buttons, he said, 'You belong to us too, sir.'

This singular answer was given without one smile. The colonel then asked Quill, was there any other motive for leaving his last regiment. 'None at all,' says Quill, 'that I know of, but that I happened, by mistake, to put some of the mess spoons into my pocket, and they would insist on my leaving them after that mistake.'

The colonel, on hearing this, rode off from him, and, when he reached the regiment, told the officers that he had met the doctor that was coming to them, who had confessed to him that he had stolen spoons from the mess-table of his former regiment. They, knowing Quill's character, had a hearty laugh at the hoax played on the colonel.

Quill soon joined them, and became the life and soul of the mess-table. Everyone who knew him, liked him, as his humours were of that nature, that he would do no man an injury.

This good fellow got into a hollow square, at the Battle of Waterloo, and was creeping about with a canteen of brandy and water from the officers to the soldiers, giving each of them a drop of it, when a shot (a twenty-four pounder) from the enemy struck close to him.[27] He looked up, and said, very coolly, 'Faith, it's time for me to go; there is more where that came from,' and immediately got out of the square, first dividing his brandy and water. This worthy man, whose wish it was to serve and amuse everyone, died lately, in the barracks of Cork.

During the time the 54th Regiment was in Holland,[28] a distressing occurrence took place; Captain Frederick had been out shooting, and, on coming into the mess-room, incautiously left his fowling-piece loaded.[29] Lieutenant McCormick taking it up, little suspecting that it was charged, it suddenly went off, and the contents were lodged in Lieutenant Campbell's[30] face, and completely disfigured him. He was a handsome, fine, and amiable young man. McCormick was wretched and inconsolable after the accident; and it was supposed for a long time that he

27 There is some exaggeration here; the largest French cannon at Waterloo were 12-pounders.

28 In the campaign of 1794-1795.

29 Captain Thomas Frederick 54th Foot was a major in the army.

30 Lieutenants Thomas McCormick and John Campbell, 54th Foot.

would not recover the shock he received by wounding his friend. Campbell got better in the course of time, and returned with me and others, at the short peace of Amiens, to England, and was appointed captain on the half-pay. McCormick, who was at the time on the full-pay, on hearing of the circumstance, immediately applied at the Horse-Guards to allow Campbell to exchange with him on the full-pay; insisting on his taking his company as the only reparation in his power for the injury he had done him. This generous act, worthy of one of the ancient Romans, did not go unrewarded; as I understood afterwards that the Duke of York gave McCormick a company in another regiment.

After the battle of Talavera, Assistant-Surgeon Rule, of the 87th Regiment, was left in charge of the wounded, and was placed over a very large French hospital, where there was a vast number of the French.[31] He was a humane attentive young man. Bonaparte visited the hospital, and in walking up and down the rooms, in which the wounded men lay, observed the great attention of Surgeon Rule to them.[32] At the moment of mounting his horse, he turned to one of his attendants, and ordered him to take 100 Napoleons to the English surgeons, and present to him with his compliments. Rule also described to me the magnificent appearance of the Emperor's staff, by which he was surrounded. In one month after, the governor of the hospital informed Rule, that by order of the Emperor, he was to give fifty Napoleons more, which he immediately received.

In the course of some time, he was ordered from Spain into France, and on to Verdun, and, on his arrival at Paris, he waited on General Clarke, the then minister of war, the present Duke of Feltre,[33] and representing that his family affairs were in the most distressed state in England; that he had an aged mother and two sisters, who required his protection; he requested a parole for two months. The general informed him, that he could not give him leave, but that he would take on himself to keep him in Paris until an answer arrived, if he would write to the Emperor. Upon this, Rule wrote to him for leave. As soon as the post could return, a passport came, signed by Bonaparte, with leave to remain as long as he pleased in England, and with an order of one hundred Napoleons, to bear his expenses. This is one of the many instances of the Emperor's generosity.

While in Cadiz, in the year 1811, I met Captain S[henley], of the British Royal Artillery, whose agreeable conversation was well known to everyone in the garrison.[34] He was a close man, and seldom dined at his own mess; but I must observe, that poor S[henley] had a wife and children to support in Ireland. He was welcome

31 Assistant Surgeon Robert Rule, 87th Foot, was made a prisoner of war in May 1810 and again in April 1814.

32 Harley has made a mistake here, Rule must have met Joseph Bonaparte, King of Spain, not his brother Napoleon Bonaparte, who never returned to Spain after early 1809.

33 Marshal Henri Jacques Guillaume Clarke, 1st Duke of Feltre (1765-1818)

34 Captain William Shenley Royal Artillery, who commanded the 5th Company of the 10th Battalion at Cadiz from April 1810 until his death there on 5 October 1813.

to all the tables of the merchants of all nations at Cadiz, and I have been often amused by his relating to me the manner he gained friends at each house. When he dined at Mr Wakeley's, the American consul, he would give his toast, '*The United States of America – no such people in the world.*' The next day, I have known him to dine at Mr Shaw's, the Scotch merchant; he would then drink, '*Success to the Scotch – the best people in the world.*' Then at Sir James Duff's, the British consul, who was very partial to the Spaniards, he would give '*Fernando Septimo-long life to the Spaniards – no nation like them.*' Another day, he would spend at Mr Fleetwood's, an English merchant, he would drink, '*Old England-John Bull – no persons like the English.*' Next day, at the table of Mr Hugh McDermott, a patriotic Irish merchant, he would give, '*The poor sod, poor Pat, and my dear Mr McDermott – no country so ill treated as Ireland, nor a more warm-hearted nation.*' By this means, he had invitations the entire week round, for he suited his conversation and toasts to the feelings of all parties. S[henley], who dined with everyone who asked him, was never to have any one at his mess; his habit was to invite his friends, when he was well convinced it was not in their power to dine with him; he frequently asked a Lieutenant Cruice, of our regiment, who is now a major in the 12th, to stop and dine with him, when he well knew he could not remain.[35] At length, Cruice and I determined, the first time we went to Cadiz, to put ourselves in the way of Captain S[henley] for an invitation, which we were sure of receiving, under the impression that we would, as usual, refuse. We accordingly mounted, and appeared leaving the city, when S[henley] came out of the artillery barracks, and asked us to dine. Cruice instantly answered, 'we would do ourselves that pleasure.' This was an answer poor S[henley] little anticipated; we accompanied him to the mess-room; no sooner had we entered, than we perceived the officers enjoying S[henley]'s disappointment. We spent a pleasant day, and we were not sparing in the best wine. I need not add, that after this, we never received another invitation. S[henley] was never known to have a dispute with any one.

When seventeen, or eighteen years of age, in 1786, I was in the habit of visiting Cork, from Limerick, and I remember meeting at every party in Cork, a gentleman of the name of Silk; he was then a dandy old bachelor, particularly neat in person, and a constant attendant at the tea-table; and what was then termed a lady's man.

Many years afterwards, and when my regiment was stationed in Kilkenny, in 1804, dining at the hospitable table of Mr Cornelius Loughnan, banker,[36] I met Mr Silk again. I perceived he did not wish to recognise me; he was still the same dandy old lad, and as attentive to the ladies. He was then making love to the banker's daughter, not more than eighteen or nineteen years of age, with a fortune of ten thousand pounds.

35 Ensign Alexander Cruice joined the 47th Foot in March 1810 and he transferred to the 12th Foot as a lieutenant in September 1812.

36 His memorial at St Canice's Cathedral gives his forename as Connell.

I reminded him of having had previously the pleasure of meeting him at a relation's of mine in Cork, a Mrs Hartness,[37] a handsome widow; telling him that that was now eighteen years ago.

This Mr Silk did not seem to relish, nor had I at the moment the most distant wish to divulge his age; for he was a pleasant gentlemanly little fellow; very unthinkingly, however, I mentioned his time of life, and very unfortunately for him, for I fear it put a stop to his getting a wife and large fortune.

It may seem a curious coincidence, that in July 1827, I dined at Clontarf Marino Crescent, near Dublin,[38] with a large party, at the house of Mr James Loughnan, son to the banker at Kilkenny.[39] This party was given, I understood, in honour of a new married couple, just arrived from England. During dinner, I frequently thought I had some recollection of the bridegroom, who sat opposite to me, and I kept racking my brain to make out where I had seen him, when a gentleman asked him to take wine, and called him Mr Silk. I then brought him to my memory, and also asked him to take wine; as soon as the cloth was removed, and before the ladies left us, 'Why sir,' said I, 'I think your name is Silk.' He wished to avoid giving an answer; but I again, and from no wish of giving pain, boasting of my own memory as superior to his, said, 'Do you not remember Mrs Hartness, in 1786, where I first met you? Then you were a pleasant fellow; but surely I met you eighteen years after that, at old Mr Loughnan's, when we were quartered in Kilkenny; and faith,' said I, 'calculating the years since we last met, that is now forty-three years ago,' leaving him at the least upwards of seventy years of age.

There was a silence, but a general smile, when his young bride turned to him, and said, 'Silk, you never told me you were half that age,' – he was vexed, and silent, wishing me, no doubt, many miles off. The company could no longer refrain from laughter.

The scene I had with Mr Silk of Clontarf, reminds me of a circumstance that occurred to me, soon after, in Dublin, in 1820, at a relation's of mine, the late Mrs Keating. Her grand-daughter, Miss Keating, a very fine woman, sat near me at dinner. I asked her if she had ever been in England. She replied that she had, and that she was educated at New Hall, in Essex, at the convent.[40] I recollected having been to see her, and reminded her of a lady and gentleman having called on her, the gentleman in regimentals – that it was my wife and I, and unfortunately calculating in my usual manner said, 'Why Miss Keating, that was in the year 1807, and you were about sixteen years old.' making her out thirty-eight years of age. Unconscious of what I was saying, I perceived the young girls in the room smiling

37 Harley writes Hartness, however the Cork directories quite clearly show that the only freemen in Cork at the time were named Hartnett.

38 This crescent of Georgian terraced houses were built in 1800 and sell now for well over 1.5 Million Euros.

39 James Loughnan was the son of Connell Loughnan (1733-1812) a banker of Kilkenny.

40 New Hall at Chelmsford was originally a palace of Henry VIII's but turned into the Convent of the Holy Sepulchre. It is now a boarding school.

and tittering; but she took it with the utmost good humour. She was convinced it could not injure her, as 'her market was made,' (as they term it in Ireland,) for she was to be married in a few days after, to the Reverend Mr N[eville], of George's Church, Dublin, a most deserving and worthy young man.[41] I shall in future be more cautious how I mention years or ages, as *I* begin to *feel* it is not an agreeable subject.

Captain W[estroppe], a most respectable old officer, and many years a wine-merchant in the city of [Cork], commanded a corps of Yeoman cavalry, composed of wealthy merchants, about the year 1812.[42] He was rather embarrassed for money to meet his engagements, which occasioned him very low spirits, under which he would have sunk, but for the talent and cleverness of his wife. One Saturday morning as they were sitting at breakfast, turning in his mind how he should meet a bill due on the following Monday, of four hundred pounds, he very naturally became unhappy. When the mail from Dublin arrived, it brought him a letter from government enclosing a bank post bill for five hundred pounds, as pay and expenses for the Yeomanry corps, under his command. Mrs W[estroppe] eyed the note with a longing look, as it lay on the table, and said, 'Mick, my dear, that would be a fine provision for your bill that will be due on Monday.' He replied 'That is impossible; it belongs to the gentlemen of the corps,' (who were then assembling in front of the house to parade). At this moment, a fine large Newfoundland dog, called Carlow, ran round the breakfast table to pick up the crumbs, when a lucky thought occurred to Mrs W[estroppe], who exclaimed, 'Mick, suppose we say the bank note stuck to a piece of bread and butter, and was unfortunately swallowed by Carlow, – I am sure the officers of the corps will not doubt what I say.' Her husband had not time to make a reply, when one of the gentlemen of the corps entered the parlour. She instantly related to him the sad accident that had occurred, with all the seeming anxiety and fright that such an event would naturally occasion, at the same time saying, poor Carlow should be killed immediately if they wished, but that she knew they were all too loyal to doubt what she said, (as loyalty at this time was a great passport in Ireland,) – to have Carlow put to death. This gentleman instantly said, 'For my part, or proportion of the pay, I would not allow poor Carlow to be molested;' and, on his return, he communicated what had taken place to the other gentlemen; when each member declared that Carlow should not be killed. My readers may judge the joy of Mrs W[estroppe] and her husband.

There lived in Newcastle, in the county Limerick, when I was a young man, an inn-keeper named Roger Shine, whose business was ruined by the hospitality of

41 The Reverend James Neville is the only clergyman in the Dublin directories between 1820-40, whose name began with an N, but he was at St Andrew's Church in Dublin. The Church Body in Dublin have confirmed that no clergyman or officer at St George's at this time had a surname beginning with an N.

42 Captain Commandant Westroppe commanded the City of Cork Cavalry (1803-12), whilst Henry Westroppe ran a Wines and Spirits Merchants at 3 Marlborough Street, Cork in 1824, these appear to be the same people.

Mr McMahon, my near relative, father to Colonel McMahon of the Irish Brigade. This gentleman then possessed eight hundred a year, which was as much as fifteen hundred a-year now. His predominant passion was to give dinners; and to such a pitch did he carry it, that he never suffered a stranger to enter the town of Newcastle without inviting him to his house, thus depriving Shine, the inn-keeper, of his guests. In consequence of Shine's loss of business, by the hospitality of Mr McMahon, he quitted the town, and took a farm in the neighbourhood of Limerick.

This change proved a fortunate one. He was at this time not worth one shilling; a heavy rent for his farm came round to be paid, and he had no means to meet it. A friend of his resided in Cork, a butter merchant, who was a native of Newcastle, named Hickey. To him, he determined to apply for accommodation, and accordingly proceeded to Cork during the summer assizes. A young gentleman, a Mr Fitzgerald, and I accompanied him, merely for our amusement. Shine was very low-spirited during the journey; whilst, on the contrary, we were all gaiety and life. On our arrival in Cork, our first object was to secure beds and make ourselves comfortable, as the hotel at the assizes was generally crowded; but Shine hastened to Hickey the merchant. My readers may judge his consternation, on finding the door closed and his friend a bankrupt; he did not return to us, as had been agreed.

The next morning, we felt uneasy at not having seen him the preceding night. Fitzgerald and I went in quest of him, and after much inquiry were directed to Shinquin's Hotel,[43] where, at twelve o'clock, we found Mr Shine still in bed.

He was silent for some moments, but at length exclaimed, 'I must be dreaming: hand me my trousers and waistcoat' (which were, on looking for them, found under his pillow). 'It is impossible!' said he. Upon our examining his pockets, to our great astonishment, and his delight, we counted out several guineas, and bank-notes, amounting to upwards of twelve hundred pounds.

He then informed us that, on finding his friend a bankrupt, and no hopes left, he was almost maddened. 'Having my wife and children at home, and knowing,' said he, 'I must be turned out of my farm for non-payment of rent, and ruin must follow, – in rambling about, unconscious of where I went, I noticed a light in a gambling house in George's Street, and having about seven or eight pounds in my pocket, the only money I possessed in the world, I determined on trying my luck, – sink or swim. I accordingly went in, and played at 'hazard' – I became a winner, and elated at my success, drank freely – from not having eaten any dinner, it had more effect on me. I still continued a winner – an old gentleman that was looking on, and saw my situation, came to me, and said, 'Sir, if you are advised by me, you will leave this; for, if you remain, you will not keep one guinea; let me call a chaise

43 The only hotel in the 1824 Cork Directory with a remotely similar name was The Skibbereen & Dublin Hotel at 5 Wintropp Street.

for you?' – I recollect allowing him to do so, and that his name was Wrickson: more I know not.'

Mr Shine then mentioned to us that he had bidden adieu to gambling for ever; and he strictly kept his word. He returned home happy, paid his rent by this lucky hit, followed his farm, and laid the foundation of the fortune his family now enjoys.[44]

I was frequently in the habit of dining with the late Mr Bridge, army agent.[45] Among the numerous guests I met at his table, was the late Sir Jerome Fitzpatrick, whose humane character and generosity are well known.[46] He was rather late for dinner, and told us he had been visiting his country women in St Giles's, remonstrating with them, on the careless manner in which they dressed, particularly noticing to them the deranged state of their hair, and pointing out the difference between the English women, and them. Their reply was, 'Sure, sir, if we had the money to buy combs, we would keep our hair as well dressed as the English ladies.' – 'I soon remedied this,' said the good Sir Jerome, 'for I distributed among them fifteen pounds, in sixpences to each:- it was this detained me so long.'

We all naturally laughed, telling the kind-hearted Sir Jerome, that by that time his sixpences were all laid out in gin. This he would not believe, but said he would investigate the matter next day. On the following morning, he proceeded to St Giles's, and found it too true: not one of his fair countrywoman had purchased a comb: he now adopted another plan, and went to a manufacturer's in Shoreditch, where he purchased four hundred combs, and had them taken to St Giles's, where he distributed them himself, begging them, for the honour of his country, that they would keep themselves neat. However, in a little time, he found that the combs, like the sixpences, had been converted into the favourite beverage.

I have now brought to a conclusion the work I proposed to offer to the public. The retrospect of one's life, and that, like mine, a long one, passed in active service, can never fail to be attended with many emotions of a very mixed nature, to a mind possessing only the ordinary sensibilities of humanity. These have I experienced in no common measure. The gay, the generous, the brave, the noble, I have had frequent occasion to associate and sympathise with; and then have witnessed their disappearance from this moving scene by the relentless hand of death. At times, my mind has been nearly overpowered, in retracing events in which those I loved and honoured bore a part more or less conspicuous, though fatal to themselves – some, indeed, to whom the ties of affection bound me with a power only to be destroyed when death itself shall have quenched my spirit. At other times,

44 Roger Shine died at Ballymacrease near Kilkenny, aged 78, on 12 November 1824.

45 This would appear to be an error, the only Army Agent of such a name being Mr John Ridge of no. 44 Charing Cross, London.

46 Sir Jerome (or Jeremiah) Fitzpatrick (1740-1810), Inspector of Health in the British Army, had sought to improve conditions on board transport ships to Australia. He also renovated Kilkenny Court House.

the drolleries and eccentricities of character I have had occasion to recall, have come upon me with all the freshness of their first impression, and have transported me back to the period of my younger days, when all was buoyant with hope. And yet these recollections would always be followed by the idea of the contrast between what I was, and what I am. Poverty, too, has pressed upon me, produced by the deception practised by others towards me, the bitterness of which is not lessened by the reflection that my own simplicity, if not folly, has concurred to render effective the arts of the designing. But, enough of this. In taking leave of my reader, whose indulgence towards the plain soldier for the imperfect execution of my task, I fear I stand greatly in need of, – I still am not without the hope that I have contributed some few hours to his amusement; and have revived recollections also, on his part, of scenes connected with the glory of his country, and in which every British subject must feel a lively interest. Nor will he, as I trust, consider deficient in interest those anecdotes, which are largely interspersed throughout the volumes, illustrative of the character of my countrymen, whose concerns, at this time, exercise so great a portion of the sympathy of the empire at large.

Appendix[1]

The 16th day of July, 1823

The bearer, John Harley, Esq is authorised by me to act as British Vice-Consul in Corunna, during my absence at Ferrol.

Given under my hand and seal, at His Britannic Majesty's Consul office in Corunna.

Richard Bartlett, Consul.

As I am obliged to go to Ferrol, I appoint John Hartley, Esq, to be Vice-consul to His Britannic Majesty, in the city.

Given under my hand, this 16th of July, 1823.

Richard Bartlett Consul.

To the Collector of the Custom House, Corunna.
Corunna, 25th September, 1824

Dear Harley,
Accept my best thanks for your sending me the trunk and newspapers: the latter were a great treasure to me, and your friends on board the Sylphide. I have now less communication than ever with England; no vessel comes here, except one occasionally with hides from Liverpool or London; even Bacolao is oppressed with such duties as to be equal to a prohibition; not a quintal will be sold this year, at this port, unless the duties are lowered. I have no news to tell you; Corunna is the same as when you left it, except that poverty and misery are more predominant. We have two French regiments, the 37th and 5th, about 2,000 men. Mrs Bartlett offers her most friendly recollections.

Believe me, very sincerely yours,

Richard Bartlett.

1 These letters were supplied by Harley as proof of his assertions regarding his periods of service.

Isle of Man, 22nd October, 1816
I certify that I have known Paymaster John Harley, of the 47th regiment, since the year 1803, and have always considered him as an attentive, good officer, zealous on all occasions to benefit His majesty's service. I particularly observed and witnessed his exertions in order to obtain volunteers from the Irish Militia, in the year 1814.
James Cumming, Major-General.

Duke Square, Parsons Town,[2]
8th of March 1834.

My dear Harley,
I was favoured with your letter, and shall have much pleasure in being named a subscriber to your book. London is the field to obtain signatures. You no doubt will recollect this day thirty-three years, our landing in Egypt, the glorious 8th of March 1801. I regret to inform you my health is fast declining, and renders me unfit for society, &c.- the vulgar saying, 'like a fish out of water.' Believe me, my dear Harley, very truly yours, Samuel Moffatt, Late Lieut. Col. 32nd Regiment.[3]

2 Now known as Birr, County Offaly.
3 Samuel Moffatt had been a Captain- Lieutenant in the 54th Foot with Harley until he went on half pay in 1802.

Index

From Reason to Revolution series – Warfare 1721-1815

http://www.helion.co.uk/published-by-helion/reason-to-revolution-1721-1815.html

The 'From Reason to Revolution' series covers the period of military history c. 1721–1815, an era in which fortress-based strategy and linear battles gave way to the nation-in-arms and the beginnings of total war.

This era saw the evolution and growth of light troops of all arms, and of increasingly flexible command systems to cope with the growing armies fielded by nations able to mobilise far greater proportions of their manpower than ever before. Many of these developments were fired by the great political upheavals of the era, with revolutions in America and France bringing about social change which in turn fed back into the military sphere as whole nations readied themselves for war. Only in the closing years of the period, as the reactionary powers began to regain the upper hand, did a military synthesis of the best of the old and the new become possible.

The series will examine the military and naval history of the period in a greater degree of detail than has hitherto been attempted, and has a very wide brief, with the intention of covering all aspects from the battles, campaigns, logistics, and tactics, to the personalities, armies, uniforms, and equipment.

Submissions

The publishers would be pleased to receive submissions for this series. Please contact series editor Andrew Bamford via email (andrewbamford18@gmail.com), or in writing to Helion & Company Limited, 26 Willow Road, Solihull, West Midlands, B91 1UE.

Titles

No 1 *Lobositz to Leuthen. Horace St Paul and the Campaigns of the Austrian Army in the Seven Years War 1756-57* Translated with additional materials by Neil Cogswell (ISBN 978-1-911096-67-2)

No 2 *Glories to Useless Heroism. The Seven Years War in North America from the French journals of Comte Maurés de Malartic, 1755-1760* William Raffle (ISBN 978-1-1911512-19-6) (paperback)

No 3 *Reminiscences 1808-1815 Under Wellington. The Peninsular and Waterloo Memoirs of William Hay* William Hay, with notes and commentary by Andrew Bamford (ISBN 978-1-1911512-32-5)

No 4 *Far Distant Ships. The Royal Navy and the Blockade of Brest 1793-1815* Quintin Barry (ISBN 978-1-1911512-14-1)

No 5 *Godoy's Army. Spanish Regiments and Uniforms from the Estado Militar of 1800* Charles Esdaile and Alan Perry (ISBN 978-1-911512-65-3) (paperback)

No 6 *On Gladsmuir Shall the Battle Be! The Battle of Prestonpans 1745* Arran Johnston (ISBN 978-1-911512-83-7)

No 7 *The French Army of the Orient 1798-1801. Napoleon's Beloved 'Egyptians'* Yves Martin (ISBN 978-1-911512-71-4)*

No 8 *The Autobiography, or Narrative of a Soldier. The Peninsular War Memoirs of William Brown of the 45th Foot* William Brown, with notes and commentary by Steve Brown (ISBN 978-1-911512-94-3) (paperback)

No 9 *Recollections from the Ranks. Three Russian Soldiers' Autobiographies from the Napoleonic Wars* Translated and annotated by Darrin Boland (ISBN 978-1-912174-18-8) (paperback)

No 10 *By Fire and Bayonet. Grey's West Indies Campaign of 1794* Steve Brown (ISBN 978-1-911512-60-8)

No 11 *Olmütz to Torgau. Horace St Paul and the Campaigns of the Austrian Army in the Seven Years War 1758-60* Translated with additional materials by Neil Cogswell (ISBN 978-1-911512-72-1)

No 12 *Murat's Army. The Army of the Kingdom of Naples 1806-1815* Digby Smith (ISBN 978-1-912390-09-0) (paperback)

No 13 *The Veteran or 40 Years' Service in the British Army. The Scurrilous Recollections of Paymaster John Harley 47th Foot – 1798-1838* John Harley, with notes and commentary by Gareth Glover (ISBN 978-1-912390-25-0) (paperback)

No 14 *Narrative of the Eventful Life of Thomas Jackson. Militiaman and Coldstream Sergeant, 1803-15* Thomas Jackson, with notes and commentary by Eamonn O'Keeffe (ISBN 978-1-912390-12-0) (paperback)

Books within this series are published in two major formats. 'Falconets' are paperbacks, page size 248mm × 180 mm, with high visual content including colour plates; 'Culverins' are hardback monographs, page size 234mm × 156mm. Books marked * in the list above are Falconets, all others are Culverins unless otherwise noted.